THE SOCIOCULTURAL CONTEXT OF ROMANTIC RELATIONSHIPS

Embedded within the sociocultural context of romantic relationships are features such as race, culture, neighborhoods, the legal system, and governmental policy. Due to the inherent difficulties with studying large structures and systems, little work has been done at the macro level in relationship science. This volume spotlights the complex interplay between romantic relationships and these structural systems, including varied insights from experts in the field. In turn, more diverse and generalizable research programs on the social ecology of relationships can be developed, helping to facilitate advances in theory. Scholars and students of relationship science in psychology, sociology, communication, and family studies will benefit from these discussions. This title is part of the Flip it Open programme and may also be available Open Access. Check our website Cambridge Core for details.

Brian G. Ogolsky is Professor of Human Development and Family Studies at the University of Illinois Urbana-Champaign, USA. He is an expert on how romantic relationships change over time with particular attention to the intersection between law, public policy, and family life. He has won many awards for his scholarship, mentorship, and instruction. He has authored two previous books, which both received international acclaim from the International Association for Relationship Research.

Advances in Personal Relationships

Christopher R. Agnew
Purdue University
John P. Caughlin
University of Illinois Urbana-Champaign
C. Raymond Knee
University of Houston
Terri L. Orbuch
Oakland University

Although scholars from a variety of disciplines have written and conversed about the importance of personal relationships for decades, the emergence of personal relationships as a field of study is relatively recent. *Advances in Personal Relationships* represents the culmination of years of multidisciplinary and interdisciplinary work on personal relationships. Sponsored by the International Association for Relationship Research, the series offers readers cutting-edge research and theory in the field. Contributing authors are internationally known scholars from a variety of disciplines, including social psychology, clinical psychology, communication, history, sociology, gerontology, and family studies. Volumes include integrative reviews, conceptual pieces, summaries of research programs, and major theoretical works. *Advances in Personal Relationships* presents first-rate scholarship that is both provocative and theoretically grounded. The theoretical and empirical work described by authors will stimulate readers and advance the field by offering new ideas and retooling old ones. The series will be of interest to upper-division undergraduate students, graduate students, researchers, and practitioners.

Other Books in the Series

Attribution, Communication Behavior, and Close Relationships
Valerie Manusov and John H. Harvey, editors

Stability and Change in Relationships
Anita L. Vangelisti, Harry T. Reis, and Mary Anne Fitzpatrick, editors

Understanding Marriage: Developments in the Study of Couple Interaction
Patricia Noller and Judith A. Feeney, editors

Growing Together: Personal Relationships Across the Lifespan
Frieder R. Lang and Karen L. Fingerman, editors

Communicating Social Support
Daena J. Goldsmith

Communicating Affection: Interpersonal Behavior and Social Context
Kory Floyd

Changing Relations: Achieving Intimacy in a Time of Social Transition
Robin Goodwin

Feeling Hurt in Close Relationships
Anita L. Vangelisti, editor

Romantic Relationships in Emerging Adulthood
Frank D. Fincham and Ming Cui, editors

Responding to Intimate Violence Against Women: The Role of Informal Networks
Renate Klein

Social Influences on Romantic Relationships: Beyond the Dyad
Christopher R. Agnew, editor

Positive Approaches to Optimal Relationship Development
C. Raymond Knee and Harry T. Reis, editors

Personality and Close Relationship Processes
Stanley O. Gaines, Jr.

The Experience and Expression of Uncertainty in Close Relationships
Jennifer A. Theiss

Contemporary Studies on Relationships, Health, and Wellness
Jennifer A. Theiss and Kathryn Greene, editors

Power in Close Relationships
Christopher R. Agnew and Jennifer J. Harman, editors

Health and Illness in Close Relationships
Ashley P. Duggan

Intimate Relationships Across Cultures: A Comparative Study
Charles T. Hill

Relationship Maintenance: Theory, Process, and Context
Brian G. Ogolsky and J. Kale Monk

On-Again, Off-Again Relationships: Navigating (In)Stability in Romantic Relationships
René M. Dailey

Interdependence, Interaction, and Close Relationships
Laura V. Machia, Christopher R. Agnew and Ximena B. Arriaga

The Sociocultural Context of Romantic Relationships

Edited by
Brian G. Ogolsky
University of Illinois Urbana-Champaign

Shaftesbury Road, Cambridge CB2 8EA, United Kingdom

One Liberty Plaza, 20th Floor, New York, NY 10006, USA

477 Williamstown Road, Port Melbourne, VIC 3207, Australia

314–321, 3rd Floor, Plot 3, Splendor Forum, Jasola District Centre, New Delhi – 110025, India

103 Penang Road, #05–06/07, Visioncrest Commercial, Singapore 238467

Cambridge University Press is part of Cambridge University Press & Assessment, a department of the University of Cambridge.

We share the University's mission to contribute to society through the pursuit of education, learning and research at the highest international levels of excellence.

www.cambridge.org
Information on this title: www.cambridge.org/9781009158664

DOI: 10.1017/9781009158657

© Cambridge University Press & Assessment 2024

This publication is in copyright. Subject to statutory exception and to the provisions of relevant collective licensing agreements, no reproduction of any part may take place without the written permission of Cambridge University Press & Assessment.

First published 2024

A catalogue record for this publication is available from the British Library

Library of Congress Cataloging-in-Publication Data
NAMES: Ogolsky, Brian G., editor.
TITLE: The sociocultural context of romantic relationships / edited by Brian G. Ogolsky, University of Illinois, Urbana-Champaign.
DESCRIPTION: Cambridge, United Kingdom ; New York, NY : Cambridge University Press, [2024] | Series: Advances in personal relationships | Includes bibliographical references and index.
IDENTIFIERS: LCCN 2023031410 | ISBN 9781009158664 (hardback) | ISBN 9781009158657 (ebook)
SUBJECTS: LCSH: Man-woman relationships. | Couples. | Interpersonal attraction. | Interpersonal relations.
CLASSIFICATION: LCC HQ801 .S6595 2024 | DDC 306.7–dc23/eng/20230902
LC record available at https://lccn.loc.gov/2023031410

ISBN 978-1-009-15866-4 Hardback

Cambridge University Press & Assessment has no responsibility for the persistence or accuracy of URLs for external or third-party internet websites referred to in this publication and does not guarantee that any content on such websites is, or will remain, accurate or appropriate.

CONTENTS

List of Contributors		*page* ix
1	The Sociocultural Context of Romantic Relationships *Ghada Kawas and Brian G. Ogolsky*	1
2	Systemic Racism and Romantic Relationships *Antoinette M. Landor and Shardé McNeil Smith*	7
3	Sociocultural Perspectives on Romantic Relationships: A View from the East and West *Susan E. Cross and MinJoo Joo*	29
4	Gender and Heteronormativity in Romantic Relationships *April L. Few-Demo and Katherine R. Allen*	55
5	Social Class, Neighborhoods, and Romantic Relationships *Kristin D. Mickelson*	71
6	Religion and Spirituality in Romantic Relationships *Annette Mahoney, James S. McGraw, and Jay R. Chinn*	90
7	The Importance of Work in Romantic Relationships *Karen Kramer, Amit Kramer, and Qiujie Gong*	115
8	History and Cohort Effects in Romantic Relationships *TeKisha M. Rice and Aran Garnett-Deakin*	135
9	The Legal Meaning of Sex (and Romantic Relationships) *Robin Fretwell Wilson, So Young Park, and Rebecca Valek*	151
10	Romantic Relationships and Traditional Media *Jesse Fox and Jessica R. Frampton*	168
11	Romantic Relationships and Social Media *Bree McEwan and Leah E. LeFebvre*	201

12	Situating Latinx Immigrant Romantic Relationships in the Context of Illegality: Using a Socioculturally Attuned Lens *Bethany L. Letiecq and J. Maria Bermudez*	226
13	Romantic Relationships during a Global Pandemic *Paula R. Pietromonaco and Nickola C. Overall*	247

Index 273

CONTRIBUTORS

Katherine R. Allen
Virginia Tech University

J. Maria Bermudez
University of Georgia

Jay R. Chinn
Bowling Green State University

Susan E. Cross
Iowa State University

April L. Few-Demo
University of Georgia

Jesse Fox
Ohio State University

Jessica R. Frampton
Illinois State University

Aran Garnett-Deakin
Virginia Tech University

Qiujie Gong
University of Illinois, Urbana-Champaign

MinJoo Joo
Iowa State University

Ghada Kawas
University of Illinois, Urbana-Champaign

Amit Kramer
University of Illinois, Urbana-Champaign

Karen Kramer
University of Illinois, Urbana-Champaign

Antoinette M. Landor
University of Missouri

Leah E. LeFebvre
University of Alabama

Bethany L. Letiecq
George Mason University

Annette Mahoney
Bowling Green State University

Bree McEwan
University of Toronto, Mississauga

James S. McGraw
Bowling Green State University

Shardé McNeil Smith
University of Illinois, Urbana-Champaign

Kristin D. Mickelson
Arizona State University

Brian G. Ogolsky
University of Illinois, Urbana-Champaign

Nickola C. Overall
University of Auckland

So Young Park
University of Missouri

Paula R. Pietromonaco
University of Massachusetts, Amherst

TeKisha M. Rice
Virginia Tech University

Rebecca Valek
University of Illinois, Chicago

Robin Fretwell Wilson
University of Illinois, Urbana-Champaign

1

The Sociocultural Context of Romantic Relationships

GHADA KAWAS AND BRIAN G. OGOLSKY

The social ecology of relationships (Huston, 2000) argues that three levels of analysis are required to understand the dynamics of romantic relationships: the individual(s), the dyad, and the society. Over the past several decades, relationship scientists have meticulously documented the individual and dyadic levels of analysis. For example, in the past ten years, the *Advances in Personal Relationships* series has published volumes on health, power, technology, interdependence, relationship maintenance, personality, and intimate partner violence. Each of these volumes documented either individual or dyadic level processes in great detail. The lost cog in relationship science, however, is the societal or macro level of influence. Very little attention has been paid to the social and cultural forces that operate on close relationships despite the critical importance of this level of analysis. Indeed, one might argue that relationships and the very individuals who make up those relationships cannot be understood without the sociocultural context in which they exist.

Thus, relationship science has a "context problem." A systematic review of 559 relationship-focused papers (771 studies) published between 2014 and 2018 showed that the average participant in relationship research is a thirty-year-old, college-educated, White American who is from a middle class background and engaged in a different-sex, same-race relationship (Williamson, 2022). Only 10 percent of the studies reviewed in this article focused on traditionally marginalized and underrepresented groups such as non-White, low-income, and/or gender and sexual minorities. This issue is further supported by findings from a systematic review of 198 articles on relationship maintenance spanning two decades (Ogolsky & Stafford, 2022). Results of their analysis showed that Western, educated, industrialized, rich, and democratic (WEIRD) samples dominated relational maintenance research, participant intersectionality was often disregarded, and that contexts such as political climate, culture, and socioeconomic status were not considered.

This problem is one that the social sciences have contended with for decades. Arnett's (2008) analysis of six prominent psychological journals between 2003 and 2007 found that over 70 percent of authors and 68 percent of samples were from the United States. Additionally, when ethnicity was reported, the samples were predominantly of European–American heritage. Thus, this research was inherently American, which neglects approximately 95 percent of the world's population. A follow-up analysis of the same journals ten years later showed little change, with American authors and samples constituting just over 60 percent of publications (Thalmayer et al., 2021). This change was primarily due to increased authorship and sample selection from other English-speaking or Western European countries. Therefore, the more recent analysis still shows that 89 percent of the world's population continues to be underrepresented in psychological research. This is especially problematic due to a tendency to generalize research results to all individuals and populations; however, WEIRD countries have been shown to have some of the least representative populations compared to other countries (Henrich et al., 2010). It also narrows the field of topics studied to those most relevant to the authors in those countries.

There are several reasons why more diverse backgrounds are not represented in the literature. Karney et al. (2004) found that recruitment of ethnically diverse samples was limited by a lower likelihood for non-White couples to respond, a lack of eligibility for non-White couples in the study criteria, and a lower likelihood for non-White couples to participate after being told they were eligible. Furthermore, it is no surprise that less work in relationship science has been done at the macro level due to the difficulties inherent in studying large structures and systems. Embedded within the sociocultural context are features such as race, culture, neighborhoods, the legal system, and governmental policy. Understanding the complex interplay between relationships and structural systems requires large, diverse, costly, interdisciplinary studies that are exceedingly rare. Yet, the time has come for us to overcome these hurdles rather than simply stating them as absolute truths. One suggestion is to diversify the voices of researchers and participants in the field by striving to include individuals of diverse genders and sexual orientations, racial and ethnic backgrounds, ages, socioeconomic statuses, and relationship approaches (Ogolsky & Stafford, 2022; Williamson et al., 2022). It is especially important to approach diversity and inclusion through an intersectional lens.

On the basis of these shortcomings, the goal of this volume is to do just that – to spotlight the topics that are often excluded or forgotten in relationship science. In doing so, the field can then continue to promote more diverse and generalizable research programs to help facilitate advances in theory. In each chapter, the goal of the author(s) was to synthesize the work in each area by providing a critical analysis of the state of the current research as well as

The Sociocultural Context of Romantic Relationships 3

directions for future research. Thus, this book as a whole paints a picture of the diversity of sociocultural forces that operate on romantic relationships. Chapter authors are from the fields of psychology, communication, sociology, law, gender and women's studies, ethnic studies, and family studies, to reflect the inherent multidisciplinary nature of the research in this area. Taken together, it is our hope that this volume be a preeminent resource for understanding the sociocultural context of romantic relationships. In the following section, we provide a brief introduction to each of the chapters.

INTRODUCTION TO THE VOLUME

The historic and systemic marginalization of individuals with minoritized racial and ethnic identities impacts various aspects of their lives, including romantic relationships. In Chapter 2, Landor and McNeil Smith investigate how systemic racism influences romantic relationship initiation, development, maintenance, and dissolution. The authors focus specifically on the experiences of Black Americans in romantic relationships to explain how racialized experiences affect how individuals understand and conduct romantic relationships within a broader sociocultural context. The chapter reviews and critiques the existing literature and provides recommendations for the future of relationship science.

Much of the research pertaining to relationship initiation, maintenance, and dissolution has been dominated by White, educated, industrialized, rich, democratic samples, omitting other cultural groups and creating a monocultural perspective in relationship science. In Chapter 3, Cross and Joo broaden the scope of relationship science and explore how sociocultural factors affect East Asian romantic relationship paradigms compared to Europeanheritage contexts. The chapter first explains broad social, ideological, and institutional factors that shape the East Asian *Confucian* cultural model of marriage and then describes how East Asian ways of thinking, feeling, and behaving form relationship processes that differ from those found in Western contexts.

Gender and sexuality are essential to relationship experience and organization. Although there is a push to recognize the fluid nature of gender and sexuality, gender essentialism, cisnormativity, and heteronormativity continue to dominate relationship science research and paradigms. In Chapter 4, Few-Demo and Allen employ an intersectional feminist theoretical approach to examine micro and macro perspectives of gender and heteronormativity in romantic relationships. They also examine the social structures and constructions that impact relationship initiation, development, maintenance, and dissolution. The chapter reviews selected trends in the literature pertaining to diverse romantic relationships and how they are aligned with or critical of heteronormative, cisnormative, and mononormative ideologies.

Romantic relationships can be a major financial undertaking, especially when media representations and dating scripts discount social class when approaching romantic relationships. In Chapter 5, Mickelson examines the impact of social class on four stages of romantic relationships: dating, cohabitation, marriage, and divorce. The chapter reviews literature from 2007 to 2022 to reveal how social class impacts stages of a relationship, how heteronormative assumptions are dominant in the literature, and how gender role expectations dominate social class.

Religion is an integral part of religious individuals' lives, often guiding their actions and interactions with others; this can be especially true for how religious individuals approach romance and intimacy. In Chapter 6, Mahoney and colleagues examine how involvement in religion impacts relationship initiation, development, maintenance, and dissolution. The chapter then further investigates the religious/spiritual factors that are tied to enhanced relationship functioning as well as those that worsen the quality of romantic relationships and partners' well-being.

Work can be a very dominant aspect of people's lives; it is bound to influence personal and romantic lives in one way or another. The ongoing conversation around workplace romantic and sexual relationships varies from romanticized conceptions to sexual harassment allegations and company rules and regulations. In Chapter 7, Kramer and colleagues examine the impact of work and romantic relationships on individuals. The chapter covers consensual and nonconsensual romantic and sexual relationships in the workplace, how organizations seek to regulate romantic relationships at work, and how work impacts individuals' personal romantic and family lives.

Relationships do not exist in a vacuum; historic, societal, and political stressors can create variations in how individuals behave with regards to romantic relationships. In Chapter 8, Rice and Garnett-Deakin discuss how historic events and sociopolitical environmental shifts in the United States impact romantic relationships and create cohort effects in generations. The chapter provides examples of specific historic events and explains the impact of each on romantic relationship initiation, maintenance, and dissolution.

Contrary to contemporary beliefs and legal changes, which seem to imply that romantic and sexual partnerships are a private matter, laws, regulations, and court opinions (especially those pertaining to marriage and marital dissolution) suggest otherwise. In Chapter 9, Wilson and colleagues examine the laws and regulations related to sexual behavior and their lasting impact on marriage, cohabitation, and parent–child relations in the United States. The chapter provides examples of court cases relating to how sex can be a condition of marriage and how that impacts marriage and marriage dissolution. It also examines the responsibilities created between adults engaging in sex and the legal consequences of sex on parent–child relationships and obligations.

A cursory scroll through the contents of major streaming services reveals dozens of fictional and reality-based shows or movies about finding love. Indeed, traditional media such as books, letters, radio, newspapers, recorded music, television, and the telephone have long been used as a method of learning about romantic relationships, initiating romantic relationships, and communicating with partners. In Chapter 10, Fox and Frampton explore how traditional media impacts relational processes. This chapter discusses media use in relationships, how its consumption influences relationships, and how people cultivate relationships with media characters.

Social spaces have always been used to meet or meet up with potential or continuing partners; the transition of these spaces to online social media platforms is no surprise given how the world has changed in the past three decades. In Chapter 11, McEwan and LeFebvre examine the positive and negative ways that romantic couples use social media to find and seek information about potential and new romantic partners. The authors further examine how social media is used to perform and communicate maintenance behaviors throughout a relationship, and during relationship dissolution. This chapter elaborates on behaviors such as "online stalking" of a potential partner, ongoing partner social media surveillance, relational curation, and "ghosting."

Although great strides have been made with research related to Latinx immigrant families residing in the United States, it is essential to consider how immigration laws and policies shape Latinx immigrant experiences in romantic relationships. In Chapter 12, Letiecq and Bermudez examine how the romantic relationships of undocumented and mixed-status Latinx immigrants in the United States are impacted by their illegality. The authors focus on how illegality conditions and constrains individuals' experiences of and opportunities for romantic relationships while they reside in the United States. The chapter explores the systemic structures and sociocultural context that impact the lived realities of immigrant families and undocumented individuals in the United States through dating and commitment making, mixed-citizenship coupling, dating violence, and relationship maintenance strategies under structural oppression.

Pandemic-related restrictions had diverging impacts for people in romantic relationships that could push them together or pull them apart (physically and/or emotionally). The long-term ramifications of the pandemic on social interaction in general, and romantic relationships specifically, can already be seen in how individuals are choosing to "return to normal," or not, even if they are able to. In Chapter 13, Pietromonaco and Overall investigate how pandemic-related stress has and continues to impact couples' relationships, relationship initiation, and relationship processes and functioning. The chapter applies a vulnerability–stress model in its approach to post-pandemic relationship navigation.

REFERENCES

Arnett, J. J. (2008). The neglected 95%: Why American psychology needs to become less American. *American Psychologist*, 63(7), 602. https://doi.org/10.1037/0003-066X.63.7.602

Henrich, J., Heine, S., & Norenzayan, A. (2010). The weirdest people in the world? *Behavioral and Brain Sciences*, 33(2–3), 61–83. https://doi.org/10.1017/S0140525X0999152X

Huston, T. L. (2000). The social ecology of marriage and other intimate unions. *Journal of Marriage and Family*, 62(2), 298–320. https://doi.org/10.1111/j.1741-3737.2000.00298.x

Karney, B. R., Kreitz, M. A., & Sweeney, K. E. (2004). Obstacles to ethnic diversity in marital research: On the failure of good intentions. *Journal of Social and Personal Relationships*, 21(4), 509–526. https://doi.org/10.1177/0265407504044845

Ogolsky, B. G., & Stafford, L. (2022). A systematic review of relationship maintenance: Reflecting back and looking to the future. *Personal Relationships*. https://doi.org/10.1111/pere.12429

Thalmayer, A. G., Toscanelli, C., & Arnett, J. J. (2021). The neglected 95% revisited: Is American psychology becoming less American? *American Psychologist*, 76(1), 116–129. https://doi.org/10.1037/amp0000622

Williamson, H. C., Bornstein, J. X., Cantu, V., Ciftci, O., Farnish, K. A., & Schouweiler, M. T. (2022). How diverse are the samples used to study intimate relationships? A systematic review. *Journal of Social and Personal Relationships*, 39(4), 1087–1109. https://doi.org/10.1177/02654075211053849

2

Systemic Racism and Romantic Relationships

ANTOINETTE M. LANDOR AND SHARDÉ McNEIL SMITH

Race at its core is a socially constructed category that differentially and hierarchically affords power, resources, and other material advantages to social groups on the basis of nationality, ethnicity, phenotype, and other markers of social difference (Williams et al., 2019). Systemic racism is the structured system that created and maintains this racial hierarchy. As writer Scott Woods framed it, "racism is the original insidious cultural disease" (Woods, 2014). From police related brutal murders of unarmed Black[1] Americans such as George Floyd, Jr. and Breonna Taylor, erasure of indigenous American history, anti-immigrant sentiment, a surge in horrific acts of hate targeting the Asian American Pacific Islander (AAPI) community, and a resurgence of blatant and unabashed white supremacy, it is clear that relationship science can no longer continue to treat romantic relationships as if they form, develop, maintain, and dissolve in a vacuum operating independently of broader sociocultural context such as systemic racism. Without inclusion of the sociocultural context of racism in relationship research, romantic relationships and the individuals who make up those relationships are isolated from the contextual forces that surround them. Thus, given the pervasive and deeply entrenched nature of racism in the United States, the importance of understanding how racism defines, structures, reinforces, and constrains romantic relationships has never been more evident as it is today.

The origins of systemic racism in the United States can be traced back to the genocide of American Indians and 400 years of oppression, dehumanization, systematic marginalization, and discrimination based on race manifesting in myriad ways including racial disparities in income and wealth, education, employment, housing, health and healthcare, and the criminal justice system (Bailey et al., 2017; Bloome, 2014; Braveman et al., 2022). Though racism operates at all societal levels, the deleterious effects of systemic racism (i.e., structural racism, institutional racism, cultural racism) must not be disregarded. Systemic racism is the fundamental driver of racial inequities. Racial inequities are indelible features in the United States and woven throughout the fabric of this country persisting because of unjust and unfair systems and structures, rooted in white supremacy, that (re)produce and sustain racial discrimination (Bonilla-Silva, 2017; Du Bois, 1899; Kendi, 2016; Omi & Winant, 2014). Murry and colleagues (2001) made clear that racism is a "ubiquitous, continuous contextual variable" (p. 917). Hence, the impact of systemic racism and racial inequities on romantic relationships is not trivial. Rather, it is essential to advancing relationship science because racialized systems and structures have always shaped romantic relationships and the narratives around these relationships – whether relationship science acknowledges this fact or not.

Despite this reality, little attention has been given to the role of systemic racism on romantic relationship development and functioning in mainstream relationship science. That is, although relationship science acknowledges multiple contexts, most previous literature and theories have offered and reinforced research and recommendations that center on individual(s)' or couples' personal attributes and abilities rather than on the embedded systemic inequalities that individuals and their relationships are situated in. For example, marriage and relationship education has focused on the skill building of Black American couples' interpersonal communication rather than attending to the systemic inequities that disrupt the development and functioning of romantic relationships. This myopic focus can be particularly dangerous due to its implications for racial equity in relationship science. Solutions at the micro-level have often resulted in labels indicative of deficit or pathology when a particular romantic relationship outcome does not occur (e.g., marriage among Black Americans). To this end, this chapter broadens the focus of relationship science by encouraging the need to situate all relationships in a racialized context that explains various experiences, decisions, and outcomes. Dismantling systemic racism must be an indispensable component of research, policies, and interventions to achieve racial equity in relationship science. By not acknowledging and accounting for the central and pervasive role of systemic racism, relationship science is playing a part in perpetuating racism.

This chapter focuses on how racial inequities at the macro level constrain opportunities for forming romantic relationships, create barriers in relationship maintenance, and exacerbate relationship instability and dissolution, resulting in unequal romantic relationship experiences of individuals and couples across the lifespan. As such, the primary aim of this chapter is to investigate how systemic racism shifts our understanding of romantic relationships at all facets of relationship initiation, development, maintenance, and dissolution. To do this, we begin by outlining the limitations in relationship science as it accounts for the role of race and racism in romantic relationships. Next, we demonstrate how racial demographic information in this area of research and a focus on interpersonal racism are only parts of the story. We then offer an overview of how historical and contemporary racialized experiences through systemic racism manifest in romantic relationships and illustrate how an incorporation of systemic racism paints a more holistic picture of romantic relationship experiences and outcomes. Finally, we conclude with recommendations for future relationship science across four key domains: conceptualization and theory, measurement, privilege exploration, and within-group heterogeneity.

The field of relationship science has seen considerable growth in romantic relationship research on racially and ethnically minoritized populations, though it is still woefully underrepresented in relationship science journals (Williamson et al., 2022). However, the goal of this chapter is not to review romantic relationship literature across every racially and ethnically marginalized group. Instead, this chapter brings to the surface the material and cultural realities of the ways in which systemic racism manifest in romantic relationships, using the experiences of Black Americans as an exemplar. We note, however, that this work has broader relevance for romantic relationships across and within other marginalized populations. Examining the extent to which macro level systemic racism is associated with romantic relationships also generalizes to other racial and ethnic groups and is an important area for further inquiry. Macro level systemic racism affects all of us – even populations racialized as white because they benefit from a racialized system that privileges whiteness. Additionally, though the scope of the chapter focuses on US romantic relationships, it is important to acknowledge that the impact of systemic racism on romantic relationships may look different in non-Western countries. Countries with similar and divergent histories of racial oppression, imperialism, and colonialism are crucial to examine. Finally, and most importantly, this chapter identifies ways forward. We build on the insights of interdisciplinary scholarship and the lessons learned over the past few decades to provide a foundation for moving this field forward. In particular, this chapter encourages more interrogation of traditional frameworks that focus exclusively on the characteristics or behaviors of individuals at the micro-level to explain romantic relationship development and functioning. Taken together, we hope that this chapter can serve as a guide for extending and enhancing the next generation of work in relationship science and advancing research and theory by moving the conversations about systemic racism to the forefront of relationship science research.

LIMITATIONS TO EXISTING RELATIONSHIP SCIENCE LITERATURE

This section identifies several ways past literature in relationship science has limited our understanding of how systemic racism manifests in romantic relationships and contributed to the lack of broad discussions in this area. First, relationship science research has mostly treated romantic relationships as if they are homogeneous, regardless of and without considerations for systemic racism.

This chapter asks: might our current knowledge of romantic relationships be one-sided, assuming homogeneity and universality? By ignoring and not considering macro level sociocultural context such as systemic racism, most of what we know about romantic relationships is often rooted only in micro-level processes and/or might not be generalizable to all populations. Past research and theory have used experiences of Western, Educated, Industrialized, Rich, Democratic (WEIRD) and extra W is for White (WWEIRD) populations focused on white, middle-class, nonimmigrant, and gendered-stereotyped models to determine normality and benchmark "healthy development" (Henrich et al., 2010). This approach raises questions about exactly whose romantic relationships are being used to generalize our understanding of relationships.

Second, some relationship science research has recognized the salience of context by incorporating ecological systems theory to guide their work. For example, the bioecological model by Bronfenbrenner (1979) was groundbreaking when it was first introduced because it acknowledged the importance of interrelated context using nested systems ranging from the microsystem to the macrosystem. Ecological models have helped the field to gain a better understanding of the influence of social context as part of the macrosystem, within which beliefs, expectations, and norms within a society are situated. In addition to its overall impact, however, a critique of this theoretical framework has been that it does not accurately account for systemic racism and often illustrates context as being neutral (Hope & Spencer, 2017). This chapter contends that macro level context is not neutral because one cannot dismiss the pervasive and entrenched role of systemic racism in shaping romantic relationship development and functioning.

Third, romantic relationship research often attends to marriage outcomes and marital behaviors. Though important, in doing this, relationship science has centered the romantic relationship experiences of the most privileged groups. By privileging marriage and diminishing the significance of nonmarital relationships, it serves to further legitimate marriage as the "primary normative frame for affective relationships" while overlooking the exploration of the detrimental effects of the marriage ideal for individuals who experience systemic racism resulting in limited opportunities to cultivate high-quality marriages (Landor & Barr, 2018; Lenhardt, 2014, p. 1343). It should not be surprising then, that despite years of research in this area, our understanding of the complexity of romantic relationships of the most marginalized groups remains incomplete and imprecise.

RACIAL DIFFERENCES IN RELATIONSHIP PATTERNS AND EFFECTS OF INDIVIDUAL RACISM: ONLY PART OF THE STORY

Most major mainstream relationship science research reveals that little attention has been given to the role of macro level sociocultural context such as systemic racism on romantic relationship development and functioning. For instance, consider the literature on marriage and union formation. Decades of relationship research has consistently shown racial and ethnic differences in union formation and marriage patterns, specifically divergent marriage patterns between Black and white individuals. Compared to other racial and ethnic groups, Black Americans have the highest rate of never married persons, report the lowest overall marriage rate, have the highest median age at first marriage, are less likely to marry compared to previous generations, and when they do marry they spend less time married than white Americans (Banks, 2012; Chambers & Kravitz, 2011; Dixon, 2009; Helm & Carlson, 2013; Raley et al., 2015; Raley & Sweeney, 2009; U.S. Census Bureau, 2022). Even when research projects forward to age forty using cohort estimates, Black people's chances of ever marrying declines significantly more than white people (Bloome & Ang, 2020). Black Americans are also more likely to experience instability, divorce, or dissolution than any other racial and ethnic group in the UnitedStates (Raley et al., 2015). Moreover, Black Americans report lower marital quality and experience more contemplation of divorce than their white counterparts, even after controlling for level of education and economic resources (Bulanda & Brown, 2007). Yet, these demographic findings are *only part of the story* in that they provide a limited and decontextualized view of how romantic relationships are experienced in the United States.

Racial and ethnic-comparative approaches to understanding romantic relationships are common in relationship science literature and are often viewed as race-neutral. However, using race to explain differences in romantic relationship development and functioning separately from racism misses the mark because race is the very function of racism. Comparing romantic relationship experiences and outcomes without accounting for systemic racism and racial inequities is problematic as it privileges white individuals and couples while ignoring, disguising, minimizing, and negating the material and cultural realities of Black individuals and couples (Collins, 2004; Landor & Barr, 2018; McNeil Smith & Landor, 2018; Murray et al., 2018). Hence, systemic racism contextualizes racial variations in romantic relationship outcomes. For example, common explanations for the racial differences highlighted above involve demographic characteristics, economic factors, and changing social attitudes at the micro-level of influence. Some scholars suggest that racial differences in marriage are due, in part, to communication patterns of couples (Allen & Helm, 2013) and broader societal changes in ideas about family arrangements making marriage optional (Raley et al., 2015), whereas other researchers point to sex-ratio imbalance, marriage market explanations (e.g., the shortage of marriageable men), or the educational advantages of Black women that reduce the incentives to marry (Banks, 2012; Tucker & Taylor, 1989). Still, none of these factors completely explain racial gaps in marriage patterns because gaps continue to exist at all levels of income, education, and family structure. Moreover, in some cases, research has theorized that racial disparities and structural factors resulting in economic disadvantage, labor market disparities, and increasing incarceration rates explain racial gaps in marriage (Bryant et al., 2010; Chambers & Kravitz, 2011; Dixon, 2009; Tucker & Mitchell-Kernan, 1995). Though structural factors contribute to the racial gap in marriage, they still fail to fully explain why. Research in this area often underemphasizes historical and contemporary systemic racism that is embedded in marriage and union formation rates and has not adequately addressed or tested these issues at a macro level of influence.

Furthermore, according to a recent systematic review of romantic couple relationships, the relatively few studies on romantic relationships that have focused on sociocultural factors involving power and oppression lacked an explanation of why these patterns existed (Galovan et al., 2022). As such, presenting decontextualized findings related to the sociodemographic rates and trends of romantic relationships, especially around marriage, can signify personal failings grounded in racial stereotypes. For example, single-parent households, particularly single-parent Black women, have been blamed for numerous "social ills" in American society (Moynihan, 1965). As such, findings that report statistics on the prevalence of single parenthood and nonmarital births among Black women without identifying macro level contextual processes for these patterns reinforce assumptions and stereotypes by questioning the values and behavioral choices of these women. In fact, research has found that Black women and men place high value on marriage and would like to be married one day (Barr & Simons, 2012, 2013). As stated in the classic work by Burton and Tucker (2009), "interpreting demographic trends as having a dysfunctional base is easy to do when a group is studied in isolation and when their behaviors are interpreted out of context" (p. 134). Demographic trends void of explanatory context often perpetuate harmful myths and negate the material and cultural realities of people of color. Although understanding romantic relationship demographic trends is vital, relationship science must also seriously grapple with how systemic racism can create unequal access to romance, dating, and marriage. Thus, alternative scholarly efforts are needed to create a paradigm shift in relationship science.

We would be remiss if we did not create space to acknowledge pioneers in this area of relationship research. Notable Black scholars, including Chalandra Bryant, Linda Burton, Averil Clarke, Patricia Hill Collins, Patricia Dixon, Shalonda Kelly, Harriet McAdoo, Velma McBride Murry, Elaine Pinderhughes, and M Belinda Tucker, have illustrated the important role of context in studying relationships and marriages of Black people. These researchers, among others, crafted new constructions of knowledge by placing greater emphasis on the ways in which sociocultural context affect Black romantic relationships. For example, these scholars have pointed out how Black Americans and Black American couples encounter a distinct set of contextual stressors (e.g., racism, socioeconomic conditions, unequal sex ratios) that have meaningful implications for marital quality, dissolution, and well-being (Burton & Tucker, 2009; Dixon, 2009; Pinderhughes, 2002). In addition, Bryant and colleagues (2010) developed a conceptual model depicting factors associated with Black American marital outcomes by including stressors and demographic characteristics such as racial discrimination, financial strain, and minority status as direct and indirect influences on couple relationships. Together, this work has been instrumental in starting the conversations to consider racial inequities in romance and love. This chapter takes these ideas a step further by directly recognizing and addressing the impact of systemic racism at the macro level on shaping romantic relationships. It is this consequential macro level factor that creates unequal access to romantic relationships experiences and outcomes.

Overall, what has been missing from this literature is a serious discussion of how systemic racism manifests in romantic relationships creating unequal romantic relationship experiences and outcomes. That is, we contend that it is systemic racism that contributes to and maintains racial differences in marriage and union formation. For instance, if focusing primarily on the micro-level perspective, one might conclude that marriage rates could be increased by teaching Black people about the value of marriage through marriage promotion policies or that divorce could be reduced by teaching Black couples more effective communications skills – all of these solutions primarily focus on personal choices or constraints and avoid placing these romantic relationships and the individuals who make them up into the macro level sociocultural context of systemic racism in which they are situated. The following section aims to provide a more accurate view of Black romantic relationships by shifting the focus to the macro level sociocultural context of systemic racism, and how it shifts, influences, and changes how Black Americans relate in their romantic relationships.

IN FULL VIEW: MANIFESTATION OF SYSTEMIC RACISM ON BLACK ROMANTIC RELATIONSHIPS

Racism is embedded in all aspects of romantic relationships creating the need for Black Americans and other minoritized groups to navigate systemic racialized barriers during the formation, development, maintenance, and dissolution of romantic relationships. Though discussions about the multiple levels in which racism operates (e.g., individual, structural) is not new, most of the empirical literature on the role of racism on romantic relationships has focused on micro-level racial discrimination (e.g., perceived interpersonal racial discrimination). To this end, across each subsection below, we briefly ground the discussion in research literature that shows how racial discrimination shapes individual attitudes towards, expectations about, and behaviors in romantic relationships at a micro-level of influence. The larger focus of this section, however, is on the insidious nature of systemic racism on romantic relationships. We argue that there is a critical need to expand empirical knowledge in relationship science by examining the extent to which macro level systems, in this case, systemic racism which is a relic of white supremacy, has been impacting the lives and romantic relationships of Black Americans, resulting in racial inequities that are often subtle (and sometimes not so subtle) against Black people, and other people of color. Specifically, we consider how systemic racism, as manifested through racial inequities across multiple sectors including the economy, education, housing, health, and the criminal legal system, have shaped the romantic relationship development and functioning of Black Americans. Although this is not an exhaustive review of racial inequities, it broadly reflects the literature in this area and recognizes the challenge to integrate studies across various disciplines, components of romantic relationships (e.g., relationship quality, relationship stability), and populations (e.g., singles, married couples, cohabiting couples).

Historical and Contemporary Racialized Experiences

To gain a full view of the manifestation of systemic racism on romantic relationships, one must first understand the historical and contemporary racialized experiences of Black Americans and Black American couples. Relative to whites, Blacks face significant disadvantages regarding income and wealth, educational attainment, employment and job status, health, and involvement in the criminal justice system. These disparities reflect and are caused by the legacy and terror of chattel slavery and racial oppression in the United States (Feagin, 2006). Moreover, Black Americans and their romantic relationships are continuously shaped by a long history of systemic racism in U.S. laws, policies (written and unwritten), and practices that advantage whites over Blacks (Hunter, 2017; Lenhardt, 2014). From enslavement without the right to legally marry, to forced breeding and sale of family members to other slave owners as property, to the Moynihan report (1965), which characterized Black families as matriarchal and dysfunctional, to U.S. government surveillance of Black romantic relationships and families to assess their suitability as citizens while establishing punishments for law violation (e.g., loss of federal aid, removal of children from the household, imprisonment), to anti-miscegenation laws and current marriage promotion policies, the historical and contemporary sociocultural context of systemic racism has always threatened the development and functioning of Black romantic relationships (Bryant et al., 2010; Burton et al., 2010; Landor & Barr, 2018; Lenhardt, 2014). Challenges in Black romantic relationships are, in fact, a function of the same systemic racism that has limited the opportunities of Black Americans in numerous areas of life including education, housing, and employment. Thus, focusing on macro level sociocultural context is important to contextualizing the romantic relationship experiences of Black Americans.

The Cost of Racism on Romantic Relationships: Initiation and Development

Theoretical evidence suggests that racism undermines the establishment of romantic relationships and worsens potential relationship development (Bryant et al., 2010). Yet, little empirical research has examined how racism, at both the micro-level and macro level of influence, directly and indirectly, relates to relationship initiation and development experiences of Black Americans. Given the connections between views of marriage and family formation, scholars have linked racial discrimination at the micro-level to attitudes and views of marriage (Clarke, 2011; Collins, 2004). For instance, using a sample of African American young adults, Simons et al. (2012) found experiences of racial discrimination were associated with negative views of marriage through the development of distrustful views of relationships. High levels of distrust can negatively influence Black Americans' decisions to initiate a relationship (Estacio & Cherlin, 2010). However, the cost of racism on romantic relationships extends beyond this micro-level of influence.

Systemic racism also takes a toll on the initiation and development of Black romantic relationships because it structures the social settings that Black Americans have to find romantic relationships. That is, systemic racism, as manifested through racial inequities across multiple sectors including the criminal legal system, the economy, and education, creates challenges to establishing romantic relationships. In particular, higher mass incarceration rates among Black males, disproportionate unemployment rates of Black males, and disparate educational attainment between Black males and females, have resulted in the systematic removal of Black men from dating and marriage markets thus contributing to disparate gender ratios and a reduction in the number of available and dateable Black men (Dixon, 2009). Black Americans account for 12 percent of the United States adult population but represent 33 percent of the prison population (Alexander, 2010). Incarceration reduces Black men's opportunity to form romantic relationships rendering them unavailable to potential partners and absent from their families (Lopoo & Western, 2005). A qualitative study of the impact the criminal-legal system had on the romantic relationship status of Black women found harmful effects on cultivating and maintaining romantic connections by creating uncertainty and extreme emotional distress (Monterrosa, 2021). In addition, Black male unemployment and lower educational attainment reduces the likelihood of upward mobility therefore significantly limiting Black men's attractiveness as dating and marriage prospects. The consequences for this systematic exclusion from dating and marriage markets then extends across the life span during young adulthood through older adulthood (Mouzon et al., 2020).

Systemic racism has also redefined the salience and meaning of marriage and intimate relationships. For example, studies show that marriage is less of a necessity for Black women, particularly women who are financially secure (Bank, 2012; Barnes, 2015; Hill, 2006). Also, Black men and women desire to marry someone with characteristics (e.g., educated, financially stable) that will provide upward mobility (King & Allen, 2009). Moreover, although Black men and women value and desire to establish and be involved in stable high-quality relationships (Barr et al., 2015), research has noted that in response to systemic racism in state-sanctioned marriage and the resulting penalties (Lenhardt, 2014), Black Americans have developed adaptive and alternative strategies for romantic relationships resulting in variations in relationship formation including singleness and singlehood (Banks, 2012).

Racism as the *Third Person* in Romantic Relationships: Maintenance/Functioning and Dissolution

Racism also has erosive effects on romantic relationships once they have developed. At the micro-level, scholars have shown that perceived racial discrimination negatively impacts a host of relationship dynamics for Black couples including relationship quality (Bryant et al., 2010; Doyle & Molix, 2014), satisfaction, and instability (Lavner et al., 2018). Furthermore, there is burgeoning research showing that racial discrimination is associated with greater spousal strain (Doyle & Molix, 2014; Priest et al., 2020) and increased difficulty in the maintenance of Black intimate romantic relationships (Awosan & Hardy, 2017; Awosan & Opara, 2016). In particular, theorists and researchers have posited that the stress from interpersonal experiences of racism through racial discrimination spill over into the relationship and consequently affect the relational health of the couple (Barton et al., 2018; Henderson et al., 2023). As such, the quality, stability, and satisfaction of Black relationships are intricately tied to the sociocultural context that these relationships are embedded in.

Most of the research in this area has focused on the inequitable interpersonal treatment experienced by romantic partners, yet there is a vital need to also document and understand how systemic racism perpetuates and maintains existing relationship experiences and inequities. From a macro level standpoint, racism impacts the maintenance, functioning, and dissolution of Black relationships through past and contemporary racialized policies and practices. Economic factors such as financial strain and instability are negatively associated with relationship quality (Barton & Bryant, 2016; Lerman, 2002) and positively associated with risk for relationship dissolution (Cutrona et al., 2011). As such, Black relationship maintenance and stability must be viewed through a context that accounts for the racialized wealth gap derived from exclusionary racist practices such as redlining, higher unemployment rates, and segregated communities. This is particularly important given evidence that neighborhood factors, such as living in a lower-income community, can compromise relational well-being of African American couples, even when controlling for individual demographic variables (Cutrona et al., 2003). Furthermore, issues of power and negotiations of gender roles within Black couple relationships are influenced by the economic realities of Black men and women in a racialized society. For example, though Black couples are described as having more egalitarian gender role attitudes and division of household labor, there is evidence to suggest that Black husbands tend to adopt more traditional gender role attitudes compared to their wives (Stanik & Bryant, 2012). Given that Black women on average are more educated than their Black male partners and Black men have significantly higher rates of unemployment, the ability for Black men to enact traditional gender roles is more difficult. Some scholars have posited that Black men may desire more traditional gender roles to "assert their dominance within the family as compensation for the oppression they face in the larger society" (Stanik & Bryant, 2012, p. 258) and Black female partners may take a one-down approach to their male partners because they are aware of the societal oppression that Black men face (Cowdery et al., 2009). Such an approach that is driven by systemic and structural factors may compromise relationships by contributing to lower marital quality for couples (Stanik & Bryant, 2012).

Dissolution of relationships must also be viewed through a systemic racism lens. Beyond demographic statistics that report higher dissolution rates among Black couples compared to other racial/ethnic groups, there is little to no examination of breakups and divorce in a racialized sociocultural context. In Amato's (2010) decade-in-review, predictors of divorce included poverty, low levels of education, premarital birth, premarital cohabitation, and parental divorce. Black Americans are disproportionately at risk of experiencing each of these risk factors, yet the structural factors that contribute to this reality are rarely unpacked. It also presents a deficit perspective as if divorce is a personal failing for Black communities when actually "many Black couples experience the unspoken unfairness embedded in intergenerational patterns of statistically fewer marriages and more divorces that are driven by structural racism" (Kelly et al., 2020, p. 1384). Furthermore, opportunities to remedy relationship decline through couple therapy is not afforded to Black couples in the same way as it is for white couples. Black couples may be reluctant to engage in couples therapy due to cultural stigma, a history of medical mistrust, and fear of having a culturally insensitive therapist (Nightingale et al., 2019).

Racism as Pulling Us Together

Romantic relationships of Black Americans have a legacy of demonstrating strength and resilience despite adversity (Dixon, 2009; Hunter, 2017; McAdoo, 2007). In Hunter's (2017) *Bound in Wedlock*, there is considerable evidence demonstrating the lengths that coupled African American men and women went to reconnect with each other and their resistance of systemic oppression throughout the transition from slavery to "freedom" in the nineteenth century. Even today, Black Americans have coped with, used their strengths, and resisted the deleterious effects of racism on their romantic relationships by enacting what Masten (2001) calls "ordinary magic." Several scholars have acknowledged the obstacles in the formation, maintenance, and stability of Black marriages while simultaneously shifting the focus on identifying the strengths inherent in these relationships (e.g., Dew et al., 2017; Marks et al., 2008; Skipper et al., 2021; Vaterlaus et al., 2017). Sparked by the controversial, inaccurate, and deficit-laden federal report by Moynihan (1965), the proclaimed "tangle of pathologies" that described African American families prompted a number of scholars to refute these claims and highlight the inherent strengths of Black families in a racialized social system (e.g., Billingsley, 1968; Hill, 1972).

To deal with the effects of individual and systemic racism, Black couples utilize a host of coping strategies, social support systems, and adaptability of family roles (McAdoo, 2007). Support from immediate family, extended family, fictive kin, and the community have continuously been instrumental in contributing to the resilience of Black couple and family relationships (Marks et al., 2008). In particular, Black couples draw on their shared cultural understanding and efforts to pull together to protect the family from the effects of societal inequality (Awosan & Hardy, 2017; Cowdery et al., 2009). There are also positive and strong Black marriages that report effective communication, flexible gender roles, and an intentional approach to financial management as resources that sustain their marriages (Marks et al., 2008; Skipper et al., 2021). Furthermore, the institution of church and a strong sense of spirituality has historically been used to promote positive Black coupling experiences through religious coping strategies (e.g., praying) and the provision of social welfare services (e.g., housing, financial assistance; Pool, 2017) and is a prominent resource today for Black relationships (Jenkins et al., 2022; Moore et al., 2021; Phillips et al., 2012). Black Greek-letter fraternities and sororities (collectively referred to as the Divine Nine), as well as Black civic organizations such as Jack and Jill and The Links also provide support and uplift the Black community from racial inequities. These organizations have served as a refuge for Black Americans living in predominately white communities or the only or one of a few Black Americans at their workplace. Collectively, these resources and more are inherent and mobilized in Black marital (Phillips et al., 2012) and cohabiting (Chaney, 2014) relationships.

MOVING FORWARD: WHAT'S NEEDED?

This chapter focused on how systemic racism constrains opportunities for forming romantic relationships, creates barriers in relationship maintenance, and exacerbates relationship instability and dissolution, resulting in unequal romantic relationship experiences of individuals and couples across the lifespan. This work explicitly contradicts the myth that relationship science is race-neutral and is unaffected by bias. Acknowledging the centrality of systemic racism as a driver of racial inequities that shape romantic relationship development and functioning will yield important theoretical and applied insights. We hope that relationship science, and family science more broadly, has reached an inflection point where understanding systemic racism is a central component.

Below we outline our recommendations for incorporating systemic racism in relationship science across four key domains: conceptualization and theory, measurement, privilege exploration, and within-group heterogeneity.

Conceptualization and Theory

Scholars must work to conceptualize and explicitly operationalize systemic racism in relationship science literature. As a first step, there must be an interrogation of whether existing relationship theories and frameworks are able to capture the presence and effects of systemic racism. In particular, scholars should begin by theorizing about the role of oppression and privilege at the macro level and how these factors contour romantic relationship development and functioning. Otherwise, important processes may remain invisible and unexplored, and erroneous assumptions and conclusions may be constructed. Such a process may include revisioning existing acontextual theories or integrating macro level critical frameworks, such as Critical Race Theory (Delgado & Stefancic, 2023) or Systemic Racism Theory (Feagin, 2006) with micro-level relationship frameworks.

In addition to improving our theorizing about romantic relationships, scholars need to ask research questions related to the historical underpinnings of contemporary realities. Work by health researchers using macro level factors such as the legacy of slavery and historical redlining provide some directions for relationship science research. For instance, a higher concentration of slavery in 1860 at the county level was associated with slower declines in heart disease mortality among Blacks in recent decades (Kramer et al., 2017). Moreover, research by Faber (2020) found that historical redlining practices underline contemporary residential segregation patterns and health inequities. What might this look like when examining how the legacy of slavery or historical redlining shape union formation and marriage rates across all racialized groups? Scholars should also consider the connections between historical and contemporary forms of systemic racism on romantic relationships given that the historical forms direct contemporary ones.

Consider Measurement at Global, National, State, and Local Levels

There continues to be a need for research that examines the role of measurement when understanding how systemic racism impacts romantic relationships. As this research expands, the development of measures of systemic racism will have to align with theory. To date, no study has empirically examined systemic racism as a determinant of relationship development and functioning. Again, relationship science should consider turning to innovative work in the field of health science. A robust body of literature in this field has demonstrated how structural racism operates to influence health in myriad ways (Bailey et al., 2017; Krieger et al., 2020; Lynch et al., 2021) and several scholars have made important contributions to the measurement of systemic racism at local, state, national, and global levels.

A similar process can and should occur in relationship science as racial inequalities manifest in institutionalized policies and practices (e.g., de jure racism of the Jim Crow era; de facto racism in mandatory sentencing) that impact romantic relationships in various ways across geographic contexts. For example, researchers can explore how indicators of structural racism (e.g., local and state-level racial disparities in education, employment, incarceration, concentration of poverty) directly and indirectly through individual discrimination influence relationship initiation, development, and maintenance. Racial disparities at the community- and state-level across domains of educational attainment, employment, judicial treatment, and political participation may be proxies for systematic exclusion of Black people from resources and mobility, which indirectly affects the formation and maintenance of romantic relationships (Lukachko et al., 2014). Census data that can capture the historical concentration of enslaved people in a specific area and current patterns of poverty can also be used as indicators of the legacy of slavery that indirectly affects family and relationship formation within particular geographics locales (Baker & O'Connell, 2022). Examining the impact of local policies and practices, which are often not race-neutral in implementation, on romantic relationships can also uncover factors that contribute to relationship maintenance and satisfaction, including but not limited to health care access, neighborhood environment, and economic stability. Finally, scholars can examine racial inequities and structural racism on a global scale – for example, explore how colonization and caste systems, which are also rooted in white supremacy, act as international forms of structural racism and racial inequities that undermine the romantic relationships of current populations across the world.

Explore Privilege and Power in Relationship Science

For centuries, systemic racism has resulted in unearned privilege and power that has protected white individuals and couples from the deleterious romantic relationship experiences and outcomes that affect Black individuals and couples. Consequently, Black Americans have unequal access to romance, dating, and marriage (Chambers & Kravitz, 2011; Dixon, 2009). Given that systemic racism permeates all sectors of society, one way for relationship science to shift this narrative is to examine the historical and contemporary advantages of romantic relationship privilege and power. This confronts systemic racism and the privilege embedded in it. Research has overlooked the effects of racial inequities on all racial and ethnic groups, including white populations. In fact, exploration of the effects of systemic racism on the romantic relationships of white populations remain less clear. White individuals and couples do not develop in a vacuum outside of the same system of racialized oppression and systemic racism. We suspect that experiencing greater privilege and relative power creates both historical and contemporary resources and opportunities that impact relationship initiation, development, maintenance, and dissolution. One might ask "how might being in the dominant racial position in the U.S. influence the romantic relationship development and functioning of white partners in relationships?" and "do whites reap romantic relationship advantages from higher levels of systemic racism?" This exploration may underscore the myriad advantages white individuals and couples experience across the lifespan. Highlighting how macro level systemic racism impacts whites may help to better understand and address the unequal distribution of romantic relationship development and functioning across all racial and ethnic populations.

New Focus on Old Issues: Within-Group Heterogeneity

Future research investigating how systemic racism affects romantic relationships must also attend to within-group heterogeneity that shapes and reinforces romantic relationships initiation, development, maintenance, and dissolution. The magnitude of within-group heterogeneity in Black romantic relationships underscores the importance of considering issues of intragroup diversity in relationship science. Past scholarship has overwhelmingly compared Black and white Americans and focused on heterosexual relationships, obscuring important variations within the Black American population that include, but are not limited to, ethnicity (e.g., Caribbean Black), skin tone (e.g., being lighter skin), and sexual orientation. Although Black Americans share sociohistorical experiences, their social location(s) illustrates variations in the degree of systemic racism. Therefore, researchers should not assume equivalent relationship processes and outcomes across all Black Americans. For instance, using a national sample of unmarried African Americans and Black Caribbeans, work by Lincoln and colleagues (2008) found that correlates of relationship satisfaction and longevity differed among African American and Black Caribbeans. Moreover, another example of within-group heterogeneity in Black romantic relationships is skin tone. Within-group differences in romantic relationship development and functioning is related to skin tone and colorism – defined as the unequal treatment and discrimination of individuals on the basis of the lightness or darkness of their skin tone. Studies show that lighter skin African Americans are more likely to marry and have higher status spouses compared to their darker skin counterparts (Burton et al., 2010; Hamilton et al., 2009; Landor & Bar, 2018; Landor & McNeil Smith, 2019). Furthermore, the intersectionality of race and sexual orientation should also be considered. A systematic review of research focused on Black American same-sex couples found that Black sexual minority women were underrepresented in the literature compared to Black sexual minority men and there is a dearth of research on same-sex couples where both partners are Black (Lassiter et al., 2022). A focus on how systemic racism intersects with within-group heterogeneity to impact romantic relationships will aid in understanding variations within racialized groups rather than comparing these groups to white Americans.

To summarize, understanding the ways in which systemic racism impacts romantic relationships is an important and timely area of inquiry. We hope to inspire a movement of relationship science toward a better understanding of the critical role played by macro level, sociocultural context like systemic racism in all facets of romantic relationships. Although there is no "one size fits all" approach to addressing systemic racism in relationship science, these common themes and actions can be implemented to move this field forward. Incorporating the study of systemic racism will provide us with a more holistic picture of romantic relationship experiences that can have equitable and beneficial research, theory, practice, and policy implications for all families.

NOTE

1 Throughout the chapter, Black is used rather than African American, unless specifically referred to in original articles, to describe the range of individuals who identify as descendants of Africa and the African Diaspora, including Africans and African Americans, among others.

REFERENCES

Alexander, M. (2010). *The new Jim crow: Mass incarceration in the age of colorblindness*. The New Press.

Allen, T., & Helm, K. M. (2013). Threats to intimacy for African American couples. In J. Carlson & K. M. Helm (Eds.), *Love, intimacy, and the African American couple* (pp. 85–116). Brunner-Routledge.

Amato, P. R. (2010). Research on divorce: Continuing trends and new developments. *Journal of Marriage and Family*, 72(3), 650–666. https://doi.org/10.1111/j.1741-3737.2010.00723.x

Awosan, C. I., & Hardy, K. V. (2017). Coupling processes and experiences of never married heterosexual black men and women: A phenomenological study. *Journal of Marital and Family Therapy*, 43(3), 463–481. https://doi.org/10.1111/jmft.12215

Awosan, C. I., & Opara, I. (2016). Socioemotional factor: A missing gap in theorizing and studying Black heterosexual coupling processes and relationships. *Journal of Black Sexuality and Relationships*, 3(2), 25–51. https://doi.org/10.1353/bsr.2016.0027

Bailey, Z. D., Krieger, N., Agénor, M., Graves, J., Linos, N., & Bassett, M. T. (2017). Structural racism and health inequities in the USA: Evidence and interventions. *The Lancet*, 389(10077), 1453–1463. https://doi.org/10.1016/S0140-6736(17)30569-X

Baker, R. S., & O'Connell, H. A. (2022). Structural racism, family structure, and Black–White inequality: The differential impact of the legacy of slavery on poverty among single mother and married parent households. *Journal of Marriage and Family*, 84(5), 1341–1365. https://doi.org/10.1111/jomf.12837

Banks, R. R. (2012). *Is marriage for white people?: How the African American marriage decline affects everyone*. Penguin.

Barr, A. B., & Simons, R. L. (2012). Marriage expectations among African American couples in early adulthood: A dyadic analysis. *Journal of Marriage and Family*, 74(4), 726–742. https://doi.org/10.1111/j.1741-3737.2012.00985.x

Barr, A. B., Simons, R. L., & Simons, L. G. (2015). Nonmarital relationships and changing perceptions of marriage among African American young adults. *Journal of Marriage and Family*, 77(5), 1202–1216.

Barnes, R. J. D. (2015). *Raising the race: Black career women redefine marriage, motherhood, and community*. Rutgers University Press.

Barton, A. W., & Bryant, C. M. (2016). Financial strain, trajectories of marital processes, and African American newlyweds' marital instability. *Journal of Family Psychology*, 30(6), 657. https://doi.org/10.1037/fam0000190

Barton, A. W., Beach, S. R., Bryant, C. M., Lavner, J. A., & Brody, G. H. (2018). Stress spillover, African Americans' couple and health outcomes, and the stress-buffering effect of family-centered prevention. *Journal of Family Psychology*, 32(2), 186–196. https://psycnet.apa.org/doi/10.1037/fam0000376

Billingsley, A. (1968). *Black families in White America*. Prentice-Hall.

Bloome, D. (2014). Racial inequality trends and the intergenerational persistence of income and family structure. *American Sociological Review*, 79(6), 1196–1225. https://doi.org/10.1177/0003122414554949

Bloome, D., & Ang, S. (2020). Marriage and union formation in the United States: Recent trends across racial groups and economic backgrounds. *Demography*, 57(5), 1753–1786. https://doi.org/10.1007/s13524-020-00910-7

Bonilla-Silva, E. (2017). What we were, what we are, and what we should be: The racial problem of American sociology. *Social Problems*, 64(2), 179–187. https://doi.org/10.1093/socpro/spx006

Braveman, P. A., Arkin, E., Proctor, D., Kauh, T., & Holm, N. (2022). Systemic and structural Racism: Definitions, examples, health damages, and approaches to dismantling. *Health Affairs*, 41(2), 171–178. https://doi.org/10.1377/hlthaff.2021.01394

Bronfenbrenner, U. (1979). *The ecology of human development: Experiments by nature and design*. Harvard University Press.

Bryant, C. M., Wickrama, K. A. S., Bolland, J., Bryant, B. M., Cutrona, C. E., & Stanik, C. E. (2010). Race matters, even in marriage: Identifying factors linked to marital outcomes for African Americans. *Journal of Family Theory & Review*, 2(3), 157–174. https://doi.org/10.1111/j.1756-2589.2010.00051.x

Bulanda, J. R., & Brown, S. L. (2007). Race-ethnic differences in marital quality and divorce. *Social Science Research*, *36*(3), 945–967. https://doi.org/10.1016/j.ssresearch.2006.04.001

Burton, L. M., & Tucker, M. B. (2009). Romantic unions in an era of uncertainty: A post-Moynihan perspective on African American women and marriage. *The Annals of the American Academy of Political and Social Science*, *621*(1), 132–148.

Burton, L. M., Bonilla-Silva, E., Ray, V., Buckelew, R., & Freeman, E. H. (2010). Critical race theories, colorism, and the decade's research on families of color. *Journal of Marriage and Family*, *72*(3), 440–459. https://doi.org/10.1111/j.1741-3737.2010.00712.x

Chambers, A. L., & Kravitz, A. (2011). Understanding the disproportionately low marriage rate among African Americans: An amalgam of sociological and psychological constraints. *Family Relations*, *60*(5), 648–660. https://doi.org/10.1111/j.1741-3729.2011.00673.x

Chaney, C. (2014). "No matter what, good or bad, love is still there": Motivations for romantic commitment among Black cohabiting couples. *Marriage & Family Review*, *50*(3), 216–245. https://:doi.org/10.1080/01494929.2013.851056

Clarke, A. Y. (2011). *Inequalities of love: College-educated Black women and the barriers to romance and family*. Duke University Press.

Collins, P. H. (2004). *Black sexual politics: African Americans, gender, and the new racism*. Routledge.

Cowdery, R. S., Scarborough, N., Knudson-Martin, C., Seshadri, G., Lewis, M. E., & Mahoney, A. R. (2009). Gendered power in cultural contexts: Part II. Middle class African American heterosexual couples with young children. *Family Process*, *48*(1), 25–39. https://doi.org/10.1111/j.1545-5300.2009.01265.x

Cutrona, C. E., Russell, D. W., Abraham, W. T., Gardner, K. A., Melby, J. N., Bryant, C., & Conger, R. D. (2003). Neighborhood context and financial strain as predictors of marital interaction and marital quality in African American couples. *Personal Relationships*, *10*(3), 389–409. https://doi.org/10.1111/1475-6811.00056

Cutrona, C. E., Russell, D. W., Burzette, R. G., Wesner, K. A., & Bryant, C. M. (2011). Predicting relationship stability among midlife African American couples. *Journal of Consulting and Clinical Psychology*, *79*(6), 814–825. https://doi.org/10.1037/a0025874

Delgado, R., & Stefancic, J. (2023). *Critical race theory: An introduction* (4th ed.). University Press.

Dew, J. P., Anderson, B. L., Skogrand, L., & Chaney, C. (2017). Financial issues in strong African American marriages: A strengths-based qualitative approach. *Family Relations*, *66*(2), 287–301. https://doi.org/10.1111/fare.12248

Dixon, P. (2009). Marriage among African Americans: What does the research reveal? *Journal of African American Studies*, *13*(1), 29–46, 9062–9065.

Doyle, D. M., & Molix, L. (2014). Perceived discrimination as a stressor for close relationships: Identifying psychological and physiological pathways. *Journal of Behavioral Medicine*, *37*(6), 1134–1144. https://doi.org/10.1007/s10865-014-9563-8

Du Bois, W. E. B. (1899). *The Philadelphia negro: A social study*. University of Pennsylvania Press.

Faber, J. W. (2020). We built this: Consequences of new deal era intervention in America's racial geography. *American Sociological Review*, *85*(5), 739–775. https://doi.org/10.1177/0003122420948464

Feagin, J. (2006). *Systemic racism: A theory of oppression*. Routledge.
Galovan, A. M., Orbuch, T. L., Shrout, M. R., Drebit, E., & Rice, T. M. (2022). Taking stock of the longitudinal study of romantic couple relationships: The last 20 years. *Personal Relationships*. Advance online publication. https://doi.org/10.1111/pere.12452
Gramlich, J. (2018). *US incarceration rate is at its lowest in 20 years*. Retrieved November, 12, 2018.
Hamilton, D., Goldsmith, A. H., & Darity Jr, W. (2009). Shedding "light" on marriage: The influence of skin shade on marriage for black females. *Journal of Economic Behavior & Organization*, 72(1), 30–50. https://doi.org/10.1016/j.jebo.2009.05.024
Helm, K. M., & Carlson, J. (Eds.). (2013). *Love, intimacy, and the African American couple*. Routledge.
Henderson, A. K., Wong, J. S., Dues, A., & Walsemann, K. M. (2023). Interpersonal discrimination and relationship quality among married mid-life and older Black adults. *Journal of Family Issues*. Advance online publication. https://doi.org/10.1177/0192513X221150988
Henrich, J., Heine, S. J., & Norenzayan, A. (2010). The weirdest people in the world?. *Behavioral and Brain Sciences*, 33(2–3), 61–83. https://doi.org/10.1017/S0140525X0999152X
Hill, R. (1972). *The strengths of Black families*. Emerson Hall.
Hill, S. A. (2006). Marriage among African American women: A gender perspective. *Journal of Comparative Family Studies*, 37(3), 421–440. https://doi.org/10.3138/jcfs.37.3.421
Hope, E. C., & Spencer, M. B. (2017). Civic engagement as an adaptive coping response to conditions of inequality: An application of phenomenological variant of ecological systems theory (PVEST). In N. J. Cabrera & B. Leyendecker (Eds.), *Handbook on positive development of minority children and youth* (pp. 421–435). Springer.
Hunter, T. W. (2017). *Bound in wedlock: Slave and free black marriage in the nineteenth century*. Harvard University Press. https://doi.org/10.1093/whq/whaa144
Hurt, T. R. (2013). Toward a deeper understanding of the meaning of marriage among Black men. *Journal of Family Issues*, 34(7), 859–884. https://doi.org/10.1177/0192513X12451737
Jenkins, A. I., Fredman, S. J., Le, Y., Mogle, J. A., & McHale, S. M. (2022). Religious coping and gender moderate trajectories of marital love among black couples. *Family Process*, 61(1), 312–325. https://doi.org/10.1111/famp.12645
Kelly, S., Jérémie-Brink, G., Chambers, A. L., & Smith-Bynum, M. A. (2020). The Black Lives Matter movement: A call to action for couple and family therapists. *Family Process*, 59(4), 1374–1388. https://doi.org/10.1111/famp.12614
Kendi, I. X. (2016). *Stamped from the beginning: The definitive history of racist ideas in America*. Hachette UK.
King, A. E. O., & Allen, T. T. (2009). Personal characteristics of the ideal African American marriage partner: A survey of adult Black men and women. *Journal of Black Studies*, 39(4), 570–588. https://doi.org/10.1177/0021934707299637
Kramer, M. R., Black, N. C., Matthews, S. A., & James, S. A. (2017). The legacy of slavery and contemporary declines in heart disease mortality in the US South. *SSM-Population Health*, 3, 609–617. https://doi.org/10.1016/j.ssmph.2017.07.004

Krieger, N., Van Wye, G., Huynh, M., Waterman, P. D., Maduro, G., Li, W., Gwynn, R., Barbot, O., & Bassett, M. T. (2020). Structural racism, historical redlining, and risk of preterm birth in New York City, 2013-2017. *American Journal of Public Health*, *110*(7), 1046-1053. https://doi.org/10.2105/AJPH.2020.305656

Landor, A. M., & Barr, A. (2018). Politics of respectability, colorism, and the terms of social exchange in family research. *Journal of Family Theory & Review*, *10*(2), 330-347. https://doi.org/10.1111/jftr.12264

Landor, A. M., & McNeil Smith, S. (2019). Skin-tone trauma: Historical and contemporary influences on the health and interpersonal outcomes of African Americans. *Perspectives on Psychological Science*, *14*(5), 797-815. https://doi.org/10.1177/1745691619851781

Lassiter, J. M., Dacus, J. D., & Johnson, M. O. (2022). A systematic review of Black American same-sex couples research: Laying the groundwork for culturally-specific research and interventions. *The Journal of Sex Research*, *59*(5), 555-567. https://doi.org/10.1080/00224499.2021.1964422

Lavner, J. A., Barton, A. W., Bryant, C. M., & Beach, S. R. H. (2018). Racial discrimination and relationship functioning among African American couples. *Journal of Family Psychology*, *32*(5), 686-691. https://doi.org/10.1037/fam0000415

Lenhardt, R. A. (2014). Marriage as Black citizenship. *Hastings Law Journal*, *66*(5), 1317-1364.

Lerman, R. I. (2002). *Impacts of marital status and parental presence on the material hardship of families with children*. Urban Institute.

Lincoln, K. D., Taylor, R. J., & Jackson, J. S. (2008). Romantic relationships among unmarried African Americans and Caribbean Blacks: Findings from the national survey of American life. *Family Relations*, *57*(2), 254-266. https://doi.org/10.1111/j.1741-3729.2008.00498.x

Lopoo, L. M., & Western, B. (2005). Incarceration and the formation and stability of marital unions. *Journal of Marriage and Family*, *67*(3), 721-734. https://doi.org/10.1111/j.1741-3737.2005.00165.x

Lukachko, A., Hatzenbuehler, M. L., & Keyes, K. M. (2014). Structural racism and myocardial infarction in the United States. *Social Science & Medicine*, *103*, 42-50. https://doi.org/10.1016/j.socscimed.2013.07.021

Lynch, E. E., Malcoe, L. H., Laurent, S. E., Richardson, J., Mitchell, B. C., & Meier, H. C. (2021). The legacy of structural racism: Associations between historic redlining, current mortgage lending, and health. *SSM-Population Health*, *14*, 100793. https://doi.org/10.1016/j.ssmph.2021.100793

Marks, L. D., Hopkins, K., Chaney, C., Monroe, P. A., Nesteruk, O., & Sasser, D. D. (2008). "Together, we are strong": A qualitative study of happy, enduring African American marriages. *Family Relations*, *57*(2), 172-185. https://doi.org/10.1111/j.1741-3729.2008.00492.x

Masten, A. S. (2001). Ordinary magic: Resilience processes in development. *American Psychologist*, *56*(3), 227-238. https://doi.org/10.1037//0003-066X.56.3.227

McAdoo, H. P. (2007). *Black families* (4th ed.). Sage Publications.

McNeil Smith, S., & Landor, A. M. (2018). Toward a better understanding of African American families: Development of the sociocultural family stress model. *Journal of Family Theory & Review*, *10*(2), 434-450. https://doi.org/10.1111/jftr.12260

Monterrosa, A. E. (2021). Romantic (in)justice: Criminal-legal system-impacted black women's romantic relationship status and quality. *Feminist Criminology*, *16*(4), 424–446. https://doi.org/10.1177/15570851211019472

Mouzon, D. M., Taylor, R. J., & Chatters, L. M. (2020). Gender differences in marriage, romantic involvement, and desire for romantic involvement among older African Americans. *PLoS One*, *15*(5), e0233836. https://doi.org/10.1371/journal.pone.0233836

Moore, T. J., Chaney, C., & Skipper, A. (2021). "Put God above all [and He] will glorify your marriage": Relational spirituality in Black couples, *Marriage & Family Review*, *57*(8), 673–699. https://doi.org/10.1080/01494929.2021.1887048

Moynihan, D. P. (1965). *The Negro family: The case for national action* (pp. 1–35). U.S. Department of Labor.

Murray, V. M., Butler-Barnes, S. T., Mayo-Gamble, T. L., & Inniss-Thompson, M. N. (2018). Excavating new constructs for family stress theories in the context of everyday life experiences of Black American families. *Journal of Family Theory & Review*, *10*(2), 384–405. https://doi.org/10.1111/jftr.12256

Murry, V. M., Brown, P. A., Brody, G. H., Cutrona, C. E., & Simons, R. L. (2001). Racial discrimination as a moderator of the links among stress, maternal psychological functioning, and family relationships. *Journal of Marriage and Family*, *63*(4), 915–926. https://doi.org/10.1111/j.1741-3737.2001.00915.x

Nightingale, M., Jones, S. C., & Smith, S. D. (2019). Black American couples' perceptions of the significance of race and racial conversations in therapy: A qualitative study. *Journal of Black Sexuality and Relationships*, *6*(2), 37–57. https://doi.org/10.1353/bsr.2019.0020

Omi, M., & Winant, H. (2014). *Racial formation in the United States*. Routledge.

Phillips, T. M., Wilmoth, J. D., & Marks, L. D. (2012). Challenges and conflicts... strengths and supports: A study of enduring African American marriages. *Journal of Black Studies*, *43*(8), 936–952. https://doi.org/10.1111/famp.12614

Pinderhughes, E. B. (2002). African American marriage in the 20th century. *Family Process*, *41*(2), 269–282.

Poole, T. G. (2017). Black families and the Black church: A sociohistorical perspective. In H. E. Cheatham & J. B. Stewart (Eds.), *Black families* (pp. 33–48). Routledge.

Priest, J. B., McNeil Smith, S., Woods, S. B., & Roberson, P. N. (2020). Discrimination, family emotional climate, and African American health: An application of the BBFM. *Journal of Family Psychology*, *34*(5), 598. https://psycnet.apa.org/doi/10.1037/fam0000621

Raley, R. K., & Sweeney, M. M. (2009). Explaining race and ethnic variation in marriage: Directions for future research. *Race and Social Problems*, *1*(3), 132–142. https://doi.org/10.1007/s12552-009-9013-3

Raley, R. K., Sweeney, M. M., & Wondra, D. (2015). The growing racial and ethnic divide in U.S. marriage patterns. *The Future of children/Center for the Future of Children, the David and Lucile Packard Foundation*, *25*(2), 89. https://doi.org/10.1353/foc.2015.0014

Simons, R. L., Simons, L. G., Lei, M. K., & Landor, A. M. (2012). Relational schemas, hostile romantic relationships, and beliefs about marriage among young African American adults. *Journal of Social and Personal Relationships*, *29*(1), 77–101.

Skipper, A. D., Marks, L. D., Moore, T. J., & Dollahite, D. C. (2021). Black marriages matter: Wisdom and advice from happily married black couples. *Family Relations*, 70(5), 1369–1383. https://doi.org/10.1111/fare.12565

Stanik, C. E., & Bryant, C. M. (2012). Marital quality of newlywed African American couples: Implications of egalitarian gender role dynamics. *Sex Roles*, 66(3–4), 256–267. https://doi.org/10.1007/s11199-012-0117-7

Tucker, M. B., & Mitchell-Kernan, C. (Eds.). (1995). *The decline in marriage among African Americans: Causes, consequences, and policy implications*. Russell Sage Foundation.

Tucker, M. B., & Taylor, R. J. (1989). Demographic correlates of relationship status among Black Americans. *Journal of Marriage and the Family*, 51(3), 655–665. www.jstor.org/stable/352165

U.S. Census Bureau. (2022). *Marriage and divorce*. Retrieved from www.census.gov/topics/families/marriage-and-divorce.html

Vaterlaus, J. M., Skogrand, L., Chaney, C., & Gahagan, K. (2017). Marital expectations in strong African American marriages. *Family Process*, 56(4), 883–899. https://doi.org/10.1111/famp.12263

Williams, D. R., Lawrence, J. A., & Davis, B. A. (2019). Racism and health: Evidence and needed research. *Annual Review of Public Health*, 40(1), 105–125. https://doi.org/10.1146/annurev-publhealth-040218-043750

Williamson, H. C., Bornstein, J. X., Cantu, V., Ciftci, O., Farnish, K. A., & Schouweiler, M. T. (2022). How diverse are the samples used to study intimate relationships? A systematic review. *Journal of Social and Personal Relationships*, 39(4), 1087–1109. https://doi.org/10.1177/02654075211053849

Woods, S. (2014, January). *5 things no one is actually saying about Ani DiFranco or plantations. Scott Woods make lists: Everything but laundry and groceries*. https://scottwoodsmakeslists.wordpress.com/2014/01/03/5-things-no-one-is-actually-saying-about-ani-difranco-or-plantations/

3

Sociocultural Perspectives on Romantic Relationships

A View from the East and West

SUSAN E. CROSS AND MINJOO JOO

A family has a three-bedroom house. The family consists of a mother, father, three sons aged fifteen, eleven, and eight, and two daughters aged fourteen and three. *Who sleeps in the same room?*

When we have posed this question to European-American audiences, the response is usually puzzled looks and comments like "Isn't it obvious?" They articulate that the "obvious" answer is that the parents get one room, the daughters get another room, and the sons get the third room. And, in fact, in the study by Shweder et al. (2003), 88 percent of participants from the United States (Illinois) gave this response. In contrast, only 47 percent of participants from Orissa, India, gave this response. Another 47 percent of the Indian participants responded with arrangements that either placed the youngest child together with the parents and the two oldest sons together (mother, father, and three-year daughter together; fourteen year old daughter and eight-year-old son together; fifteen and eleven-year-old sons together) or separated the mother and father to sleep with same sex children, giving the oldest sons their own room (father and eight-year-old son together; mother and two daughters together; fifteen and eleven-year-old sons together).

Why would the Indians expect a married couple to share a room with a young child, or separate them entirely? Shweder and his colleagues (2003) argue that different belief systems in the United States and India shape these responses. In the United States, there is a widespread belief in the "sacred couple;" couple privacy is paramount (to the point of often putting infants in a separate room). In India, in contrast, concerns about protection of the very young (e.g., the youngest child should sleep in the same room as an adult), anxiety over female chastity (e.g., one must always chaperone unmarried adolescent girls), and respect for hierarchy (e.g., the oldest son should not have to sleep with the youngest son) frame decisions about who sleeps by whom.

This example illustrates that cultural phenomena, such as values, beliefs, attitudes, and practices, shape key aspects of romantic relationships. It also highlights how cultures may tend to see their own traditional practices as "natural" or "obvious." One benefit of cross-cultural investigations of human behavior is that they reveal cultural assumptions and values that often go unexamined by scholars embedded within a particular context. To date, the prevalent theories of romance, marriage, and close relationships have been developed by Western researchers, and they may take for granted values, beliefs, and social conditions that have created a unique approach to romantic relationships when compared to other parts of the world.

Cultural groups vary in many ways, and to do justice to the ways that culture influences romantic relationships would require much more than a single chapter. Instead, in this chapter, we have used the developing literature on East Asian ways of thinking, feeling, and relating to suggest avenues for further investigation of culturally-defined relationships. Our chapter focuses on research from countries that largely share a Confucian heritage and Taoist ways of thinking (People's Republic of China (PRC), Taiwan, South Korea, and Japan; Nisbett, 2003; Therborn, 2004a). We acknowledge that historical, economic, ecological, and other factors have led to diverse policies, practices, and attitudes about marriage within and across these countries. However, their shared legacies of Confucianism and dialectical thinking contribute to core similarities in relationship patterns that diverge from those found in Western contexts marked by Judeo-Christian heritage, Enlightenment values, and analytical ways of thinking. (For perspectives on romantic relationships in other regions of the world, we recommend Campos & Kim, 2017; Hewitt & Churchill, 2020; Karandashev, 2017; Schmitt, 2005, 2010; Therborn, 2004a).

The topics that are central to this book – relationship initiation, maintenance, and dissolution – take different forms in different cultural contexts. For example, dating is not universal across cultures (some societies still widely practice variations of arranged marriage; and dating can look very different in diverse cultural contexts; de Munck, 1998); pair-bonding and marriage come in a variety of forms (e.g., unmarried people who cohabit; polygamous families); and romance may not be a central feature of relationship initiation or maintenance in some contexts (Lam et al., 2016; Levine et al., 1995).

This chapter focuses primarily on how sociocultural factors shape East Asian models of romantic relationships, with comparisons to the dominant model of relationships in European-heritage contexts (such as the United States, Canada, Western European, New Zealand, and Australia). We first focus on relatively broad social, ideological, and institutional factors that shape the East Asian *Confucian* cultural model of marriage, then we drill down to describe how East Asian ways of thinking, feeling, and behaving result in relationship processes that diverge from those observed in Western contexts. We conclude with comments and suggestions for scholars who seek to expand their own research to include cross-cultural perspectives.

CULTURAL MODELS OF ROMANTIC RELATIONSHIPS

Cultural models have been defined as "Presupposed, taken-for-granted models of the world that are widely shared (although not always to the exclusion of other, alternative models) by the members of a society and that play an enormous role in their understanding of that world and their behavior in it" (Quinn & Holland, 1987, p. 4). These widely shared understandings are shaped throughout childhood and beyond by stories, injunctions, morality tales, media, traditions, and everyday practices; over time, they become tacit, "natural" or "obvious" ways of understanding the world (i.e., the Western cultural model of the *sacred couple*).

East Asian Models of Romantic Relationships

In East Asian contexts (China, Japan, Korea, and Taiwan), ideals, practices, and traditions are founded in Confucian ethics and values, which include loyalty to one's family and group, conformity to social expectations and obligations, and respect for those with higher rank or age (Hwang, 2014; Ikels, 2004). Confucian ethics spell out proper behavior in five cardinal relationships and the ordering of these relationships or roles in terms of importance: ruler and minister, father and son, husband and wife, brother to brother, and between friends (Ho, 1996). As this ordering indicates, the relation between children and their parents is traditionally more important than that of spouses. In traditional Confucian-influenced contexts, marriages are embedded in a web of relational obligations. East Asian families (especially those in China and Taiwan) are founded on the framework of *filial piety* (which is termed, *xial*, in China). Filial piety refers to the importance of continuing the family line, and it imposes several obligations on individuals. First, adult children are obligated to show gratitude, respect, and care for their parents until their deaths (Ho, 1996; Ikels, 2004; Wu et al., 2016; Yeh, 2003). Second, children must continue the family line by having children. Finally, children are expected to behave in ways that bring honor and respect to their families. Filial piety has been referred to as the "essential core of Confucian ethics for ordinary people" (Hwang & Han, 2010, p. 486); it is the foundation for putting one's family's needs before one's own (Hwang, 2014; Xu et al., 2017).

Filial piety is a well-articulated cultural value in East Asian contexts, but the *Confucian* model of relationships also involves other dimensions of cultural variation. In particular, East Asian contexts are relatively *tight*, which means the range of acceptable behavior in everyday situations is fairly narrow and there is little tolerance of deviations from the norm (Gelfand, 2018; Gelfand et al., 2011). In contrast, in *looser* societies (e.g., New Zealand, the Netherlands), social norms are relatively weak; there is a broader range of acceptable behavior within situations and deviant behavior is more acceptable. Cultural tightness has been traced to historical and ecological threats, such as resource scarcity, disease prevalence, natural disasters, and dense populations (Gelfand et al., 2011). Consequently, there are relatively firm, strictly held norms for individuals and families with respect to romantic relationships in East Asian contexts; people who deviate from these norms may be harshly criticized, sanctioned by their families, and punished by their workplaces, communities, or the government.

Western, European-Heritage Models of Romantic Relationships

The cultural model that frames Western, middle-class marriages focuses on the sacred couple (Shweder et al., 2003). Western relationships tend to build on Judeo-Christian and enlightenment values, which emphasize individual choice of marriage partners and prioritization of the couple and the nuclear family over the extended family. Therborn (2004a, 2006, 2014) argues that in the Western European family model (what Therborn terms the *Christian-European* family model), marriage is not universal (i.e., singleness and celibacy are celebrated for some, such as among priests and nuns in the Catholic church); dissolution of romantic relationships and marriages is relatively easy; and gender equality is frequently enshrined in laws. These societies are relatively loose, allowing for a variety of relationship types (e.g., same sex marriages; couples who chose not to have children, short- and long-term cohabitation). The sacred couple model of marriage stipulates a boundary between the nuclear family (the couple and their children) and their extended families. Of course, there is variation in European-heritage countries in the extent to which this cultural model is lived out, with considerable differences between North-Western European (e.g., Sweden, Denmark) and Eastern and Southern European countries (e.g., Slovenia, Italy, and Greece; Kalmijn, 2007; Švab et al., 2012; see also Thornton, 2005).

Legal Influences on Models of Marriage

A country's laws around marriage and children also shape or frame the ways that marriage is initiated and proceeds. They often stipulate the minimum age for marriage, who is allowed to marry (e.g., whether same-sex couples may marry; whether an already married person may take another spouse), property rights, and the responsibilities of parents. Although many countries have instituted laws to give women equal rights as men in marriage, as of 2020 10 percent of countries continue to legally require women to obey their husbands (Gautier, 2020). Similarly, 24 percent of countries do not provide women the same rights as men in obtaining a divorce or in remarrying.

European-heritage and richer countries have legally given women more equality, especially compared to Middle Eastern and North African countries (Gautier, 2020).

Family law in the East Asia region is fairly diverse, partly due to the division between the more democratic countries of South Korea, Japan, and Taiwan, compared to the communist influences in the PRC. In many of these Confucian-heritage countries, families are viewed as the bedrock of society, and laws have traditionally served to maintain family stability (rather than individual rights; Chin et al., 2014; Zhou, 2017). Thus, although equal rights are enshrined in law in these countries, men's rights and wishes continue to be privileged over those of women (Ji, 2015). For example, in the PRC, women were officially given equal rights in the marriage laws of 1950 (which were updated in the 1980 Marriage Law); in practice, women may still be discriminated against in the case of a divorce. Chinese laws also require adult children to provide financial and emotional support for their parents (Xu & Xia, 2014; see Hwang, 2014 for Taiwanese family policy)

China also has many registration laws that shape family life, especially for families that emigrate from rural areas to urban areas to work. Individuals whose registration (termed *hukou*, in China) is in a rural area do not have equal access to social services, educational recourses, or other support available in an urban *hukou* (Wang & Xia, 2020). Cohabitation can be very costly in terms of limiting the partners' professional opportunities and restricting their access to government services; the children born to unmarried couples may not be registered and do not have the same educational opportunities as other children (Chin et al., 2014; Xu, 2017). Furthermore, the PRC's effort to reduce population growth by enforcing a single child law for families gave rise to an imbalanced sex ratio, with 120 men of marriageable age for every 100 women (Xu et al., 2017). This has resulted in a greater number of unmarried men, especially among those in the lower socio-economic rungs of Chinese society (Wang & Xia 2020; see also Raymo et al., 2015).

In contrast, laws in Western cultural contexts privilege the individual over the family, and they increasingly permit a variety of nontraditional family configurations. The frequency of cohabitation without marriage is increasing in European-heritage countries (Lesthaeghe, 2020), and in many Latin American countries (Esteve et al., 2022). In some Western-heritage countries, more than half of all births are to non-married women (e,g, France, Norway, Sweden, Denmark; OECD Family Database, 2020; Ortiz-Ospina & Roser, 2020). At the end of 2021, legal partnerships or marriages among same-sex couples were legal in thirty-one countries; most of these are in Northwestern Europe and other European-heritage countries (Australia, New Zealand, Canada, and the United States), with growing acceptance in South American countries (e.g., Brazil, Uruguay, Argentina; Hewitt & Churchill, 2020; Navarre & Trimble, 2021).

MATE SELECTION EAST AND WEST

In many non-western contexts, mate selection is the job of one's parents (Buunk et al., 2008; Therborn, 2004a). In general, parents are more involved in young people's mate selection in collectivist societies than in individualistic societies (Buunk et al., 2010), and in societies where the extended family systems prevail over the nuclear family (Lee & Stone, 1980).

In Confucian contexts, marriage was traditionally viewed as the union of two families, and the selection of appropriate mates for one's children was a central parental responsibility. Young people were thought to be too inexperienced to make such decisions themselves. Although the primary purpose of marriage is continuation of the family line, one can better ensure the success of one's family if the marriage enhances the family's resources. Thus, accumulation of property, advantageous business alliances, and useful political ties often have been the foundation of marriages (Hsu, 1963). Traditionally, the primary criterion for mate selection is the compatibility of the young people's family backgrounds. This is known as *men tang hu tui*, which means "the doors of the two families should be of similar texture and the houses must face each other." (Chu, 1985, p. 264; Xia & Zhou, 2003). To the Chinese, this means that the partners should come from similar socio-economic backgrounds. The assumption is that this similarity of backgrounds will ensure an easy adjustment to the marriage and the likelihood of compatibility. Furthermore, East Asians assume that any reasonably competent man and woman can forge a good partnership because people are able to adjust and change to fit each other (Chiu et al., 1997; Joo et al., 2022). Thus, finding one's "soulmate" or "being in love" are not always the criteria for finding a partner. Instead, pragmatic concerns may have priority over romance and emotion in mate selection.

Like many aspects of life in East Asian contexts, individuals' and their family's expectations and preferences for marital partners are changing. Young people in China, for example, expect to choose their own partners with the guidance of their families (Zhang & Kline, 2009). When Chinese or Taiwanese young people are asked to describe their ideal partner, men, and women both are interested in partners who will sacrifice for the sake of the family, who exhibit filial piety (Xu & Xia, 2014), who are kind and honest, who are acceptable to their parents, and who they love (Chen et al., 2015; Guo et al., 2017; Jankowiak et al., 2015; Lam et al., 2016; Zhang & Kline, 2009; Zhou, 2017) Women are more likely than men to seek a partner with higher social status and economic standing than themselves (Schmitt, 2004). Parents of young people, however, are more likely than their offspring to value attributes related to the future son/daughter-in-law's political, educational, and religious background and their social status (Guo et al., 2017). A comparison of parent-offspring preferences for the offspring's future partner found that there was more convergence among Chinese parent-offspring pairs than among a similar group of American parent-offspring pairs

(Guo et al., 2017); this reflects a tighter society in China with more agreement about the attributes desired in an ideal partner.

Given that a child's first responsibility is to demonstrate filial piety in Confucian contexts by producing children and raising them successfully, unmarried adults are often stigmatized (Xu & Xia, 2014). Indeed, unmarried people over the age of thirty in China are negatively labeled "leftover" or "bare-branches" (Ji, 2015; Jin & Guo, 2011). In South Korea, marriage marks the achievement of adulthood, so unmarried adults may be considered "underage" (Park & Hong, 2012, cited by Chin et al., 2014). As of 2010, the proportion of never-married adults aged 30–44 in China was about 5 percent (Chen & Tong, 2021), compared to 28 percent in the United States in 2018 (US Census Bureau, 2020). Marriage rates in the PRC have stayed about the same since 1980, despite great increases in affluence and increased rural-urban migration (Lesthaeghe, 2020; Wang & Xia, 2020), whereas marriage rates in Japan are much lower than in China (Hewitt & Churchill, 2020). Married offspring tend to have more resources to share with aging parents than do unmarried children (Jin & Guo, 2011), which may also be part of the reason that Chinese parents, who often have little access to pensions or state welfare programs, pressure their children to marry. As a result of this bias against unmarried people, many Chinese cities have a gathering place for parents to post fliers seeking a mate for their child (Zhou, 2017).

In Western contexts, because individuals are selecting romantic partners themselves, mutual love and attraction are the primary grounds for mate selection (Buunk et al., 2010). As Buunk et al. (2008) articulate, many of the existing theories of mate selection, particularly evolutionary theories, operate under the assumption that individuals have complete freedom to select their own mates. Much of this work has been conducted in individualistic and in loose cultural contexts, where there are fewer social norms and expectations around marriage. Marriage rates in Western European countries are low relative to the rest of the world, although US marriage rates are higher than in Western Europe and other Western heritage countries (e.g., New Zealand, Australia, Canada; Hewitt & Churchill, 2020). Some of the reasons for low marriage rates in Western contexts include acceptance of singleness as a legitimate personal choice and greater incidence of cohabitation and of children born outside marriage (Horowitz et al., 2019; Lesthaeghe, 2020; Thornton & Young-DeMarco, 2001).

HOW DO CULTURALLY DISTINCTIVE WAYS OF THINKING AND FEELING INFLUENCE RELATIONSHIP PROCESSES?

Independent and Interdependent Models of the Self

As individuals grow up, they become accustomed to the cultural model – a constellation of norms, values, and practices that direct the ways individuals relate to and interpret the world (Cross & Lam, 2017; Quinn & Holland, 1987).

These cultural models are building blocks for developing the normative pattern of social interactions, including how one views the self and maintains relationships with close others (Markus & Kitayama, 2010). One of the most influential theories in cultural psychology is cultural models of independent and interdependent self (Markus & Kitayama, 1991). People with an independent self recognize themselves as a separate and unique whole. Therefore, it is ideal to be autonomous, to choose personal values over social obligations, and to express one's authentic self consistently across time and situations. In contrast to individuals with the independent self, for those who have an interdependent model of self, the self is a part of a web of close relationships, fundamentally connected with important others. Hence, the cultural ideal is to fit in, to be appropriate, and to be flexible to maintain harmony with the social environment. Whereas the independent self is prevalent in Western societies, the interdependent model of the self is prevalent in non-Western societies such as East Asian cultural contexts. It is important to note that the emphasis on independent vs. interdependent self is relative. For instance, people from the United States and Western European contexts are more likely to endorse the independent self, compared to those in East Asian cultures (Markus & Kitayama, 1991). Within the United States, European Americans are more likely to be independent than African American groups, whose culture facilitates interdependence (Brannon et al., 2015).

As the models of the self explain the ways individuals navigate the social world, they should be closely tied to cultural models of close relationships. However, relatively few studies have examined how culturally normative ways of being a person manifest in one's close relationships. In this section, we examine how cultural models guide the formation and maintenance of close relationships.

Predispositions

Individuals bring in their distinctive tendencies to close relationships, such as their personality or expectations about close others. Cultural differences in cognition and emotion can influence people's predispositions that carry over to their relationship dynamic. One important example of such predisposition is one's attachment style (Bowlby, 1973). Attachment theory has been applied extensively in various areas such as legal settings and counseling contexts but researchers have remained relatively indifferent to exploration of cultural variations (but see Keller et al., 2006; Morelli et al., 2017). Among the limited number of studies on culture and attachment, most focus on differences in attachment styles. For instance, individuals from East Asian, interdependent cultures were found to be high in anxious and avoidant attachment styles compared to their Western counterparts (Schmitt, 2004; Wei et al., 2004; You & Malley-Morrison, 2000). However, this tendency in individuals from interdependent cultures should not be viewed as unhealthy or insecure, as fundamental assumptions in attachment theory may reflect Western ideals about close relationships. Indeed, compared to people in the United States, Taiwanese individuals viewed an insecure attachment style as more ideal (Wang & Mallinckrodt, 2006). This cultural difference may partly be due to Chinese relational norms that suppress direct expression of emotion and identity, in contrast to Western norms that encourage open communications with the romantic partner (Wang & Mallinckrodt, 2006).

A few studies have shed light on cultural differences in the basic assumptions of attachment theory. According to the theory, the romantic partner serves as the central figure in one's relationship network. People prioritize their partner over anyone else, mainly turn to them in times of need, and serve as each other's basis of self-growth (e.g., Zeifman & Hazan, 2008). However, whether individuals around the world form their strongest attachment to their romantic partner is questionable. For instance, in a daily diary study, US individuals in dating relationships tended to turn to the romantic partner over other relationships for more severe negative events, demonstrating the centrality of the attachment bond with the romantic partner. In contrast, this difference between the romantic partner and other relationships was not found among Korean individuals (Joo, 2021). When Taiwanese and US participants were asked the hypothetical question of whether they would save their mother or their spouse from a burning house, the Taiwanese participants were far more likely than the Americans to choose to save their mother (Wu et al., 2016). Further, residential mobility has been identified as a possible mechanism for such cultural differences. Yilmaz et al. (2022) found that Turkish individuals who frequently relocate are more likely to confide in their romantic partner on important matters compared to those who do not, suggesting that dense social connections may attenuate the importance of the romantic partner. These findings emphasize the need to consider relationship networks holistically rather than focusing on the romantic relationship exclusively, especially in cultural contexts with low relational mobility and strong interdependence.

People also bring a set of expectations to their close relationships, which are largely based on cultural norms and ideals. For instance, studies have found that individuals from collectivistic cultural backgrounds, such as Indians (Bejanyan et al., 2014), Taiwanese (Lam et al., 2016), and South Asian Canadians (Lalonde et al., 2004) tend to prefer potential mates who have traditional characteristics (e.g., gender roles, chastity, etc.) compared to their Western counterparts. Such differences were often attributed to an interdependent model of self; if individuals include their close others in the self, they are more likely to employ traditional and normative standards. In a similar vein, endorsement of family values also explained the cultural difference between Indians and Americans in ideal characteristics (Bejanyan et al., 2014). Further, the emphasis on family relationships in some cultures leads individuals to explicitly prefer potential mates who are family-oriented. Indeed, individuals from Taiwan were more likely to consider those who endorse extended family-oriented beliefs (e.g., who look after each other's parents) as ideal marriage partners compared to those from the United States (Lam et al., 2016).

Partner Perception and Evaluation

Across cultures, couples strive to form and maintain happy relationships. In so doing, they engage in processes such as evaluation, conflict management, and expression of emotion. Cultural factors guide and provide the basis on which these processes operate. For instance, culture influences how individuals perceive and evaluate their romantic partner. In Western cultures, it has been consistently found that individuals tend to view their romantic partner in a positive light (Fletcher, 2015). European Americans often perceive their romantic partner more positively than the partner views themselves (e.g., Murray et al., 1996a, 1996b). In turn, this positive directional bias has been consistently linked to positive consequences such as high relationship quality (Fletcher & Kerr, 2010). However, researchers have found that this positive bias is weaker among East Asian couples, and it is attributable to the cultural theory of dialecticism. Individuals from East Asian cultural contexts tend to endorse the lay belief that the world is full of contradictions that work together to form a harmony (i.e., *naïve dialecticism*; Peng & Nisbett, 1999). Hence, they tolerate contradictions and ambivalence better than Western individuals, and this tendency permeates into one's close relationships (for a review, see Cross & Lam, 2018). For instance, Lam and colleagues (2016) found that compared to their European American peers, Hong Kong Chinese individuals not only rated partners more ambivalently on an explicit level, describing them as having both positive and negative characteristics, but also were more ambivalent toward their partners on an implicit level; they associated their partner with both positive and negative words. In addition, Hong Kong Chinese individuals were less likely to evaluate a partner in a more positive light than the partner's self-view (i.e., lower positive directional bias) compared to European Americans (Cross & Lam, 2018).

The cultural difference in the partner assessment is also related to different normative strategies to maintain relationships under independent and interdependent cultural models. For instance, positive bias can make the partner feel good about themselves, thereby strengthening the relationship (Murray et al., 1996b). This aligns with the promotion-oriented relationship maintenance strategy often used among individuals with independent models of self. Because relational ties are often weak, people must constantly engage in behaviors that confirm their intimacy and support for their partner (Kito et al., 2017). In contrast, when problems appear, positive bias can easily shift to negative directional bias, making the relationship vulnerable to dissolution (Fletcher, 2015; Le et al., 2010). Therefore, an ambivalent attitude would reduce the risk of the relationship ending, which is consistent with the use of prevention-focused strategies in close relationships among those with interdependent self (Li et al., 2015). Indeed, East Asian people tend to develop the feeling of being embedded in close-knit social networks, and they engage in prevention strategies such as avoiding conflict by suppressing emotions (Cross & Lam, 2017).

Emotional Experience and Expression

One of the important ways such promotion vs. prevention strategies are manifested is through emotional experience and expression in romantic relationships. Individuals with an independent model of the self must keep recognizing and expressing their love and intimacy to maintain the relationship because relationships are relatively mobile (Schug et al., 2010).

Indeed, studies found that individuals from Western cultural contexts tended to feel more intimate with their close others than Polish people (Rybak & McAndrew, 2006) and Chinese Canadians (Marshall, 2008). Also, individuals from Western, independence-oriented cultures reported higher passion and love toward their romantic partner compared to those from non-Western, interdependence-oriented cultures (Goodwin & Findlay, 1997; Sprecher, Sullivan, et al., 1994). One possible reason behind such cultural patterns of love among East Asian individuals is the tendency to see the "bad in the good." Individuals from East Asian cultures tend to show a dialectical understanding of emotion (for a review, see Goetz et al., 2008). They tend to experience mixed and ambivalent emotions more frequently compared to Western individuals in close relationships (Tsai, Levenson, et al., 2006). For example, after engaging in a structured discussion, Chinese American couples were more likely to experience both love and negative emotions (e.g., anger), but European American couples were more likely to experience either love or negative emotions (Shiota et al., 2010).

Not only are individuals with an independent self-concept more likely to experience high intimacy but they also are more likely to directly express their affection, compared to those with an interdependent model of the self. For instance, Americans are more likely to say "I love you" to close others than are Chinese individuals (Caldwell-Harris et al., 2013). Such cultural differences are also evident in media; both verbal and nonverbal affection are more likely to be found in American books than in Chinese books (Wu et al., 2019). In contrast to the Western emphasis on direct expression of affection, in interdependence-oriented cultures, implicit communication is valued over direct emotional expression because the latter can disrupt group harmony (Gao et al., 1996; Hofstede, 2001). For example, African Americans and Asian Americans are less likely to consider self-expressive skills as a crucial factor in close relationships than are European Americans (Samter et al., 1997). For African American individuals, simply keeping the company of close others could be considered a good conversation. Similarly, Chinese individuals were less likely to use verbal expressions of love but were more likely to use an indirect method of expressing gratitude (e.g., offering advice) or love (e.g., gift-giving) compared to US individuals (Beichen & Murshed, 2015; Bello et al., 2010). Taken together, close relationships among those with an interdependent model of the self may not be so much rooted in explicit emotional expression but in companionship and implicit reciprocity (Burleson, 2003).

Relationship Maintenance

Cultural norms influence how individuals deal with difficulties in relationships. At a fundamental level, the meaning of conflict differs across cultures. In independence-oriented cultures, conflict is perceived as a chance to strengthen the relationship if managed effectively. Hence, the ability to voice one's thoughts and anger constructively to negotiate conflicting goals between partners is critical to the well-being of the relationship (Greenberg & Goldman, 2008). In these contexts, a primary focus is on expressing and maintaining the authentic self throughout the conflict management process (Knee et al., 2013). In interdependence-oriented societies, in contrast, surfaced disagreement denotes the failure of the relationship. Therefore, individuals strive to avoid conflicts by reading their partner's mind so they can fulfill the partner's needs before being asked, or by suppressing their own thoughts and emotions (Rothbaum et al., 2000). Indeed, Koreans were more likely to use passive conflict management strategies such as neglecting the situation, compared to the United States individuals (Yum, 2000).

Another important process behind relationship maintenance is the regulation of the self and the partner. Being able to protect and maintain one's self-concept is critically important in Western cultural contexts (Cross et al., 2003). Therefore, attempts to change or improve the partner's behavior could make the partner feel negatively regarded and could decrease relationship quality among Western individuals (for a review, see Overall, 2012). However, changing the self for the partner may come naturally for individuals in interdependence-fostering cultures as they tend to use prevention-oriented strategies. In societies with high social interdependence, people prioritize avoiding conflicts by adjusting themselves to situations rather than by expressing themselves and influencing the situation (Morling et al., 2002). This tendency carries over to self- and partner-regulation in romantic relationships. For instance, Joo et al. (2022) found that compared to US married couples, Chinese couples perceived that they had changed more in their relationships because they were more likely to value obligatory adjustments (e.g., "[It is important to] go along with one's partner even if one does not agree with his or her point of view"). Furthermore, the degree to which individuals changed in the relationship was related to higher relationship quality among Chinese individuals but not among US individuals. The results of the study suggest that attempts to change the partner's behavior and thoughts may not be as harmful in East Asian contexts as in Western contexts.

SOCIOCULTURAL INFLUENCES AND RELATIONSHIP DISSOLUTION

Laws and Norms Related to Divorce and Dissolution

A society's views of divorce and relationship dissolution intertwine traditional cultural viewpoints, social and family concerns, and legal options. In most East Asian contexts, people who divorce face considerable stigma, as do their children (Xu & Xia, 2014). Children from divorced families may face discrimination in finding marriage partners, so parents often decide to stay together for the sake of their children (Soumuchou, 1987, cited in Rothbaum, Rosen et al., 2002). This perspective is reflected in courts' decisions whether or not to grant a divorce; despite laws providing for no-fault divorce in China, for example, judges may be reluctant to grant a divorce due to beliefs that the welfare and development of children depend on an intact family (Wang & Xia, 2020).

Since 1990, divorce rates have increased in East Asian contexts; in China, this rise is often attributed to urbanization and increased unemployment rates (Zhang et al., 2014, cited in Wang & Xia, 2020). Chinese couples cite other reasons for seeking a divorce, including domestic violence, family dysfunction, gender inequality, and property rights disputes (Johnson et al., 2015; Liu et al., 2019; Wang & Xia, 2020; Yang et al., 2018). Taiwan and South Korea have instituted no-fault divorce laws (Chin et al., 2014; Hwang, 2014). Nevertheless, the net divorce rates in East Asian contexts are still considerably lower than in Western contexts (Hewitt & Churchill; 2020).

These sociocultural influences in East Asian contexts serve as *centripetal forces* (i.e., outside influences acting on the couple) that keep the couple together. Laws, social stigma, and family pressure may work together to offset *centrifugal forces* (i.e., influences from within the couple that might cause them to separate). Rothbaum and his colleagues (2000) describe the external forces that keep Japanese couples together as "an incentive structure, enforced by the social network, that surrounds all relationships within the group and serves to support those relationships" (2000, p. 1133; see also the notion of *structural commitment* by Johnson, 1991; Johnson et al., 1999). With strong centripetal forces keeping the couple together, there is less expectation that the marriage needs intimacy, romance, or passion to thrive (Iwao, 1993).

In contrast, in Western cultural contexts, the centripetal forces of norms, expectations, and laws that hold a marriage together are weaker; no-fault divorce, legal gender equality, affluence, and declines in stigma and discrimination against divorced people make the dissolution of a marriage much easier to contemplate than in the past (Brown & Wright, 2019; Gillath & Keefer, 2016). Western or European-heritage countries have been exposed to broad social changes (e.g., increased individualism, greater residential mobility, increases in women's rights, greater participation of women in the workforce) longer than have most East Asian countries, and these social changes contribute to rising rates of divorce (Vignoli et al., 2018; Wang & Schofer, 2018). Likewise, social norms and attitudes within Western societies, such as increased focus on personal satisfaction, self-fulfillment, intimacy, and romantic love, have contributed to higher expectations of a marriage partner, and consequently to higher rates of divorce (Cherlin, 2004; Finkel et al., 2014). In short, the centripetal forces acting to keep a couple together have weakened, whereas the centrifugal forces (e.g., higher expectations of self-fulfillment and increased acceptance of divorce) have tended to push couples apart, leading to high levels of divorce in Western contexts.

COUPLE-LEVEL FACTORS THAT INFLUENCE THE DISSOLUTION OF RELATIONSHIPS AND MARRIAGE

A relationship can come to an end because of one's feelings or decisions (e.g., lack of love and intimacy) or due to contextual factors (e.g., bad relationships with extended family). As has been discussed throughout this chapter, one's internal motivation and choice play more important roles in relationship processes among individuals with independent versus interdependent self-concepts. Two widely examined internal motivators of relationship dissolution are (loss of) love and relationship satisfaction (Rodrigues et al., 2013).

Often, love is considered to be fundamental to long-lasting relationships. Especially in Western, independence-oriented cultures, romantic and passionate love serve as the foundation for marriage (Finkel et al., 2014; Kephart, 1967; Sprecher, Aron et al., 1994). Indeed, individuals who get divorced tend to show diminished love and affection toward their partner (Huston et al., 2001).

Meanwhile, any intervention of external factors such as marriage arrangement by family carries a negative connotation. Even though arranged marriages can signify compatibility, the reduced role of love seems to discount the sacredness of such marriage (Eastwick, 2013). In contrast, in interdependence-oriented cultures, prioritizing the feeling of love over harmony with one's social environment is viewed as being immature (Shaver et al., 1992). In such cultural contexts, relationships are built upon the individual as well as social compatibility rather than romantic love. For instance, individuals from Chinese backgrounds were more likely to value the relationship with extended family and relational harmony compared to those from European heritage backgrounds (Hiew et al., 2015; Lam et al., 2016). Furthermore, a study found that Chinese couples had high cohesiveness even though they did not endorse romantic love as the building block of their marriage (Xu & Ye, 1999). The role of relationship satisfaction in relationship dissolution is also subject to cultural influence. Low satisfaction in relationships has consistently been linked to a high risk of relationship dissolution in Western cultures (Gager & Sanchez, 2003; Karney & Bradbury, 1995). Happiness is constitutive of relationships; thus, low satisfaction signals the inability of the relationship to serve its core function. However, research has shown that those with interdependent self-construals tend to care less about satisfaction with their partner and more about fulfilling obligations and meeting social expectations. For example, East Asian couples tend to report lower relationship satisfaction and higher negative emotions in relationships than their Western counterparts (Cross & Lam, 2018; Schoebi et al., 2010; Tsai, Knutson, et al., 2006; Williamson et al., 2012). More importantly, Broman (2002) found that marital satisfaction was a significant predictor of divorce for European-heritage Americans but not for African Americans, whose culture tends to foster interdependence (Brannon et al., 2015).

CONCLUSIONS

Romantic relationships in East Asian and Western contexts have many similarities and many differences. We have focused primarily on differences here because most of relationship science has assumed similarities. Western scientists have seldom examined the assumptions embedded in their theories and research, or whether these assumptions might vary cross-culturally. Relationships involve people's thoughts and attitudes, their emotional reactions, their motives, and goals, and mounting research shows that these and other basic processes (e.g., cognition, emotion, brain activity) vary cross-culturally (Cohen & Kitayama, 2019; Kitayama & Uskul, 2011; Masuda et al., 2019; Tsai & Clobert, 2019).

Ideally, a chapter like this would have included information from a broader range of cultural contexts. We focused on East Asian relationships because there is an established literature on cultural variation in basic psychological processes in this region and a growing research base applying that literature to romantic and family relationships. Creative scholars in other cultural contexts are also contributing to a broader understanding of romantic relationships (e.g., the Philippines [Vazhappily & Reyes, 2016]; the Middle East [Alhuzail, 2022; Sadeghi et al., 2012; Yilmaz et al., 2022]; S. Asia [Fonseca et al., 2018; Iqbal et al., 2019]; Latin America [Bravo & Martinez, 2016; Esteve et al., 2022; Falconier & Epstein, 2011]; and Africa [Nwoye, 2000; Osei-Tutu et al., 2021; Salter & Adams, 2012; Therborn, 2004b]).

Relationship scientists who want to be on the cutting edge of our discipline have many opportunities to expand into new cultural contexts, but they must go beyond simply seeking to generalize existing Western theories in non-Western contexts. We encourage scholars to partner with indigenous researchers who can bring to the investigation the key cultural concepts, values, and beliefs about relationships in that context, and who can point out the cultural assumptions in existing theories and research. Research that combines indigenous concepts, beliefs, and processes with existing Western theories and approaches will be most successful in developing a more global and equitable science of relationships (see Zhang & Kline, 2020, for more suggestions for cross-cultural research in relationships). We encourage investigators venturing into unfamiliar cultural contexts to approach their work with a sense of humility: Western scholars need to be willing to consider non-Western relationships from within that culture's worldview and perspective, looking for the ways culturally specific beliefs and practices have developed over time and their functions in maintaining families and societies. As our opening example of assigning family members to rooms illustrates, a decision that seems odd or unusual to a Westerner will often have deep cultural roots based in long-standing values and beliefs. We recognize that thinking outside the Western-focused relationship science "box" has many challenges, and that it is safer, faster, and cheaper to study easily accessed populations in the United States, Canada, and Western Europe. Doing research with romantic couples at all is difficult and expensive. But the time has come to recognize that if relationship science is to be a *human* science, it must be a *global* science.

REFERENCES

Alhuzail, N. A. (2022). The meaning of the marital relationship in the lives of three generations of Bedouin women. *Journal of Cross-Cultural Psychology*, 53(6), 683–702. https://doi.org/10.1177/00220221221099593

Beichen, L., & Murshed, F. (2015). Culture, expressions of romantic love, and gift-giving. *Journal of International Business Research*, 14(1), 68.

Bejanyan, K., Marshall, T. C., & Ferenczi, N. (2014). Romantic ideals, mate preferences, and anticipation of future difficulties in marital life: A comparative studXy of young adults in India and America. *Frontiers in Psychology*, 5, 1355. https://doi.org/10.3389/fpsyg.20

Bello, R. S., Brandau-Brown, F. E., Zhang, S., & Ragsdale, J. D. (2010). Verbal and non-verbal methods for expressing appreciation in friendships and romantic relationships: A cross- cultural comparison. *International Journal of Intercultural Relations*, 34(3), 294–302. https://doi.org/10.1016/j.ijintrel.2010.02.007

Bowlby, J. (1973). Attachment and loss: Volume II: Separation, anxiety and anger. In *Attachment and loss: Volume II: Separation, anxiety and anger*. The Hogarth Press and the Institute of Psycho-Analysis.

Brannon, T. N., Markus, H. R., & Taylor, V. J. (2015). "Two souls, two thoughts," two self-schemas: Double consciousness can have positive academic consequences for African Americans. *Journal of Personality and Social Psychology, 108*(4), 586–609. https://doi.org/10.1037/a0038992

Bravo, C. S., & Martinez, A. W. (2016). Profiles using indicators of marital communication, communication styles, and marital satisfaction in Mexican couples. *Journal of Sex & Marital Therapy, 43*(4), 361–376. https://doi.org/10.1080/0092623x.2016.1168332

Broman, C. L. (2002). Thinking of divorce, but staying married: The interplay of race and marital satisfaction. *Journal of Divorce & Remarriage, 37*(1–2), 151–161. https://doi.org/10.1300/J087v37n01_09

Brown, S. L., & Wright, M. R. (2019). Divorce attitudes among older adults: Two decades of change. *Journal of Family Issues, 40*(8), 1018–1037. https://doi.org/10.1177/0192513X19832936

Burleson, B. R. (2003). The experience and effects of emotional support: What the study of cultural and gender differences can tell us about close relationships, emotion, and interpersonal communication. *Personal Relationships, 10*(1), 1–23. https://doi.org/10.1111/1475-6811.00033

Buunk, A. P., Park, J. H., & Dubbs, S. L. (2008). Parent-offspring conflict in mate preferences. *Review of General Psychology, 12*(1), 47–62. https://doi.org/10.1037/1089-2680.12.1.47

Buunk, A. P., Park, J. H., & Duncan, L. A. (2010). Cultural variation in parental influence on mate choice. *Cross-Cultural Research: The Journal of Comparative Social Science, 44*(1), 23–40. https://doi.org/10.1177/1069397109337711

Caldwell-Harris, C., Kronrod, A., & Yang, J. (2013). Do more, say less: Saying "I love you" in Chinese and American cultures. *Intercultural Pragmatics, 10*(1), 41–69. https://doi.org/10.1515/ip-2013-0002

Campos, B., & Kim, H. S. (2017). Incorporating the cultural diversity of family and close relationships into the study of health. *American Psychologist, 72*(6), 543–554. https://doi.org/10.1037/amp0000122

Chen, D., & Tong, Y. (2021). Marriage for the sake of parents? Adult children's marriage formation and parental psychological distress in China. *Journal of Marriage and Family, 83*(4), 1194–1211. https://doi.org/10.1111/jomf.12749

Chen, R., Austin, J. P., Miller, J. K., & Piercy, F. P. (2015). Chinese and American individuals' mate selection criteria: Updates, modifications, and extensions. *Journal of Cross-cultural Psychology, 46*(1), 101–118. https://doi.org/10.1177/0022022114551793

Cherlin, A. J. (2004). The deinstitutionalization of American marriage. *Journal of Marriage and Family, 66*(4), 848–861.

Chin, M. J., Lee, J., Lee, S., Son, S., & Sung, M. (2014). Family policy in S. Korea: Development, implementation, and evaluation. In M. Robila (Ed.), *Handbook of family policies across the Globe*. Springer. https://doi.org/10.1007/978-1-4614-6771-7_20

Chiu, C., Hong, Y., & Dweck, C. S. (1997). Lay dispositionism and implicit theories of personality. *Journal of Personality and Social Psychology, 73*(1), 19–30.

Chu, G. C. (1985). The changing concept of self in contemporary China. In A. J. Marsella, G. deVos & F. L. K. Hsu (Eds.), *Culture and self: Asian and western perspectives* (pp. 252–277). Tavistock.

Cohen, D., & Kitayama, S. (2019). *Handbook of cultural psychology* (2nd ed.). Guilford Press.

Cross, S. E., & Lam, B. C. P. (2017). Cultural models of self: East-West differences and beyond. In A. T. Church (Ed.), *The Praeger handbook of personality across cultures* (pp. 1–34). ABC-CLIO.

Cross, S. E., & Lam, B. C. P. (2018). Dialecticism in close relationships and marriage. In J. Spencer-Rodgers & K. Peng (Eds.), *The psychological and cultural foundations of East Asian cognition* (1st ed., pp. 353–381). Oxford University Press. https://doi.org/10.1093/oso/9780199348541.003.0012

Cross, S. E., Gore, J. S., & Morris, M. L. (2003). The relational-interdependent self-construal, self-concept consistency, and well-being. *Journal of Personality and Social Psychology, 85*(5), 933–944. https://doi.org/10.1037/0022-3514.85.5.933

de Munck, V. C. (1998). Lust, Love, and arranged marriages in Sri Lanka. In V. C. de Munck (Ed.), *Romantic love and sexual behavior* (pp. 285–300). Praeger.

Eastwick, P. W. (2013). Cultural influences on attraction. In J. A. Simpson & L. Campbell (Eds.), *The Oxford handbook of close relationships* (pp. 161–182, Chapter xvii, 846 Pages). Oxford University Press.

Esteve, A., Castro-Martin, T., Castro Torres, A. F. (2022). Families in Latin America: Trends, singularities and contextual factors. *Annual Review of Sociology, 48*, 485–505.

Falconier, M. K., & Epstein, N. B. (2011). Female-demand/male-withdraw communication in Argentinian couples: A mediating factor between economic strain and relationship distress. *Personal Relationships, 18*, 586–603. https://doi.org/10.1111/j.1475-6811.2010.01326.x

Finkel, E. J., Hui, C. M., Carswell, K. L., & Larson, G. M. (2014). The suffocation of marriage: Climbing mount Maslow without enough oxygen. *Psychological Inquiry, 25*(1), 1–41. https://doi.org/10.1080/1047840X.2014.863723

Fletcher, G. J. O. (2015). Accuracy and bias of judgments in romantic relationships. *Current Directions in Psychological Science, 24*(4), 292–297. https://doi.org/10.1177/0963721415571664

Fletcher, G. J. O., & Kerr, P. S. G. (2010). Through the eyes of love: Reality and illusion in intimate relationships. *Psychological Bulletin, 136*(4), 627–658. https://doi.org/10.1037/a0019792

Fonseca, A. L., Kamble, S., Duggi, D., Flores, M., & Butler, E. A. (2018). Daily emotion regulation in American and Asian-Indian romantic couples. *Journal of Comparative Family Studies, 49*(4), 487–512.

Gager, C. T., & Sanchez, L. (2003). Two as one? Couples' perceptions of time spent together, marital quality, and the risk of divorce. *Journal of Family Issues, 24*(1), 21–50. https://doi.org/10.1177/0192513X02238519

Gao, G., Ting-Toomey, S., & Gudykunst, W. B. (1996). Chinese communication processes. In M. H. Bond (Ed.), *The handbook of Chinese psychology* (pp. 280–293). Oxford University Press.

Gautier, A. (2020). Family law across cultures (comparative family law). In W. K. Halford & F. van de Vijver (Eds.), *Cross-cultural family research and practice* (pp. 143–184). Elsevier Press.

Gelfand, M. J. (2018). *Rule makers, rule breakers: How tight and loose cultures wire our world*. Scribner.

Gelfand, M. J., Raver, J. L., Nishii, L., Leslie, L. A., Lun, J., Lim, B. C., Duan, L., Almaliach, A., Ang, S., Arnadottir, J., Aycan, Z., Boehnke, K., Boski, P., Cabecinhas, R., Chan, D., Chhokar, J., D'Amato, A., Ferrer, M., Fischlmayr, I. C., … Yamaguchi, S. (2011). Differences between tight and loose cultures: A 33-nation study. *Science*, 332(6033), 1100–1104. https://doi.org/10.1126/science.1197754

Gillath, O., & Keefer, L. A. (2016). Generalizing disposability: Residential mobility and the willingness to dissolve social ties. *Personal Relationships*, 23(2), 186–198. https://doi.org/10.1111/pere.12119

Goetz, J. L., Spencer-Rodgers, J., & Peng, K. (2008). Dialectical emotions: How cultural epistemologies influence the experience and regulation of emotional complexity. In R. M. Sorrentino & S. Yamaguchi (Eds.), *Handbook of motivation and cognition across cultures* (pp. 517–538). Elsevier Publishing.

Goodwin, R., & Findlay, C. (1997). "We were just fated together"… Chinese love and the concept of yuan in England and Hong Kong. *Personal Relationships*, 4(1), 85–92. https://doi.org/10.1111/j.1475-6811.1997.tb00132.x

Greenberg, L. S., & Goldman, R. N. (2008). *Emotion-focused couples therapy: The dynamics of emotion, love, and power*. American Psychological Association.

Guo, Q., Li, Y., & Yu, S. (2017). In-law and mate preferences in Chinese society and the role of traditional cultural values. *Evolutionary Psychology*, 15(3), 1–11.

Hewitt, B., & Churchill, B. (2020). Convergence and difference: Marriage and family life from a cross-cultural perspective. In W. K. Halford and F. van de Vijver (Eds.), *Cross-cultural family research and practice* (pp. 57–102). Elsevier Publishing.

Hiew, D. N., Halford, W. K., van de Vijver, F. J. R., & Liu, S. (2015). The Chinese–Western intercultural couple standards scale. *Psychological Assessment*, 27(3), 816. https://doi.org/10.1037/pas0000090

Ho, D. (1996). Filial piety and its psychological consequences. In M. H. Bond (Ed.), *The handbook of Chinese psychology* (pp. 155–165). Oxford University Press.

Hofstede, G. (2001). *Culture's consequences: Comparing values, behaviors, institutions, and organizations across nations* (2nd ed.). Sage.

Horowitz, J., Graf, N., & Livingston, G. (2019, November 6). "Marriage and cohabitation in the U.S. Pew Research Center." Downloaded from www.pewresearch.org/social-trends/2019/11/06/marriage-and-cohabitation-in-the-u-s/

Hsu, F. L. K. (1963). *Clan, caste, club*. D. Van Nostrand Co., Inc.

Huston, T. L., Caughlin, J. P., Houts, R. M., Smith, S. E., & George, L. J. (2001). The connubial crucible: Newlywed years as predictors of marital delight, distress, and divorce. *Journal of Personality and Social Psychology*, 80(2), 237. https://doi.org/10.1037/0022-3514.80.2.237

Hwang, K. K., & Han, K. H. (2010). Face and morality in Confucian society. In M. H. Bond (Ed.), *The handbook of Chinese psychology* (pp. 479–498). Oxford University Press.

Hwang, S. H. (2014). Family policies in Taiwan: Development, implementation, and assessment. In M. Robila (Ed.), *Handbook of family policies across the globe* (pp. 273–287). Springer.

Ikels, C. (2004). *Filial piety: Practice and discourse in contemporary East Asia*. Stanford University Press.

Iqbal, S., Ayub, N., van de Vijver, F., & Halford, W. K. (2019). Couple relationship standards in Pakistan. *Couple and Family Psychology: Research and Practice, 8*(4), 208–220. https://doi.org/10.1037/cfp0000124

Iwao, S. (1993). *The Japanese woman: Traditional image and changing reality.* Free Press.

Jankowiak, W., Shen, Y., Yao, S., Wang, C., & Volsche, S. (2015). Investigating love's universal attributes: A research report from China. *Cross-Cultural Research, 49*(4), 422–436.

Ji, Y. C. (2015). Between tradition and modernity: "Leftover" women in Shanghai. *Journal of Marriage and Family, 77*(5), 1057–1073.

Jin, X., & Guo, Q. (2011). Intergenerational economic support of unmarried male in rural area. *Northwest Population, 32*(4), 38–42.

Joo, M. J. (2021). *Structural and functional differences in support in close relationships between the East Asian and the Western cultural contexts.* Iowa State University.

Joo, M. J., Lam, B. C. P., Cross, S. E., Chen, S. X., Lau, V. C. Y., Ng, H. K. Y., & Gunsoy, C. (2022). Cross-cultural perspectives on self-change in close relationships: Evidence from Hong Kong Chinese and European Americans. *Personality and Social Psychology Bulletin, 48*(7), 1118–1133. https://doi.org/10.1177/01461672211026129

Johnson, M. D., Nguyen, L., Anderson, J. R., Liu, W., & Vennum, A. (2015). Pathways to romantic relationship success among Chinese young adult couples: Contributions of family dysfunction, mental health problems, and negative couple interaction. *Journal of Social and Personal Relationships, 32*(1), 5–23.

Johnson, M. P. (1991). Commitment to personal relationships. In W. H. Jones & D. W. Perlman (Eds.), *Advances in personal relationships* (Vol. 3, pp. 117–143). Jessica Kingsley.

Johnson, M. P., Caughlin, J. P., & Huston, T. L. (1999). The tripartite nature of marital commitment: Personal, moral, and structural reasons to stay married. *Journal of Marriage and the Family, 61*(1), 160–177.

Kalmijn, M. (2007). Explaining cross-national differences in marriage, cohabitation, and divorce in Europe, 1990–2000. *Population Studies, 61*(3), 243–263. https://doi.org/10.1080/00324720701571805

Karandashev, V. (2017). *Romantic love in cultural contexts.* Springer. https://doi.org/10.1007/978-3-319-42683-9_8

Karney, B. R., & Bradbury, T. N. (1995). The longitudinal course of marital quality and stability: A review of theory, methods, and research. *Psychological Bulletin, 118*(1), 3. https://doi.org/10.1037/0033-2909.118.1.3

Keller, H., Lamm, B., Abels, M., Yovsi, R., Borke, J., Jensen, H., Papaligoura, Z., Holub, C., Lo, W., Tomiyama, A. J., Su, Y., Wang, Y., & Chaudhary, N. (2006). Cultural models, socialization goals, and parenting ethnotheories: A multicultural analysis. *Journal of Cross-Cultural Psychology, 37*(2), 155–172. https://doi.org/10.1177/0022022105284494

Kephart, W. M. (1967). Some correlates of romantic love. *Journal of Marriage and the Family, 29*(3), 470–474. https://doi.org/10.2307/349585

Kitayama, S., & Uskul, A. K. (2011). Culture, mind, and the brain: Current evidence and future directions. *Annual Review of Psychology, 62*(1), 419–449. https://doi.org/10.1146/annurev-psych-120709-145357

Kito, M., Yuki, M., & Thomson, R. (2017). Relational mobility and close relationships: A socioecological approach to explain cross-cultural differences. *Personal Relationships*, 24(1), 114–130. https://doi.org/10.1111/pere.12174

Knee, C. R., Hadden, B. W., Porter, B., & Rodriguez, L. M. (2013). Self-determination theory and romantic relationship processes. *Personality and Social Psychology Review*, 17(4), 307–324. https://doi.org/10.1177/1088868313498000

Lalonde, R. N., Hynie, M., Pannu, M., & Tatla, S. (2004). The role of culture in interpersonal relationships: Do second generation South Asian Canadians want a traditional partner? *Journal of Cross-Cultural Psychology*, 35(5), 503–524. https://doi.org/10.1177/0022022104268386

Lam, B. C. P., Cross, S. E., Wu, T. F., Yeh, Wang, Y. C., & Su, J. C. (2016). What do you want in a marriage? Examining marriage ideals in Taiwan and the United States. *Personality and Social Psychology Bulletin*, 42(6), 703–722. https://doi.org/10.1177/0146167216637842

Le, B., Dove, N. L., Agnew, C. R., Korn, M. S., & Mutso, A. A. (2010). Predicting nonmarital romantic relationship dissolution: A meta-analytic synthesis. *Personal Relationships*, 17(3), 377–390. https://doi.org/10.1111/j.1475-6811.2010.01285.x

Lee, G. R., & Stone, L. H. (1980). Mate-selection systems and criteria: Variation according to family structure. *Journal of Marriage and Family*, 42(2), 319–326. https://doi.org/10.2307/351229

Lesthaeghe, R. J. (2020). The second demographic transition: Cohabitation. In W. K. Halford & F. van de Vijver (Eds.), *Cross-cultural family research and practice* (pp. 103–141). Academic Press.

Levine, R., Sato, S., Hashimoto, T., & Verma, J. (1995). Love and marriage in eleven cultures. *Journal of Cross-Cultural Psychology*, 26(5), 554–571.

Li, L. M. W., Adams, G., Kurtiş, T., & Hamamura, T. (2015). Beware of friends: The cultural psychology of relational mobility and cautious intimacy. *Asian Journal of Social Psychology*, 18(2), 124–133. https://doi.org/10.1111/ajsp.12091

Liu, J., Bell, E., & Zhang, J. (2019). Conjugal intimacy, gender and modernity in contemporary China. *The British Journal of Sociology*, 70(1), 283–305.

Markus, H. R., & Kitayama, S. (1991). Culture and the self: Implications for cognition, emotion, and motivation. *Psychological Review*, 98(2), 224–253. https://doi.org/10.1037/0033-295X.98.2.224

Markus, H. R., & Kitayama, S. (2010). Cultures and selves: A cycle of mutual constitution. *Perspectives on Psychological Science*, 5(4), 420–430. https://doi.org/10.1177/1745691610375557

Marshall, T. C. (2008). Cultural differences in intimacy: The influence of gender-role ideology and individualism–collectivism. *Journal of Social and Personal Relationships*, 25(1), 143–168. https://doi.org/10.1177/0265407507086810

Masuda, T., Russell, M. J., Li, L. M. W., & Lee, H. (2019). Cognition and perception. In D. Cohen & S. Kitayama (Eds.), *Handbook of cultural psychology* (2nd ed., pp. 222–245). The Guilford Press.

Morelli, G. A., Chaudhary, N., Gottlieb, A., Keller, H., Murray, M., Quinn, N., Rosabal-Coto, M., Scheidecker, G., Takada, A., & Vicedo, M. (2017). A pluralistic approach to attachment. In H. Keller & K. Bard (Eds.), *The cultural nature of attachment: Contextualizing relationships and development* (pp. 140–169). The MIT Press.

Morling, B., Kitayama, S., & Miyamoto, Y. (2002). Cultural practices emphasize influence in the United States and adjustment in Japan. *Personality and Social Psychology Bulletin, 28*(3), 311–323. https://doi.org/10.1177/0146167202286003

Murray, S. L., Holmes, J. G., & Griffin, D. W. (1996a). The benefits of positive illusions: Idealization and the construction of satisfaction in close relationships. *Journal of Personality and Social Psychology, 70*(1), 79. https://doi.org/10.1037/0022-3514.70.1.79

Murray, S. L., Holmes, J. G., & Griffin, D. W. (1996b). The self-fulfilling nature of positive illusions in romantic relationships: love is not blind, but prescient. *Journal of Personality and Social Psychology, 71*(6), 1155. https://doi.org/10.1037/0022-3514.71.6.1155

Navarre, B., & Trimble, M. (2021). "Same-sex marriage legalization by country." *U.S. News*. Downloaded from www.usnews.com/news/best-countries/articles/countries-where-same-sex-marriage-is-legal

Nisbett, R. E. (2003). *The geography of thought: How Asians and Westerners think differently, and why*. Free Press.

Nwoye, A. (2000). Building on the indigenous: Theory and method of marriage therapy in contemporary eastern and western Africa. *Journal of Family Therapy, 22*(4), 347–359. https://doi.org/10.1111/1467-6427.00157

OECD Family Database. (2020). www.oecd.org/els/family/SF_2_4_Share_births_outside_marriage.pdf

Ortiz-Ospina, E.& Roser, M. (2020)."Marriages and divorces". Published online at OurWorldInData.org. Retrieved from: https://ourworldindata.org/marriages-and-divorces [Online Resource]

Osei-Tutu, A., Affram, A. A., & Dzokoto, V. A. (2021). "I reported my wife to her mother…" An analysis of transgressions within child- and parent-in-law relationships in Ghana. *Journal of Comparative Family Studies, 52*, 94–116 . https://doi.org/10.3138/jcfs.52.1.007

Overall, N. C. (2012). The costs and benefits of trying to change intimate partners. In P. Noller & G. C. Karantas (Eds.), *The Wiley-Blackwell handbook of couples and family relationships* (pp. 234–247). Wiley-Balckwell. https://doi.org/10.1002/9781444354119.ch16

Park, H., & Hong, H. (2012). *Korean life history*. Korea National Open University Press.

Peng, K., & Nisbett, R. E. (1999). Culture, dialectics, and reasoning about contradiction. *American Psychologist, 54*(9), 741–754. https://doi.org/10.1037/0003-066X.54.9.741

Quinn, N., & Holland, D. (1987). Culture and cognition. In D. Holland & N. Quinn (Eds.), *Cultural models in language and thought* (Vol. 1, pp. 3–40). Cambridge University Press.

Raymo, J. M., Park, H., Xie, Y. & Yeung, W-J. J. (2015), Marriage and family in East Asia: Continuity and change. *Annual Review of Sociology, 41*, 471–492. https://doi.org/10.1146/annurev-soc-073014-112428

Rodrigues, A. E., Hall, J. H., & Fincham, F. D. (2013). What predicts divorce and relationship dissolution? In M. A. Fine & J. H. Harvey (Eds), *Handbook of divorce and relationship dissolution* (pp. 101–128). Psychology Press.

Rothbaum, F., Pott, M., Azuma, H., Miyake, K., & Weisz, J. (2000). The development of close relationships in Japan and the United States: Paths of symbiotic harmony and generative tension. *Child Development, 71*(5), 1121–1142. https://doi.org/10.1111/1467-8624.00214

Rothbaum, F., Rosen, K., Ujiie, T., & Uchida, N. (2002). Family systems theory, attachment theory and culture. *Family Process*, 41(3), 328–350. https://doi.org/10.1111/j.1545-5300.2002.41305.x

Rybak, A., & McAndrew, F. T. (2006). How do we decide whom our friends are? Defining levels of friendship in Poland and the United States. *The Journal of Social Psychology*, 146(2), 147–163. https://doi.org/10.3200/SOCP.146.2.147-163

Sadeghi, M. S., Mazaheri, D. A., Motabi, D. F., & Zahedi, K. (2012). Marital interaction in Iranian couples: Examining the role of culture. *Journal of Comparative Family Studies*, 43, 281–300. https://doi.org/10.3138/jcfs.43.2.281

Salter, P. S., & Adams, G. (2012). Mother or wife? An African dilemma tale and the psychological dynamics of sociocultural change. *Social Psychology*, 43(4), 232–242. https://doi.org/10.1027/1864-9335/a000124

Samter, W., Whaley, B. B., Mortenson, S. T., & Burleson, B. R. (1997). Ethnicity and emotional support in same-sex friendship: A comparison of Asian-Americans, African-Americans, and Euro-Americans. *Personal Relationships*, 4(4), 413–430. https://doi.org/10.1111/j.1475-6811.1997.tb00154.x

Schmitt, D. P. (2004). The Big Five related to risky sexual behaviour across 10 world regions: Differential personality associations of sexual promiscuity and relationship infidelity. *European Journal of Personality*, 18(4), 301–319. https://doi.org/10.1002/per.520

Schmitt, D. P. (2005). Fundamentals of human mating strategies. In D. M. Buss (Ed.), *The handbook of evolutionary psychology* (pp. 258–291). John Wiley & Sons, Inc.

Schmitt, D. P. (2010). Romantic attachment from Argentina to Zimbabwe: Patterns of adaptive variation across contexts, cultures, and local ecologies. In P. Erdman & K. Ng (Eds.), *Attachment: Expanding the cultural connections; attachment* (pp. 211–226). Routledge/Taylor & Francis Group.

Schoebi, D., Wang, Z., Ababkov, V., & Perrez, M. (2010). Affective interdependence in married couples' daily lives: Are there cultural differences in partner effects of anger? *Family Science*, 1(2), 83–92. https://doi.org/10.1080/19424620903471681

Schug, J., Yuki, M., & Maddux, W. (2010). Relational mobility explains between- and within-culture differences in self-disclosure to close friends. *Psychological Science*, 21(10), 1471–1478. https://doi.org/10.1177/0956797610382786

Shaver, P. R., Wu, S., & Schwartz, J. C. (1992). Cross-cultural similarities and differences in emotion and its representation. In M. S. Clark (Ed.), *Emotion* (pp. 175–212). Sage Publications, Inc.

Shiota, M. N., Campos, B., Gonzaga, G. C., Keltner, D., & Peng, K. (2010). I love you but...: Cultural differences in complexity of emotional experience during interaction with a romantic partner. *Cognition and Emotion*, 24(5), 786–799. https://doi.org/10.1080/02699930902990480

Shweder, R. A., Balle-Jensen, L., & Goldstein, W. (2003). Who sleeps by whom revisited. In R. A. Shweder (Ed.), *Why do men barbecue?* (pp. 46–73). Harvard University Press.

Soumuchou, S. T. H. (1987). *Nippon no kodomo to hahaoya.* [Children and mothers in Japan.] Okurashou Insatsu Kyoku.

Sprecher, S., Aron, A., Hatfield, E., Cortese, A., Potapova, E., & Levitskaya, A. (1994). Love: American style, Russian style, and Japanese style. *Personal Relationships*, 1(4), 349–369. https://doi.org/10.1111/j.1475-6811.1994.tb00070.x

Sprecher, S., Sullivan, Q., & Hatfield, E. (1994). Mate selection preferences: Gender differences examined in a national sample. *Journal of Personality and Social Psychology*, 66(6), 1074. https://doi.org/10.1037/0022-3514.66.6.1074

Švab, A., Rener, T., & Kuhar, M. (2012). Behind and beyond hajnal's line: Families and family life in Slovenia. *Journal of Comparative Family Studies*, 43(3), 419–437.

Therborn, G. (2004a). *Between sex and power: Family in the world, 1900–2000*. Routledge.

Therborn, G. (2004b). *African families in a Global context*. Nordiska Afrikainstitutet.

Therborn, G. (2006). Family's in today's world- and tomorrow's, international. *Journal of Health Services*, 36(3), 593–603.

Therborn, G. (2014). Family systems of the world: Are they converging? In J. Treas, J. Scott, and M. Richards (Eds.), *Wiley Blackwell companion to the sociology of families* (pp. 3–19). John Wiley.

Thornton, A. (2005). *Reading history sideways: The fallacy and enduring impact of the developmental paradigm on family life*. The University of Chicago Press.

Thornton, A., & Young-DeMarco, L. (2001). Four decades of trends in attitudes toward family issues in the United States: The 1960s through the 1990s. *Journal of Marriage and the Family*, 63(4), 1009–1037.

Tsai, J. L., & Clobert, M. (2019). Cultural influences on emotion: Established patterns and emerging trends. In D. Cohen & S. Kitayama (Eds.), *Handbook of cultural psychology* (2nd ed., pp. 292–318, Chapter xiii, 930 Pages). The Guilford Press.

Tsai, J. L., Knutson, B., & Fung, H. H. (2006). Cultural variation in affect valuation. *Journal of Personality and Social Psychology*, 90(2), 288–307. https://doi.org/10.1037/0022-3514.90.2.288

Tsai, J. L., Levenson, R. W., & McCoy, K. (2006). Cultural and temperamental variation in emotional response. *Emotion*, 6(3), 484–497. https://doi.org/10.1037/1528-3542.6.3.484

US Census Bureau. (2020). Marital status in the United States. https://statisticalatlas.com/United-States/Marital-Status.

Vazhappily, J. J., & Reyes, M. E. (2016). Couples' communication as a predictor of marital satisfaction among selected Filipino couples. *Psychological Studies*, 61(4), 301–306. https://doi.org/10.1007/s12646-016-0375-5.

Vignoli, D., Matysiak, A., Styrc, M. & Tocchioni, V. (2018). The positive impact of women's employment on divorce: Context, selection, or anticipation? *Demographic Research*, 38, 1059–1109.

Wang, C. D. C., & Mallinckrodt, B. S. (2006). Differences between Taiwanese and US cultural beliefs about ideal adult attachment. *Journal of Counseling Psychology*, 53(2), 192–204. https://doi.org/10.1037/0022-0167.53.2.192

Wang, C. T. L., & Schofer, E. (2018). Coming out of the penumbras: World culture and cross-national variation in divorce rates. *Social Forces*, 97(2), 675–704. https://doi.org/10.1093/sf/soy070

Wang, D. & Xia, Y. (2020). Couple relationships in China. In A. Abela et al. (Eds.), *Couple relationships in a global context* (pp. 107–124). Springer. https://doi.org/10.1007/978-3-030-37712-0_7

Wei, M., Russell, D. W., Mallinckrodt, B., & Zakalik, R. A. (2004). Cultural equivalence of adult attachment across four ethnic groups: Factor structure, structured means, and associations with negative mood. *Journal of Counseling Psychology*, 51(4), 408–417. https://doi.org/10.1037/0022-0167.51.4.408

Williamson, H. C., Ju, X., Bradbury, T. N., Karney, B. R., Fang, X., & Liu, X. (2012). Communication behavior and relationship satisfaction among American and Chinese newlywed couples. *Journal of Family Psychology*, 26(3), 308–315. https://doi.org/10.1037/a0027752

Wu, M. S., Li, B., Zhu, L., & Zhou, C. (2019). Culture change and affectionate communication in China and the United States: Evidence from Google digitized books 1960–2008. *Frontiers in Psychology*, 10, 1110. https://doi.org/10.3389/fpsyg.20

Wu, T.-F., Cross, S. E., Wu, C.-W., Cho, W., & Tey, S.-H. (2016). Choosing your mother or your spouse: Close relationship dilemmas in Taiwan and the United States. *Journal of Cross-cultural Psychology*, 47(4), 558–580. DOI: 10.1177/0022022115625837

Xia, Y., & Zhou, Z. (2003). Chinese mate selection. In R. R. Hamon & B. B. Ingoldsby (Eds.), *Couple formation across cultures* (pp. 231–246). Sage

Xu, A. (2017). The establishment and dissolution of marriage. In A. Xu, J. DeFrain, & W. Liu (Eds.), *The Chinese family today* (pp. 129–168). Routledge.

Xu, A., & Xia, Y. (2014). The changes in mainland Chinese families during the social transition: A critical analysis. *Journal of Comparative Family Studies*, 45(1), 31–53.

Xu, A., & Ye, W. (1999). *Research on marital quality in China*. Social Sciences Publication House.

Xu, A., DeFrain, J., & Liu, W. (2017). *The Chinese family today*. Routledge.

Yang, T., Poon, A. W. C., & Breckenridge, J. (2018). Estimating the prevalence of intimate partner violence in mainland China – Insights and challenges. *Journal of Family Violence*, 34(2), 93–105

Yeh, K.-H. (2003). The beneficial and harmful effects of filial piety: An integrative analysis. In K. S. Yang, K. K. Hwang, P. B. Pederson, & I. Daibo (Eds.), *Asian social psychology: Conceptual and empirical contributions* (pp. 67–82). Greenwood Publishing Group, Inc.

Yilmaz, C., Selcuk, E., Gunaydin, G., Cingöz-Ulu, B., Filiztekin, A., & Kent, O. (2022). You mean the world to me: The role of residential mobility in centrality of romantic relationships. *Social Psychological and Personality Science*. https://doi.org/10.1177/19485506211061017

You, H. S., & Malley-Morrison, K. (2000). Young adult attachment styles and intimate relationships with close friends a cross-cultural study of Koreans and Caucasian Americans. *Journal of Cross-Cultural Psychology*, 31(4), 528–534. https://doi.org/10.1177/0022022100031004006

Yum, Y. (2000). *Cross-cultural comparisons of links among relational maintenance behaviors, exchange factors, and individual characteristics in close relationships*. The Pennsylvania State University.

Zeifman, D., & Hazan, C. (2008). Pair bonds as attachments: Reevaluating the evidence. In J. Cassidy & P. R. Shaver (Eds.), *Handbook of attachment: Theory, research, and clinical applications* (pp. 436–455). The Guilford Press.

Zhang, C., Wang, X., & Zhang, D. (2014). Urbanization, unemployment rate and China's rising divorce rate. *Chinese Journal of Population Resources and Environment*, 12(2), 157–164.

Zhang, S., & Kline, S. (2009). Can I make my own decision? A cross-cultural study of social network influence in mate selection. *Journal of Cross-Cultural Psychology*, 40(1), 3–23.

Zhang, S., & Kline, S. (2020). Couple communication in a cross-cultural perspective. In W. K. Halford & F. van de Vijver (Eds.), *Cross-cultural family research and practice* (pp. 211–247). Elsevier Inc.

Zhou, P. (2017). Love. In X. Zhou (Ed)., *Inner experience of the Chinese people* (pp. 113–122). Springer.

4

Gender and Heteronormativity in Romantic Relationships

APRIL L. FEW-DEMO AND KATHERINE R. ALLEN

INTRODUCTION

Gender and sexuality are two primary ways in which relationships are organized and experienced. Once considered immutable, gender and sexuality have proven to be highly volatile and contentious concepts, engaging scholars, politicians, parents, students, and many others over the Internet in critical debates about what is natural, what is socially constructed, and what is systemically enforced. Despite the volatile nature of the debates about gender and sexuality, in most societies, some vestige of gender essentialism – the belief in the immutable nature of maleness and femaleness – still dominates intimate relationships of all types. For example, we see the pervasiveness of a binary approach to gender in the popular and often dangerous practice of gender reveal parties as well as in current legislation across many US states restricting the rights of transgender youth and athletes. Gender inequities have also been prominent in the new research about the impact of COVID-19 on how women's lives from diverse backgrounds have been disrupted due to shouldering the responsibilities for homeschooling during lockdown (Collins et al., 2021), not having designated space in the home for their own work lives (Waismel-Manor et al., 2021), or having worries about childcare because they cannot afford to stay home (Chaney, 2020). Gender asymmetry continues to be present on the world stage, including the dismantling of state sponsored collectivist child, elder, and health care systems in China and thus forcing working mothers back home (Ji et al., 2017), and transnational carework for primarily female domestic workers from developing nations, who migrate from their home countries and families to work for wealthy families in developed countries (Allen & Henderson, 2023; Lutz, 2011).

In this chapter, we examine how social structures at the macro level and social constructions at the microlevel influence selected issues regarding relationship initiation, development, maintenance, and dissolution. We emphasize how relational scripts influence gender dynamics and gender expression in romantic relationships at individual and interactional levels (Ogolsky et al., 2017). We review trends in the literature concerning diverse romantic relationships and how they adhere to or critique heteronormative ideologies.

We are guided by an intersectional feminist theoretical approach (Few-Demo & Allen, 2020), which we employ to critique heteronormativity and heterodominant discourses in relational and family science in order to examine the plethora of relationships formed in the context of gender, identity, and sexuality. An intersectional feminist approach brings a critical lens to this review of gender and romantic relationships. Our review of the changing landscape of romantic relationships will highlight "the social embeddedness ... of Western intellectual traditions fomented by political, cultural, and social norms that valorize androcentricity, heteronormativity, cisgenderism, and Whiteness over other identities and forms of social order (Few-Demo & Allen, 2020, p. 328). Critical perspectives disrupt majority discourses and give voice to the previously silenced and invisible experience of those whose experiences do not adhere to what is referred to as "normative" (Allen & Henderson, 2023; Few-Demo et al., 2022). Thus, in this review, we examine diverse heteronormative and cisnormative relationships as well as a variety of queer relationships. We include the romantic relationships of sexual minorities not only as an active critique of heteronormativity, but also to keep gender at the center of our analysis. We select examples of diverse relationships by race, ethnicity, class, and sexual orientation to examine recent literature on relationship initiation, development, maintenance, and dissolution.

MACRO LEVEL TRENDS AND GENDERED RELATIONSHIPS

Gender performance, relations, and display, much like romantic relationships, are influenced by shifts in cultural norms and legal consequences resulting from various sociopolitical trends. For example, the past two decades have witnessed a series of court rulings and federal and state laws in regard to the legitimacy of same-gender relationships and LGBTQ+ individuals as a protected class. Monk and Ogolsky (2019) theorized that "ambiguous sociopolitical contexts could create uncertainty about relational acceptance, recognition, norms, and future relationship status for individuals," (p. 244) thereby impacting individuals' commitment and engagement in intimate relationships. Monk and Ogolsky defined *sociopolitical uncertainty* as,

a state of (a) having doubts about legal recognition bestowed on individuals and families by outside systems, (b) being unsure about social acceptance of marginalized relationships, and (c) being unsure about how "traditional" social norms and roles pertain to marginalized relationships or how alternative scripts might unfold. (p. 244)

They further argued that sociopolitical uncertainty influences the value that people place on relationships that fall outside of heteronormative standards.

Another consideration impacting individuals' timing and pursuit of romantic relationships at the macrosystemic level is downward economic trends and changes in women's access to wealth and education. For instance, the gender wage gap is growing narrower among younger workers nationally. According to the Pew Research Center, women under the age of 30 are earning the same amount as or more than men in 22 of 250 US metropolitan areas (Fry, 2022). Moreover, women have increased their presence in the housing market, with their homeownership rate of households increasing while the homeownership rate of households led by men continued to drop (Goodman et al., 2021). Goodman and colleagues (2021) also reported that since the COVID-19 pandemic, single men were more likely to be unemployed, financially insecure, and lack a college degree than men who had a partner. They also noted that by 2019, households headed by women accounted for 50 percent of all households and that this homeownership trend held across all racial and ethnic groups. Of special note, households led by African American women were the highest share of households led by women (i.e., 60 percent; Goodman et al., 2021). Women are owning and having more access to resources and assets than ever before, impacting their decisions to enter or leave relationships, the timing of relationship formation and dissolution, as well as their decisions to delay marriage.

Furthermore, gender does not operate in a vacuum. The overarching context of intimate relationships occurs under the dominating lens of heteronormativity. Heteronormativity refers to the beliefs, rules, privileges, and sanctions that are derived from heterosexuality and cisnormativity that dictate the nature and experience of gendered intimacy between romantic partners (Allen et al., 2009; Oswald et al., 2009; Reczek, 2020). Heteronormativity not only presumes the compulsory preference for a fixed gender binary to ensure biological procreation, but it also encourages serial monogamy between partners over the life span. Under this ideology, sexuality and sexual orientation are fixed identities; sexual fluidity and pansexual eroticism are deemed unnatural and do not occur within committed relationships or families (Few-Demo & Allen, 2020; Reczek, 2020).

THEORIZING ABOUT GENDER

Gender is a ubiquitous concept in personal identity, intimate relationships, family systems, and social institutions, present across history and all societies. Long considered one of the building blocks of social organization, gender ideologies, and gendered behaviors are found at all levels of society (Lorber, 2012). The traditional conceptualization of gender as either male or female permeates our understanding of gender as a master status, an individual identity, an interactional context, and an institutional system (Allen et al., 2022). In recent years, however, challenges to the gender binary, gender hierarchy, and gender system have sought to dismantle, and even purge, the very idea of gender as relevant (Risman, 2018). How can we understand these tremendous swings in gender ideologies, the performance of gender, and gender as part of an intersectional matrix, along with race, class, sexuality, and other systems of domination (Few-Demo & Allen, 2020; Few-Demo et al., 2022)? We ask, if gender no longer matters, then why is it at the front and center of so many political and identity debates, particularly among youth (Allen, 2022; Chamberlain, 2017; Jackson et al., 2020)? In light of this controversy, we share some of the history of how gender has been theorized in recent decades, setting the stage for the uncertainty and volatility, as well as the possibilities that characterize the current moment.

From Gender Differences to Gender Roles to Gender Theory

The presumption of gender differences is a primary way of organizing knowledge, experience, and power (Rhode, 1990). Even before a child is born, the question of gender is so primary that it is emblazoned in the popular imagination. The foundation of the gender structure can be linked to the belief that gender is a biological certainty, where maleness and femaleness result from the predetermined nature of sexual differentiation (Fausto-Sterling, 1985). Genetics and biological sex characteristics (e.g., the nature of chromosomes, gonads, hormones, internal reproductive systems, and external genitalia; Lips, 2018) are offered as proof of the immutability of gender and justification for its deterministic quality.

Over time, and given feminist critiques of the presumption of biological differences, thinking in the social and behavioral sciences has evolved beyond a simplistic belief in gender as biological given, in which "sex roles" are preordained, to a reconceptualization now defined as gender theory (Few-Demo & Allen, 2020). That is, a pure linkage between biological sex and socialized behavior (e.g., as in the belief that women are natural caregivers, and men are natural protectors) has been dismantled (Allen et al., 2009). We now understand that gender is a social construction, where people are taught to perform in gendered ways. That is, we are taught to "do gender" (West & Zimmerman, 1987). For example, when social attitudes or technological advances inspire, expand, or contradict cultural notions about gender and sexuality, the processual performativity of how we do relationships may shift (Cherlin, 2020; Sassler & Lichter, 2020). In other words, the scripts for how we initiate, maintain, and dissolve close relationships may shift to follow alternative, but accessible, scripts. For example, a shift in how relationships are done may include adult partners who choose to establish non-marital committed romantic relationships, which may or may not include the "blending of families" and choose to reside in different and separate households. Another example of how contemporary adults are redefining gender and familial expectations are those adults who voluntarily choose singlehood and/or to be childfree. Risman (2004) further elaborated on gender theory as a system of social stratification, similar to the economic system and the political system, in which the ideologies and behavioral rules about how people perform gender are structured from the top down and thus infiltrate individual and family experience.

From Binary Thinking about Gender to Feminist Intersectional Theorizing

Feminist family scholars have been instrumental in naming the detrimental nature of binary thinking on individual development and family relationships (Allen et al., 2022; Oswald et al., 2009). The use of binaries is a heuristic strategy that divides the world into two mutually exclusive types, where one type is conceptualized and treated as better than the other and consequently afforded greater prestige, privilege, and power (Allen, 2022). For example, gender has been characterized as a binary of male and female. The gender binary means that gender consists of two categories that do not overlap, such that men's lives and women's lives are more dissimilar than androgynous. The gender binary is also linked to cultural beliefs and practices, where children are socialized and indoctrinated into gendered roles according to biological sex. Further, the gender binary is linked to social organization and institutional structures that delimit educational and occupational opportunities according to gender.

Other heuristic uses of binary include white/black, straight/gay, cisgender/transgender, rich/poor, young/old, and able-bodied/disabled. Indeed, in her classic essay titled, "Age, Race, Class, and Sex: Women Redefining Difference," Audre Lorde (1984) described the origin and dehumanizing consequences of binary categories by explaining:

> Much of Western European history conditions us to see human differences in simplistic opposition to each other: dominant/subordinate, good/bad, up/down, superior/inferior. In a society where the good is defined in terms of profit rather than in terms of human need, there must always be some group of people who, through systematized oppression, can be made to feel surplus, to occupy the place of the dehumanized inferior. Within this society, that group is made up of Black and Third World people, working class people, older people, and women. (p. 114)

Taking Lorde's (1984) lead, dismantling binary thinking has led to intersectional feminist theorizing, which Crenshaw (1991) pointed out is rooted in the intertwined experiences of violence that Black women confront, where racism and sexism intersect to reinforce the structures of social inequality. Bringing critical social theory to bear upon intersectionality, (Collins, 2019) identified the core constructs of relationality, power, social inequality, social context, complexity, and social justice, and the four guiding premises of intersectionality as theory and practice:

(1) Race, class, gender, and similar systems of power are interdependent and mutually construct one another.
(2) Intersecting power relations produce complex, interdependent social inequalities of race, class, gender, sexuality, nationality, ethnicity, ability, and age.
(3) The social location of individuals and groups within intersection power relations shapes their experiences within and perspectives on the social world.
(4) Solving social problems within a given local, regional, national, or global context requires intersectional analyses. (p. 44)

Queering Gender: Beyond the Male/Female Binary

Another critique of binary categorization is to dismantle the presumption that individuals are straight *or* gay. Instead, we queer gender *and* sexuality, which means to utilize both critical and constructivist paradigms to show the intersection of gender and sexuality, as performance, relational, and socially constructed (Allen & Henderson, 2023; Few-Demo & Allen, 2020). Using a queer perspective, gender can be liberated from the male/female binary (Oswald et al., 2005), which promotes a homonormative stance that privileges the "right" kind of gay male as married and cisgender, for example (as opposed to nonbinary, consensually nonmonogamous, or trans; Allen & Mendez, 2018). These pathways open up a variety of new perspectives for featuring gender, revisioning gender, and muting gender.

ANALYZING GENDER AND HETERONORMATIVITY: RELATIONAL PERSPECTIVES

Our intersectional feminist design aims to be inclusive of a variety of relationships in our brief review of highlighting how gender unfolds and heteronormativity is rejected or embraced in contemporary romantic relationships. In this section, we provide selected examples (rather than an exhaustive array) of recent literature regarding dyadic relationships and multi-partner relationships.

Gender-as-Relational

Contemporary research on romantic relationships more often than not is framed by a *gender-as-relational* theoretical approach (Thomeer et al., 2020), with its roots in feminist theorizing as described above. This is a model that extends theorizing about relational dynamics beyond the siloed notions of Bernard's (1972) "her and his marriage" to viewing relationship dynamics as interactional at multiple levels. A *gender-as-relational* approach assumes that within close relationships, the ways in which gender is enacted is determined by the interaction of one's own understanding of gender, the partner's enactment of gender, and the gendered relational context, or rather how dynamic gender relations unfold (Thomeer et al., 2020). Thus, one's understanding and enactment of gender is contingent upon the interpretation of gender beliefs, values, and roles for partners.

The gender-as-relational approach can be interpreted as an inherently feminist tool in that it can be applied to highlight how privilege and oppression manifest in romantic relationships. For example, researchers can utilize this approach to examine how heteronormativity, homophobia, sexism, white supremacy, ageism, and ableism may influence interactions and reactions between romantic partners. This framework posits the aforementioned discriminating and marginalizing systems of oppression and privilege have specific implications for how one performs gender within a romantic relationship regardless of the gender and sexual identities of the partners (Thomeer et al., 2020). Moreover, gender roles may evolve over the life course due to changes in and exchanges of relational power that occur during different events (e.g., childrearing, empty nest), changes within state and federal policies and regulation (e.g., same gender marriage recognition; anti-trans legislation) as well as changes in structural compositions (e.g., dating, divorce, remarriage) over the life course. This conceptualization is mindful of not only how couples involving diverse gender and sexual minority identities may experience these relational shifts over time but also differential levels of institutional regulation regarding couple identity, access, and legal protections (e.g., full faith and credit clauses). Finally, the gender-as-relational approach requires the dyadic collection and analysis of relationship data, such that all romantic partners involved in the targeted relationship are informants in the study.

It is no longer sufficient to make inferences about behaviors and motivations in romantic relationships using data from one partner alone. The empirical literature over the past twenty+ years has shifted toward dyadic analyses in order to capture nuances in motivations, perceptions, and behaviors that are grounded in/reflect heteronormative, cisnormative, and or queer ideologies regarding relationship enactment. For example, the Actor–Partner Interdependence Model (APIM, Kenny & Kashy, 2014) is a model of dyadic relationships that considers interdependence in two-person relationships while using actor and partner variables as predictors of relationship outcomes. When APIM is applied to heterosexual couples, the models typically distinguish dyad members based on the gender of a partner, examining "female partner effects" and "male partner effects." In analyzing multilevel models that involve same-gender couples, a factorial method must be deployed to discern gender effects (Kroeger & Powers, 2019; West et al., 2008).

However, it is important to note that contemporary relationship researchers push social science beyond the typical accounting of female/male differences by using a gender-as-relational lens to interpret nuance in how different-sex partners influence the behavior of one another in relationships. To illustrate,

Curran et al. (2015) examined how daily fluctuations in emotion work for both relational partners predicted individuals' relationship quality. Seventy-four different-sex couples in dating, cohabiting, or married relationships were recruited, with over 750 days of diary entries collected. Using APIM, Curran et al. (2015) examined actor and partner effects of emotion work and tested for gender differences. This approach allowed predictability on three features of relationship quality: average levels, daily fluctuations, and volatility. They included six types of daily relationship quality as outcomes: love, commitment, satisfaction, closeness, ambivalence, and conflict. The study revealed three patterns. First, emotion work predicted relationship quality for different-sex people in dating, cohabiting, or married relationships. Second, gender differences were actually minimal for fixed effects in that trait and state emotion work predicted higher average scores on, and positive daily increases in, individuals' own positive relationship quality and lower average ambivalence. Finally, the volatility outcome was where gender differences were most distinct. For actor effects, they found that having a partner who reported higher average emotion work predicted lower volatility in love, satisfaction, and closeness for women versus greater volatility in love and commitment for men. Curran et al. (2015) inferred that this difference could be for men whose partners overperformed emotion work; they might feel they are receiving more support than they wanted or needed and/or experienced feelings of demasculinization given a perception of a loss in relational power in the relationship. Later, Pollitt and Curran (2022) reflected upon the study's results, stating that this study provided "evidence of how relationship satisfaction can be enhanced when both partners perform emotion work … [as well as] … the gendered ways in which women and men interact with one another can have nuanced impacts on their romantic relationships." This contemporary study is an example not only of the ways in which some partners in different-sex couples were adhering to heteronormative expectations toward the management of emotionality and linking those expectations to perceptions of relationship quality, but it also provided snapshot insights into how couples "do" relationship maintenance on a weekly basis.

We would be remiss if we did not present debates about whether to use single-partner versus dyadic designs to conduct relationship research. For instance, Barton et al. (2020) provided multiple considerations for researchers who are studying relationships and trying to decide about whether collecting single-partner or dyadic data. They suggested that if questions of partner effects, or discrepancies between partners, are of central focus of the study, then dyadic data collection efforts are perhaps best. They also advised that if the nature of the romantic relationships being studied were those that were "at risk" or otherwise unstable, then single-partner data collection is recommended. Of course, Barton et al. (2020) also briefly mentioned having both data collection designs. In addition, they cautioned, just as many other scholars have done, that *participation bias* cannot be overlooked. They argued that participation bias may occur more among two-partner studies than single-partner studies due to a disproportionate number of high-functioning couples and individuals who are very satisfied with their relationship being drawn to and willing to participate in studies (e.g., Yucel & Gassanov, 2010).

Creative Approaches to Committed Relationships

Romantic couples who are involved in living apart together relationships, or LAT, present a radical example of not only how couples circumvent traditional ways of forming relationships and maintaining relationships, but also how they avoid or eliminate certain gendered obligations and expectations for how gender "should" unfold during midlife and later life. Initiating, forming, and maintaining a committed LAT relationship may be a particularly attractive choice for some single older adults who find themselves living alone for a variety of reasons (e.g., divorce, widowhood, empty nest, voluntary singlehood) and do not wish to cohabitate or reside with a romantic partner, but still seek intimacy with another person. Reasons for embracing this type of living arrangement include preserving one's autonomy; financial independence and privacy; avoiding long-term care partnering responsibilities; preferring aging in place instead of relocation; maintaining contact with adult children from previous unions; and housing security (e.g., owning a rent-controlled apartment; Carr & Utz, 2020; Strohm et al., 2009). These relationships are creatively radical in that different-sex and same-gender partners, but specifically, women, employ an agentic means to circumvent heteronormative and sociocultural expectations that women should care for others, and especially their partners, in later life. This type of non-residential committed relationship requires an ongoing negotiation of roles, responsibilities, emotions, boundaries, and intimacy. Moreover, cultural, economic, and institutional constraints influence how LAT couples navigate these complex negotiations and feelings resulting from these negotiations (e.g., ambivalence) throughout the relationship–its formation, stability, or dissolution (Connidis et al., 2017).

Multi-Partner Relationships and Consensual Non-Monogamy

Schippers (2020) argued that with the critical examination of polysexualities, researchers were afforded an opportunity to pivot or reorient our theorizing about the intersection of gender, race, and sexuality. Consensual non-monogamous (CNM) relationships are relationships in which romantic partners engage in sexual or emotional relationships with extradyadic partners other than their primary partners with the consent and knowledge of the primary partner (Cohen & Wilson, 2017). Other forms of CNM relationships include triads or quads (i.e., three or four partners romantically linked), V-structures (i.e., one partner is equally involved with two partners), and poly "webs" or families (Barker & Langdridge, 2010).

Multi-partner relationships represent a rejection of heteronormative monogamy or ways of doing marriage or romantic pairings, complicating the structure and composition of family. As such, these relationships have been stigmatized and those engaged in CNM relationships have identified several ways in which they and their families have been marginalized and drawn discrimination. For instance, CNM couples who have disclosed their relationship arrangement to family, friends, and health care providers have experienced rejection from family members, criticisms about how they are raising their children, accusations of immorality (Moors et al., 2013), threats of losing custody of their children (Kimberly & Hans, 2017; Sheff, 2015), and warnings against living a risky sexual health lifestyle (Vaughan et al., 2019). Empirical studies on CNM relationships, however, reveal a different reality of relational dynamics. For example, several studies indicate that individuals engaged in CNM relationships report equal levels of relationship satisfaction, trust, commitment, and psychological health as individuals in monogamous relationships (Conley et al., 2017). People in these relationships also have reported low levels of jealousy and relationship insecurity (Conley et al., 2017) as well as getting a broader array of their needs fulfilled by diverse committed partners (Moors et al., 2017). CNM relationships queer and debunk notions supporting the superiority of heteronormative dyadic romantic relationships, eroticism, and relationship quality.

How Lesbians Queer Gender and Heteronormativity in Relationships

We now turn to examine gender in same-sex partnerships, focusing primarily on lesbian relationships, given the intensity of emotions found among them. Gay men in committed relationships typically have more money than lesbian couples, due to the privileging of male gender and the greater opportunities men have for financial success (Goldberg et al., 2020). As we know of middle-class marriages among heterosexuals, economic security contributes to marital stability (Cherlin, 2020). In contrast, lesbian relationships are often characterized by emotional intensity, perhaps linked to a double dose of gender socialization that promotes closeness, intimacy, and communication (Riggle et al., 2016; Rothblum, 2009). At the same time, lesbian relationships face particular challenges, in that two women in a relationship often means greater financial insecurity than if two male incomes were available (Allen & Goldberg, 2020). Cultural differences are part of the intersectional matrix for lesbian mothers. For example, Figueroa and Tasker (2020) found that lesbian mothers faced severe discrimination when religion and culture intersected with gender, sexuality, and family.

Recent qualitative and quantitative research on the relational dissolution of lesbian mothers has found that breakups can be just as intense as the beginning of lesbian relationships, when the partners were first falling in love (Allen & Goldberg, 2020; Balsam et al., 2017; Farr, 2017). Now that the field has amassed several decades of research on lesbian relationships, we are seeing some forays into these more invisible aspects. Although there has been a reluctance to examine problems and difficulties in lesbian relationships for fear of further stigmatizing already marginalized relationships, this area of research has been maturing and numerous ways of more fully examining these relationships exist. For example, lesbian relationships are the most likely to break up, compared to heterosexual relationships and those of gay men (Farr, 2017; Goldberg & Garcia, 2015). In a qualitative study of lesbians who were in the process of relational dissolution, Allen and Goldberg (2020) found a variety of discourses in their explanations, which is evidence that lesbians do not have to abide by the "we're perfect" scenario. These discourses disrupted the gendered, heteronormative narratives of marriage, motherhood, and divorce: (a) the ideology of the good mother; (b) divorce is bad for children; (c) marriage is the ideal way to live; (d) couples should stay together for the children; and (e) lesbian ex-lovers should be lifelong friends. Yet, relational conflict among LGBTQ+ couples remains a relatively taboo topic. From an intersectional feminist perspective, any deviation from the mythic norm of "happy marriage/happy family" can open LGBTQ+ families to negative public scrutiny, a concern that divorcing lesbians mothers acknowledge (Allen & Goldberg, 2020). The research on relational formation, development, maintenance, and dissolution among lesbian partners, who have a double dose of gender socialization that both intensifies and challenges their interactions, is prescient for the field in general. Rather than centering heteronormative relationships as the standard bearer, it is wise to examine ways in which lesbians and others who queer family relationships experience and navigate the difficulties and the joys in their emotional connections.

FUTURE THEORIZING AND RESEARCH DIRECTIONS

In this chapter, we have examined gender and heteronormativity in romantic relationships from micro to macro perspectives. Our intersectional feminist approach is derived from critical theorizing, in which the status quo is decentered so that previously invisible or neglected topics can be examined. We selectively reviewed several areas of current relationship research that challenge gender and sexuality norms, and instead examine ways in which relational partners are both queering and challenging taken-for-granted assumptions about doing gender and sexuality in relationships.

The exemplars we provided, including gender-as-relational for heterosexual couples, long-term living together committed partnerships for mid-life and older couples, consensual nonmonogamous relationships, and lesbian relationship intensity and dissolution are only the tip of the iceberg for studying gender and heteronormativity in relationships. For example, an emerging area of research and theorizing is what some might consider as the antithesis of romantic relationships: asexuality. Asexuality is an umbrella term to describe individuals who do not experience sexual attraction to any gender. Asexuality is thus one of the most misunderstood, invisible, and marginalized of all sexual and relational identities (Carroll, 2020). In terms of defining asexuality, it is more common to identify individuals by their absence of sexual attraction, and not by their absence of sexual behavior. Instead, those who do not engage in sexual relations are celibate (Carroll, 2020). Yet, asexuality does not preclude the establishment of romantic or other forms of intimate relationships in which gender is apparent. We simply need to understand more about how gender and sexuality operate for such evolving identities.

An intersectional feminist lens demands that future research move toward analyzing the fluidity of exchanges of relational power and disempowerment between and among partners over the course of a relationship – initiation, formation, maintenance, and dissolution. We see a need to disentangle sexuality, partnering, and parenting from normative understandings of gender in romantic relationships because heteronormative standards are inherently value-laden, prejudicial, and discriminatory.

We also suggest bringing in greater attention to social justice activist movements and the interface of the life of the scholar with activism, particularly given the urgent needs of contemporary society. A feature of contemporary intersectional feminist theorizing is the use of the Internet and all forms of social media to politicize new forms of intimacy and bringing personal and relational issues into political awareness and activism (Jackson et al., 2020). In addition, the reflexive, autoethnographic analysis of one's own life course – especially in terms of living outside the boundaries of society's norms – is a feature of the reflexive turn among scholar-activists who study intimate life (Allen, 2022). Indeed, Hoskin (2020) incorporates her lived experiences with critical femininity to challenge traditional conceptualizations of gender and sexuality. Intersectional feminist thinking began in the lived experience of sexism, racism, homophobia, and ageism (Lorde, 1984) and has much to teach scholars and activists who wish to challenge the status quo and promote justice and integrity for all.

REFERENCES

Allen, K. R. (2022). Feminist theory, method, and praxis: Toward a critical consciousness for family and close relationship scholars. *Journal of Social and Personal Relationships*. Advance online publication. https://doi.org/10.1177/02654075211065779

Allen, K. R., & Goldberg, A. E. (2020). Lesbian women disrupting gendered, heteronormative discourses of motherhood, marriage, and divorce. *Journal of Lesbian Studies*, 24(1), 12–24. https://doi.org/10.1080/10894160.2019.1615356

Allen, K. R., Goldberg, A. E., & Jaramillo-Sierra, A. L. (2022). Feminist theories: Knowledge, method, and practice. In K. Adamsons, A. L. Few-Demo, C. Proulx, & K. Roy (Eds.), *Sourcebook of family theories and methodologies*. Springer.

Allen, K. R., Lloyd, S. A., & Few, A. L. (2009). Reclaiming feminist theory, methods, and practice for family studies. In S. A. Lloyd, A. L. Few, & K. R. Allen (Eds.), *Handbook of feminist family studies* (pp. 3–17). Sage.

Allen, S. H., & Mendez, S. N. (2018). Hegemonic heteronormativity: Toward a new era of queer family theory. *Journal of Family Theory & Review, 10*(1), 70–86. https://doi.org/10.1111/jftr.12241

Balsam, K. F., Rostosky, S. S., & Riggle, E. D. B. (2017). Breaking up is hard to do: Women's experience of dissolving their same-sex relationship. *Journal of Lesbian Studies, 21*(1), 30–46. https://doi.org/10.1080/10894160.2016.1165561

Barker, M., & Langdridge, D. (Eds.). (2010). *Understanding non-monogamies*. Routledge.

Barton, A. W., Lavner, J. A., Stanley, S. M., Johnson, M. D., & Rhoades, G. K. (2020). "Will you complete this survey too?" Differences between individual versus dyadic samples in relationship research. *Journal of Family Psychology, 34*(2), 196–203. https://doi.org/10.1037/fam0000583

Bernard, J. (1972). *The future of marriage*. Bantam.

Carr, D., & Utz, R. L. (2020). Families in later life: A decade in review. *Journal of Marriage and Family, 82*(1), 346–363. https://doi.org/10.1111/jomf.12609

Carroll, M. (2020). Asexuality and its implications for LGBTQ-parent families. In A. E. Goldberg & K. R. Allen (Eds.), *LGBTQ-parent families: Innovations in research and implications for practice* (2nd ed., pp. 185–198). Springer.

Chamberlain, P. (2017). *The feminist fourth wave: Affective temporality*. Palgrave.

Chaney, C. (2020). Family stress and coping among African Americans in the age of COVID-19. *Journal of Comparative Family Studies, 51*(3–4), 254–273. https://doi.org/10.3138/jcfs.51.3-4.003

Cherlin, A. J. (2020). Degrees of change: An assessment of the deinstitutionalization of marriage thesis. *Journal of Marriage and Family, 82*(1), 62–80. https://doi.org/10.1111/jomf.12605

Cohen, M. T., & K. Wilson. (2017). Development of the consensual non-monogamy attitude scale (CNAS). *Sexuality and Culture, 21*(1), 1–14. https://doi.org/10.1007/s12119-016-9395-5

Collins, C., Ruppanner, L., Landivar, L. C., & Scarborough, W. J. (2021). The gendered consequences of a weak infrastructure of care: School reopening plans and parents' employment during the COVID-19 pandemic. *Gender & Society, 35*(2), 180–193. https://doi.org/10.1177/08912432211001300

Collins, P. H. (2019). *Intersectionality as critical social theory*. Duke University Press.

Conley, T. D., Matsick, J., Moors, A. C., & Ziegler, A. (2017). The investigation of consensually non-monogamous relationships: Theories, methods and new directions. *Perspectives on Psychological Science, 12*(2), 205–232. https://doi.org/10.1177/1745691616667925

Connidis, I. A., Borell, K., & Karlsson, S. G. (2017). Ambivalence and living apart together in later life: A critical research proposal. *Journal of Marriage and Family, 79*(5), 1404–1418. https://doi.org/10.1111/jomf.12417

Crenshaw, K. (1991). Mapping the margins: Intersectionality, identity politics, and violence against women of color. *Stanford Law Review, 43*, 1241–1299. https://doi.org/10.2307/1229039

Curran, M. A., McDaniel, B. T., Pollitt, A. M., & Totenhagen, C. J. (2015). Gender, emotion work, and relationship quality: A daily diary study. *Sex Roles, 73*(3–4), 157–173. https://doi.org/10.1007/s11199-015-0495-8

Farr, R. H. (2017). Factors associated with relationship dissolution and post-dissolution adjustment among lesbian adoptive couples. *Journal of Lesbian Studies, 21*(1), 88–105. https://doi.org/10.1080/10894160.2016.1142354

Fausto-Sterling, A. (1985). *Myths of gender: Biological theories about women and men.* Basic Books.

Few-Demo, A. L., & Allen, K. R. (2020). Gender, feminist, and intersectional perspectives on families: A decade in review. *Journal of Marriage and Family, 82*(1), 326–345. https://doi.org/10.1111/jomf.12638

Few-Demo, A. L., Hunter, A. G., & Muruthi, B. A. (2022). Intersectionality theory: A critical theory pushing family science forward. In K. Adamsons, A. L. Few-Demo, C. Proulx, & K. Roy (Eds.), *Sourcebook of family theories and methodologies.* Springer.

Figueroa, V., & Tasker, F. (2020). Familismo, lesbophobia, and religious beliefs in the life course narratives of Chilean Lesbian mothers. *Frontiers in Psychology, 11*, Article 516471. https://doi.org/10.3389/fpsyg.2020.516471

Fry, R. (2022, March 28). *Young women are out-earning young men in several U.S. cities.* Retrieved from https://pewrsr.ch/3qGHyzH

Goldberg, A. E., & Garcia, R. (2015). Predictors of relationship dissolution in lesbian, gay, and heterosexual adoptive parents. *Journal of Family Psychology, 29*(3), 394–404. https://doi.org/10.1037/fam0000095

Goldberg, A. E., Allen, K. R., & Carroll, M. (2020). "We don't exactly fit in, but we can't opt out": Gay fathers' experiences navigating parent communities in schools. *Journal of Marriage and Family, 82*(5), 1655–1676. https://doi.org/10.1111/jomf.12695

Goodman, L., Choi, J. H., & Zhu, J. (2021, March 16). *More women have become homeowners and heads of household. Could the pandemic undo that progress?* Retrieved from www.urban.org/urban-wire/more-women-have-become-homeowners-and-heads-household-could-pandemic-undo-progress

Hoskin, R. A. (2020). "Femininity? It's the aesthetic of subordination": Examining femmephobia, the gender binary, and experiences of oppression among sexual and gender minorities. *Archives of Sexual Behavior, 49*(7), 2319–2339. https://doi.org/10.1007/s10508-020-01641-x

Jackson, S. J., Bailey, M., & Welles, B. F. (2020). *#HashtagActivism: Networks of race and gender justice.* MIT Press.

Ji, Y., Wu, X., Sun, S., & He, G. (2017). Unequal care, unequal work: Toward a more comprehensive understanding of gender inequality in post-reform urban China. *Sex Roles, 77*(11–12), 765–778. https://doi.org/10.1007/s11199-017-0751-1

Kenny, D. A., & Kashy, D. A. (2014). The analysis of data from dyads and groups. In H. T. Reis & C. M. Judd (Eds.), *Handbook of research methods in social and personality psychology* (pp. 589–607, 2nd ed.). Cambridge University Press.

Kimberly, C., & Hans, J. D. (2017). From fantasy to reality: A grounded theory of experiences in the swinging lifestyle. *Archives of Sexual Behavior, 46*(3), 789–799. https://doi.org/10.1007/s10508-015-0621-2

Kroeger, R. A., & Powers, D. A. (2019). Examining same-sex couples using dyadic data methods. In R. Schoen (Ed.), *Analytical family demography* (pp. 157–186). Springer.

Lips, H. M. (2018). *Gender: The basics* (2nd ed.). Routledge.

Lorber, J. (2012). *Gender inequality: Feminist theories and politics* (5th ed.). Oxford University Press.

Lorde, A. (1984). *Sister outsider: Essays & speeches*. Crossing Press.

Lutz, H. (2011). *The new maids: Transnational women and the care economy*. Zed Books.

Monk, J. K., & Ogolsky, B. G. (2019). Contextual relational uncertainty model: Understanding ambiguity in a changing sociopolitical context. *Journal of Family Theory & Review, 11*(2), 234–261. https://doi.org/10.1111/jftr.12325

Moors, A. C., Matsick, J., & Schechinger, H. (2017). Unique and shared relationship benefits of consensually non-monogamous and monogamous relationships: A review and insights for moving forward. *European Psychologist, 22*(1), 55–71. https://doi.org/10.1027/1016-9040/a000278

Moors, A. C., Matsick, J. L., Ziegler, A., Rubin, J., & Conley, T. D. (2013). Stigma toward individuals engaged in consensual non-monogamy: Robust and worthy of additional research. *Analyses of Social Issues and Public Policy, 13*(1), 52–69.

Ogolsky, B. G., Monk, J. K., Rice, T. M., Theisen, J. C., & Maniotes, C. R. (2017). Relationship maintenance: A review of research on romantic relationships. *Journal of Family Theory & Review, 9*(3), 275–306. https://doi.org/10.1111/jftr.12205

Oswald, R. F., Blume, L. B., & Marks, S. R. (2005). Decentering heteronormativity: A model for family studies. In V. L. Bengtson, A. C. Acock, K. R. Allen, P. Dilworth-Anderson, & D. M. Klein (Eds.), *Sourcebook of family theory and research* (pp. 143–165). Sage.

Oswald, R., Kuvalanka, K., Blume, L., & Berkowitz, D. (2009). Queering "the family". In S. A. Lloyd, A. L. Few, & K. R. Allen (Eds.), *Handbook of feminist family studies* (pp. 43–55). Sage.

Pollitt, A., & Curran, M. (2022). How a gender-as-relational perspective has been applied in quantitative studies of emotion work in romantic relationships. In K. Adamsons, A. L. Few-Demo, C. Proulx, & K. Roy (Eds.), *Sourcebook of family theories and methodologies*. Springer.

Reczek, C. (2020). Sexual- and gender-minority families: A 2010–2020 decade in review. *Journal of Marriage and Family, 82*(1), 300–325. https://doi.org/10.1111/jomf.12607

Rhode, D. L. (Ed.). (1990). *Theoretical perspectives on sexual difference*. Yale University Press.

Riggle, E. D. B., Rothblum, E. D., Rostosky, S. S., Clark, J. B., & Balsam, K. F. (2016). "The secret of our success": Long-term same-sex couples' perceptions of their relationship longevity. *Journal of GLBT Family Studies, 12*(4), 319–334. https://doi.org/10.1080/1550428X.2015.1095668

Risman, B. J. (2004). Gender as a social structure: Theory wrestling with activism. *Gender & Society, 18*(4), 429–450. https://doi.org/10.1177/0891243204265349

Risman, B. J. (2018). *Where the millennials will take us: A new generation wrestles with the gender structure*. Oxford University Press.

Rothblum, E. D. (2009). An overview of same-sex couples in relation ships: A research area still at sea. In D. A. Hope (Ed.), *Nebraska symposium on motivation: Vol. 54.*

Contemporary perspectives on lesbian, gay, and bisexual identities (pp. 113–139). Springer.

Sassler, S., & Lichter, D. T. (2020), Cohabitation and marriage: Complexity and diversity in union-formation patterns. *Journal of Marriage and Family, 82*(1), 35–61. https://doi.org/10.1111/jomf.12617

Schippers, M. (2020). *Polyamory, monogamy, and American dreams: The stories we tell about poly lives and the cultural production of inequality.* Routledge

Sheff, E. (2015). *Polyamorists next door: Inside multiple-partner relationships and families.* Rowman & Littlefield.

Strohm, C. Q., Seltzer, J. A., Cochran, S. D., & Mays, V. M. (2009). "Living apart together" relationships in the United States. *Demographic Research, 21*(7), 177–214. www.jstor.org/stable/26349343

Thomeer, M. B., Umberson, D., & Reczek, C. (2020). The gender-as-relational approach for theorizing about romantic relationships of sexual and gender minority mid- to later-life adults. *Journal of Family Theory & Review, 12*(2), 220–237. https://doi.org/10.1111/jftr.12368

Vaughan, M. D., Jones, P., Taylor, B. A., & Roush, J. (2019). Healthcare experiences and needs of consensually non-monogamous people: Results from a focus group study. *Journal of Sexual Medicine, 16*(1), 42–51. https://doi.org/10.1016/j.jsxm.2018.11.006

Waismel-Manor, R., Wasserman, V., & Shamir-Balderman, O. (2021). No room of her own: Married couples' negotiation of workspace at home during COVID-19. *Sex Roles, 85*(11–12), 636–649. https://doi.org/10.1007/s11199-021-01246-1

West, C., & Zimmerman, D. H. (1987). Doing gender. *Gender & Society, 1*(2), 125–151. https://doi.org/10.1177/0891243287001002002

West, T. V., Popp, D., & Kenny, D. A. (2008). A guide for the estimation of gender and sexual orientation effects in dyadic data: An actor-partner interdependence model approach. *Personality and Social Psychology Bulletin, 34*(3), 321–336. https://doi.org/10.1177/0146167207311199

Yucel, D., & Gassanov, M. A. (2010). Exploring actor and partner correlates of sexual satisfaction among married couples. *Social Science Research, 39*(5), 725–738. http://doi.org/10.1016/j.ssresearch.2009.09.002

5

Social Class, Neighborhoods, and Romantic Relationships

KRISTIN D. MICKELSON

INTRODUCTION

We all know the formula for a good romantic comedy movie – couple meets, conflict tears couple apart, couple resolves conflict and ends up together. Aside from the fact that the vast majority of those couples are heterosexual and White, there is another common characteristic of the couples – they are usually upper middle-class professionals. The main characters almost always live in amazing apartments in the best parts of big cities and have exciting jobs with seemingly unlimited flexibility in work hours. Dates often take place in expensive restaurants or venues (e.g., cultural events like the opera or sporting events with great seats). Weddings are grand, in beautiful locations with catered gourmet food and decorations. If there is a divorce, neither character ever mentions financial issues related to the breakup – they miraculously end up with a new fabulous, fully furnished apartment. If we only learned about romantic relationships from these movies, we might believe that those in lower socioeconomic classes do not experience romance. Not only does Hollywood typically ignore the role of social class in romantic relationships, the overwhelming majority of empirical studies on intimate relationships also ignores the role of social class and place in how we experience our romantic relationships. Obviously, we know romantic relationships are not simply experienced by the middle-class and those with wealth. But, how does social class influence the development, maintenance, and dissolution of intimate relationships? This chapter will focus on four stages of romantic relationships (dating, cohabitation, marriage, and divorce) and the role of social class (i.e., income and education) and place (i.e., neighborhood characteristics) in each stage. In terms of the literature review, I restrict my focus to the past fifteen years (i.e., since 2007).

MONEY AND THE DATING GAME

In US society, dating is not cheap; often a date entails going out for a meal and/or drink and seeing a movie – not to mention gas for the car or paying for a taxi or carshare ride. In fact, in 2019, the average date night in the United States was estimated at around $116 – ranging from $143 in San Francisco to $83 in Omaha (Watson, 2019). Moreover, dating has generally followed a heteronormative expectation of the male (or the individual who requested the date) to pay for any expenses related to the date (e.g., Lever et al., 2015). So, how does socioeconomic status impact how individuals initiate and begin a romantic relationship?

First and foremost, where do individuals find their dating partners? Traditionally, research has suggested that one of the strongest predictors of attraction and relationship initiation is proximity (Sprecher, 1998). Thus, it makes sense that individuals would find their dating partners from the same neighborhoods, schools, or workplaces they occupy (Couch & Koeninger, 2016). Yet, some interesting research from the National Longitudinal Study of Adolescent Health, a nationally representative study of 14–17-year-old students in the United States during the 1994–1995 academic year, throws this idea into question. Grieger et al. (2014) argued that in addition to peer groups, the larger schools and neighborhood environments can shape the norms and rules around risky sexual behaviors, and as such it is important to understand whether adolescents tend to find their romantic partners within their school or neighborhood. In preliminary descriptive analyses, they found that around half of students in this study (47 percent female, 51 percent male) found a romantic partner from their school or neighborhood. What is striking is that half of the students found their romantic partner *outside* of their neighborhood or school, but it is not known whether this means that they are crossing social class boundaries or simply finding partners from other similarly situated neighborhoods and schools. Moving away from adolescents to adults, a recent review of socioeconomic status and intimate relationships (Karney, 2021) argues that there is evidence to support the idea that place and SES matter in relationship formation. Specifically, Karney reviews research that finds low-SES couples are more likely to meet in public, shared spaces, which serves to "exacerbate their disadvantages," whereas higher-SES couples are more likely to meet in selective and private spaces, which serve to "consolidate their advantages."

With the emergence of online dating apps, this mode of relationship formation has begun to supplant traditional offline ways of meeting potential romantic partners discussed in Karney's review – and possibly making place less important. Rosenfeld et al. (2019) found in a 2017 nationally representative survey of US adults that almost 40 percent of heterosexual adults reported meeting their partner online. Although most online dating apps are free at a basic level (e.g., Bumble, Tinder, Match.com), they all offer a premium version with upgrades (e.g., unlimited swipes, see who likes you before you swipe, better filtering) for a price. Some researchers have sought to understand whether there are social class differences in who accesses online dating. Valkenburg and Peter (2007) found that neither income nor education significantly predicted frequency of visiting dating apps or posting profiles among a sample of Dutch adults. But, Sautter and colleagues (2010) argue that it is more appropriate to frame the discussion around the "digital divide." Specifically, studies failing to show income and education as significant predictors of online dating behavior usually test this idea among those with access to the internet. Instead, they argue and find in their research that income and education predict access to the internet, but once internet access is controlled for, these social class factors no longer predict online dating behavior. Although access to siub and the internet has expanded significantly in the past decade, the digital divide continues, especially in rural America. Furthermore, when examining access to broadband (defined as download speeds of at least 25 megabytes per second [Mbps] and upload speeds of at least 3 Mbps), which is now considered essential for reliable and rapid access to the internet, approximately 45 percent of US households making less than $30,000 per year do not have broadband (Winslow, 2019). Thus, it is clear that in the current environment, social class can impact one's ability to participate in online dating apps as a means of relationship formation.

Another way of viewing the role of social class and dating is by examining dating partner preferences. Almost forty years ago, Buss and Barnes (1986) famously examined human dating preferences, replicating a common finding that women more so than men *"preferred mates who showed good earning potential and who were college educated"* (p. 569). As dating apps have emerged, the thought is that this preference would replicate online. In a study of a Chinese dating app, Ong and Wang (2015) constructed fake dating profiles and found that males of various income levels visited females' profiles without focus on their income level, whereas females of all income levels were more likely to visit higher-income males' profiles – in fact, males' profiles with the highest income level received ten times more visits than the lowest income level. In another study, Ong (2016) found a similar pattern for education – such that it does not appear to matter for females' profiles but does for males' profiles. Similarly, in a US sample, Hitsch and colleagues (2010) found that women preferred income over physical attributes more than men. However, more recent research conducted in Canada with female participants found that although income was influential in both short-term and long-term online dating preferences, it was a weaker predictor than physical attractiveness. Moreover, physical appearance acted as an initial filter, such that income was considered after screening for the most physically attractive profiles (Woloszyn et al., 2020). Thus, the literature remains equivocal about whether social class matters for dating preferences in the online world of dating.

When examining the literature on social class and specific dating behaviors, much of it tends to focus primarily on adolescents and college students (e.g., Allison & Risman, 2014; Bartoli & Clark, 2006; Brimeyer & Smith, 2012; Owen et al., 2010; Sprecher & Regan, 2002). In a paper using the National Longitudinal Study of Adolescent Health, Meier and Allen (2009) found that social class plays a role in the type of romantic relationships US adolescents experience; specifically, low-SES adolescents in the study were less likely to experience a steady exclusive dating relationship, but more likely to have sexual intercourse in their most recent relationship (Meier & Allen, 2009). In another paper by Meier and Allen (2008), social class differences were found for sexual experiences but not for those who said they had a *"special romantic relationship"* (self-defined by participants). In other words, they argue that social class (e.g., family background and income) impacts both the *"nature and timing of adolescent and young adult intimate relationship"* (p. 30).

A number of studies have examined other sexual behaviors common in dating relationships. Several studies have found that those from lower SES groups are less likely to engage in hookups (Allison & Risman, 2014; Hamilton & Armstrong, 2009; Owen et al., 2010). On the other hand, Brimeyer and Smith (2012) found that social class was neither predictive of number of dates nor hookups in a college sample. Similarly, Manning et al. (2005) found that, among adolescents, family income was not related to hooking up. However, when examining other risky sex behaviors, researchers have found that lower family income is related to increased casual sex and unplanned pregnancy for adolescents (e.g., Miller et al., 2001), and low SES is a significant risk factor for unintended pregnancy among adult women (e.g., Iseyemi et al., 2017). Furthermore, although beyond the scope of this chapter, there is a robust literature examining the role of social class on condom use and sexually transmitted diseases, which suggests that lower SES individuals (especially adolescents and certain race/ethnic groups) are more likely to engage in risky sex behaviors (see Harding, 2007, for a review).

Aside from sexual behaviors in dating, another common focus in the literature is on social class and dating violence. Dating violence is widespread and present in all social classes, with approximately 30 percent of adolescents reporting experience with dating violence (Rennison & Welchans, 2000). Although some research has not found a link between SES and dating violence victimization or perpetration (e.g., Lavoie et al., 2002), other research has shown a link between low-SES and increased dating violence among adolescents and college students (e.g., Pflieger & Vazsonyi, 2006). Pflieger and Vazsonyi (2006) further found that low self-esteem mediated the association between poor parenting and dating violence behaviors (both victimization and perpetration) for low-SES adolescents, whereas for high-SES adolescents it only mediated between poor parenting and dating violence beliefs.

To conclude, the dating game is not free from social class influences. An individual's socioeconomic status has been shown to impact who an individual prefers to date, where and how one meets, and what individuals do in terms of dating behaviors. Unfortunately, there is a lack of research on whether these social class influences extend to dating among LGBTQ individuals, although it is not unreasonable to assume that many of these results will generalize. In other words, money influences our initial attraction and interactions with potential romantic partners. Even though the first stage of intimate relationships is tied to one's social class, does social class continue to exert an influence as a relationship moves to the next stage of commitment?

MY PLACE OR YOURS OR NO PLACE

As a relationship develops into a more serious commitment, cohabitation becomes a common consideration. Viewed from a middle-class lens, this often takes the form of one individual moving into the other's place or finding a new place together. However, for individuals with less means, their options for cohabitation may be more constrained. Alternately, cohabitation may be broached earlier in some couples as a means of saving money.

Cohabitation (or living together) has changed dramatically in the past few decades. Once seen as going against social norms (particularly religious mores; see The LeClair Affair in 1968 at Barnard College), couples today are more likely to cohabitate prior to or in place of marrying than twenty years ago. In the United States, cohabitation in the past two decades among unmarried couples has nearly tripled from 6 million to 17 million (US Census Bureau, 2019) and that number is even more striking when compared to 1980 when there were only 1.6 million cohabiting couples in the United States (Spanier, 1983). In terms of demographic differences, the most recent US Census report (2019) finds most cohabiting individuals are fairly equally split between young adults (18–34 years old; 48.5 percent) and middle adults (35–64 years old; 45.5 percent), two-thirds are White (67 percent) with Hispanics (16 percent) and Blacks (11 percent) accounting for a roughly quarter combined. With respect to education, a shift has occurred over the prior twenty years with individuals cohabiting in 2017 being more highly educated (59 percent with at least some college) than in 1996 (43 percent with at least some college). However, with respect to income, although there has been a decline in the past two decades, those making less than $30,000 per year still make up the majority of cohabiting individuals (63.8 percent in 1996 vs. 52.7 percent in 2017). Moreover, support for cohabitation among high school seniors has almost doubled since the mid-1970s (from 40 percent to 71 percent; Anderson, 2016). Approximately 60 percent of young women (particularly Whites as opposed to Blacks) expect to cohabit with a partner before marrying (Manning et al., 2014). And, having a baby is no longer seen as a motivating reason to get married among young adults (Sassler et al., 2009).

But, why do couples choose to cohabit, and could this be related to social class? Some couples cohabit to "test the waters" of compatibility before moving onto marriage, whereas other couples may cohabit out of financial necessity. Sassler and Miller (2011) found that couples with lower-SES may be quicker to cohabit in order to pool their financial resources as a way to improve their economic security. Sassler and colleagues (2016) similarly found that men and women with lower-SES were more likely to move rapidly to cohabitation than their counterparts with higher-SES. Through living together, individuals can reduce food costs, improve housing quality, and have a ready source of emotional support (Edin et al., 2004; Sassler & Miller, 2017). Additionally, cohabiting can greatly decrease the expenses associated with dating.

Although cohabitation is often mentioned as a precursor to marriage, that is not necessarily borne out in the literature. Indeed, cohabiting is increasingly viewed as an alternative form of union (Guzzo, 2020). When examining through the lens of social class, those in lower SES groups are less likely to move from cohabitation to marriage. Specifically, those without a college education who are cohabiting are significantly less likely to get engaged or marry than those with a college education who are cohabiting (Sassler et al., 2018). As Karney (2021) so succinctly states: *"For those who complete college, escalating commitments take time but proceed steadily from sex to cohabitation to marriage and, finally, to first parenthood. For those without a college education, sex happens quickly after meeting, cohabitation soon after that, and first parenthood is mostly likely to precede marriage, if marriage happens at all"* (p. 398).

As gay marriage has only been legal in the United States since 2015, cohabitation has been the traditional form of union for same-sex couples. As a result, research on cohabitation and social class for same-sex couples is virtually nonexistent. I located one recent study that examined the sociodemographic differences between same-sex cohabiting and married couples using the Current Population Survey from 2015/2016 and 2017/2018. Manning and Payne (2021) found that almost half of same-sex couples were married (45 percent), but that cohabitating versus married same-sex couples differed on several important characteristics. Similar to different-sex couples, cohabiting same-sex couples were less likely to have children, were younger, more mobile, more likely to rent their home, and, most relevant to this chapter, earned less income than their married counterparts.

Prior research has suggested that cohabiting relationships are less stable and committed compared to marriages (see Wagner & Weiss, 2006, for a review), which led to oft repeated claims in academia and popular media that living together was connected to higher divorce rates and was bad for society in general (e.g., Focus on the Family (Morse, 2001) – *The Problem with Living*

Together; Morgan's (2000) book – *Marriage Lite: The Rise of Cohabitation and Its Consequences;* New York Times Opinion (Jay, 2012) – *The Downside of Cohabiting before Marriage*). However, more recent research has debunked this idea (Kuperberg, 2019), with some research showing that increased cohabitation is actually likely to lead to more discriminant selection into marriage, which would lead to declining or stabilizing divorce rates (Kennedy & Ruggles, 2014). Other research has shown that once observed (e.g., age, education, religiosity) and unobserved selection effects are controlled for cohabitation is actually related to lower risk of divorce (Kulu & Boyle, 2010; Kuperberg, 2019). Still, others note that the direction of effect may be reversed such that divorce leads to increased cohabitation due to second unions and changing norms, expectations, and attitudes (e.g., Perelli-Harris et al., 2017). However, there are social class differences in this research as well. Cohabiting couples with lower-SES appear to be at greater risk of relationship dissolution than cohabiting couples with higher-SES because they move in together much quicker (e.g., Kuperberg, 2019; Sassler et al., 2018).

Although cohabitation is becoming a common form of union for many young couples across the social class spectrum, research has consistently shown that couples with less income and education are quicker to make the jump to living together for economic reasons and with less intent to move towards marriage. And, this faster trajectory towards cohabitation is related to greater likelihood for relationship dissolution.

MARRIAGE OF EQUALS?

As we see from the above discussion, the child's rhyme of "first comes love, then comes marriage..." is less accurate today than in the past. However, most individuals do end up marrying at least once in their lifetime. In the United States, 50.4 percent of adults eighteen years or older live with a spouse (US Census Bureau, 2021). Aside from the common reason of love, there are many reasons couples marry including companionship, children, and financial considerations (Horowitz et al., 2019). Regardless of the reason, marriage is the merger of two independent individuals into a dyad. In this dyad, each individual brings to the relationship their own contribution and expectation of the other's contribution.

Today, we often hear the phrase a "marriage of equals." The literature on assortative mating backs up this phrase showing that individuals match up based on both education and income, and assortative mating has increased substantially since 1960 (Greenwood et al., 2014; Schwartz & Mare, 2005). More importantly, this assortative mating has been linked with increased income inequality in the United States (Greenwood et al., 2014; Schwartz, 2010). In other words, homogamy is deepening and solidifying the income divide in America.

But, what happens when two people enter a marriage from different socio-economic backgrounds (i.e., heterogamy)? Theory and prior research suggest that those from different backgrounds have different cultural experiences and values (Hanel et al., 2018); thus, heterogamous couples (regardless of the domain) are likely to experience more conflict and less stability due to the cultural differences in experience and values (e.g., Hohmann-Marriott & Amato, 2008). Specifically, symbolic interactionism states that the salient advantage for homogamous couples is that their "stock of experience" is organized similarly (Berger & Kellner, 1970).

Much of the research on heterogamy focuses on those from different ethnic (e.g., Hohmann-Marriott & Amato, 2008) or religious backgrounds (e.g., McClendon, 2016), or different ages (e.g., Pyke & Adams, 2010). With respect to social class heterogamy, many of the studies are conducted in European countries. In one study examining educational heterogamy in twenty-nine European countries, there was no connection between educational heterogamy and self-assessed health (Huijts et al., 2010). Another study conducted in Finland found educational heterogamy was related to greater likelihood of cohabitation (Mäenpää & Jalovaara, 2014). Finally, a study of Dutch parents found that educational heterogamy was related to cultural differences in childrearing (Eeckhaut et al., 2014).

With respect to income heterogamy, given the persistent gender wage gap in the United States with women making eighty-two cents on the dollar to men (Payscale, 2022), dual-earner heterosexual couples are unlikely to be equal in terms of income contributions to the household. A marriage of unequals (particularly in regards to income) is most likely to impact division of household labor. There is strong evidence that a wife's relative income contribution affects division of household labor, with those contributing less than their husbands doing more of the housework and childcare (e.g., see Gupta, 2006, for a review). This finding would lead us to believe that income homogamy would lead to an equitable division of household labor. However, there is an interesting reversal when a wife's income contribution matches or exceeds her husband's contribution. Specifically, wives whose incomes are the same or more than their husband's actually do more housework and childcare (Bittman et al., 2003; Schneider, 2011; Syrda, 2022). This result is likely due to gender role norm violations leading couples to try to reinforce them within the area of household labor – referred to in the literature as "gender deviance neutralization" (e.g., Syrda, 2022).

But, what about same-sex couples? Prior research has shown that same-sex couples are more likely to be heterogamous than different-sex couples on a number of sociodemographic characteristics (e.g., race/ethnicity, education, age), but not on income for example, (Manning et al., 2016; Schwartz & Graf, 2009). Yet, do differences in income contribution dictate division of household labor for same-sex couples? Although only a few studies have examined this idea, they have consistently shown that proportion of income does not translate into a greater or lesser share of housework for same-sex couples (Civettini, 2016; Solomon et al., 2005). Instead, Civettini (2016) found that housework division was related to non-normative gender displays, such that femininity for gay men and masculinity for lesbians was predictive of housework division. Moreover, Civettini (2015) and Downing and Goldberg (2011) found support for time availability, such that greater paid work hours was predictive of a smaller share of the housework for same-sex couples, which is similar to findings for different-sex couples (e.g., Cunningham, 2007).

To conclude, homogamy is a double-edged sword. Assortative mating strongly suggests that those with similar social and cultural backgrounds are most likely to marry and these marriages are more successful than those that are heterogamous. However, homogamy (especially in social class) has been shown to maintain, if not widen, the income inequality in society. Yet, heterogamy is increasing as interracial/interethnic and mixed religion coupling is becoming more commonplace in society. Moreover, with the gender pay gap, heterosexual couples (but not same-sex couples) are likely to be somewhat heterogamous with respect to income. We see from the literature that heterosexual individuals with different incomes navigate a marriage by trying to maintain gender role norms and expectations. In other words, increasing equality in income leads to a more equitable division of household labor but only to a point; once the woman makes the same or more than the man that benefit disappears and she ends up doing more housework to neutralize the gender role deviance. Interestingly, the impact of relative resources does not seem to impact same-sex couples' division of housework; rather inequity in housework for same-sex couples is more likely to be related to time availability (i.e., paid work hours) and non-normative gender displays.

TOO POOR TO DIVORCE

What does the research tell us about the link between socioeconomic status and divorce? According to the United States Census Bureau, both the rate of marriage and divorce declined in the United States from 2009 to 2019 (Anderson & Scherer, 2020). In other words, even though fewer people are marrying, fewer are also divorcing. When these numbers are broken down by income level, based on the 2019 American Community Survey, we see that divorce rates drop from a high of around 45 percent among those in poverty (i.e., making less than $10,000 annually) to a low of around 30 percent for those making $200,000 or more annually (Yau, 2021). Moreover, as suggested in the prior section, inequality in income within heterosexual couples – specifically if wives make more than their husbands – is linked with higher divorce rates. According to Nock (2001), wives who are equal contributors (i.e., 40 percent – 59 percent) in terms of family earnings are less committed (defined as viewing separation/divorce being associated with an improvement in various areas of life) and more likely to initiate divorce. As has been suggested in prior research, whereas men benefit from the marital status, women typically only benefit from marriage if it is high quality (Nock, 2001; Sayer & Bianchi, 2000). Researchers have proposed that the increased divorce initiation among women who are equal contributors is partially due to their increased sensitivity to the quality of the marriage; because they have more power within the relationship than women with less income, they are able to leave a low-quality marriage (Nock, 2001).

The conclusion that many researchers and laypeople espouse with regard to the higher divorce rates among individuals with lower SES is that they are less skilled at marriage or value marriage less (e.g., Small et al., 2010) than individuals with higher SES. However, Trail and Karney (2012) showed in their study of income and marriage that these assumptions are wrong. Specifically, in a sample of US individuals, they found that those with lower incomes endorse similar or more traditional values compared to those with higher incomes – especially with respect to divorce. Furthermore, they reported similar or slightly lower expectations for marriage than those with higher incomes. Finally, in terms of relationship problems, the two income groups did not differ with respect to communication, sex, parenting, household chores, or in-laws; however, those with lower incomes did report more problems with money, substance use, fidelity, and friends. Thus, it is not that lower income groups value marriage less, have unrealistic expectations, or are less skilled, but, rather, that they are more likely to encounter economic and social issue difficulties related to their income level (Trail & Karney, 2012). Relatedly, other research has shown that couples with lower income are more likely to cite "instrumental" reasons for dissolution or divorce such as substance abuse, domestic violence, and lack of contribution to the household, whereas couples with higher income cite more relationship-oriented reasons such as problems with communication, incompatibility, lack of intimacy or personality differences (see Karney, 2021, for a review). These issues are not unique to different-sex couples; indeed, prior research suggests that the correlates of relationship dissolution/divorce are the same for same-sex couples, including relationship dissatisfaction, lack of commitment, being young or partner age gaps, discrepancy in income or low income, and low education (Farr & Goldberg, 2019).

Fifty years ago, many women stayed in low quality marriages because their economic situation did not allow for them to divorce and divorce laws around the United States punished women financially (Leopold, 2018). This situation has changed dramatically over the decades, with more advantageous divorce laws (e.g., moving away from alimony in favor of shared assets; no-fault or unilateral divorce laws vs. fault divorce laws requiring proof of wrongdoing, such as cruelty, adultery, or desertion) and the increasing numbers of dual-income couples making it easier both legally and financially to divorce (Nock, 2001).

However, this typically assumes a middle class or upper middle-class social status. Even though individuals in higher SES groups do not suffer the same financial loss as those in lower SES groups, other research has shown that, regardless of social class, divorce is predictive of drops in wealth and financial security – especially for women (Hogendoorn et al., 2020). But, what about later financial recovery following divorce? Here social inequity continues to have an impact. Specifically, as reviewed by Karney (2021), those who are college educated and have higher SES are more likely to remarry and rebound financially than those who are less educated and have lower SES. In other words, the social divide continues to grow even after divorce and remarriage.

GAPS AND FUTURE DIRECTIONS

The literature reviewed in this chapter also highlights several gaps and future directions. First, the vast majority of the existing research on social class and romantic relationships is on heterosexual couples. We know next to nothing about how social class may impact LGBTQ relationships. Although there is no reason to expect that social class would have a different impact on these relationships, it is likely that sexual orientation and social class may intersect and produce multiplicative effects on initiation, maintenance, and/or dissolution. Future research is needed on the intertwining role of sexual orientation and social class during relationship formation and development.

Another gap is that a substantial portion of the literature on several of the topics discussed in this chapter is conducted in European or Asian countries as opposed to the United States. Although Western Europe and the United States share similar cultural orientations, Asian countries have a more collectivist perspective, which may lead to different results with respect to the social class and romantic relationships. A focus on family and community over the individual may buffer people from the effects of low SES on romantic relationships. Cross-cultural research is desperately needed to provide a more nuanced understanding of the intersection of culture and class on romantic relationships.

Relatedly, even within the United States, place is rarely considered in research on romantic relationships. When I speak of place, I am not only referring to urbanicity but also geographic region. In fact, often urbanicity and region are interconnected in our lexicon – when we think of the American Midwest it is usually referring to suburban neighborhoods, whereas the Northeast is often synonymous with urban centers, and the South is interchangeable with rural. Researchers have argued that different cultural norms and values emerge based on place (Van de Vliert, 2007). For example, Shifrer and Sutton (2014) found region and urbanicity differences in locus of control. They found that adolescents from the rural South were less likely to have an internal locus of control, whereas urban and rural adolescents from the

Northeast were more likely to have an internal locus of control. Furthermore, they argued that these differences might be due to cultural differences between these two regions. Finally, their results appeared to indicate that region was more strongly associated with differences in locus of control than urbanicity – specifically, the West and Northeast promote greater internal locus of control than the Midwest and South. Prior research has established a link between locus of control and relationship satisfaction, such that those with an internal locus of control report greater sexual satisfaction (Asgharianji et al., 2015) and marital satisfaction (Lee & McKinnish, 2019).

But, how would this relate to social class and romantic relationships? Social class and place are often confounded. Consider the inner city, which is disproportionately lower income and minority-identifying versus the suburbs, which are middle-class and overwhelmingly White. Sociologists have long argued that neighborhood and place are intimately tied to culture, and we know that culture shapes norms and values, which feed directly into our social organization and, ultimately, our social interactions – including our intimate relationships. Harding and Hepburn (2014) argue in their review of the cultural mechanisms on neighborhood effects for the importance of understanding *"how to characterize the cultural context of disadvantaged neighborhoods and how being embedded in such contexts affects individuals"* (p. 22). In other words, even though research on place and romantic relationships is still emerging; future studies are needed to separate the influence of urbanicity from region and culture from neighborhood.

Finally, it goes without saying that race/ethnicity and social class are often interconnected in American society. The disadvantaged are disproportionately from Black and Hispanic race/ethnic groups. Although there is quite a bit of research on race/ethnicity and romantic relationships (see Chapter 2 in this book), it would be beneficial to examine whether the race/ethnic differences in marriage and divorce are due primarily to social class differences or cultural differences or some other contributing factor.

CONCLUSION

This chapter has reviewed the literature from the past fifteen years on social class and the different stages of romantic relationships from meeting a potential partner, to cohabitation, marriage, and divorce. Although by no means an exhaustive review of the literature, three recurring themes are present in each stage. First, the *"rich get richer and the poor get poorer"* is apparent even within intimate relationships. Specifically, we see that those with less financial means are likely to meet and marry those from a similar social background, which widens the income divide. Even following divorce, those who are better off financially are more likely to remarry and emerge as financially sound as before, if not better. Second, gender differences in romantic relationships persist regardless of social class (albeit likely exacerbated by SES). In other words, women are still the main caretakers in heterosexual relationships, and the influence of gender norms on initiation, paying, and housework are still pervasive across the socioeconomic spectrum. Rich or poor – women still do the majority of relationship care and household labor. Third, and most important, relationship expectations are not influenced by social class. As shown in prior research, most individuals regardless of SES expect to fall in love, get married, and start a family. Stated differently, money cannot buy love – but it can make it easier to date, marry, and divorce.

ACKNOWLEDGMENT

A special thanks to Victoria Klennert and Tylie Henderson for their assistance with formatting and preparing this chapter.

REFERENCES

Allison, R., & Risman, B. J. (2014). "It goes hand in hand with the parties": Race, class and residence in college student negotiations of hooking up. *Sociological Perspectives*, *57*(1), 102–123. https://doi.org/10.1177/0731121413516608

Anderson, L. R. (2016). *High school seniors' attitudes on cohabitation as a testing ground for marriage*. Bowling Green State University, National Center for Family & Marriage Research. Retrieved from www.bgsu.edu/ncfmr/resources/data/family-profiles/anderson-hs-seniors-attitudes-cohab-test-marriage-fp-16-13.html

Anderson, L. R., & Scherer, Z. (2020). *See how marriage and divorce rates in your state stack up*. Census.gov. Retrieved from www.census.gov/library/stories/2020/12/united-states-marriage-and-divorce-rates-declined-last-10-years.html

Asgharianji, A., Vardanyan, K., & Navabinejad, S. (2015). The interrelationship among locus of control, sexual satisfaction and marital satisfaction. *Journal of Asian Scientific Research*, *5*(2), 60–72. https://doi.org/10.18488/journal.2/2015.5.2/2.2.60.72

Bartoli, A. M., & Clark, M. D. (2006). The dating game: Similarities and differences in dating scripts among college students. *Sex Cult*, *10*(4), 54–80. https://doi.org/10.1007/s12119-006-1026-0

Berger, P. L., & Kellner, H. (1970). Marriage and the construction of reality. In H. Dreitzel (Eds.), *Recent sociology: Patterns of communicative behavior* (No. 2) (pp. 49–73). Macmillan.

Bittman, M., England, P., Sayer, L., Folbre, N., & Matheson, G. (2003). When does gender trump money? Bargaining and time in household work. *American Journal of Sociology*, *109*(1), 186–214. https://doi.org/10.1086/378341

Brimeyer, T. M., & Smith, W. L. (2012). Religion, race, social class, and gender differences in dating and hooking up among college students. *Sociological Spectrum*, *32*(5), 462–473. https://doi.org/10.1080/02732173.2012.694799

Buss, D. M., & Barnes, M. (1986). Preferences in human mate selection. *Journal of Personality and Social Psychology*, *50*(3), 559–570. https://doi.org/10.1037/0022-3514.50.3.559

Civettini, N. (2015). Gender display, time availability, and relative resources: Applicability to housework contributions of members of same-sex couples. *International Social Science Review*, *91*(1), 1–34.

Civettini, N. (2016). Housework as non-normative gender display among lesbians and gay men. *Sex Roles*, *74*(5), 206–219. https://doi.org/10.1007/s11199-015-0559-9

Couch, L. L., & Koeninger, A. L. (2016). Attraction: The many factors that draw us to like, lust, and love. In R. W. Summers (Ed.), *Social psychology: How other people influence our thoughts and actions* (vol. 2, pp. 299–314). ABC-CLIO.

Cunningham M. (2007). Influences of women's employment on the gendered division of household labor over the life course: Evidence from a 31-year panel study. *Journal of Family Issues*, *28*(3), 422–444. https://doi.org/10.1177/0192513X06295198

Downing, J. B., & Goldberg, A. E. (2011). Lesbian mothers' constructions of the division of paid and unpaid labor. *Feminism & Psychology*, *21*(1), 100–120. https://doi.org/10.1177/0959353510375869

Edin, K., Kefalas, M. J., & Reed, J. M. (2004). A peek inside the black box: What marriage means for poor unmarried parents. *Journal of Marriage and Family*, *66*(4), 1007–1014. https://doi.org/10.1111/j.0022-2445.2004.00072.x

Eeckhaut, M. C. W., Putte, B. V., Gerris, J. R. M., & Vermulst, A. A. (2014). Educational heterogamy: Does it lead to cultural differences in child-rearing? *Journal of Social and Personal Relationships*, *31*(6), 729–750. https://doi.org/10.1177/0265407513503594

Farr, R. H., & Goldberg, A. E. (2019). Same-sex relationship dissolution and divorce: How will children be affected? In A. E. Goldberg & A. P. Romero (Eds.), *LGBTQ divorce and relationship dissolution: Psychological and legal perspectives and implications for practice* (pp. 151–172). Oxford University Press.

Greenwood, J., Guner, N., Kocharkov, G., & Santos, C. (2014). Marry your like: Assortative mating and income inequality. *American Economic Review*, *104*(5), 348–353. https://doi.org/10.1257/aer.104.5.348

Grieger, L., Kusunoki, Y., & Harding, D. J. (2014). The social contexts of adolescent romantic relationships. *Focus*, *31*(1), 15–17.

Gupta, S. (2006). Her money, her time: Women's earnings and their housework hours. *Social Science Research*, *35*(4), 975–999. https://doi.org/10.1016/j.ssresearch.2005.07.003

Guzzo, K. B. (2020). A research brief on prospective marital expectations among cohabitors with initial marital intentions. *Journal of Family Issues*, *41*(11), 1979–2001. https://doi.org/10.1177/0192513X20909145

Hamilton, L., & Armstrong, E. A. (2009). Gendered sexuality in young adulthood: Double binds and flawed options. *Gender & Society*, *23*(5), 589–616. https://doi.org/10.1177/0891243209345829

Hanel, P. H. P., Maio, G. R., Soares, A. K. S., Vione, K. C., de Holanda Coelho, G. L., Gouveia, V. V., Patil, A. C., Kamble, S. V., & Manstead, A. S. R. (2018). Cross-cultural differences and similarities in human value instantiation. *Frontiers in Psychology*, *9*, Article 849. https://doi.org/10.3389/fpsyg.2018.00849

Harding, D. J. (2007). Cultural context, sexual behavior, and romantic relationships in disadvantaged neighborhoods. *American Sociological Review*, *72*(3), 341–364. https://doi.org/10.1177/000312240707200302

Harding, D. J., & Hepburn, P. (2014). Cultural mechanisms in neighborhood effects research in the United States. *Sociol Urbana Rurale (Testo Stamp)*, *103*, 37–73. https://doi.org/10.3280/SUR2014-103004

Hitsch, G. J., Hortaçsu, A., & Ariely, D. (2010). What makes you click? Mate preferences in online dating. *Quantitative Marketing and Economics*, *8*(4), 393–427. https://doi.org/10.1007/s11129-010-9088-6

Hogendoorn, B., Leopold, T., & Bol, T. (2020). Divorce and diverging poverty rates: A risk-and-vulnerability approach. *Journal of Marriage and Family*, *82*(3), 1089–1109. https://doi.org/10.1111/jomf.12629

Hohmann-Marriott, B. E., & Amato, P. (2008). Relationship quality in interethnic marriages and cohabitations. *Social Forces*, *87*(2), 825–855. https://doi.org/10.1353/sof.0.0151

Horowitz, J. M., Graf, N., & Livingston, G. (2019). Why people get married or move in with a partner. *Pew Research Center*. Retrieved from www.pewresearch.org/social-trends/2019/11/06/why-people-get-married-or-move-in-with-a-partner/

Huijts, T., Monden, C., & Kraaykamp, G. (2010). Education, educational heterogamy, and self-assessed health in Europe: A multilevel study of spousal effects in 29 European countries. *European Sociological Review*, *26*(3), 261–276. https://doi.org/10.1093/esr/jcp019

Iseyemi, A., Zhao, Q., McNicholas, C., & Peipert, J. F. (2017). Socioeconomic status as a risk factor for unintended pregnancy in the contraceptive CHOICE project. *Obstetrics & Gynecology*, *130*(3), 609–615. https://doi.org/10.1097/AOG.0000000000002189

Jay, M. (2012). The downside of cohabiting before marriage. *The New York Times*. www.nytimes.com/2012/04/15/opinion/sunday/the-downside-of-cohabiting-before-marriage.html

Karney, B. R. (2021). Socioeconomic status and intimate relationships. *Annual Review of Psychology*, *72*(1), 391–414. https://doi.org/10.1146/annurev-psych-051920-013658

Kennedy, S., & Ruggles, S. (2014). Breaking up is hard to count: The rise of divorce in the United States, 1980–2010. *Demography*, *51*(2), 587–598. https://doi.org/10.1007/s13524-013-0270-9

Kulu, H., & Boyle, P. J. (2010). Premarital cohabitation and divorce: Support for the "trial marriage" theory? *Demographic Research*, *23*(31), 879–904. https://doi.org/10.4054/DemRes.2010.23.31

Kuperberg, A. (2019). *From countercultural trend to strategy for the financially insecure: Premarital cohabitation and premarital cohabitors, 1956–2015 – Council on contemporary families*. Council on Contemporary Families. Retrieved from https://thesocietypages.org/ccf/2019/07/16/from-countercultural-trend-to-strategy-for-the-financially-insecure-premarital-cohabitation-and-premarital-cohabitors-1956-2015/

Lavoie, F., Hebert, M., Tremblay, R., Vitaro, F., Vezina, L., & McDuff, P. (2002). History of family dysfunction and perpetration of dating violence by adolescent boys: A longitudinal study. *Journal of Adolescent Health*, *30*(5), 375–383. https://doi.org/10.1016/S1054-139X(02)00347-6

Lee, W., & McKinnish, T. (2019). Locus of control and marital satisfaction: Couple perspectives using Australian data. *IZA Discussion Paper*, No. 12599. https://dx.doi.org/10.2139/ssrn.3457643

Leopold, T. (2018). Gender differences in the consequences of divorce: A study of multiple outcomes. *Demography*, 55(3), 769–797. https://doi.org/10.1007/s13524-018-0667-6

Lever, J., Frederick, D. A., & Hertz, R. (2015). Who pays for dates? Following versus challenging gender norms. *SAGE Open*, 5(4), 2158244015613110. https://doi.org/10.1177/2158244015613107

Mäenpää, E., & Jalovaara, M. (2014). Homogamy in socio-economic background and education, and the dissolution of cohabiting unions. *Demographic Research*, 30, 1769–1792. https://doi.org/10.4054/DemRes.2014.30.65

Manning, W. D., & Payne, K. K. (2021). Measuring marriage and cohabitation: Assessing same-sex relationship status in the current population survey. *Demography*, 58(3), 811–820. https://doi.org/10.1215/00703370-9162213

Manning, W. D., Brown, S. L., & Stykes, J. B. (2016). Same-sex and different-sex cohabiting couple relationship stability. *Demography*, 53(4), 937–953. https://doi.org/10.1007/s13524-016-0490-x

Manning, W. D., Longmore, M. A., & Giordano, P. C. (2005). Adolescents' involvement in non-romantic sexual activity. *Social Science Research*, 34(2), 384–407. https://doi.org/10.1016/j.ssresearch.2004.03.001

Manning, W. D., Smock, P. J., Darius, C., & Cooksey, E. (2014). Cohabitation expectations among young adults in the United States: Do they match behavior? *Population Research and Policy Review*, 33(2), 287–305. https://doi.org/10.1007/s11113-013-9316-3

McClendon, D. (2016). Religion, marriage markets, and assortative mating in the United States. *Journal of Marriage and Family*, 78(5), 1399–1421. https://doi.org/10.1111/jomf.12353

Meier, A., & Allen, G. (2008). Intimate relationship development during the transition to adulthood: Differences by social class. *New Directions for Child and Adolescent Development*, 2008(119), 25–39. https://doi:10.1002/cd.207

Meier, A., & Allen, G. (2009). Romantic relationships from adolescence to young adulthood: Evidence from the national longitudinal study of adolescent health. *The Sociological Quarterly*, 50(2), 308–335. https://doi.org/10.1111/j.1533-8525.2009.01142.x

Miller, B. C., Benson, B., & Galbraith, K. A. (2001). Family relationships and adolescent pregnancy risk: A research synthesis. *Developmental Review*, 21(1), 1–38. https://doi.org/10.1006/drev.2000.0513

Morgan, P. (2000). *Marriage-lite: The rise of cohabitation and its consequences*. Institute for the Study of Civil Society.

Morse J.R., (2001). *The problem with living together*. Focus on the Family. www.focusonthefamily.com/marriage/the-problem-with-living-together/

Nock, S. L. (2001). The marriages of equally dependent spouses. *Journal of Family Issues*, 22(6), 755–775. https://doi.org/10.1177/019251301022006005

Ong, D. (2016). Education and income attraction: An online dating field experiment. *Applied Economics*, 48(19), 1816–1830. https://doi.org/10.1080/00036846.2015.1109039

Ong, D., & Wang, J. (2015). Income attraction: An online dating field experiment. *Journal of Economic Behavior & Organization*, 111, 13–22. https://doi.org/10.1016/j.jebo.2014.12.011

Owen, J. J., Rhoades, G. K., Stanley, S. M., & Fincham, F. D. (2010). "Hooking up" among college students: Demographic and psychosocial correlates. *Archives of Sexual Behavior*, 39(3), 653–663. https://doi.org/10.1007/s10508-008-9414-1

Payscale. (2022). *2022 state of the gender pay gap report*. www.payscale.com/research-and-insights/gender-pay-gap/

Perelli-Harris, B., Berrington, A., Sánchez Gassen, N., Galezewska, P., & Holland, J. A. (2017). The rise in divorce and cohabitation: Is there a link? *Population and Development Review*, 43(2), 303–329. https://doi.org/10.1111/padr.12063

Pflieger, J. C., & Vazsonyi, A. T. (2006). Parenting processes and dating violence: The mediating role of self-esteem in low- and high-SES adolescents. *Journal of Adolescence*, 29(4), 495–512. https://doi.org/10.1016/j.adolescence.2005.10.002

Pyke, K., & Adams, M. (2010). What's age got to do with it? A case study analysis of power and gender in husband-older marriages. *Journal of Family Issues*, 31(6), 748–777. https://doi.org/10.1177/0192513X09357897

Rennison, C. M., & Welchans, S. (2000). *Intimate partner violence*. Bureau of Justice Statistics. https://bjs.ojp.gov/press-release/intimate-partner-violence-0

Rosenfeld, M. J., Thomas, R. J., & Hausen, S. (2019). Disintermediating your friends: How online dating in the United States displaces other ways of meeting. *Proceedings of the National Academy of Sciences*, 116(36), 17753–17758. https://doi.org/10.1073/pnas.1908630116

Sassler, S., & Miller, A. J. (2011). Waiting to be asked: Gender, power, and relationship progression among cohabiting couples. *Journal of Family Issues*, 32(4), 482–506. https://doi.org/10.1177/0192513X10391045

Sassler, S., & Miller, A. (2017). *Cohabitation nation: Gender, class, and the remaking of relationships*. University of California Press. https://doi.org/10.1525/9780520962101

Sassler, S., Cunningham, A., & Lichter, D. T. (2009). Intergenerational patterns of union formation and relationship quality. *Journal of Family Issues*, 30(6), 757–786. https://doi.org/10.1177/0192513X09331580

Sassler, S., Michelmore, K., & Holland, J. (2016). The progression of sexual relationships. *Wiley Online Library*, 78(3), 587–597. https://doi.org/10.1111/jomf.12289

Sassler, S., Michelmore, K., & Qian, Z. (2018). Transitions from sexual relationships into cohabitation and beyond. *Demography*, 55(2), 511–534. https://doi.org/10.1007/s13524-018-0649-8

Sautter, J. M., Tippett, R. M., & Morgan, S. P. (2010). The social demography of internet dating in the United States. *Social Science Quarterly*, 91(2), 554–575. https://doi.org/10.1111/j.1540-6237.2010.00707.x

Sayer, L. C., & Bianchi, S. M. (2000). Women's economic independence and the probability of divorce: A review and reexamination. *Journal of Family Issues*, 21(7), 906–943. https://doi.org/10.1177/019251300021007005

Schneider, D. (2011). Market earnings and household work: New tests of gender performance theory. *Journal of Marriage and Family*, 73(4), 845–860. https://doi.org/10.1111/j.1741-3737.2011.00851.x

Schwartz, C. R., (2010). Earnings inequality and the changing association between spouses' earnings. *American Journal of Sociology*, 115(5), 1524–1557. https://doi.org/10.1086/651373

Schwartz, C. R., & Graf, N. L. (2009). Assortative matching among same-sex and different-sex couples in the United States, 1990–2000. *Demographic Research, 21,* 843–878. https://doi.org/10.4054/demres.2009.21.28

Schwartz, C. R., & Mare, R. D. (2005). Trends in educational assortative marriage from 1940 to 2003. *Demography, 42*(4), 621–646. https://doi.org/10.1353/dem.2005.0036

Shifrer, D., & Sutton, A. (2014). Region-urbanicity differences in locus of control: Social disadvantage, structure, or cultural exceptionalism? *Sociological Inquiry, 84*(4), 570–600. https://doi.org/10.1111/soin.12046

Small, M. L., Harding, D. J., & Lamont, M. (2010). Reconsidering culture and poverty. *The Annals of the American Academy of Political and Social Science, 629*(1), 6–27. https://doi.org/10.1177/0002716210362077

Solomon, S. E., Rothblum, E. D., & Balsam, K. F. (2005). Money, housework, sex, and conflict: Same-sex couples in civil unions, those not in civil unions, and heterosexual married siblings. *Sex Roles, 52*(9), 561–575. https://doi.org/10.1007/s11199-005-3725-7

Spanier, G. B. (1983). Married and unmarried cohabitation in the United States: 1980. *Journal of Marriage and Family, 45*(2), 277–288. https://doi.org/10.2307/351507

Sprecher, S. (1998). Insiders' perspectives on reasons for attraction to a close other. *Social Psychology Quarterly, 61*(4), 287–300. https://doi.org/10.2307/2787031

Sprecher, S., & Regan, P. C. (2002). Liking some things (in some people) more than others: Partner preferences in romantic relationships and friendships. *Journal of Social and Personal Relationships, 19*(4), 463–481. https://doi.org/10.1177/0265407502019004048

Syrda, J. (2022). Gendered housework: Spousal relative income, parenthood and traditional gender identity norms. *Work, Employment and Society, 37*(3). https://doi.org/10.1177/09500170211069780

Trail, T. E., & Karney, B. R. (2012). What's (not) wrong with low-income marriages. *Journal of Marriage and Family, 74*(3), 413–427. https://doi.org/10.1111/j.1741-3737.2012.00977.x

U.S. Census Bureau. (2019). *Cohabitation over the last 20 years: Measuring and understanding the changing demographics of unmarried partners, 1996–2017.* Census.gov. www.census.gov/library/working-papers/2019/demo/SEHSD-WP2019-10.html

U.S. Census Bureau. (2021). *America's families and living arrangements.* Census.gov. www.census.gov/data/tables/2021/demo/families/cps-2021.html

Valkenburg, P. M., & Peter, J. (2007). Who visits online dating sites? Exploring some characteristics of online daters. *CyberPsychology & Behavior, 10*(6), 849–852. https://doi.org/10.1089/cpb.2007.9941

Van de Vliert, E. (2007). Climatoeconomic roots of survival versus self-expression cultures. *Journal of Cross-Cultural Psychology, 38*(2), 156–172. https://doi.org/10.1177/0022022106297298

Wagner, M., & Weiss, B. (2006). On the variation of divorce risks in Europe: Findings from a meta-analysis of European longitudinal studies. *European Sociological Review, 22*(5), 483–500. https://doi.org/10.1093/esr/jcl014

Watson, S. (2019). The price of love: What does a typical date night cost? *Elite Singles.* Retrieved from www.elitesingles.com/mag/relationship-advice/date-night-cost

Winslow, J. (2019). *America's digital divide*. The Pew Charitable Trusts. www.pewtrusts.org/en/trust/archive/summer-2019/americas-digital-divide

Woloszyn, M. R., Clyde, K., & Corno, D. (2020). The relative impact of looks, income, warmth, and intelligence on female online dating preferences. *Social Sciences & Humanities Open*, 2(1), 100089. https://doi.org/10.1016/j.ssaho.2020.100089

Yau, N. (2021). *Divorce rates and income*. FlowingData. https://flowingdata.com/2021/05/04/divorce-rates-and-income/

6

Religion and Spirituality in Romantic Relationships

ANNETTE MAHONEY, JAMES S. McGRAW, AND JAY R. CHINN

> Well, we believe He brought us together. You know, so He played a role in the start. And I don't think that we'd be together anymore if we didn't have God in the middle. – heterosexual couple in long-term marriage
> (Lambert & Dollahite, 2008, p. 601)

> [My partner] would always say, "I feel like God has given us this relationship," or "I feel like this is meant to be, that this was a gift to us"... Our relationship has really made me feel blessed in a way that I have not felt since I was maybe a little bitty girl. – lesbian woman in same-sex union
> (Rostosky et al., 2008, p. 393)

In the first session of marriage therapy, the wife asked that "God and/or religion be left out of therapy" ... The therapist wondered if the request hinted that "God had been used in a punishing, manipulative, or destructive way" ... The wife affirmed that "God has been just a club to hit me over the head with." (Gardner et al., 2008; Seedall, 2008, p. 162).

Numerous scientific studies over the past 40–50 years have linked higher involvement in religious groups to greater marital satisfaction and commitment. However, as the quotes above illustrate, different specific religious or spiritual (RS) beliefs or behaviors can be helpful or harmful for romantic relationships. Our chapter aims to facilitate a nuanced understanding about this dual-natured intersection of RS functioning and romantic relationships. We begin by delineating findings that link global RS factors to the formation (i.e., partner selection, decisions to cohabit or marry) and maintenance (i.e., union satisfaction, infidelity, domestic violence) and dissolution (i.e., divorce) of romantic relationships. We then discuss four specific RS processes that have been empirically tied to better relational functioning within committed romantic unions: sanctification, spiritual intimacy, petitionary prayer for partner, and positive RS coping. Next, we explore three RS processes that are likely to undermine the well-being of romantic unions and/or partners: desecration/sacred loss, spiritual one-upmanship, and negative RS coping such as demonization when dealing with relationship problems, breakups, or divorce.

RELATIONAL SPIRITUALITY FRAMEWORK (RSF)

Overview

We estimate that since 1980 at least 300 empirical studies published in peer-reviewed journals have focused on RS factors and romantic relationship functioning based on prior reviews of studies from 1980 to 2010 (Mahoney, 2010; Mahoney et al., 2001) and our literature search for this book chapter of such studies published since 2009. Mahoney (2010, 2013) created the Relational Spirituality Framework (RSF) to synthesize key quantitative findings and gaps in this wide-reaching literature. Analogous to Pargament and Mahoney's (2017) conception of spirituality as the discovery, conservation, and transformation of what people perceive as sacred, the RSF heuristically sorts RS and couple/family literature into three recursive, overlapping stages: (a) formation – creating a particular relationship, (b) maintenance – preserving an established relationship, and (c) transformation – reforming or terminating a distressed relationship. The RSF also divides the literature into two general approaches to assessing RS factors. The first involves assessing *global* RS factors, often with one or two items, such as an individual's frequency of religious attendance or overall rating of importance of religion in their lives. The second approach to research on RS factors and close relationships involves assessing and thus disentangling *specific* RS factors that could be expected to enhance or undermine relational and/or individual well-being. That is, the RSF differentiates both helpful and harmful RS factors embedded within individuals' relationships with (a) perceived supernatural figures (e.g., deity, immortal ancestor), (b) other individuals (e.g., romantic partner, spouse), and (c) the religious community (e.g., religious leaders and coreligionists) that could impact relational and personal well-being. In this chapter, we illustrate both RS resources and risk factors in the context of romantic unions.

Overlap of RS Factors

Before proceeding, two points are worth discussing about the overlap of religious (R) and spiritual (S) factors in scientific research on romantic couples. First, few if any studies to date on RS factors and romantic relationships have sharply distinguished "being religious" from "being spiritual." Hence in this chapter, we use religious/spiritual (RS) to refer to variables that have been framed in research as reflective of being religious/religion/religiousness and/or being spiritual/spirituality. Consistent with this decision, a clear consensus does not exist among social scientists about the boundaries between an individual's religiousness and spirituality (Hill & Edwards, 2013; Kapuscinski & Masters, 2010; Oman, 2013). In general, being religious is portrayed within social science literature as public engagement in a given organized sociocultural-historical religious tradition; adherence to orthodox beliefs, dogmas, or rituals, especially having perceived relationships with supernatural entities; and external pressure to conform to social or moral norms promoted by a religious group(s) (Pargament et al., 2013). Being spiritual tends to be framed as a personal search for a connection to divine entities or supernatural phenomena; a private quest for moral virtues or non-theistic enlightenment; and/or internal motivation to seek out meaning, purpose, and self-transcendence within or outside of the self or organized religious groups. However, religious institutions remain the primary cultural context that promotes the integration of theistic (deity-centered) and non-theistic spirituality into daily life. This includes people's decision-making, beliefs, and behaviors tied to dating, cohabitation, sexuality, marriage, divorce, and other relational topics.

Second, wide variation exists within and between organized religious groups on controversial relationship issues. Thus, people can seek out support from leaders or members within a preferred religious group(s) that reinforce their values about romantic unions. For example, both mixed and same-sex couples can find religious communities who affirm the sanctity of their bond despite the historical emphasis in major world religions of promoting heterosexual marriage and restricting sexual activity to these unions. The goodness of fit between individuals and their faith community(ies) likely determines whether people access soothing RS resources or encounter painful RS struggles tied to romantic relationships. Notably, although scientific studies on RS factors tied to marital well-being focus on heterosexuals, some RS factors have also been tied to relational well-being for dating, cohabiting, and/or same-sex unions (for elaboration of theory and findings, see Mahoney and Krumrei, in press).

GLOBAL RS FACTORS AND ROMANTIC RELATIONSHIPS

This section highlights quantitative findings on global RS factors and relationships based on peer-reviewed studies published since 1980 and features recent illustrative studies. For more details on studies published from 1980 to 1999, see Mahoney et al. (2001); from 2000 to 2009, see Mahoney (2010, 2013), and from 2010 to 2018, see Mahoney and Boyatzis (2019). For readers interested in rich qualitative depictions of highly religious married heterosexuals with adolescents, see Dollahite and Marks's (2021) book that synthesizes their extensive publications (over 100) based on interviews with around 200 devout couples drawn from numerous monotheistic, ethnic communities (e.g., Asian American, Black, Catholic, Mainline Protestant, Evangelical or Orthodox Christian; Jewish; Latter-day Saint; and Muslim).

Formation of Romantic Unions

Partner Selection

Considerable research suggests that RS global factors help to shape decisions about selecting a romantic partner, with people deciding early in their courtship whether (non)religious compatibility matters. For example, a similar percentage of US women (ages 15–44) in 1995 reported having the same religious affiliation (e.g., "none," Catholic, Protestant) as their partner regardless of whether the couple was dating, being sexually intimate, cohabiting, or married (Blackwell & Lichter, 2004). In addition, similarity between partners in (non)RS engagement emerged as one of the top three desired shared qualities, along with education and intelligence, for the romantic unions of Americans from mid-adolescence into young adulthood from 1994 to 2007 (i.e., Eastwick et al., 2017). The subjective belief that RS factors shape one's life decisions has also been robustly tied to whether and whom to marry per a 2006 data set of US adults (Sigalow et al., 2012). Finally, cross-culturally, men and women rank similarity in religious affiliation as an important factor when selecting a marital partner (Mahoney, 2013; Mahoney et al., 2001). For instance, McClendon (2016) tracked young US adults born between 1980 and 1984 across fifteen years and those in favorable markets for religious assortative mating (i.e., a relatively high number of potentially similar RS partners) were more likely to get married and marry a partner with a similar religious affiliation whereas those in less favorable markets delayed marriage rather than marry a partner with a different affiliation. Overall, our above review of rigorous social science studies indicate that people tend to gravitate toward romantic partners who share their (non)RS values and cultural identity.

Cohabitation

Although major world religions have for centuries sanctioned marriage as the only legitimate context for couples to cohabit and have sexual intercourse, unmarried cohabitation has surpassed marriage as the most common union experience in young adulthood in the United States, with 68 percent of unmarried women anticipating they will live with a romantic partner outside of marriage (Manning et al., 2019). Some RS factors seem to push back against such modern shifts. For instance, based on recent national surveys (2011–2015), viewing religion as important, but not religious attendance, lowered young women's future expectations they would cohabit rather than marry (Manning et al., 2019). Yet, according to 2006–2010 surveys, only half (49 percent) of unmarried US White and Black women who report attending religious services several times per month or more "think that it's better to get married than stay single" (Wilcox & Wolfinger, 2016). Furthermore, many unmarried men and women who attend religious services at least several times per month report having engaged in sex in the past year, with base rates of

47 percent–48 percent for White attendees and 65 percent–69 percent for non-White attendees as compared to 75 percent–76 percent and 81 percent–82 percent, respectively, of non-attenders (Wilcox & Wolfinger, 2016). In turn, higher sexual activity amongst highly religious young adults is tied to their higher endorsement of cohabitation (Willoughby & Carroll, 2010).

Marriage or Remarriage

Some RS factors appear to promote the formation of mixed-sex marital unions. Specifically, longitudinal analyses tracking adolescents into adulthood from 1994 to 2007 found that teens from conservative Protestant or Latter-day Saint families (particularly women), and anyone who viewed religion as highly important, more frequently entered marriage and at a relatively early age (Uecker, 2014). Similarly, based on pooled 2006–2010 surveys, American men and women affiliated with conservative Protestant traditions reported being more likely than their unaffiliated and Catholic peers to remarry following divorce; greater worship service attendance, but not religious importance, across religious denominations was correlated with an accelerated pace of remarriage (Xu & Bartkowski, 2017). Yet, in a 1996–2010 longitudinal study of middle-aged American female nurses, frequent service attendance predicted future remarriage only after being widowed, not after divorce or marital separation (Li et al., 2018). Finally, before the legalization of same-sex marriage, sexual minorities more engaged in RS practices also more often cemented their bond via legal contracts (e.g., wills, mortgages; Oswald et al., 2008). However, studies have yet to be conducted on whether global RS factors increase the formation of same-sex legal or religious marriages.

Structuring Heterosexual Marriages

Empirical findings on how RS factors impact the formation of egalitarian versus traditional heterosexual marriages defy easy generalizations. For example, Muslims and conservative Christian Protestants living in the United States hold far more diverse and flexible attitudes about feminism, women's participation in paid work, and familial hierarchy than implied by conservative religious teachings that encourage patriarchal relations between men and women (Edgell, 2005). Even more revealing are studies focused on behavioral indices of egalitarianism between couples, which find virtually no differences in how married heterosexuals who belong to socially liberal versus socially conservative religious groups manage decision making or divide general household labor (Mahoney, 2010). However, RS factors are tied to how married Americans structure their roles as co-parents. Specifically, after the transition to parenthood, greater religious attendance, Biblical conservatism, and the sanctification of parent-infant relationships are associated with married heterosexual adopting a traditional division of child care where mothers take a primary position over fathers (DeMaris et al., 2011).

In summary, romantic partners pair up partly based on global RS factors, a winnowing process that could remain robust, especially if cultural polarization accelerates between those who do and do not identify with socially conservative religious traditions. RS factors may also continue to facilitate getting married or remarried, despite the fact half or more of unmarried American adults who often attend religious services also engage in cohabitation and sexual intercourse outside of marriage.

Maintenance of Romantic Unions

Although marked differences exist within and across religious traditions on the morality of same-sex and sexually active non-marital relationships, many theological worldviews endorse virtuous processes (e.g., love, commitment, fidelity) that help maintain romantic relationships. This section reviews mixed evidence that global RS factors are tied to such desirable processes.

Marital Satisfaction and Commitment

Up through 2010, higher global RS involvement by married Americans fairly consistently correlated, albeit to a modest degree, with greater marital satisfaction and commitment (Mahoney, 2010; Mahoney et al., 2001). Recent studies have echoed (Fincham et al., 2018) and extended these findings to married individuals outside of the United States (Cirhinlioğlu et al., 2018). Young American adults' higher personal RS has also been correlated with their relational satisfaction and commitment within dating or cohabiting unions (Aragoni et al., 2021; Langlais & Schwanz, 2017). Furthermore, although gender traditionalism is generally tied to lower relationship satisfaction, this link disappears for highly religiously engaged American women who may embrace traditional gender roles rather than egalitarianism between wives and husbands (Perry & Whitehead, 2016). Notably, these generalizations are largely based on cross-sectional studies that have intentionally examined RS-romantic relationship linkages, with mixed or null findings often occurring in longitudinal studies (see, Cutrona et al., 2011; Day & Acock, 2013; Rose et al., 2018; Wolfinger et al., 2009).

An additional set of social science studies have treated religious attendance or importance as one of many demographic control variables in complex multi-variate studies that target other predictors; these studies rarely, if ever, spotlight RS findings. However, a 2020 large-scale project that used machine learning to identify the most robust self-report predictors of relationship quality across forty-three longitudinal couples studies (Joel et al., 2020) offers insights about RS involvement as one of many individual difference variables (e.g., personal satisfaction with life, depression) embedded within large data sets. Specifically, actors' or partner's overall religiosity emerged as the 12th out of 32 individual difference factors that predicted actor's later relational satisfaction and commitment, being significant in 48 percent of the sixteen cases where assessed (Joel et al., 2020). Of course, whether one views this RS result as a "half-full" or "half-empty" outcome is debatable.

Another major takeaway from Joel et al.'s (2020) study was that relationship specific variables (e.g., perceived partner commitment, intimacy) are far more important than individual difference factors in predicting future relationship quality. Consistent with this point, studies have begun to closely examine dyadic RS factors, such as (dis)similar RS activities between partners. As would be expected, dyadic RS factors tend to yield more consistent findings than one partner's RS functioning. For example, partner's (dis)similarity in religious affiliation, attendance, and salience were robustly correlated to greater relationship satisfaction for American adults in cohabiting or dating unions in 2006 (Henderson et al., 2018). Similarly, Gurrentz (2017) followed newlyweds from 1998 to 2004 and found that couples, where wives were markedly higher than husbands on RS engagement, reported greater conflict and the lowest marital quality compared to couples where both spouses endorsed either high or no RS engagement. Joint activities between spouses, such as praying or reading scriptures together, were also tied to greater marital satisfaction and lower negative marital interactions for highly religiously homogenous Protestant Christian couples surveyed in 2012–2013 (Wilmoth & Riaz, 2019). However, in a recent rigorous study using 2010–2011 national US data, shared religious activities in the home or similar religious (non)attendance were not consistently tied to marital commitment and negative or positive marital interactions (Dew et al., 2020); this result underscores the potential value of using more in-depth measures to identify robust dyadic RS factors that predict marital satisfaction and commitment amongst contemporary couples.

Intimate Partner Violence

A complex set of studies has attempted to address concerns that greater RS engagement may foster intimate partner physical aggression, especially toward women. On one hand, in research of RS subgroups where intimate partner violence has already occurred, female survivors often report that their male partners used socially conservative RS rhetoric to defend their aggression (Johnson, 2015; Nason, 2018), a finding consistent with disclosures made by male perpetrators in a parish-based invention program (Davis & Jonson-Reid, 2020). On the other hand, in fifteen studies published up to 2010 and using primarily US data from the 1980 to early 2000s, general RS involvement was either unrelated or tied to *lower* (not higher) rates of physical aggression within married and unmarried couples (see Mahoney, 2010; Mahoney et al., 2001; Todhunter & Deaton, 2010). In a 2018 large cross-cultural survey of Australia, Latin, and North American, and European countries, RS (dis) similarity within couples was also unrelated to intimate partner violence toward women (DeRose et al., 2021). However, in a recently published online convenience study of 260 American adult men, higher RS commitment was associated with *more* frequent minor and major acts of physical aggression toward their partners (Renzetti et al., 2017). In efforts to reconcile these mixed findings, some studies suggest that public RS activities done for extrinsic motives (e.g., gain prestige or avoid shame) versus intrinsic purposes (e.g., gain closeness to God) may differentially be tied to intimate partner violence (Pournaghash-Tehrani et al., 2009) or moderate the link between economic disadvantage and violence (Pitt & DeMaris, 2019) by men and women. Overall, this literature underscores the need to disentangle specific RS factors that foster or inhibit partners' physical aggression toward each other in general as well as within dysfunctional relationships.

Infidelity

Another complicated body of research pertains to sexual infidelity in marriage. More frequent religious attendance was correlated with lower rates of extramarital sex based on several studies using 1980–1990s US national surveys (Mahoney, 2010). A longitudinal study of married American nurses from 1988 to 1992 also found that higher RS engagement predicted less infidelity (Tuttle & Davis, 2015). In addition, married US Christians who were strongly attached to any denomination during 1991–2004 engaged in less infidelity than their less devout co-believers (Burdette et al., 2007). But several qualifications pertain to these findings. For instance, higher religious attendance does not curb infidelity for maritally dissatisfied Americans who may feel more trapped by RS marital vows (Atkins et al., 2001). In addition, the odds of marital infidelity increase for high worship attendees who do not feel close to God and for low worship attenders who do feel close to God (Atkins & Kessel, 2008), implying that strong connections to God and a RS community must work in concert. Similarly, based on a 2006 US survey, only individuals who relied on their RS beliefs to decide whom to marry and viewed religion as highly important in their lives had a lower risk of infidelity; higher levels of only one of these factors or religious attendance alone did not reduce infidelity (Esselmont & Bierman, 2014). Overall, congruence across different facets of RS functioning may be key to sustain sexual fidelity within marriage.

Questions arise as to whether RS factors decrease infidelity for contemporary romantic unions because we located no published RS findings for married couples using data gathered after 2006, and we located contrary or null findings for young unmarried couples with more recent data. Unexpectedly, for example, the more dating college students in southeastern US reported that their RS identity was central to their lives, the *more* often they engaged in physical and emotional acts of intimacy with a person outside of their romantic relationship (Norona et al., 2016). Also, null findings emerged between global RS variables and infidelity in recent cross-sectional and longitudinal studies of dating or unmarried adults (Maddox Shaw et al., 2013; Negash et al., 2019). Finally, based on a large 2018 cross-cultural data set of married and cohabiting couples (combined), dyads where the two partners had nominal or unequal levels of RS (less/mixed religious couples) had higher rates of infidelity than either highly RS couples or non-RS couples (shared secular couples; DeRose et al., 2021). Taken together, more up-to-date research is needed to identify specific RS factors that robustly discourage infidelity given inconclusive findings using global RS variables.

Dissolution of Romantic Unions

Divorce Rates

In numerous studies published prior to 2000 that involved people who are now elderly or deceased, lower divorce rates were linked to attending religious services and being religiously affiliated (Mahoney, 2010; Mahoney et al., 2001). Subsequent longitudinal studies using national American or British data collected from the 1980s to early 2000s replicated that higher religious attendance predicted lower future divorce for older adults and/or women (Brown et al., 2008; Village et al., 2010; Woods & Emery, 2002), although null results emerged for a combined sample of men and women (Tuttle & Davis, 2015). To illustrate, married American nurses in their fifties in 1996 who attended services more than once a week had a 50 percent lower risk of divorce by 2010 than non-attenders (Li et al., 2018). Also, in a study of middle-aged married or cohabiting African Americans with children, greater RS salience predicted less relationship dissolution for women, but not men, from 1997 to 2003 (Cutrona et al., 2011).

Once again, caveats are in order about global RS indices and divorce. Cutrona et al. (2011) also found that African American women's personal RS devotion increased marrying the biological co-parent of their child, which was then tied to lower marital stability. In addition, although several global RS variables each predicted lower divorce rates from 1971 to 2005 for middle-aged or older, mostly White Californians as they aged, none of the RS factors remained uniquely predictive after controlling for each other and demographics (McDaniel et al., 2013); this result highlights the need to clarify what particular RS constructs may impact divorce. For instance, southern US communities with large concentrations of conservative Protestants produced higher divorce rates in 2000 than others, both because conservative Protestants themselves exhibited higher divorce risk and because individuals in communities dominated by conservative Protestants faced numerous higher divorce risk factors; notably, early cessation of education in favor of marriage and childbearing due was identified as the critical RS cultural mechanism (Glass & Levchak, 2014).

Beyond personal RS factors, such as individual religious attendance, two high quality longitudinal studies offer mixed evidence that dyadic (dis)similarity in RS engagement predicts divorce. Specifically, compared to the modest effect of each partner's religious attendance on marital dissolution from 1987 to 1994, Vaaler et al. (2009) found a markedly high future divorce rates for US couples with RS differences, such as when the husbands attended religious services more often than wives, and when wives were more conservative in their biblical beliefs or Christian affiliation than husbands. Furthermore, these patterns persisted after controlling for demographic covariates, marital duration, and marital quality. However, using 1998–2004 national data, newlywed couples where both spouses or only the wife exhibited RS engagement had lower rates of future divorce compared to couples where neither spouse identified as being RS (Gurrentz, 2017). Such findings imply that mixed faith couples who tend to experience greater marital distress also more often remain married whereas distressed secular couples may more often split up.

Summary and Limitations about Global RS Factors and Romantic Relationships

Taken together, higher endorsement of global RS variables has been cross-sectionally linked to desirable romantic relational outcomes for married, cohabiting, and dating mixed-sex couples. However, most findings have relied on a few single RS items and data sets with people now in their mid-sixties or much older. Furthermore, mixed or null findings have often emerged in longitudinal studies. These methodological issues raise many questions about whether, why, and how greater involvement in organized religious groups are tied with better relational functioning. Perhaps greater involvement in a supportive faith community signals greater internalization of RS beliefs that reinforce that community's valued family goals (e.g., getting and remaining married) or virtues (e.g., love, commitment, fidelity) which, in turn, strengthens romantic bonds. More longitudinal research is needed to clarify such hypotheses.

We also want to emphasize that the reliance on single global RS as well as multi-item RS measures that simply ask more general questions about general RS activities (e.g., frequency of prayer or Scripture reading) fail to disentangle specific RS beliefs and behaviors focused on romantic relationships that are helpful or harmful. This confounding creates three major problems in understanding why RS may matter for romantic unions. First, skeptics can easily argue that any apparent associations between higher RS functioning and relational well-being are merely due to partners' basic psychosocial strengths, such as having strong moral values or social networks, which people can develop and access within or outside of organized religious participation. From this conceptual vantage point, greater RS engagement, such as attending religious services, is interchangeable with involvement in other cultural subgroups; that is, RS involvement is not necessarily beneficial because of unique, substantive RS beliefs or practices utilized as an individual or dyad. Second, and conversely, critics can easily attribute associations between global RS indices and relational problems to specific RS beliefs, such as the idea that scriptural passages or a deity condone spousal maltreatment or staying married at all costs. Third, global RS indices allow those with indiscriminately pro-religious worldviews to accentuate only the advantages tied to identifying as being RS because global RS indices can conceal rare but toxic forms of faith, especially in large national or community samples of mostly non-distressed couples.

SPECIFIC HELPFUL AND HARMFUL RS FACTORS FOR ROMANTIC RELATIONSHIPS

One solution to problems embedded within global RS measures is for researchers to disentangle specific RS factors that can enhance or undermine relational functioning across diverse types of romantic relationships. Delving into both types of factors can help build better theoretical models, yield more consistent and stronger effect sizes, and be more useful for educational and intervention programs than findings yielded by global RS measures. Thus, in this section, we highlight studies on specific RS processes and romantic relationships. Unless otherwise noted, these studies have thus far been conducted with US samples of predominantly middle-class, White Christians. Such sampling is similar to overall US demographics, but it obscures the roles these RS processes may (or may not) play within other demographic or religious subgroups.

Helpful RS Factors and Relational Functioning

Sanctification of Romantic Relationships

Sanctification refers to the degree to which a relationship is perceived (a) as a manifestation of God or Higher Powers (i.e., theistic sanctification) and/or (b) as imbued with sacred qualities (i.e., nontheistic sanctification). In a meta-analysis of correlational findings through mid-2019, Mahoney et al. (2021) found that greater sanctification of various types of close relationships was consistently associated with more positive relational adjustment (i.e., average r = 0.24, CI = 0.20–0.29) and lower rates of relational problems (average r = −0.12, CI = −0.06 to −0.18). Below we highlight a few findings from around fifty-five qualitative and quantitative studies on sanctification and relational well-being in couples and family relationships that have been conducted as of 2022.

Married heterosexuals (Mahoney et al., 2009) as well as individuals in same-sex unions (Phillips et al., 2017) and dating and cohabiting relationships (Henderson et al., 2018) often view their relationship as having sacred qualities and/or as being a manifestation of a deity's presence. For all three types of romantic relationships, greater perceived sanctification of the couple relationship has been tied to greater relationship satisfaction and commitment (Henderson et al., 2018; Phillips et al., 2017), even after controlling for positive relationship behaviors (e.g., forgiveness and sacrifice; Sabey et al., 2014). Greater sanctification has also been found to be linked to less partner-focused revenge (Davis et al., 2012), to buffer against the adverse impact of life stress on relationship quality (Ellison et al., 2011), and to predict more supportive partner behaviors and in turn greater relationship happiness (Rusu et al., 2015). Furthermore, cross-sectional and longitudinal evidence indicates that greater sanctification of marriage predicts better observed communication skills (by both spouses) and intimacy during conflictual marital interactions (Kusner et al., 2014; Rauer & Volling, 2015) and emotionally vulnerable conversations (Padgett et al., 2019).

At least four studies have extended findings on sanctification of marriage beyond predominantly Christian US couples. Consistent with experimental findings on unmarried college students (Fincham et al., 2010), greater relational sanctification has been tied to lower infidelity thoughts and behaviors among married Iranians seeking counseling (Reich & Kalantar, 2018). Also among married Iranians, greater sanctification of marriage uniquely predicted both greater marital satisfaction after controlling for religious/spiritual coping (Fallahchai et al., 2021) and more frequent prayer for one's partner (Reich & Kalantar, 2018). Furthermore, among Christian Orthodox couples from Romania, higher marital sanctification has been associated with better marital satisfaction and with more supportive marital interactions (Rusu et al., 2015).

The value of delving into specific RS processes like sanctification is vividly illustrated by studies focused on sexuality within intimate unions. For decades, higher global RS engagement has been linked to greater sex guilt and more inhibition of sexual activity outside of marriage (Hernandez et al., 2013), implying that generally being RS mainly functions to suppress sexual well-being. However, greater sanctification of sexuality predicts greater sexual satisfaction cross-sectionally among married and unmarried partners (Leonhardt et al., 2021) and longitudinally among newlyweds (Hernandez-Kane & Mahoney, 2018). Greater sanctification is also tied to lower sex guilt among mixed-sex, same-sex, and cohabiting partners (Leonhardt et al., 2019; Phillips et al., 2017) and to lower odds of physical and emotional cheating, even after controlling for plausible alternate explanations (general RS factors, problematic alcohol use, trait self-control; McAllister et al., 2020).

Spiritual Disclosure and Intimacy

Whereas sanctification captures an individual's private perceptions of a given relationship, dyads can also have explicit dialogues about each party's RS views. In an initial study on this topic, Brelsford and Mahoney (2008) assessed how much college students and parents openly discussed their RS views and struggles. Labeled spiritual disclosure, this process was associated with higher relationship satisfaction and lower verbal hostility, both in mother-child and father-child pairs. However, many people may avoid revealing information about their (non)RS thoughts or feelings to others, due to fear of being dismissed, ridiculed, or misunderstood (Brelsford & Mahoney, 2008). Kusner et al. (2014) therefore created a measure to assess both dyadic spiritual disclosures and spiritual support (i.e., responding to a partner's spiritual disclosures in an empathic, nonjudgmental way), labeling this combined process spiritual intimacy. Greater spiritual intimacy predicted both partners displaying less negativity and more positivity during observations of couples discussing major conflicts (Kusner et al., 2014) as well as less self-reported conflict at home, less stalemating by both spouses, and more collaborative communication by husbands (Mahoney et al., 2021); these associations persisted after accounting for couples' stable characteristics (e.g., education level, personality traits, and family background). Moreover, in a longitudinal study, spiritual intimacy predicted observations of new parents being more emotionally supportive of one another during emotionally vulnerable conversations (Padgett et al., 2019). Finally, spiritual intimacy between dating couples has been tied to greater relationship satisfaction and commitment, even after accounting for emotional intimacy (Flint, 2021).

Petitionary Prayer for Partner

Individuals can privately turn to a perceived relationship with God to help sustain their adult union (Fincham & Beach, 2014). For example, several studies have found that, in generally well-functioning relationships, benevolent prayer for one's partner reliably facilitates that relationship's quality (Fincham et al., 2010; Fincham & Beach, 2013, 2014). Indeed, in longitudinal studies of US college students in a dating relationship, those who privately prayed for their romantic partner's well-being have reported increased relationship satisfaction and decreased risk of infidelity over time (for review, see Fincham & Beach, 2013). Similarly, among Iranians seeking marital counseling, partner-focused prayer was tied to lower infidelity, even after controlling for sanctification (Reich & Kalantar, 2018). Experimental studies have also found that praying for someone with whom one has a romantic or close relationship increases the praying person's levels of selfless concern, gratitude, and forgiveness of the person for whom they are praying (Fincham & Beach, 2013). In addition, in a randomized experiment with a community sample of married African Americans, Beach et al. (2011) randomly assigned couples to one of three conditions: (a) an evidence-supported marital education program, (b) the same program supplemented with a module focused on partner-focused prayer, and (c) self-help reading materials only. In the experimental condition, partner-focused prayer enhanced marital outcomes for wives (but not husbands) over time, beyond the beneficial effects of the other two conditions. However, for both spouses in the experimental condition, partner-focused prayer predicted each partner's higher marital satisfaction, which also mediated (explained) the effect of partner-focused prayer on increased marital commitment (Fincham & Beach, 2014).

Positive RS Coping

Rooted in Pargament's (1997) seminal book, extensive research exists on the role of positive RS coping for individual well-being (Abu-Raiya & Pargament, 2015). Measures of positive RS coping largely assess how much people cope with stressful life events by drawing on a benevolent and secure relationship with God (divine coping) and on support from coreligionists (fellow religious believers). Such resources tend to correlate with better psychological adjustment, especially stress-related growth (Abu-Raiya & Pargament, 2015). Likewise, positive RS coping with personal and interpersonal stressors could potentially be tied to relational well-being (Mahoney, 2010, 2013). Two studies of married couples offer preliminary support of this possibility. Specifically, for married Iranians, higher positive RS coping predicted greater marital satisfaction after controlling for prayer for partner (Reich & Kalantar, 2018) as well as the sanctification of marriage and global indices of RS (frequency of prayer, religious pilgrimages, fasting, reciting the Quran; Fallahchai et al., 2021).

Summary on Helpful RS Factors and Romantic Unions

To recap, greater sanctification of romantic relationships and benevolent prayer for a partner have been robustly tied to better relational and sexual satisfaction. These findings have emerged for studies of non-distressed couples inside and outside of marriage. Initial studies also suggest spiritual disclosure, spiritual intimacy, and positive religious/spiritual coping may help sustain healthy romantic unions. Such RS processes are likely to be reciprocally linked to a secure attachment to God/higher powers as well as involvement with a religious group that affirms one's romantic relationship of choice and promotes social values, norms, and role models that help reinforce positive couple dynamics.

Harmful RS Factors and Relational Functioning

We now explore RS factors that could exacerbate relational or personal suffering. With regard to forming unions, people could encounter stressful RS conflicts internally, with others, or with God/higher powers as they decide with whom, when, and how to create romantic unions. Individuals raised or currently involved in families affiliated with socially conservative religious groups may especially face painful RS struggles about the moral legitimacy of forming same-sex, cohabiting, or sexually-active nonmarital relationships that hamper the development of such unions. Problematic RS processes could also occur when people encounter major difficulties either maintaining healthy romantic unions, such as experiencing infidelity, partner violence, or chronic dysfunctional interaction patterns (e.g., contempt, gas-lighting), or dissolving marriages and serious romances. Although not yet often examined in couples literature, the following studies illustrate RS factors that could increase distress as people navigate major relationship challenges.

Sacred Loss and Desecration

People may often interpret relational problems as a sacred loss (e.g., the loss of something once viewed as sacred or intended by God) or desecration (e.g., willful destruction or attack of a sacred aspect of life). For example, 74 percent divorced adults whose overall involvement in religious groups was on par with national norms viewed their divorce as a sacred loss and desecration some degree (Krumrei et al., 2011a). As expected, such appraisals longitudinally predicted higher personal psychological distress and dysfunctional conflict tactics between ex-spouses (Krumrei et al., 2011a). Likewise, the more college students viewed a prior romantic break up as a sacred loss/desecration and experienced spiritual struggles over the event, the more emotional distress they reported over time (Hawley et al., 2015). Such linkages were particularly robust if students had engaged in more premarital sexual activity with their ex-partner and more often attended services and saw religion as important. Finally, college students who recalled experiencing their parental divorce as a spiritual loss and desecration reported greater current personal and family-related distress (Warner et al., 2009).

Spiritual One-Upmanship

On the flip side of spiritual intimacy, couples may engage in RS dialogues that would be expected to be destructive and distancing. For example, Mahoney et al. (2021) assessed ways spouses draw upon deities or RS (dis)beliefs to reinforce their own superiority when the pair had conflictual interactions (formerly mislabeled as only theistic triangulation). The more frequently both parties used such strategies, the more both engaged in stonewalling and husbands were verbally aggressive. This study begins to corroborate Gardner et al.'s (2008) insightful descriptions of various strategies clinically-distressed couples use to triangulate (non)RS beliefs or God into their conflicts. Another strategy worth investigation is people privately praying to God as an ineffectual way to try to change or tolerate a partner's dysfunctional behavior instead of directly confronting problems. Such RS processes may be especially toxic for distressed couples even if relatively rare in the general public.

Negative RS Coping

As a counterpart to positive RS coping, negative RS coping refers to ways that coping with major life stressors can trigger distressing RS thoughts and feelings about supernatural figures (e.g., anger toward God, feeling punished by the devil), religious groups (e.g., conflicts with co-believers), or one's self (e.g., feeling morally conflicted), processes that are also increasingly referred to as "spiritual struggles" (Exline et al., 2014). A meta-analysis of thirty-two longitudinal studies clearly demonstrates that spiritual struggles lead to declines in individuals' psychological adjustment (Bockrath et al., 2021). Initial efforts have extended this research to married couples. For example, married Canadian women, but not men, who reported more spiritual struggles in general also reported lower marital satisfaction (Tremblay et al., 2002). For both Iranian men and women, this RS factor was uniquely tied to lower marital satisfaction after controlling sanctification and positive religious coping (Fallahchai et al., 2021). In two intriguing studies of Iranian women seeking counseling after infidelity by their husbands, higher spiritual struggles were robustly tied to stronger desires to divorce (Hassannezhad et al., 2022; Khazaei & Babaie, 2022). Studies of divorce also vividly illustrate the relevance of negative religious coping with specific relationship problems, not just generally. For example, around 80 percent of adults who had recently divorced experienced spiritual struggles about the divorce internally, with God, and other people over the dissolution (Krumrei et al., 2011a), and higher levels longitudinally predicted their greater depressive and anxiety symptoms. Honing in on demonization, 48 percent viewed their divorce in least one of the following three ways: believed their ex-spouse was operating under demonic influences (43 percent), viewed themselves as under the control of demonic forces (31 percent), and demonized the divorce itself (36 percent). Greater anger and post-traumatic anxiety symptoms, such as intrusive negative thoughts and avoidance, covaried with all three forms of demonization (Krumrei et al., 2011b).

Summary of Harmful RS Factors and Romantic Unions
In summary, studies have begun to identify desecration/sacred loss, spiritual one-upmanship, and negative RS coping as examples of specific RS processes that undermine the well-being of romantic unions and/or partners. Although such toxic RS processes are less commonplace than adaptive RS processes, it is important to recognize that these and likely other specific maladaptive RS factors deserve attention by researchers and clinicians when trying to fully understand romantic relationships.

GLOBAL AND FUTURE CHALLENGES

Integrative reviews of scientific studies of RS and marriage up through 2010 consistently suggested that global RS variables, such religious attendance or importance, were reciprocally tied to the formation and maintenance of marital relationships (Mahoney, 2010; Mahoney et al., 2001). Our updated review of this literature as of early 2022, including studies of non-marital unions, yielded more a complex and inconclusive picture of the intersection of RS factors and contemporary romantic unions. Simplistic generalizations that being more RS is tied to greater marital satisfaction, commitment, and stability as well as lower infidelity or domestic violence are no longer easily made. Rather a major theme of this chapter is that researchers are urged to disentangle specific RS factors that enhance versus undermine the creation and maintenance of romantic relationships across diverse types of couples (mixed and same-sex, dating and cohabiting) and cultural contexts dominated by one or more religious institutions (e.g., Christian, Muslim, Buddhist, Hindu). For example, compelling cross-sectional and longitudinal evidence shows that some specific RS cognitions (e.g., sanctification of marriage or sexuality within committed unions) or behaviors (e.g., praying for one's partner) predict better relationship functioning for unmarried and married couples. These specific RS constructs are likely portable beyond US samples. Emerging evidence also points to spiritual intimacy as an additional RS resource tied to relational well-being. Other specific RS constructs may be helpful but still need to be investigated, such as each partner having a secure attachment to God. Conversely, more rare but problematic RS processes, such as spiritual one-upmanship and negative RS coping (e.g., demonization), can intensify relational and personal distress, and such processes may be especially salient in a context of relationship dysfunction or dissolution. Importantly, RS resources or risks are impossible to decipher based on global RS variables.

Taking a further step back, we close by noting that US national and global religious and political cultural forces will likely accelerate polarizing rhetoric about secular versus religious worldviews in upcoming decades. The heavy focus thus far on white, heterosexual, Christians in scientific research on RS and romantic relationships could, unfortunately, play into counterproductive stereotypes and biases that obscure the roles that particular RS factors play for diverse couples. We urge researchers and practitioners need to avoid perpetuating unsubstantiated assumptions when they anticipate the types of romantic partners for whom RS helps or harms. Namely, higher mean levels or base rates can emerge for a given RS factor for one subgroup (e.g., married, heterosexual Christians; African American or Latinx Americans) versus another subgroup (e.g., cohabiting, LBGTQ Christians; European Americans or Asian Americans), but such group differences do not imply that this RS factor only predicts enhanced or impaired relational functioning for one of the groups. Rather specific RS resources or struggles may impact individuals with different RS identities or religious group affiliations similarly, even if the rates of various RS processes are significantly different between the subgroups. In addition, focusing on RS differences within couples (i.e., between paired partners) may be very fruitful. Generating more nuanced research findings across all types of couples can usefully inform relationship education programs for the general public and clinical interventions with dysfunctional unions. Furthermore, a balanced perspective could help social scientists build bridges with diverse religious organizations that hold socially liberal to conservative views on sexual morality and marriage (Mahoney & Krumrie, in press; Mahoney et al., 2019). In conclusion, we hope this chapter helps readers appreciate the roles of religion and spirituality, for better and worse, for romantic relationships.

REFERENCES

Abu-Raiya, H., & Pargament, K. I. (2015). Religious coping among diverse religions: Commonalities and divergences. *Psychology of Religion and Spirituality*, 7(1), 24–33. https://doi.org/10.1037/a0037652

Aragoni, H. K., Stanley, S. M., Smith-Acuña, S., & Rhoades, G. K. (2021). Religiosity and relationship quality in dating relationships. *Couple and Family Psychology: Research and Practice*. 12(2). Advance online publication. https://doi.org/10.1037/cfp0000177

Atkins, D. C., & Kessel, D. E. (2008). Religiousness and infidelity: Attendance, but not faith and prayer, predict marital fidelity. *Journal of Marriage and Family*, 70(2), 407–418. https://doi.org/10.1111/j.1741-3737.2008.00490.x

Atkins, D. C., Baucom, D. H., & Jacobson, N. S. (2001). Understanding infidelity: Correlates in a national random sample. *Journal of Family Psychology*, 15(4), 735–749. https://doi.org/10.1037/0893-3200.15.4.735

Beach, S. R. H, Hurt, T. R., Fincham, F. D., Kameron J., Franklin, K. J., McNair, L. M., & Stanley, S. M. (2011). Enhancing marital enrichment through spirituality: Efficacy data for prayer focused relationship enhancement. *Psychology of Religion and Spirituality*, 3(3), 201–216. https://doi.org/10.1037/a0022207

Blackwell, D. L., & Lichter, D. T. (2004). Homogamy among dating, cohabiting, and married couples. *The Sociological Quarterly*, 45(4), 719–737. https://doi.org/10.1111/j.1533-8525.2004.tb02311.x

Bockrath, M. F., Pargament, K. I., Wong, S., Harriott, V. A., Pomerleau, J. M., Homolka, S. J., Chaudhary, Z. B., & Exline, J. J. (2021). Religious and spiritual struggles and their links to psychological adjustment: A meta-analysis of longitudinal studies. *Psychology of Religion and Spirituality*. Advance online publication. https://doi.org/10.1037/rel0000400

Brelsford, G. M., & Mahoney, A. (2008). Spiritual disclosure between older adolescents and their mothers. *Journal of Family Psychology*, 22(1), 62–70. https://doi.org/10.1037/0893-3200.22.1.62

Brown, E., Orbuch, T. L., & Bauermeister, J. A. (2008). Religiosity and marital stability among Black American and White American couples. *Family Relations*, 57(2), 186–197.

Burdette, A. M., Ellison, C. G., Sherkat, D. E., & Gore, K. A. (2007). Are there religious variations in marital infidelity? *Journal of Family Issues*, 28(12), 1553–1581. https://doi.org/10.1177/0192513X07304269

Cirhinlioğlu, F. G., Cirhinlioğlu, Z., & Tepe, Y. K. (2018). The mediating role of religiousness in the relationship between the attachment style and marital quality. *Current Psychology*, 37(1), 207–215. https://doi.org/10.1007/s12144-016-9504-5

Cutrona, C. E., Russell, D. W., Burzette, R. G., Wesner, K. A., & Bryant, C. M. (2011). Predicting relationship stability among midlife African American couples. *Journal of Consulting and Clinical Psychology*, 79(6), 814–825.

Davis, D. E., Hook, J. N., Van Tongeren, D. R., & Worthington, E. L. (2012). Sanctification of forgiveness. *Psychology of Religion and Spirituality*, 4(1), 31–39. https://doi.org/10.1037/a0025803

Davis, M., & Jonson-Reid, M. (2020). The dual use of religious-faith in intimate partner abuse perpetration: perspectives of Latino men in a parish-based intervention program. *Social Work & Christianity*, 47(4), 71–95. https://doi.org/10.34043/swc.v47i3.109

Day, R. D., & Acock, A. (2013). Marital well-being and religiousness as mediated by relational virtue and equality. *Journal of Marriage and Family*, 75(1), 164–177. https://doi.org/10.1111/j.1741-3737.2012.01033.x

DeMaris, A., Mahoney, A., & Pargament, K. I. (2011). Doing the scut work of childcare: Does religiousness encourage greater father involvement? *Journal of Marriage and Family*, 73(2), 354–368. https://doi.org/10.1111/j.1741-3737.2010.00811.x

DeRose, L. F., Johnson, B. R., Wang, W., & Salazar-Arango, A. (2021). Couple religiosity, male headship, intimate partner violence, and infidelity. *Review of Religious Research*, 63(4), 607–627. https://doi.org/10.1007/s13644-021-00461-2

Dew, J. P., Uecker, J. E., & Willoughby, B. J. (2020). Joint religiosity and married couples' sexual satisfaction. *Psychology of Religion and Spirituality*, 12(2), 201–212. https://doi.org/10.1037/rel0000243

Dollahite, D. C., & Marks, L. D. (2021). *Strengths in diverse families of faith: Exploring religious differences*. Routledge.

Eastwick, P. W., Harden, K. P., Shukusky, J. A., Morgan, T. A., & Joel, S. (2017). Consistency and inconsistency among romantic partners over time. *Journal of Personality and Social Psychology*, 112(6), 838–859. https://doi.org/10.1037/pspi0000087

Edgell, P. (2005). *Religion and family in a changing society*. Princeton University Press.

Ellison, C. G., Henderson, A. K., Glenn, N. D., & Harkrider, K. E. (2011). Sanctification, stress, and marital quality. *Family Relations* 60(4), 404–420. https://doi.org/10.1111/j.1741-3729.2011.00658.x

Esselmont, C., & Bierman, A. (2014). Marital formation and infidelity: An examination of the multiple roles of religious factors. *Sociology of Religion*, 75(3), 463–487. https://doi.org/10.1093/socrel/sru036

Exline, J. J., Pargament, K. I., Grubbs, J. B., & Yali, A. M. (2014). The religious and spiritual struggles scale: Development and initial validation. *Psychology of Religion and Spirituality*, 6(3), 208–222. https://doi.org/10.1037/a0036465

Fallahchai, R., Fallahi, M., Moazenjami, A., & Mahoney, A. (2021). Sanctification of marriage, religious coping and marital adjustment of Iranian couples. *Archive for the Psychology of Religion*, 43(2), 121–134. https://doi.org/10.1177/0084672421996826

Fincham, F. D., & Beach, S. R. H. (2013). Can religion and spirituality enhance prevention programs for couples? In K. I. Pargament, A. Mahoney, & E. Shafranske (Eds.), *APA handbook of psychology, religion, and spirituality: Vol II* (pp. 461–480). American Psychological Association.

Fincham, F. D., & Beach, S. R. H. (2014). I say a little prayer for you: Praying for partner increases commitment in romantic relationships. *Journal of Family Psychology*, 28(5), 587–593. https://doi.org/10.1037/a0034999

Fincham, F. D., Lambert, N. M., & Beach, S. R. H. (2010). Faith and unfaithfulness: Can praying for your partner reduce infidelity? *Journal of Personality and Social Psychology*, 99(4), 649–659. https://doi.org/10.1037/a0019628

Fincham, F. D., Rogge, R., & Beach, S. R. H. (2018). Relationship satisfaction. In A. L. Vangelisti & D. Perlman (Eds.), *The Cambridge handbook of personal relationships* (pp. 422–436). Cambridge University Press.

Flint, D. D. (2021). *Dating couples' spiritual intimacy predicts relationship satisfaction and commitment beyond emotional intimacy*. (Unpublished dissertation, Bowling Green State University).

Gardner, B. C., Butler, M. H., & Seedall, R. B. (2008). En-gendering the couple-deity relationship: Clinical implications of power and process. *Contemporary Family Therapy*, 30(3), 152–166.

Glass, J., & Levchak, P. (2014). Red states, blue states, and divorce: Understanding the impact of conservative Protestantism on regional variation in divorce rates. *American Journal of Sociology*, 119(4), 1002–1046. https://doi.org/10.1086/674703

Gurrentz, B. T. (2017). Religious dynamics and marital dissolution: A latent class approach. *Marriage & Family Review*, 53(2), 185–205. https://doi.org/10.1080/01494929.2016.118421

Hassannezhad, M., Zolfaghari, H., & Manouchehri, K. (2022). Marital infidelity and betrayal experiences: The role of executive functions and religious coping strategies in predicting divorce of women. *Journal of Positive School Psychology*, 6(2), 4123–4131.

Hawley, A. R., Mahoney, A., Pargament, K. I., & Gordon, A. K. (2015). Sexuality and spirituality as predictors of distress over a romantic breakup: Mediated and moderated pathways. *Spirituality in Clinical Practice*, 2(2), 145–159. https://doi.org/10.1037/scp0000034

Henderson, A. K., Ellison, C. G., & Glenn, N. D. (2018). Religion and relationship quality among cohabiting and dating couples. *Journal of Family Issues*, 39(7), 1904–1932. https://doi.org/10.1177/0192513X17728982

Hernandez, K. M., Mahoney, A., Pargament, K. I. (2013). The sacred dance between sexuality and religion: Scientific insights from the 21st century. In D. L. Tolman & L. Diamond (Eds.), *APA handbook of sexuality and psychology* (pp. 425–447). American Psychological Association. http://doi.org/10.1037/14194-013

Hernandez-Kane, K. M., & Mahoney, A. (2018). Sex through a sacred lens: Longitudinal effects of sanctification of marital sexuality. *Journal of Family Psychology*, 32(4), 425–434. https://doi.org/10.1037/fam0000392

Hill, P. C., & Edwards, E. (2013). Measurement in the psychology of religiousness and spirituality. In K. I. Pargament, J. J. Exline, & J.W. Jones (Eds.), *APA handbook of psychology, religion, and spirituality: Context, theory, and research* (Vol. 1, pp. 51–78). American Psychological Association. https://doi.org/10.1037/14045-003

Joel, S., Eastwick, P. W., Allison, C. J. Arriaga, X. B. Baker, Z. G. Bar-Kalifa, E., Bergeron, S., Birnbaum, G. E., Brock, R. L., Brumbaugh, C. C., & Carmichael, C.L. (2020). Machine learning uncovers the most robust self-report predictors of relationship quality across 43 longitudinal couples studies. *Proceedings of the National Academy of Sciences, 117*(32), 19061–19071

Johnson, A. J. (2015). *Religion and men's violence against women*. Springer.

Kapuscinski, A. N., & Masters, K. S. (2010). The current status of measures of spirituality: A critical review of scale development. *Psychology of Religion and Spirituality, 2*(4), 191–205. https://doi.org/10.1037/a0020498

Khazaei, S., & Babaie, M. (2022). The role of cognitive flexibility and religious coping strategies in predicting divorce of women with betrayal experiences (Persian). *Human Relations Studies, 2*(4), 4–12. https://doi.org/10.22098/jhrs.2022.1407

Krumrei, E. J., Mahoney, A., & Pargament, K. I. (2011a). Spiritual stress and coping model of divorce: A longitudinal study of a community sample. *Journal of Family Psychology, 25*(6), 973–985. https://doi.org/10.1037/a0025879.

Krumrei, E. J., Mahoney, A., & Pargament, K. I. (2011b). Demonization of divorce: Prevalence rates and links to postdivorce adjustment. *Family Relations, 60*(1), 90–103. https://doi.org/10.1111/j.1741-3729.2010.00635.x

Kusner, K. G., Mahoney, A., Pargament, K. I., & DeMaris, A. (2014). Sanctification of marriage and spiritual intimacy predicting observed marital interactions across the transition to parenthood. *Journal of Family Psychology, 28*(5), 604–614. https://doi.org/10.1037/a0036989

Lambert, N. M., & Dollahite, D. C. (2008). The threefold cord: Marital commitment in religious couples. *Journal of Family Issues, 29*(5), 592–614. https://doi.org/10.1177/0192513X07308395

Langlais, M. R., & Schwanz, S. J. (2017). Centrality of religiosity of relationships for affectionate and sexual behaviors among emerging adults. *Sexuality & Culture, 22*(2), 405–421. https://doi.org/10.1007/s12119-017-9474-2

Leonhardt, N. D., Busby, D. M., & Willoughby, B. J. (2019). Sex guilt or sanctification? The indirect role of religiosity on sexual satisfaction. *Psychology of Religion and Spirituality, 12*(2), 213–222. https://doi.org/10.1037/rel0000245

Leonhardt, N. D., Busby, D. M., Hanna-Walker, V. R., & Leavitt, C. E. (2021). Sanctification or inhibition? Religious dualities and sexual satisfaction. *Journal of Family Psychology, 35*(4), 433–444. http://doi.org/10.1037/fam0000796

Li, S., Kubzansky, L. D., VanderWeele, T. J. (2018). Religious service attendance, divorce, and remarriage among U.S. nurses in mid and late life. *PLoS ONE 13*(12), e0207778. https://doi.org/10.1371/journal.pone.0207778

Maddox Shaw, A. M., Rhoades, G. K., Allen, E. S., Stanley, S. M., & Markman, H. J. (2013). Predictors of extradyadic sexual involvement in unmarried opposite-sex relationships. *Journal of Sex Research, 50*(6), 598–610. https://doi.org/10.1080/00224499.2012.666816

Mahoney, A. (2010). Religion in families 1999-2009: A relational spirituality framework. *Journal of Marriage and Family, 72*(4), 805–827. https://doi.org/10.1111/j.1741-3737.2010.00732.x

Mahoney, A. (2013). The spirituality of us: Relational spirituality in the context of family relationships. In K. Pargament, J. J. Exline, J. Jones, A. Mahoney, & E. Shafranske

(Eds.), *APA handbook of psychology, religion, and spirituality* (Vol. 2, pp. 365–389). American Psychological Association. https://doi.org/10.1037/14045-020

Mahoney, A., & Boyatzis, C. J. (2019). Parenting, religion, and spirituality. In M. Bornstein (Ed.), *Handbook of parenting* (Vol. 5, 3rd ed., pp. 515–552). Routledge.

Mahoney, A., & Krumrei, E. J. (in press). Questions left unaddressed by religious familism: Is spirituality relevant to non-traditional families? L. Miller (Ed.), *The Oxford handbook of the psychology of spirituality* (2nd ed.). Oxford University Press.

Mahoney, A., Pargament, K. I., & DeMaris, A. (2009). Couples viewing marriage and pregnancy through the lens of the sacred: A descriptive study. *Research in the Social Scientific Study of Religion, 20*, 1–45. https://doi.org/10.1163/ej.9789004175624.i-334.7

Mahoney, A., Pargament, K. I., & DeMaris, A. (2021). Spiritual intimacy, spiritual one-upmanship, and marital conflict across the transition to parenthood. *Journal of Family Psychology, 35*(4), 552–558. https://doi.org/10.1037/fam0000795

Mahoney, A., Pargament, K. I., Swank, A., & Tarakeshwar, N. (2001). Religion in the home in the 1980s and '90s: A meta-analytic review and conceptual analysis of religion, marriage, and parenting. *Journal of Family Psychology, 15*(4), 559–96. https://doi.org/10.1037//0893-3200.15.4.559

Mahoney, A., Pomerleau, J. M., & Riley, A. (2019). Transcending barriers to build bridges between family psychology and religious organizations. In B. H. Fiese, M. Celano, K. Deater-Deckard, E. N. Jouriles, & M. A. Whisman, (Eds.), *APA handbook of contemporary family psychology* (Vol. 2, pp. 315–335). APA Publications.

Mahoney, A., Wong, S., Pomerleau, J. M., & Pargament, K. I. (2021). Sanctification of diverse aspects of life and psychosocial functioning: A meta-analysis of studies from 1999 to 2019. *Psychology of Religion and Spirituality. 14*(4), 585–598. Advance online publication. https://doi.org/10.1037/rel0000354

Manning, W. D., Smock, P. J., & Fettro, M. N. (2019). Cohabitation and marital expectations among single millennials in the U.S. *Population Research and Policy Review, 38*(3), 327. https://doi.org/10.1007/s11113-018-09509-8

McAllister, P., Henderson, E., Maddock, M., Dowdle, K., Fincham, F. D., & Braithwaite, S. R. (2020). Sanctification and cheating among emerging adults. *Archive of Sexual Behavior, 49*(3), 1177–1188. https://doi.org/10.1007/s10508-020-01657-3

McClendon, D. (2016). Religion, marriage markets, and assortative mating in the United States. *Journal of Marriage and Family, 78*(5), 1399–1421. https://doi.org/10.1111/jomf.12353

McDaniel, S., Boco, A. G., & Zella, S. (2013). Changing patterns of religious affiliation, religiosity, and marital dissolution: A 35-year study of three-generation families. *Journal of Divorce & Remarriage, 54*(8), 629–657.

Nason, C. N. (2018). Presidential address: Going public: The art and science of researching domestic violence and religion. *Journal for the Scientific Study of Religion, 57*(1), 7–23. https://doi.org/10.1111/jssr.12504

Negash, S., Veldorale-Brogan, A., Kimber, S. B., & Fincham, F. D. (2019). Predictors of extradyadic sex among young adults in heterosexual dating relationships: A multivariate approach. *Sexual and Relationship Therapy, 34*(2), 153–172. https://doi.org/10.1080/14681994.2016.1219334

Norona, J. C., Pollock, B. E., Welsh, D. P., & Bolden, J. (2016). Religiosity and intimacy with an extradyadic partner in emerging adulthood: A developmental perspective. *Journal of Adult Development*, 23(1), 45–50. https://doi.org/10.1007/s10804-015-9220-7

Oman, D. (2013). Defining religion and spirituality. In R. F. Paloutzian & L. Park (Eds.), *Handbook of the Psychology of Religion and Spirituality* (2nd ed., pp. 23–47). Guildford Press.

Oswald, R. F., Goldberg, A., Kuvalanka, K., & Clausell, E. (2008). Structural and moral commitment among same-sex couples: Relationship duration, religiosity, and parental status. *Journal of Family Psychology*, 22(3), 411–419. https://doi.org/10.1037/0893-3200.22.3.411

Padgett, E., Mahoney, A., Pargament, K. I., & DeMaris, A (2019). Marital sanctification and spiritual intimacy predicting married couples' observed intimacy skills across the transition to parenthood. *Religions*, 10(3), 177–193. https://doi.org/10.3390/rel10030177

Pargament, K. I. (1997). *The psychology of religion and coping: Theory, research, practice*. Guilford Press.

Pargament, K. I., & Mahoney, A. (2017). Spirituality: The search for the sacred. In C. R. Snyder, S. J. Lopez, L. M. Edwards, & S. C. Marques (Eds.), *The Oxford handbook of positive psychology* (3rd ed., pp. 878–891). Oxford University Press. https://doi.org/10.1093/oxfordhb/9780199396511.013.51

Pargament, K. I., Mahoney, A., Exline, J. J., Jones, J. W., & Shafranske, E. (2013). Envisioning an integrative paradigm for the psychology of religion and spirituality: An introduction to the APA handbook of psychology, religion and spirituality. In K. I. Pargament, J. J. Exline, & J. W. Jones (Eds.), *APA handbook of psychology, religion, and spirituality* (Vol. 1, pp. 3–19). American Psychological Association.

Perry, S. L., & Whitehead, A. L. (2016). For better or for worse? Gender ideology, religious commitment, and relationship quality. *Journal for the Scientific Study of Religion*, 55(4), 737–755. https://doi.org/10.1111/jssr.12308

Phillips, R. E., Avant, S., Kalp, D., Cenkner, D., Lucci, M., Herndon, R., & Maccarelli, A. (2017). Initial validation of measures of sanctification in same-sex romantic relationships and sexual behavior. *Journal for the Scientific Study of Religion*, 56(4), 836–851. https://doi.org/10.1111/jssr.12488

Pitt, C., & DeMaris, A. (2019). Religiosity as a buffer in the association between economic disadvantage and violence. *Interdisciplinary Journal of Research on Religion*, 15(1), 1–28.

Pournaghash-Tehrani, S., Ehsan, H. B., & Gholami, S. (2009). Assessment of the role of religious tendency in domestic violence. *Psychological Reports*, 105(3 Pt 1), 675–684. https://doi.org/10.2466/PR0.105.3.675-684.

Rauer, A., & Volling, B. (2015). The role of relational spirituality in happily married couples' observed problem-solving. *Psychology of Religion and Spirituality*, 7(3), 239–249. https://doi.org/10.1037/rel0000022

Reich, N., & Kalantar, S. M. (2018). The role of praying for the spouse and sanctification of marriage in reducing infidelity. *Mental Health, Religion & Culture*, 21(1), 65–76. https://doi.org/10.1080/13674676.2018.1447555

Renzetti, C. M., DeWall, C. N., Messer, A., & Pond, R. (2017). By the grace of God: Religiosity, religious self-regulation, and perpetration of intimate partner violence. *Journal of Family Issues, 38*(14), 1974–1997. https://doi.org/10.1177/0192513X15576964

Rose, A., Anderson, S., Miller, R., Marks, L., Hatch, T., & Card, N. (2018). Longitudinal test of forgiveness and perceived forgiveness as mediators between religiosity and marital satisfaction in long-term marital relationships. *American Journal of Family Therapy, 46*(4), 356–374. https://doi.org/10.1080/01926187.2018.1547667

Rostosky, S. S., Riggle, E. D. B., Brodnicki, C., & Olson, A. (2008). An exploration of lived religion in same-sex couples from Judeo-Christian traditions. *Family Process, 47*(3), 389–403. https://doi.org/10.1111/j.1545-5300.2008.00260.x

Rusu, P. P., Hilpert, P., Beach, S. R. H., Turliuc, M. N., & Bodenmann, G. (2015). Dyadic coping mediates the association of sanctification with marital satisfaction and well-being. *Journal of Family Psychology, 29*(6), 843–849. https://doi.org/10.1037/fam0000108

Sabey, A. K., Rauer, A. J., & Jensen, J. F. (2014). Compassionate love as a mechanism linking sacred qualities of marriage to older couples' marital satisfaction. *Journal of Family Psychology, 28*(5), 594–603. https://doi.org/10.1037/a0036991

Sigalow, E., Shain, M., & Bergey, M. R. (2012). Religion and decisions about marriage, residence, occupation, and children. *Journal for the Scientific Study of Religion, 51*(2), 304–323. https://doi.org/10.1111/j.1468-5906.2012.01641.x

Todhunter, R. G., & Deaton, J. (2010). The relationship between religious and spiritual factors and the perpetration of intimate personal violence. *Journal of Family Violence, 25*, 745–753. http://doi.org/10.1007/s10896-010-9332-6

Tremblay, J., Sabourin, S., Lessard, J.-M., & Normandin, L. (2002). The predictive value of self other differentiation and religious coping strategies in the study of marital satisfaction. *Canadian Journal of Behaviroal Science, 34*(1), 19–27. https://doi.org/10.1037/h0087151

Tuttle, J. D., & Davis, S. N. (2015). Religion, infidelity, and divorce: Reexamining the effect of religious behavior on divorce among long-married couples. *Journal of Divorce & Remarriage, 56*(6), 475–489. https://doi.org/10.1080/10502556.2015.1058660

Uecker, J. E. (2014). Religion and early marriage in the United States: Evidence from the Add Health Study. *Journal for the Scientific Study of Religion, 53*(2), 392–415. https://doi.org/10.1111/jssr.12114

Vaaler, M. L., Ellison, C. G., & Powers, D. A. (2009). Religious influences on the risk of marital dissolution. *Journal of Marriage and Family, 71*(4), 917–934. https://doi.org/10.1111/j.1741-3737.2009.00644.x

Village, A., Williams, E., & Francis, L. J. (2010). Does religion make a difference? assessing the effects of Christian affiliation and practice on marital solidarity and divorce in Britain, 1985–2005. *Journal of Divorce & Remarriage, 51*(6), 327–338. https://doi.org/10.1080/10502551003652041

Warner, H. L., Mahoney, A., & Krumrei, E. J. (2009). When parents break sacred vows: The role of spiritual appraisals, coping, and struggles in young adults' adjustment to parental divorce. *Psychology of Religion and Spirituality, 1*(4), 233–248. https://doi.org/10.1037/a0016787

Wilcox, W. B., & Wolfinger, N. H. (2016). *Soul mates: Religion, sex, love, and marriage among African Americans and Latinos*. Oxford University Press.

Willoughby, B. J., & Carroll, J. S. (2010). Sexual experience and couple formation attitudes among emerging adults. *Journal of Adult Development*, *17*(1), 1–11.

Wilmoth, J. D., & Riaz, M. (2019). Religious activities, Christian media consumption and marital quality among Protestants. *Religions*, *10*(2), 119. https://doi.org/10.3390/rel10020119

Wolfinger, N. H., Wilcox, W. B., & Hernandez, E. (2009). 'Bendito Amor' (Blessed Love): Religion and relationships among married and unmarried Latinos in urban America. *Journal of Latino-Latin American Studies*, *3*(4), 171–188.

Woods, L. N., & Emery, R. E. (2002). The cohabitation effects on divorce: Causation or selection? *Journal of Divorce & Remarriage*, *37*(3–4), 101–119.

Xu, X. H., & Bartkowski, J. P. (2017). Remarriage timing: Does religion matter? *Religions*, *8*(9), 160. https://doi.org/10.3390/rel8090160

7

The Importance of Work in Romantic Relationships

KAREN KRAMER, AMIT KRAMER, AND QIUJIE GONG

Working in a law firm in Chicago, Michelle Robinson was assigned as a mentor to a new hire that recently joined the law firm. After spending several weeks together, the new hire asked Michelle on a date. Michelle refused – she was his boss and did not think it was appropriate. But the new hire was persistent and kept asking her out. Michelle Robinson finally agreed to date him. In 1992, three years after starting to work together, Michelle and Barack Obama got married (Obama, 2021).

Romantic relationships at work are common, with some surveys estimating that over 50 percent of employees were engaged in an intimate relationship with a colleague at work (Elsesser, 2019). After all, working individuals spend a significant amount of time at work and interact daily with people who they many times perceive as similar to them across different characteristics. The idea that "birds of feather flock together" is well-documented in relationship research and relies on the similarity-attraction framework (Byrne, 1971; Montoya et al., 2008; Newcomb, 1961). The workplace, which brings together similar people, is, therefore, a fertile ground for the formation of romantic relationships (Reich & Hershcovis, 2011).

Romantic relationships are also affected by work. Beyond financial resources that can be a source of both satisfaction and dissatisfaction in romantic relationships (Ward et al., 2021), work competes with romantic relationships on resources like time, energy, and attention but also provides individuals with resources that may positively affect romantic relationships like self-esteem, meaning, and the development of different skills that may be applied to romantic relationships. Importantly, the work domain is influential in romantic relationships not only because people spend a significant amount of their life at work. The work domain is part of a system of social institutions (Turner, 1997) that shape human behavior and are embedded with values, norms, and rules that direct and reproduce human behavior. In this chapter, we provide an overview of romantic relationships at work and their corollaries, both positive outcomes such as the formation of romantic relationships, and negative outcomes, such as sexual harassment.

The chapter is divided into three parts. In Part I we discuss romantic relationships at work, work sexual harassment, and the ways in which organizations attempt to regulate romantic relationships at work. These policies have a role in romantic relationships in and out of work. Organizational policies and norms can be directly related to romantic relationships; for example, human resources policies that specify "dos and don'ts" at work may be part of a broader policy at work (e.g., sexual harassment and abuse of power policies). Relationships may even be a part of a policy not intended to regulate romantic relationship (e.g., policies about the nature of interactions between employees at a work). Government policies also play a role in romantic relationships at work, though their effect is more distal. For example, sexual harassment laws that protect individuals might also deter individuals from forming romantic relationships at work.

In Part II of the chapter, we discuss the influence work has on romantic relationships outside work – how different aspects of work spill over to family life and affect romantic relationships. The spillover of work into romantic relationships can be both negative and positive. For example, a negative impact of work on romantic relationships is competition and conflict between work and romantic relationships (e.g., competition and conflict over finite time and energy resources) as well as spillover of negative emotions from the work to the romantic relationship. A positive impact of work on romantic relationships can include resources that are generated at work (e.g., compensation, learned skills) and positively influence the romantic relationship or spillover of positive emotions, moods, and feelings from the work domain to the romantic relationship.

Finally, in Part III, we take an economic perspective on romantic relationships. We begin by shortly reviewing an economic perspective on marriage markets (Becker, 1973) and apply it to the workplace, as a local marriage market (Lichter et al., 1991). We apply the economic principles of rational choice, supply and demand, and utility maximization to provide a view of romantic relationships that is driven by economic principles. We then discuss the role of outcomes of work, wages, and status in the formation of romantic relationships and the relative bargaining power individuals have in romantic relationships.

ROMANTIC RELATIONSHIPS AT WORK

Definition and Prevalence

Romantic relationships at work consist of mutually desired non-platonic relationships between two members of the organization. We define these relationships broadly, as a non-platonic relationship in which affection is communicated, sexual attraction is present, and both members perceive the relationship to extend beyond a professional relationship (Chory & Hoke, 2020; Pierce & Aguinis, 2001; Pierce et al., 2004). The prevalence of romantic relationships at work is quite significant, with surveys reporting more than 70 percent of employees in the United Kingdom (Clarke, 2006) and 58 percent of American employees have experienced a romantic relationship at work, including 82 percent of those who are fifty years old or over (Elesser, 2019). Furthermore, it is estimated that about 10 percent of employees have married a person they met at work (SHRM, 2011). Surprisingly, relative to its frequent occurrence, romantic relationships at work have not received significant research attention. This is especially surprising given the potential impact these relationships may have on individuals, families, and organizations.

Differentiating Hierarchical and Lateral Romantic Relationships at Work

Romantic relationships at work are typically divided into two types: *lateral romantic relationships* between employees who have a similar organizational status and *hierarchical romantic relationship* between employees who differ in their organizational status (Pierce & Aguinis, 1997, 2003). Society, organizations, and employees perceive hierarchical romantic relationships more negatively, as they entail a greater potential for both abuse and favoritism (Pierce & Aguinis, 2003). These negative perceptions of hierarchical romantic relationships have increased substantially with the rise of the #MeToo movement (Cavico & Mujtaba, 2021; Green, 2019), which was founded in 2006 to increase people's awareness to the prevalence of sexual assault and harassment in society, especially among women in minority groups and in low-income communities. The #MeToo movement has had a profound impact on workplaces and perceptions of sexual harassment and abuse of power at work (Murphy, 2019). Lateral romantic relationships receive little attention in the literature, which might be surprising given the implications any relationship might have on individuals' work outcomes (e.g., coworker trust; Chory & Hoke, 2020) and non-work outcomes (e.g., psychological well-being; Khan et al., 2017).

The difference between hierarchical and lateral romantic relationships extends beyond a simple categorization and the potential for abuse and favoritism. The differences in power and status in hierarchical romantic relationships also intersect with gender, race, and ethnicity. Specifically, white men are much more likely to be in positions of power in organizations than women and people of color. For example, the Bureau of Labor Statistics (2022) reports that among executives, 85.7 percent are white and 70.9 percent are male. Only 5.9 percent of executives are Black and 6.8 percent are Hispanic or Latino. As such, hierarchical romantic relationships at work are likely to replicate power and status differences in society and reinforce gender and racial inequality at work and outside.

Indeed, past research on romantic relationships at work is heavily focused on hierarchical relationships because of their potential to be exploitive and lead to both favoritism and sexual harassment. Mainiero (2020) discusses the relationship between sexuality and power in the workplace, and the emphasis brought by the #MeToo movement to the gendered nature of these relationships. Studies preceding the rise of the #MeToo movement (e.g., Anderson & Hunsaker, 1985; Mainiero, 1986) have suggested that regardless of power status, women will be more negatively evaluated than men when engaging in a romantic relationship at work. These gendered outcomes might be a result of a gendered attribution of success and failure. Specifically, men's successes are more likely to be attributed to relatively fixed factors like knowledge, skills, and abilities whereas men's failures are more likely to be attributed to externalities (e.g., luck). Women's successes, however, are more likely to be attributed to externalities (e.g., luck, having a good team) whereas their failures are more likely to be attributed to fixed factors (Lopez & Ensari, 2014; Mainiero, 1986; Seo et al., 2017). Again, work replicates power structures in society and applies normative perceptions of gender inequality to the work domain.

Differentiating Romantic Relationships from Sexual Harassment at Work

A point of contention in research and organizational practices on romantic relationships at work is concerned with distinguishing courting and romantic relationships at work from sexual harassment. In many cases, the sexual harassment and abuse of power are clear and appalling such as the case with Corey Coleman, the personnel chief of FEMA, who allegedly hired some women as possible sexual partners for male employees (Rein, 2018), or Harvey Weinstein who required sexual relations as a *quid pro quo* and was also convicted on several felony sex crimes, including rape (NY Times, 2020). However, in some cases, what might begin as a consensual romantic relationship at work, might develop over time to sexual harassment (Pierce & Aguinis, 2009). We, therefore, provide a short review of sexual harassment at work to differentiate it from romantic relationships at work and continue with a review of organizational practices that attempt to accommodate romantic relationships at work while preventing sexual harassment.

Sexual Harassment

Sexual harassment in the workplace can occur at the individual level and also be present as part of the organizational climate. At the individual level, sexual harassment is defined as "unwelcome sexual advances, requests for sexual favors, and other verbal or physical harassment of a sexual nature" (U.S. Equal

Employment Opportunity Commission, 2022). To be illegal, harassment needs to be frequent or severe. creating an intimidating, hostile, or abusive working environment or to result in an adverse employment decision (U.S. Equal Employment Opportunity Commission, 2022). For example, although asking a person at work on a date is not considered sexual harassment, requiring a date as a condition for promotion, or requiring any sexual conduct in exchange for refraining from an employment related decision (e.g., firing) are types of sexual harassment.

Sexual harassment can also extend to the climate of the organization or a unit within the organization when it creates a hostile or offensive work environment. For example, when several employees repeatedly make offensive comments about women in general (U.S. Equal Employment Opportunity Commission, 2022), sexual harassment can take the form of an organizational climate in which an individual's performance and well-being, at work and outside work, are negatively affected by the work environment. Such climate occurs, for example, when the work environment includes repeated inappropriate touching, suggestive remarks, sexual jokes, or display of sexually suggestive symbols or photos (Dessler, 2010; Griffith, 2019). Implied by these two categories of sexual harassment is that people in power have more opportunities to harass their employees because they are less likely to suffer from negative work and social sanctions and can allocate organizational rewards and penalties. However, supervisors, coworkers, subordinates, and even people outside the organization (e.g., customers) of any gender can be harassers or victims (Center for American Progress, 2018).

A feminist perspective takes a broader view and analyzes sexual harassment at work through the lenses of power, privilege, and gender inequality (Seo et al., 2017). Using this perspective, sexual harassment at work is not only a result of differences in power between managers (usually men) and subordinates (men and/or women) but also a result of the threat men feel from the presence of women in the workplace, especially women in power positions. Specifically, from a feminist perspective, sexual harassment at work is used to restore the power dynamics between men and women that are weakened by women present in the workplace and especially when women advance to managerial positions of power (Berdahl, 2007). Feminist scholars thus suggest that women, more than men, are likely to be sexually harassed at the workplace, regardless of their position. Data from the EEOC support this claim, showing that women file 83.5 percent of sexual harassment charges and are more likely to report sexual harassment when they work in male-dominated industries. Approximately 28 percent of women working in male-dominated industries reporting they had personally experienced sexual harassment at work compared to 20 percent of women in female-dominated industries (Parker, 2018).

Many organizations are well aware of the threats sexual harassment at work presents to their employees and the organization (e.g., liability).

Organizations, therefore, use different training modules and policies that are meant to educate their workforce and prevent sexual harassment from occurring. At the same time, most organizations are also aware of the inevitability of romantic relationships at work, the negative perceptions of hierarchical romantic relationships at work, and the potential for consensual romantic relationships to develop to sexual harassment. As a result, many organizations have policies and guidance concerning romantic relationships at work, which we discuss in the next section.

Organizational Policies about Romantic Relationships at Work

What do Jeff Zucker (former CNN president), Steve Easterbrook (former McDonald's CEO), Katie Hill (former US representative for California's 25th congressional district), Brian Krzanich (former Intel CEO), Darren Houston (former Priceline CEO), and Brian Dunn (former Best Buy CEO) have in common? They lost their jobs, and many of them, their careers, because they were engaged in a romantic relationship at work.

Being aware of the inevitability of romantic relationships at work, as well as the ethical and legal issues they present, organizations devise different policies that put formal structure around romantic relationships at work, aiming to prevent abuse of power, favoritism, discrimination, and sexual harassment. At the same time, organizations also train their employees and supervisors about the importance of harassment-free work environment (Nagele-Piazza, 2018). Still, because of the potential for a romantic relationship at work to transform to a case of sexual harassment, organizations apply a wide spectrum of policies, ranging from a complete ban on relationships between a subordinate and any superior, to specific policies about dating and reporting.

Although no descriptive assessment of the frequency of policies regarding romantic relationships at work exists, some policies are more common than others. For example, many organizations mandate a formal disclosure of a romantic relationship to the human resource department (Cavico & Mujtaba, 2021), assuming transparency would make favoritism and abuse of power less likely. Other common policies include clear guidelines regarding public display of affection within the workplace, guidelines regarding making advances at work, training about romantic relationships and sexual harassment, and clear policies surrounding relationships between a subordinate and a supervisor (Uzialko, 2023). Overall, the policies seem to focus on greater transparency when two employees are involved in a romantic relationship. For example, in many organizations, all romantic relationships must be reported to human resources. These policies allow the organization to identify and prevent favoritism or abuse of power. Policies also have specific rules regarding banning of certain relationships and behaviors. For example, worker-manager romantic relationships or public display of affection are not allowed and may result in dismissal in order to avoid potential favoritism and abuse of power and maintain a comfortable work environment for other workers. In many organizations, policies exist to create a clear line between romantic relationships at work and sexual harassment. For example, many organizations offer training about romantic relationships at work and sexual harassment concurrently and have policies that also make this distinction. Google, Facebook, and Airbnb, for example, allow employees to ask another coworker out, but only once, to avoid claims of sexual harassment (MarketWatch, 2019). In addition, organizations often ask employees who are involved in a romantic relationship to sign a "consensual relationship agreement" often referred to as a "love contract" (Cavico & Mujtaba, 2021), which specifies "dos" and "don'ts" at work as well as work expectations if the romantic relationship ends.

WORK AND ROMANTIC RELATIONSHIPS OUTSIDE WORK

As one of the main domains of activity in many people's life, work has a significant impact on other life domains, including romantic relationships (Bianchi & Milkie, 2010; Perry-Jenkins & Gerstel, 2020; Voydanoff, 2004). Multiple studies have shown that work characteristics and attributes are related to the quality of romantic relationships both negatively and positively. For example, shift work and work overload are negatively related to romantic relationships quality (e.g., Crouter et al., 2001; Maume & Sebastian, 2012; Perry-Jenkins et al., 2007; Presser, 2000) whereas other facets of work, such as job satisfaction and income are positively related to romantic relationship quality and stability (Jackson et al., 2017; Rogers & May, 2003; Whillans et al., 2018). It is also important to note that although we focus on spillover from work to romantic relationships as a unidirectional relationship, these relationships are likely to be mutual and flow between these two domains in both directions (Rogers & May, 2003; van Steenbergen et al., 2011).

How Does Work Impact Romantic Relationships?

In this section, we focus on three main areas in which work affects romantic relationships: choices about time allocation between the two domains and the ability to control time allocation, monetary and non-monetary resources obtained at work, and the spillover of affect from one's work to one's romantic relationship.

Time Allocation and the Ability to Control Time and Romantic Relationships

As a finite resource, the allocation of time is often perceived as a zero-sum game between work and other life domains, including romantic relationships. Many couples choose a gendered allocation of time to address the scarcity of time resources, with men, on average, allocating more time to paid work and women, on average, allocating more time to unpaid work – doing household chores and taking care of children (Bianchi & Raley, 2006; Craig & Mullan, 2010). Still, because 46.8 percent of households in the United States are comprised of dual earners (Bureau of Labor Statistics, 2022), time allocation is an important issue in romantic relationships.

There is no clear research support for a direct relationship between time spent at work and the quality of romantic relationships, though indirect relationships have been shown in multiple studies. For example, time spent at work is related to other family outcomes such as work-family conflict (e.g., Adkins & Premeaux, 2012; Hill et al., 2010), which are in turn related to couple relationship quality (Fellows et al., 2016), but the direct relationship between working hours and different indicators of the quality of romantic relationships is often null (e.g., Minnotte et al., 2015; Unger et al., 2015). Researchers have tried to explain these null findings and concluded that the work time itself (number of hours people spend at work) is less important than the ability to control the allocation of this work time. Specifically, romantic relationships are affected by individuals' ability to control different aspects of their work, including their work time, by having more autonomy and discretion as to when, where, and how to perform their work (Perry-Jenkins & Gerstel, 2020).

Control over work and time at work can take different forms. Researchers have defined control over work as the ability to determine, at least partly, how, when, and where work is performed. Control over work is an employee-driven job flexibility (Gerstel & Clawson, 2018), which is different from flexible work arrangements that are employer-driven and controlled (Gerstel & Clawson, 2018). When considering control over work time as an antecedent of the quality of romantic relationships, a clearer relationship emerges. For example, employees who work non-standard schedules like night and rotating shifts, have lower quality romantic relationships (Crouter et al., 2001; Maume & Sebastian, 2012; Perry-Jenkins et al., 2007; Presser, 2000). Similarly, more subjective measures of time spent at work such as work overload and overwork (e.g., Kulik & Liberman, 2022; Shafer et al., 2018) as well as ability to take longer breaks from work when needed, for example, for a birth of child (Kramer et al., 2019; Petts & Knoester, 2020), were also shown to be related to the quality of romantic relationships.

Monetary and Non-monetary Resources Generated by Work and Romantic Relationships

Work requires the investment of many resources by individuals. Individuals invest time, physical, cognitive, and emotional effort at work that might come at the expense of romantic relationships that also require investment of similar resources. Likewise, work might also provide individuals with rewards that may enhance romantic relationships. For example, monetary rewards from work can be used to "buy time" for investment in romantic relationships (e.g., buying prepared food or cleaning services) and allow leisure activities that nurture romantic relationships and create shared experiences that promote couple functioning (Johnson et al., 2006; Shahvali et al., 2021). In addition to direct monetary rewards, work can also provide non-monetary rewards that may positively affect romantic relationships (Greenhaus & Powell, 2006). For example, individuals may acquire skills at work that can be used to enhance romantic relationships (e.g., time management skills, conflict resolution techniques).

Research on the association between income and romantic relationship quality supports the notion that money does not buy higher quality romantic relationships, but it does help (Dakin & Wampler, 2008). Monetary rewards from work and the use into which couples put them, have been shown to relate positively to marital and relationship satisfaction, and negatively to relationship stress, and separation. For example, when couples can make time-saving purchases, such as household services (e.g., housecleaning services) they have higher relationship satisfaction and are able to spend more quality time together (Whillans et al., 2018) and create shared experiences that improve couple's functioning (Shahvali et al., 2021). Greater consumption of goods is also related to greater satisfaction (Headey et al., 2008). On the flip side, lack of financial resources is related to negative outcomes in romantic relationships. The relationship between lack of financial resources and negative outcomes in romantic relationship is consistent with Conger's Family Stress model (Conger & Conger, 2002). It suggests that couples who face greater economic pressure and strain suffer from higher levels of stress and pressure, which create more psychological distress. With higher psychological distress, couples are more likely to experience greater marital conflict and marital distress (e.g., Conger et al., 1999; Falconier & Epstein, 2010; Randall et al., 2017), though gender differences exist in those relationships. Finally, there is also empirical evidence showing that employment and macro-economic conditions are related to relationship formation and separation, with unemployment rate and economic downturns being negatively related to both the marriage rate (González-Val & Marcén, 2018; Schneider & Hastings, 2015) and the divorce rate (Amato & Beattie, 2011; Killewald, 2016; Poortman, 2005).

Non-monetary aspects of work are also related to the quality of romantic relationships. For example, work-family enrichment, the extent to which experiences in the work role improve the quality of the family role and performance in that role (Greenhaus & Powell, 2006) has been shown to increase marital satisfaction of both the focal individual and their partner (Gopalan et al., 2018; Liu et al., 2016; van Steenbergen et al., 2014) as well as positively relate to positive marital behaviors, such as making enjoyable interactions and engaging friends and family in activities (van Steenbergen et al., 2014).

Spillover of Affect from Work to Romantic Relationships

The spillover of affect from work to family life and romantic relationships has long been recognized in the literature (e.g., Bronfenbrenner & Crouter, 1982; Small & Riley, 1990). An underlying assumption in this line of research is that the boundaries between work and life outside work are permeable and therefore affect that is generated in one domain spills over to other domains. Research provides strong support for the permeability of these boundaries. The growing blur between boundaries as technology allows individuals to work anytime and anywhere, including when they spend time with their romantic partners (Hertlein, 2012; Kramer & Kramer, 2021; McDaniel & Coyne, 2016; Pak et al., 2022; Paulin et al., 2017). Although we recognize that affect spillover can also occur from romantic relationships to the work domain (Rogers & May, 2003), in this chapter we focus on spillover of affect from work to the romantic relationship.

In recent years, studies using various designs, most prominently experience sampling methods (ESM), have revealed how affective states at work and romantic relationships are interrelated. For example, Judge and colleagues (2006) showed that work-family conflict led to feelings of guilt and hostility that had a negative relationship with marital satisfaction. Multiple studies have shown that both positive and negative momentary moods spill over from work to romantic relationships (e.g., Heller & Watson, 2005; Jones & Fletcher, 1996; Song et al., 2008). Other studies have shown that stress, overload, expectation of stigma (e.g., for being part of the LGBTQ community), and incivility at work are negatively related to emotional and behavioral reactions that are at the core of romantic relationships (e.g., overt expressions of anger, disregard of a partner's needs, lower affection and disclosure, social undermining of the partner, and overall relationship satisfaction and quality; Dispenza, 2015; King et al., 2018; Meier & Cho, 2019; Sears et al., 2016). Furthermore, this spillover has been shown to crossover to the partner and influence their affective state and behaviors as well (Sears et al., 2016; Song et al., 2008). More recently, a growing area of research examines how the diffusion of work to the relationship domain using internet connected devices (ICTs) affects romantic relationships (e.g., Aljasir, 2022; Carlson et al., 2018; McDaniel et al., 2018, 2021). This is a growing area of research that becomes increasingly important as the development of ICTs and their use by individuals outside work makes the boundaries between work and romantic relationships more blurred than ever and with it, the potential for greater interference of work in romantic relationships.

ROMANTICS RELATIONSHIP FROM AN ECONOMIC PERSPECTIVE

In the 1960s, economists increasingly started using economic theory to explain behavior outside the traditional boundaries of monetary markets (Becker, 1973). Building on social exchange theory (Thibaut & Kelley, 1959), they started analyzing families using an economic analysis. Understanding families became one of the most prominent areas to which economists applied their theoretical and analytical tools, providing a different perspective on choices made by individuals regarding mate selection, marriages, births, divorce, division of household labor, among others (Becker, 1991). Broadly speaking, two main principles guided this economic analysis. First, individuals' decisions follow the principles of rational choice outside monetary markets just as they guide decisions and choices in monetary markets. Second, the principles of supply and demand also operate in a similar way outside monetary markets. Applying these economic principles to marriages, Becker (1973) suggested a framework of "marriage markets" in which individuals decide to marry when the utility they expect from it exceeds the utility of remaining single, while taking into account the potential supply of relevant matches. Similarly, divorce decisions are also a result of a utility analysis – when the utility of becoming single exceeds the expected losses of a divorce, individuals would make a separation decision.

Over time, Becker's analysis of marriage markets was criticized for oversimplifying the decision to marry or separate. Key weaknesses of Becker's model include the assumptions that people make purely rational choices (Tversky & Kahneman, 1986), that all post-marriage decisions are determined, like in monetary markets, by binding agreements in the marriage market (Pollak, 2019), that couples pool their resources to maximize family-level utility (Lundberg et al., 1997), that paid and unpaid work provide the same bargaining power (Anderson & Eswaran, 2009), and that gender (and race) have no role in marriage markets decisions (Hitsch et al., 2010; Lundberg & Pollak, 2015). With the understanding of the limitations and critique of economic approaches, we continue with an introduction to the economic perspective on romantic relationships.

An Economic Perspective on Romantic Relationships

At its core, an economic perspective on romantic relationships does not consider "romance" as relevant for the formation and maintenance of romantic relationships. Dating, marriage, and divorce are all a result of maximizing the individual utility given the supply of desirable matches and the demand by other actors in the market. Any choices are a result of rational decisions taking into account utility maximization, supply, and demand. A key assumption is that men and women prefer marrying people who are similar to them on social, demographic, and economic characteristics (Qian & Lichter, 2018). Further, an economic approach often tries to understand romantic relationships by observing long-term trends in marriage and divorce like age of first marriage, marriage, and divorce rates, similarities between couples across a host of demographic characteristics and human capital, and the importance of social class in romantic relationships. As such, this approach does not pay any attention to individual level variables that go beyond demographics characteristics like personality, attachment style, and other intra-individual and couple-level variables, such as marital conflict and the quality of communication between couples.

A common area of research that is analyzed using economic principles concerns the decrease in marriage rates since the 1950s, especially among low-income communities (Lundberg & Pollak, 2015). Economists, sociologists, and demographers that use an economic perspective suggest that one of the reasons for the decline in marriage rate is change in the supply of suitable matches across different socioeconomic groups. For example, the increased education of women relative to men, especially in low-income communities, reduces the supply of good matches for low-income women, making it less likely for them to get married because the utility that they can gain by marrying a man with lower education is insufficient relative to the cost of marriage (e.g., Gibson-Davis et al., 2005). Supply and demand also play a role in romantic relationships among high earners. Due to structural inequality, men are much more likely to be top earners than women. Men desire a "good match" – a professional, highly educated woman – but the supply of these women is low. Therefore, top-earner women can be more selective in their choice of marriage and find a "better" partner, for example, one that will be more egalitarian when it comes to sharing household chores and childcare (Carbone & Cahn, 2014). Other examples of the importance of supply and demand in romantic relationship markets is demonstrated by studies showing that when college women account for a higher proportion of a college campus, they go on fewer traditional dates, are less likely to have boyfriends, and are more likely to have casual sex (Uecker & Regnerus 2010); that men are likely to marry sooner and women are less likely to work when the supply of men is greater than women when migration flows occur (Angrist, 2002); that following wars, when the supply of men is low, men are less likely to settle for lower quality matches (Abramitzky et al., 2014); and, that Chinese parents accumulate more savings when there is greater competition for women (less women relative to men) in marriage markets (Wei & Zhang, 2011).

In general, economic approaches assign value to desired characteristics in the marriage market and explain romantic relationships, or matches, by the value of the desired characteristics each partner brings to the marriage. For example, because "single" has a higher value than "divorced" in the marriage market (Qian & Lichter, 2018), previously married people are at a disadvantage relative to never-married people, have less supply of potential matches, and are therefore less likely to get married relative to singles. Furthermore, when divorced people remarry, they are likely to settle for a lower quality match (Qian & Lichter, 2018), casting a wider net and having more heterogenous pairings. For example, people who remarry are more likely to marry a person that is less educated than they are, compared to people who are first married. Overall, by using insights from economics such as supply and demand, rational choice, and maximization of utility, researchers provide a different perspective on the formation and dissolution of romantic relationships. Treating romantic relationships as economic markets takes a macro perspective on trends in marriage, divorce, and fertility, and complements the more micro perspectives that are better suited for understanding the intra-couple complexities and intricacies of romantic relationships.

SUMMARY

Romantic relationships are important to most individuals. So is their work and career. It is no wonder that these two important domains are therefore influenced by each other. In this chapter, we provided a review of how workplaces perceive romantic relationship as unavoidable and potentially harmful and their attempt to control romantic relationship at work, how work and romantic relationships interact to affect each other, and an economic perspective of romantic relationship as an exchange relationship motivated by utility maximization.

It is important to note that although research on the intersection of romantic relationships and work is growing, some areas of research require more attention. For example, minorities in the workplace, and specifically sexual minorities, face additional constraints when attempting to reconcile work and romantic relationship (e.g., Holman et al., 2022; Stavrou & Ierodiakonou, 2018). Another topic that requires additional attention is the development of relationship between work and romantic relationships over the life course. It is not clear if associations observed between work and romantic relationships in emerging adults (e.g., Luyckx et al., 2014) persist over the life course, or whether, for example, one domain is more dominant at a younger age whereas another takes priority at an older age.

Romantic relationships and work are often portrayed as competing with one another (Fellows et al., 2016). Such perspective views romantic relationships and work as competing for the same resources: participation and investment in one domain is depleting resources (time, energy, affect) that are not available anymore for investment in the other domain. This zero-sum game view is common when using economics perspectives of romantic relationships and work that applies analytical tools that focus on competing demands and competition for limited and finite resources. However, romantic relationships and work can also enhance and strengthen one another (e.g., Gareis et al., 2009), and more research is needed to further understand how these two important domains in people's life can be fulfilled.

REFERENCES

Abramitzky, R., Boustan, L. P., & Eriksson, K. (2014). A nation of immigrants: Assimilation and economic outcomes in the age of mass migration. *Journal of Political Economy*, 122(3), 467–506.

Adkins, C. L., & Premeaux, S. F. (2012). Spending time: The impact of hours worked on work–family conflict. *Journal of Vocational Behavior*, 80(2), 380–389.

Aljasir, S. (2022). Present but absent in the digital age: Testing a conceptual model of phubbing and relationship satisfaction among married couples. *Human Behavior and Emerging Technologies*. https://doi.org/10.1155/2022/1402751

Amato, P. R., & Beattie, B. (2011). Does the unemployment rate affect the divorce rate? An analysis of state data 1960-2005. *Social Science Research*, 40(3), 705–715.

Anderson, C., & Hunsaker, P. (1985) Why there's romancing at the office and why it's everyone's problem. *Personnel*, 62(2), 57–63.

Anderson, S., & Eswaran, M. (2009). What determines female autonomy? Evidence from Bangladesh. *Journal of Development Economics*, 90(2), 179–191.

Angrist, J. (2002). How do sex ratios affect marriage and labor markets? Evidence from America's second generation. *The Quarterly Journal of Economics*, 117(3), 997–1038.

Becker, G. S. (1973). A theory of marriage: Part I. *Journal of Political Economy*, 81(4), 813–846.

Becker, G. S. (1991). *A treatise on the family: Enlarged edition*. Harvard University Press.

Berdahl, J. L. (2007). The sexual harassment of uppity women. *Journal of Applied Psychology*, 92(2), 425–437.

Bianchi, S. M., & Milkie, M. A. (2010). Work and family research in the first decade of the 21st century. *Journal of Marriage and Family*, 72(3), 705–725.

Bianchi, S. M., & Raley, S. B. (2006). Time allocation in families. In S. M. Bianchi, L. M. Casper, & R. B. King (Ed.), *Work, family, health, and well-being* (pp. 31–52). Routledge.

Bronfenbrenner, U., & Crouter, A. C. (1982). Work and family through time and space. In Sheila B. Kamerman & Cheryl D. Hayes (Eds.), *Families that work: Children in a changing world*. National Academy Press.

Bureau of Labor Statistics. (2022). *Labor force statistics from the Current Population Survey. Table 11: Employed persons by detailed occupation, sex, race, and Hispanic or Latino ethnicity*. www.bls.gov/cps/cpsaat11.htm

Byrne, D. E. (1971). *The attraction paradigm*. Academic Press.

Carbone, J., & Cahn, N. (2014). *Marriage markets: How inequality is remaking the American family*. Oxford University Press.

Carlson, D. S., Thompson, M. J., Crawford, W. S., Boswell, W. R., & Whitten, D. (2018). Your job is messing with mine! The impact of mobile device use for work during family time on the spouse's work life. *Journal of Occupational Health Psychology*, 23(4), 471–482.

Cavico, F. J., & Mujtaba, B. G. (2021). Workplace romance and sexual favoritism in the #MeToo workplace: Legal and practical considerations for management. *Equality, Diversity and Inclusion: An International Journal*, 40(6), 667–689.

Center for American Progress (2018). *Gender matters: Women disproportionately report sexual harassment in male-dominated industries.* www.americanprogress.org/article/gender-matters/

Chory, R. M., & Gillen Hoke, H. (2020). Coworkers' perceptions of, and communication with, workplace romance participants: Proposing and testing a model. *International Journal of Business Communication,* 2329488420908321. https://doi.org/10.1177/2329488420908321

Clarke, L. (2006). Sexual relationships and sexual conduct in the workplace. *Legal Studies, 26,* 347–368.

Conger, R. D., & Conger, K. J. (2002). Resilience in midwestern families: Selected findings from the first decade of a prospective, longitudinal study. *Journal of Marriage and Family, 64,* 361–373. https://doi.org/10.1111/j.1741-3737.2002.00361.x

Conger, R. D., Rueter, M. A., & Elder Jr, G. H. (1999). Couple resilience to economic pressure. *Journal of Personality and Social Psychology, 76*(1), 54.

Craig, L., & Mullan, K. (2010). Parenthood, gender and work-family time in the United States, Australia, Italy, France, and Denmark. *Journal of Marriage and Family, 72*(5), 1344–1361.

Crouter, A. C., Bumpus, M. F., Head, M. R., & McHale, S. M. (2001). Implications of overwork and overload for the quality of men's family relationships. *Journal of Marriage and Family, 63,* 404–416.

Dakin, J., & Wampler, R. (2008). Money doesn't buy happiness, but it helps: Marital satisfaction, psychological distress, and demographic differences between low-and middle-income clinic couples. *The American Journal of Family Therapy, 36*(4), 300–311.

Dessler, G. (Ed.) (2010). *Fundamentals of human resource management* (4th ed.). McGraw-Hill/Irwin.

Dispenza, F. (2015). An exploratory model of proximal minority stress and the work-life interface for men in same-sex, dual-earner relationships. *Journal of Counseling & Development, 93*(3), 321–332.

Elsesser, K. (2019, February 14). These 6 surprising office romance stats should be a wake-up call for organizations. *Forbes Magazine,* www.forbes.com/sites/kimelsesser/2019/02/14/these-6-surprising-office-romance-stats-should-be-a-wake-up-call-to-organizations/?sh=3f6cee6223a2

Falconier, M. K., & Epstein, N. B. (2010). Relationship satisfaction in Argentinean couples under economic strain: Gender differences in a dyadic stress model. *Journal of Social and Personal Relationships, 27*(6), 781–799.

Fellows, K. J., Chiu, H. Y., Hill, E. J., & Hawkins, A. J. (2016). Work–family conflict and couple relationship quality: A meta-analytic study. *Journal of Family and Economic Issues, 37*(4), 509–518.

Gareis, K. C., Barnett, R. C., Ertel, K. A., & Berkman, L. F. (2009). Work-family enrichment and conflict: Additive effects, buffering, or balance? *Journal of Marriage and Family, 71*(3), 696–707.

Gerstel, N., & Clawson, D. (2018). Control over time: Employers, workers, and families shaping work schedules. *Annual Review of Sociology, 44,* 77–97.

Gibson-Davis, C. M., Edin, K., & McLanahan, S. (2005). High hopes but even higher expectations: The retreat from marriage among low-income couples. *Journal of Marriage and Family, 67*(5), 1301–1312.

González-Val, R., & Marcén, M. (2018). Unemployment, marriage and divorce. *Applied Economics*, 50(13), 1495–1508.

Gopalan, N., Grzywacz, J. G., & Cui, M. (2018). Role of work and family enrichment in the relationship between environment factors and outcomes in work and non-work domains. *Journal of Organizational Psychology*, 18(4). https://doi.org/10.33423/jop.v18i4.82

Green, M. Z. (2019). A new# MeToo result: Rejecting notions of romantic consent with executives. *Employement Rights & Employement Policy Journal*, 23(1), 115.

Greenhaus, J. H., & Powell, G. N. (2006). When work and family are allies: A theory of work-family enrichment. *Academy of Management Review*, 31(1), 72–92.

Griffith, J. (2019). The sexual harassment–suicide connection in the US military: Contextual effects of hostile work environment and trusted unit leaders. *Suicide and Life-Threatening Behavior*, 49(1), 41–53.

Headey, B., Muffels, R., & Wooden, M. (2008). Money does not buy happiness: Or does it? A reassessment based on the combined effects of wealth, income and consumption. *Social Indicators Research*, 87(1), 65–82.

Heller, D., & Watson, D. (2005). The dynamic spillover of satisfaction between work and marriage: The role of time and mood. *Journal of Applied Psychology*, 90(6), 1273–1279.

Hertlein, K. M. (2012). Digital dwelling: Technology in couple and family relationships. *Family Relations*, 61(3), 374–387.

Hill, E. J., Erickson, J. J., Holmes, E. K., & Ferris, M. (2010). Workplace flexibility, work hours, and work-life conflict: Finding an extra day or two. *Journal of Family Psychology*, 24(3), 349.

Hitsch, G. J., Hortaçsu, A., & Ariely, D. (2010). Matching and sorting in online dating. *American Economic Review*, 100(1), 130–163.

Holman, E. G., Ogolsky, B. G., & Oswald, R. F. (2022). Concealment of a sexual minority identity in the workplace: The role of workplace climate and identity centrality. *Journal of Homosexuality*, 69(9), 1467–1484.

Jackson, G. L., Krull, J. L., Bradbury, T. N., & Karney, B. R. (2017). Household income and trajectories of marital satisfaction in early marriage. *Journal of Marriage and Family*, 79(3), 690–704.

Johnson, H. A., Zabriskie, R. B., & Hill, B. (2006). The contribution of couple leisure involvement, leisure time, and leisure satisfaction to marital satisfaction. *Marriage & Family Review*, 40(1), 69–91.

Jones, F., & Fletcher, B. (1996). Taking work home: A study of daily fluctuations in work stressors, effects on moods and impacts on marital couples. *Journal of Occupational and Organizational Psychology*, 69(1), 89–106.

Judge, T. A., Ilies, R., & Scott, B. A. (2006). Work–family conflict and emotions: Effects at work and at home. *Personnel Psychology*, 59(4), 779–814.

Khan, M. A. S., Jianguo, D., Usman, M., & Ahmad, M. I. (2017). Moderated mediation model of interrelations between workplace romance, wellbeing, and employee performance. *Frontiers in Psychology*, 8, 2158.

Killewald, A. (2016). Money, work, and marital stability: Assessing change in the gendered determinants of divorce. *American Sociological Review*, 81(4), 696–719.

King, V., Wickrama, K. K., O'Neal, C. W., & Lorenz, F. O. (2018). Adverse work experiences and marital outcomes in middle years: Role of self-esteem. *Personal Relationships*, 25(1), 50–64.

Kramer, A., & Kramer, K. Z. (2021). Putting the family back into work and family research. *Journal of Vocational Behavior*, 126, 103564.

Kramer, K. Z., Bae, H., Huh, C. A., & Pak, S. (2019). The positive spillover and crossover of paternity leave use: A dyadic longitudinal analysis. *Journal of Vocational Behavior*, 115, 103310.

Kulik, L., & Liberman, G. (2022). Stressors at the work-family interface and satisfaction with the quality of the couple relationship: A comparative analysis of men and women. *Journal of Family Studies*, 28(1), 255–276.

Lichter, D. T., LeClere, F. B., & McLaughlin, D. K. (1991). Local marriage markets and the marital behavior of black and white women. *American Journal of Sociology*, 96(4), 843–867.

Liu, H., Ngo, H. Y., & Cheung, F. M. (2016). Work–family enrichment and marital satisfaction among Chinese couples: A crossover-spillover perspective. *International Journal of Stress Management*, 23(2), 209.

Lopez, E. S., & Ensari, N. (2014). The effects of leadership style, organizational outcome, and gender on attributional bias toward leaders. *Journal of Leadership Studies*, 8(2), 19–37.

Lundberg, S. J., & Pollak, R. A. (2015). The evolving role of marriage: 1950–2010. *The Future of Children*, 25(2), 29–50.

Lundberg, S. J., Pollak, R. A., & Wales, T. J. (1997). Do husbands and wives pool their resources? Evidence from the United Kingdom child benefit. *Journal of Human Resources*, 32(3), 463–480.

Luyckx, K., Seiffge-Krenke, I., Schwartz, S. J., Crocetti, E., & Klimstra, T. A. (2014). Identity configurations across love and work in emerging adults in romantic relationships. *Journal of Applied Developmental Psychology*, 35(3), 192–203.

Mainiero, L. A. (1986). A review and analysis of power dynamics in workplace romances. *Academy of Management Review*, 11(4), 750–762. https://doi.org/10.2307/258394.

MarketWatch (2019). *Google, Facebook and Airbnb employees only get one shot to ask a co-worker on a date*. www.marketwatch.com/story/at-google-facebook-and-airbnb-you-cant-ask-a-coworker-out-on-a-date-twice-2019-07-01/?msclkid=0e561863b9da11ec8ba91aae2df0564b

Maume, D. J., & Sebastian, R. A. (2012). Gender, nonstandard work schedules, and marital quality. *Journal of Family and Economic Issues*, 33(4), 477–490.

McDaniel, B. T., & Coyne, S. M. (2016). "Technoference": The interference of technology in couple relationships and implications for women's personal and relational well-being. *Psychology of Popular Media Culture*, 5(1), 85.

McDaniel, B. T., Galovan, A. M., Cravens, J. D., & Drouin, M. (2018). "Technoference" and implications for mothers' and fathers' couple and coparenting relationship quality. *Computers in Human Behavior*, 80, 303–313.

McDaniel, B. T., Galovan, A. M., & Drouin, M. (2021). Daily technoference, technology use during couple leisure time, and relationship quality. *Media Psychology*, 24(5), 637–665.

Meier, L. L., & Cho, E. (2019). Work stressors and partner social undermining: Comparing negative affect and psychological detachment as mechanisms. *Journal of Occupational Health Psychology, 24*(3), 359–372.

Minnotte, K. L., Minnotte, M. C., & Bonstrom, J. (2015). Work–family conflicts and marital satisfaction among US workers: Does stress amplification matter? *Journal of Family and Economic Issues, 36*(1), 21–33.

Montoya, R. M., Horton, R. S., & Kirchner, J. (2008). Is actual similarity necessary for attraction? A meta-analysis of actual and perceived similarity. *Journal of Social and Personal Relationships, 25*(6), 889–922.

Murphy, M. (2019). Introduction to "# MeToo movement". *Journal of Feminist Family Therapy, 31*(2–3), 63–65.

Nagele-Piazza, L. (2018). *How to revamp your harassment prevention program.* www.shrm.org/ResourcesAndTools/legal-and-compliance/employment-law/Pages/How-to-Revamp-Your-Harassment-Prevention-Program.aspx

Newcomb, T. M. (1961). *The acquaintance process.* Holt, Rinehart & Winston.

NY Times (2020). Harvey Weinstein is found guilty of rape. *NY Times,* February 24, 2020. www.nytimes.com/2020/02/24/nyregion/harvey-weinstein-verdict.html

Obama, M. (2021). *Becoming.* Crown Publishing.

Pak, S., Kramer, A., Lee, Y., & Kim, K. J. (2022). The impact of work hours on work-to-family enrichment and conflict through energy processes: A meta-analysis. *Journal of Organizational Behavior, 43*(4), 709–743.

Parker, K. (2018). Women in majority-male workplaces report higher rates of gender discrimination. *Pew Research Center.* www.pewresearch.org/fact-tank/2018/03/07/women-in-majority-male-workplaces-report-higher-rates-of-gender-discrimination/

Paulin, M., Lachance-Grzela, M., & McGee, S. (2017). Bringing work home or bringing family to work: Personal and relational consequences for working parents. *Journal of Family and Economic Issues, 38*(4), 463–476.

Perry-Jenkins, M., & Gerstel, N. (2020). Work and family in the second decade of the 21st century. *Journal of Marriage and Family, 82*(1), 420–453.

Perry-Jenkins, M., Goldberg, A. E., Pierce, C. P., & Sayer, A. G. (2007). Shift work, role overload, and the transition to parenthood. *Journal of Marriage and Family, 69,* 123–138.

Petts, R. J., & Knoester, C. (2020). Are parental relationships improved if fathers take time off of work after the birth of a child? *Social Forces, 98*(3), 1223–1256.

Pierce, C. A., & Aguinis, H. (1997). Bridging the gap between romantic relationships and sexual harassment in organizations. *Journal of Organizational Behavior: The International Journal of Industrial, Occupational and Organizational Psychology and Behavior, 18*(3), 197–200.

Pierce, C. A., & Aguinis, H. (2001). A framework for investigating the link between workplace romance and sexual harassment. *Group & Organization Management, 26*(2), 206–229.

Pierce, C. A., & Aguinis, H. (2003). Romantic relationships in organizations: A test of a model of formation and impact factors. *Management Research, 1*(2), 161–169.

Pierce, C. A., & Aguinis, H. (2009). Moving beyond a legal-centric approach to managing workplace romances: Organizationally sensible recommendations for HR leaders. *Human Resource Management, 48*(3), 447–464.

Pierce, C. A., Broberg, B. J., McClure, J. R., & Aguinis, H. (2004). Responding to sexual harassment complaints: Effects of a dissolved workplace romance on decision-making standards. *Organizational Behavior and Human Decision Processes*, 95(1), 66–82.

Pollak, R. A. (2019). How bargaining in marriage drives marriage market equilibrium. *Journal of Labor Economics*, 37(1), 297–321.

Poortman, A. R. (2005). How work affects divorce: The mediating role of financial and time pressures. *Journal of Family Issues*, 26(2), 168–195.

Presser, H. B. (2000). Nonstandard work schedules and marital instability. *Journal of Marriage and the Family*, 62, 93–110.

Qian, Z., & Lichter, D. T. (2018). Marriage markets and intermarriage: Exchange in first marriages and remarriages. *Demography*, 55(3), 849–875.

Randall, A. K., Totenhagen, C. J., Walsh, K. J., Adams, C., & Tao, C. (2017). Coping with workplace minority stress: Associations between dyadic coping and anxiety among women in same-sex relationships. *Journal of Lesbian Studies*, 21(1), 70–87.

Reich, T. C., & Hershcovis, M. S. (2011). Interpersonal relationships at work. In S. Zedeck (Ed.), *APA handbook of industrial and organizational psychology, Vol. 3. Maintaining, expanding, and contracting the organization* (pp. 223–248). American Psychological Association. https://doi.org/10.1037/12171-006

Rein, L. (2018, July 20). FEMA personnel chief harassed women, hired some as possible sexual partners for male employees, agency leader says. *Washington Post*. www.washingtonpost.com/politics/fema-official-harassed-women-hired-some-as-possible-sexual-partners-for-male-employees-agency-chief-says/2018/07/30/964da518-9403-11e8-80e1-00e80e1fdf43_story.html

Rogers, S. J., & May, D. C. (2003). Spillover between marital quality and job satisfaction: Long-term patterns and gender differences. *Journal of Marriage and Family*, 65(2), 482–495.

Schneider, D., & Hastings, O. P. (2015). Socioeconomic variation in the effect of economic conditions on marriage and nonmarital fertility in the United States: Evidence from the Great Recession. *Demography*, 52(6), 1893–1915.

Sears, M. S., Repetti, R. L., Robles, T. F., & Reynolds, B. M. (2016). I just want to be left alone: Daily overload and marital behavior. *Journal of Family Psychology*, 30(5), 569.

Seo, G., Huang, W., & Han, S. H. C. (2017). Conceptual review of underrepresentation of women in senior leadership positions from a perspective of gendered social status in the workplace: Implication for HRD research and practice. *Human Resource Development Review*, 16(1), 35–59.

Shafer, E. F., Kelly, E. L., Buxton, O. M., & Berkman, L. F. (2018). Partners' overwork and individuals' wellbeing and experienced relationship quality. *Community, Work & Family*, 21(4), 410–428.

Shahvali, M., Kerstetter, D. L., & Townsend, J. N. (2021). The contribution of vacationing together to couple functioning. *Journal of Travel Research*, 60(1), 133–148.

SHRM Online Staff. (2011, February 11). Every day is Valentine's for some workers. *SHRM*. www.shrm.org/hr-today/news/hr-news/pages/valentinesday.aspx

Small, S. A., & Riley, D. (1990). Toward a multidimensional assessment of work spillover into family life. *Journal of Marriage and the Family*, 52(1), 51–61.

Song, Z., Foo, M. D., & Uy, M. A. (2008). Mood spillover and crossover among dual-earner couples: A cell phone event sampling study. *Journal of Applied Psychology*, 93(2), 443–452.

Stavrou, E., & Ierodiakonou, C. (2018). Expanding the work–life balance discourse to LGBT employees: Proposed research framework and organizational responses. *Human Resource Management*, 57(6), 1355–1370.

Thibaut, J. W., & Kelley, H. H. (1959). *The social psychology of groups*. Routledge.

Turner, R. E. (1997). Wetland loss in the northern Gulf of Mexico: Multiple working hypotheses. *Estuaries*, 20(1), 1–13.

Tversky, A., & Kahneman, D. (1986). Rational choice and the framing of decisions. *The Journal of Business*, 59(4), S251–S278. www.jstor.org/stable/2352759

Uecker, J. E., & Regnerus, M. D. (2010). Bare market: Campus sex ratios, romantic relationships, and sexual behavior. *The Sociological Quarterly*, 51(3), 408–435.

Unger, D., Sonnentag, S., Niessen, C., & Kuonath, A. (2015). The longer your work hours, the worse your relationship? The role of selective optimization with compensation in the associations of working time with relationship satisfaction and self-disclosure in dual-career couples. *Human Relations*, 68(12), 1889–1912.

U.S. Bureau of Labor Statistics. (2020). *Comparing characteristics and selected expenditures of dual- and single-income households with children*. www.bls.gov/opub/mlr/2020/article/pdf/comparing-characteristics-and-selected-expenditures-of-dual-and-single-income-households-with-children.htm

U.S. Equal Employment Opportunity Commission. (2022). *Sexual harassment*. www.eeoc.gov/sexual-harassment

Uzialko, A. (2023, January 23). How to manage workplace relationships. *Business News Daily*. www.businessnewsdaily.com/7764-co-workers-dating.html

Van Steenbergen, E. F., Kluwer, E. S., & Karney, B. R. (2011). Workload and the trajectory of marital satisfaction in newlyweds: Job satisfaction, gender, and parental status as moderators. *Journal of Family Psychology*, 25(3), 345.

van Steenbergen, E. F., Kluwer, E. S., & Karney, B. R. (2014). Work–family enrichment, work–family conflict, and marital satisfaction: A dyadic analysis. *Journal of Occupational Health Psychology*, 19(2), 182.

Voydanoff, P. (2004). The effects of work demands and resources on work-to-family conflict and facilitation. *Journal of Marriage and Family*, 66(2), 398–412.

Ward, D. E., Park, L. E., Walsh, C. M., Naragon-Gainey, K., Paravati, E., & Whillans, A. V. (2021). For the love of money: The role of financially contingent self-worth in romantic relationships. *Journal of Social and Personal Relationships*, 38(4), 1303–1328.

Wei, S. J., & Zhang, X. (2011). The competitive saving motive: Evidence from rising sex ratios and savings rates in China. *Journal of Political Economy*, 119(3), 511–564.

Whillans, A. V., Pow, J., & Norton, M. I. (2018). *Buying time promotes relationship satisfaction*. Harvard Business School, Working paper 18-072.

8

History and Cohort Effects in Romantic Relationships

TEKISHA M. RICE AND ARAN GARNETT-DEAKIN

Relationship science has traditionally occupied itself with the characteristics of satisfying relationships along with the antecedents and consequences of relationship dissolution. Yet, even in its genesis, relationship science has been critiqued for neglecting the changing environments that relationships exist within (Berscheid, 1999). According to Berscheid (1999), relationship science must transcend individual, monodisciplinary perspectives in order to be a "cohesive force" in identifying aspects of the environment that support and undermine relationship functioning. More than two decades later, how far have scholars come? What aspects of historical context and what cohort effects have relationship scholars examined and overlooked? This chapter discusses historical and cohort effects in romantic relationships in relation to sociohistorical events. In doing so, we review extant research and highlight the interplay between the historical context that relationships operate within and the interactions of romantic partners.

Much of scholars' understanding of the historical context of marriage comes from the work of family historians. These scholars highlight the lack of novelty in the ways we do family, while underscoring the novelty of co-occurring family forms. For example, Coontz (2016) describes families as "the way we never were," highlighting the inconsistencies in idealistic views of traditional family structure and realities of modern family structure. Although diverse family structures are not new, Coontz describes a "rapidly changing and diversifying family environment" that has influenced the social role of marriage (Coontz, 2015, p. 10). Historically, marriage was a central social institution that organized political and economic rights in society and provided a structure for the transfer of assets within families (Coontz, 2004). Today, marriage is less central to economic and political rights – although married individuals have access to certain rights, privileges, and responsibilities that unmarried people do not – a phenomenon deemed the "deinstitutionalization of marriage" (Cherlin, 2004). The changing social and political environment of marriage has created a social landscape where multiple ways of coupling exist simultaneously, even if they are not all legally recognized. Notably, rather than experiencing uncertainty around the norms governing marriage, individuals may question whether they should squeeze their way of doing partnering into the institutionalized version of marriage (Lauer & Yodanis, 2010).

Alongside changes in how people "do" marriage came adjustments in what individuals expected from romantic partners. Rather than seeking a partner to secure basic needs like security, people began to seek partners for emotional fulfillment (Coontz, 2004). These increased demands came with more satisfying relationships, as long as partners were able to meet higher order needs (Finkel et al., 2014). Notably, there is wide variation in how individuals may (or may not) rely on intimate partnerships to meet higher order needs (Pietromonaco & Perry-Jenkins, 2014). Although couples with the capacity to meet higher expectations may experience greater satisfaction within their relationships (McNulty, 2016), data capturing what individuals desire from their romantic partnerships across relationship structures (e.g., monogamous vs. pluralistic partnering), lifespan, culture, and other critical intersectional social positions is slim. Understanding contemporary expectations of intimate partnerships requires a multi-pronged approach. Scholars must employ several tools in the researchers' toolbox, including qualitative data, within-group analyses, and prospective and retrospective assessments – all while considering social, political, and historical context.

Although family historians have made great strides in examining how the meaning, structure, and functions of romantic partnering have changed (and stayed the same) across time, less is understood about how aspects of the historical context continue to impact romantic partnering. The historical intertwinement of marriage with social and political systems should also make marriage susceptible to the influences of the macro-system. Thus, the idea that marriage, as an institution and the dynamics within it, can be influenced by historical events is neither novel nor surprising. What is surprising, given the standing acknowledgment of historical influences, is the lack of empirical research examining how characteristics of the macro-system trickle down to individuals' experiences within their relationships. On one hand, scholars have considered various cohort effects in family life. This research describes how a specific group of individuals experience different trajectories based on a specific event. For example, scholars have examined reasons for staying in abusive relationships among women who matured during the women's rights movement. Findings suggest that compared to the younger women in the sample, older women expressed more commitment to marriage as an institution and had unique concerns around their ability to acquire employment and thus, provide for themselves economically (Zink et al., 2003).

Alternatively, we discuss historic effects as events that become a part of shared knowledge and maintain lingering effects within and across generations. From this perspective, *cohort effects become historic effects*. One event may simultaneously be a cohort effect for individuals in one developmental period *and* an historic effect for individuals in another developmental period. Relative to historic effects, cohort effects are likely greater in intensity and contribute to more observable associations and testable hypotheses. In this chapter, we discuss events that have likely transitioned from being cohort effects to a historic context that influences romantic partnering. Specifically, we suggest that scholars should examine relationships within historical context by considering the psychological meaning attributed to socio-historical events. We argue that discrete historical events and those with significant psychosocial meaning are encased within systems of power and have the capacity to influence decision making within relationships. In addition, we urge scholars to consider that the hypotheses and research questions regarding the cohort effects associated with a particular event may need to be shifted as it transitions into a historic event.

Theoretical and Conceptual Considerations

Symbolic interactionism (LaRossa & Reitzes, 2009) and life course theory (Elder, 1994) lend credence to the linkages between historical events and lived experiences within romantic relationships. Symbolic interactionism suggests that human behavior relies on meanings created through social processes and the interaction between individual freedom and societal constraint. Individuals apply shared symbols and create meanings that contribute to identities, roles, and behaviors (LaRossa & Reitzes, 2009). Individuals present their roles and identities when moving through everyday life and simultaneously make inferences about others and the ways in which they respond to this presentation. The context, community, and social location of an individual are vital when examining the connection between shared meanings and actions (Stryker, 2008). Context is especially relevant to socio-historical events as it refers to the societal and cultural settings within which individuals interact with the roles and identities of others (LaRossa & Reitzes, 2009).

Life course theory (Elder, 1994) is also useful in assessing the relevance of sociohistorical context to romantic relationships. Its primary thesis is that families operate within a macrosocial context of society and history. Two components of life course theory specifically inform how scholars can examine relationships in a sociohistorical context: linked lives and historical embeddedness. The concept of linked lives references how events that one person experiences may influences others in their networks (Gee et al., 2012). Research on racial discrimination provides an example of linked lives, indicating that one person's experience of discrimination can affect their romantic partner's mental health (McNeil Smith et al., 2020) and relationship satisfaction (Jenkins et al., 2020). Related to the concept of linked lives is that of historical embeddedness and changes across time (Elder & George, 2016). Relationships develop across ontogenetic (i.e., individual development) and historical (i.e., broader social context) time (Bengston & Allen, 1993). Groups of individuals who simultaneously experience historical events during similar developmental periods can be defined as distinct cohorts. Young adulthood (approximately ages 18–30) may be a particularly impactful developmental period for defining cohorts relevant to relationship development. Bühler and Nikitin (2020) argue that aspects of the social environment, including historical events, are especially formative in young adulthood as individuals establish their identity and roles within society. At the same time, life course theory emphasizes how shared history may define how people experience linked lives and historical embeddedness (Bengston & Allen, 1993; Elder, 1994). When combined with the ecological focus on macro time (i.e., changing values, expectations, and events in society; Bronfenbrenner, 1986) and the intersectional emphasis on historical events and institutions that designate (dis)advantage (Crenshaw, 1991; Few-Demo, 2014) across social positions, theoretical significance of historical and cohort effects cannot be overlooked.

The concept of *historical trauma* helps describe the relevance of historical context to experiences within romantic relationships. Historical trauma references the collective traumatic events experienced by individuals who share a group identity or affiliation (Evans-Campbell, 2008). From this perspective, events that occurred in the past are viewed as parts of a single trajectory, facilitating the interpretation of contemporary experiences through the lens of historical events. Thus, historical events are expected to have complex, ongoing influences on individual and family health and identity (Evans-Campbell 2008; Gone, 2013). Historical trauma is characterized by widespread events (i.e., affecting several individuals), generate collective distress, and are inflicted by outsiders with "purposeful and often destructive intent" (Evans-Campbell, 2008, p. 321). Historical context becomes relevant to contemporary romantic partners who interpret current experiences within their relationships through the lens of historic events and those who have a shared history. Relationship maintenance may be especially important for community resilience and coping among historically marginalized groups. For example, Stamps and colleagues (2021) collected open-response data from 410 Black individuals on shifts in relational dynamics during the COVID-19 pandemic. Findings indicate that Black individuals displayed collective resilience and coping in the context of the COVID-19 pandemic by gathering virtually, engaging in ritual celebrations (e.g., birthdays) from a distance, and meeting the material needs of family and community members (e.g., meal sharing, grocery deliveries). These seemingly mundane relationship maintenance behaviors may have enhanced significance when considered in the context of Black Americans' historical trauma in the United States.

From this view, the historical mistreatment of Black individuals in the United States may contribute to the type of relationship maintenance strategies that romantic partners use. Yet, responses to historical trauma within romantic relationships has received little explicit empirical attention. Extant research indicates that Black romantic partners have engaged in gendered power dynamics to facilitate respect (Cowdrey et al., 2009) in part, to avoid replicating the race-based devaluation that partners experience in other environments (work, community). Moreover, contemporary experiences of discrimination can act as reminders of the historical mistreatment. For example, Black partners with a shared understanding of the historical context of slavery are intentional about responding to their partners' disclosure of discrimination with affirmation and support (Rice, in press). Thus, the discussion that proceeds is intended to be illustrative rather than exhaustive.

COHORT AND HISTORIC INFLUENCES IN (CONTEMPORARY) ROMANTIC PARTNERING

The relationship experiences of any given cohort are shaped by ongoing and historical conditions in the environment. According to the Pew Research Center, 9/11 was reported as the most important historical event across four generations: silent generation (1928–1945), baby boomers (1946–1964), generation X (1965–1980), and millennials (1981–1998) (Pew Research Center, 2016). Little research in the fields of family and relationship science assessed how the significance of this historical event translated to experiences within romantic relationships. However, symbolic interactionism and life course perspectives would suggest that the meaning individuals attributed to the salience of these events may emerge from their interactions with close others and societal intuitions. For example, the September 11, 2001 attacks on the world trade center may be considered collective trauma for individuals who were emerging adults or older. Those in romantic partnerships at the time may have experienced shifting or discrepant values in response to the event that influenced couples' decisions. For instance, decisions around residential proximity to large cities may have been a source of strain for partners. Younger cohorts of couples may have partnered within an increasingly polarized sociopolitical environment, which may further elevate the importance of concordance in values and decision making. Research assessing the significance of the election of Donald Trump on relationships indicates that partners who voted differently from one another had lower levels of relationship maintenance and communal orientation (Afifi et al., 2018). Although some individuals reported feeling closer, Bayne and colleagues' (2020) found that the election was also a source of tension for people in politically divided relationships. Participants reported avoiding political discussion, withdrawing from relationships, and attempting change their partners' political opinions. Of note, such discrete events may be experienced as a cohort effect (with more direct implications for navigating romantic relationships) for individuals in one developmental period and experienced as an historic influence – and thus having indirect implications on relationships – for individuals in different developmental periods. In the sections that follow, we discuss illustrative cohort and historic influences romantic relationships.

Interracial Partnering and Racial Trauma

Race and ethnicity-based stress and trauma has a long history in the United States, from the genocide and oppression of indigenous populations to the enslavement, lynching, and erection of institutions that systemically exclude Black Americans. The prohibition and legal recognition of interracial partnering presents one example of a cohort-to-historic effect on romantic partnering. The initial prohibition of interracial marriage occurred in 1661, predating the formal establishment of the United States (Martin, 1979). Despite a common goal of prohibiting sexual relationships between white and non-white individuals, the language around anti-miscegenation laws varied by state (de Guzman & Nishina, 2017; Martin, 1979). Whereas some states like Virginia banned white individuals from marrying any non-white individuals, others specifically banned Black individuals from marrying non-Black individuals. Although the goals were unified (maintaining the purity of the white race), the syntax of the laws meant that in some states, marriages between Black and Filipino individuals, for example, would be legal whereas marriages between Black and white individuals would not be legally recognized. Individuals found in violation of anti-miscegenation laws were subject to forced annulments and Black individuals, in particular, could face punishment by imprisonment or death.

Importantly, interracial parings were not uncommon during US history – some were voluntary and others were involuntary. Enslaved Black women were subject to rape by white slave owners, and subsequent mistreatment by white wives of slave owners. Enslaved Black men faced dire consequences from consensual interracial pairings when their white female partners accused them of rape to avoid the social rejection. Thus, the historic sociopolitical climate around interracial partnering not only discouraged contemporary relationship initiation among interracial couples, but also hindered when, how, and what maintenance behaviors were used by couples. The landmark *Loving v. Virginia* decision federally recognized interracial marriage as a legal right in 1967, however, state-level bans remained across the United States (though they were not actionable) until 2000 when Alabama removed this language from their state constitution. Since the 1960s, social perception has become more positive regarding interracial relationships with interracial couples making up 15 percent of marriages in 2012 compared to 6.7 percent in 1980 (Murty & Roebuck, 2015).

Given the growing multiracial population in the United States (United States Census Bureau, 2021), it is critical to understand the historic implications of anti-miscegenation laws for contemporary interracial couples. Despite more than fifty years of legal precedent, individuals in interracial pairings continue to anticipate social rejection that motivates the modification or abandonment of relationship initiation and maintenance strategies. For example, in a study of 120 men and women, there were three distinct ways that individuals modified relationship initiation strategies: those who did not change initiation strategies based on race, those who were moderately influenced, and those who significantly changed strategy based on the race of the other individual (Brooks & Lynch, 2019; Harris & Kalbfleisch, 2000). Of the group that said they would not change initiation strategy based on race, about one half said that there was little chance they would date outside of their racial group. Additionally, a majority of this group was made up of white individuals. This attitude is largely attributed to the participants having a color-blind racial ideology where it is believed that everyone should be treated the same, regardless of race and life experiences (Brooks & Lynch, 2019). This racial ideology largely erases the historic impacts of personal and structural racism and can lead to people of color experiencing microaggressions in their own relationships (Killian, 2002). Moreover, individuals who are just initiating interracial relationships may downplay this sense of connectedness to buffer potential negation of experiences by a potential partner that espouses a color-blind world view (Brooks & Lynch, 2019).

Research also demonstrates how interracial couples may consciously or unconsciously engage in topic avoidance as a way to maintain their relationships. In a qualitative assessment of twelve interracial couples, Killan (2002) found that Black partners in interracial couples avoided discussing instances of discrimination with their white partners. Black partners worried that their white partners may not be empathetic to these instances of discrimination. Research also indicates that interracial partners may avoid engaging in leisure activities together and experience isolation from family, friends, and work colleagues (Hibbler & Shinew, 2002). When interracial partners do discuss race, they may focus on topics external to the relationship such as race-related discourse in media and social networks (Brooks et al., 2021a). Recent research also highlights the importance of understanding the racial and ethnic world view of interracial partners. Couples who struggle to articulate a cohesive worldview may experience conflict in their relationships (Byrd & Garwick, 2006). Partners with a multicultural worldview – which positively assesses the cultural heritage of several groups (Berry & Kalin, 1995) – are less likely to avoid discussion of race, more likely to initiate race-related discussions that include references to systemic racism, and three times more likely to identify race-reacted issues that influencing dynamics within and outside of their relationships (Brooks et al., 2021a, 2021b). The historic context of interracial pairings continues to linger in the social climate and influences how interracial couples maintain their relationships and anticipate social stress. Notably, individuals may view others' rejections of their interracial pairing as a stressor and report minimal to no impact on their relationship (Brooks et al., 2021b). That is, although the historical influence of the prohibition of interracial marriage creates a climate where couples continue to anticipate rejection, the felt impact of the historic context may be minimal.

Same-Gender Marriage

The historic influence of anti-miscegenation laws and *Loving v. Virginia* facilitates important theorizing around same-gender couples, heterosexism, and the landmark *Obergefell v. Hodges* (2015) decision that federally recognized same-sex marriage. The history of marriage equality in the United States is rife with public and political resistance. Indeed, homosexuality was considered a mental illness until 1980 (American Psychiatric Association, 1980), only to be considered legally invalid (Defense of Marriage Act, 1996) before gaining supportive legal recognition – all within a socially sanctioned context. If the influences of anti-miscegenation laws remain more than half a century after being overturned, do same-gender couples face a similar fate? If so, how might the historical ban on same-gender marriage continue to influence relationship development and maintenance?

Just as the United States population has become increasingly multi-racial, larger proportions of younger generations report more diverse sexual orientations and gender identities (Gallup, 2021). The *Obergefell v. Hodges* decision is a prime example of a cohort effect that may transition to a historic effect. One might expect a sharp distinction in the ways same-gender and queer inclusive mixed-gender couples engage in relationship maintenance prior to, shortly after, and generations after the federal recognition of same-gender marriage. For example, whereas prior to 2015, cohorts of same gender couples may have avoided public affection or leisure activities together, after 2015 cohorts of couples may have been more likely to publicly engage in maintenance behaviors with a measured degree of caution. Indeed, data collected prior to 2015 indicate that greater levels of minority stress were associated with fewer public displays of affection among same-gender couples with lower levels of commitment (Hocker et al., 2021). More recent research highlights that individuals in same-gender and gender-diverse relationships desired public affection more than those in mixed-gender relationships. However, individuals in same-gender and gender-diverse relationships engaged in public affection less frequently and were more vigilant about doing so (Blair et al., 2022).

Similarly, although we know little about the impact of overturned marriages (Oswald & Kuvalanka, 2008) some same-gender couples promptly married after it became legal in their state for fear that the right to marry may soon disappear (Rostosky et al., 2016). Given this history, couples may be uncertain about the future legal recognition of their relationship at the state and federal levels (Monk & Ogolsky, 2019). Indeed, Black, white, and Latinx sexual and gender minority women expressed fear that marriage equality would be in jeopardy after the election of the Trump administration (Riggle et al., 2021). Even couples who obtained civil marriages reported ongoing vigilance, anticipation of rejection, and concern about whether to conceal their relationships in certain settings (Rostosky et al., 2016). Although same-gender couples with legal recognition report less psychological distress, better well-being (Riggle et al., 2010), less vigilance, and fewer feelings of isolation (Rostosky et al., 2016) than those in less committed relationships, uncertainty regarding the permanence of that legal recognition may counteract the psychological benefits associated with it (Riggle et al., 2010). Thus, legal recognition in and of itself does not protect couples from minority stress or its adverse influences (Rostosky et al., 2016; Todosijevic et al., 2005) but may improve the social climate that same-gender couples must navigate (Ogolsky et al., 2019). Despite increasing social acceptance and political support of same-gender partnering, ongoing fear of rejection and aggression may have a lasting influence in how same-gender couples navigate social stress in their relationships, albeit lower in intensity overtime as support increases. Perhaps like individuals in interracial relationships, heterosexism will become a recognizable stressor for partners that has little felt impact over the next few decades.

Technological Advancements and Online Dating

Advances in technology such as online dating and social media mean that individuals have unprecedented access to the personal information of potential partners. Prior to the Internet, strangers meeting for the first time were restricted by a limited impression formed after an initial meeting (Finkel et al., 2012). Instead of gradually obtaining information over time, individuals can now instantly learn a range of intimate details about potential partners.

Additionally, online dating services have fundamentally changed how relationships are initiated. We identified two waves of online dating services. The initial wave came into the mainstream around 1995 and involved web-based profiles (e.g., Match.com, eHarmony, etc.) that connected individuals based on similarities and differences in interests and relationship needs. For example, eHarmony provides users with a combability score based on several questions assessing relationship attitudes, communication style, and psychological and behavioral traits (eHarmony, n.d.). Initially, online dating was viewed as an act of desperation with concerns around the possibility of users being deceptive (i.e., catfishing) or predatory (see Finkel et al., 2012; Simmons & Lee, 2020). Over time, individuals expressed more acceptance of online dating despite ongoing safety concerns (Anderson et al., 2020; Rosenfeld et al., 2019; Smith & Duggan, 2013).

The second wave of online dating appeared around 2012 with geospatial apps (e.g., Grindr, Tindr, Bumble) that originally connected individuals based on algorithms, spatial proximity, and shared identities. For example, Grindr was the first geospatial app introduced in 2012 and was created to increase the ease, safety, and certainty associated with dating as a gay man (see Redina et al., 2014). Although online dating and dating apps carry a level of stigma such as only being used for hookups (Lefebvre, 2018; Monto & Carey, 2014) there are benefits that come with online dating services. Online dating services and dating apps offer access to larger pools of potential partners (Regan, 2015), the ability to communicate prior to meeting, and the ability to find partners who match based on perceived compatibility regardless of geographic location (Billedo et al., 2015).

Expanded identities along with polarizing global events have led to more specialized dating platforms that focus on both shared values and shared lived experiences. For instance, there are dating sites and apps dedicated to shared religious identity (Christian Mingle), political identity (The Right Stuff, Bernie Singles), racial identity (Black People Meet), occupation (Farmer's Only), sexual orientation (Grindr), STI status (Herpes Fish), and food allergies (Gluten Free Singles) to name a few. Though these choices can be overwhelming and complicated to sift through, such platforms can be havens for those seeking partners with specific ideals or experiences. For example, in a qualitative study of twenty dating app users in Hong Kong, Chan (2021) found that people conveyed their own political views and attempted to identify the political views of prospective partners when online dating. Individuals deduced political affiliations based on non-political information presented on dating profiles like occupation industry. People also asked strategic questions to deduce political affiliation and initiated explicit discussions around political affiliation. Suspected political affiliations signaled approval or disapproval of political beliefs and actions, which allowed respondents to identify politically likeminded partners. This study demonstrates how historic changes in technology interact with the sociopolitical environment in ways that may influence relationship initiation decisions.

EXAMINING COHORT AND HISTORIC EFFECTS IN ROMANTIC PARTNERING: CHALLENGES AND POSSIBILITIES

The challenges and possibilities that come with examining the impact on historical and other macro-social events on interpersonal relationships are not mutually exclusive. On one hand, historical events may be so distal that their theoretical and practical influence on relationships can be difficult to capture (Kelley, 1992). Yet scholars must wrestle with identifying the theoretical and practical significance of understanding how historical context shapes experiences within romantic relationships. Doing so may help direct scholars to questions that advance knowledge. One way to address this issue is by having scholars examine contemporary consequences of historical events within a modern, and relevant, context. Simply acknowledging the historical context of modern social phenomena may be a fruitful opportunity for understanding historical and cohort effects on romantic relationships (e.g., Awosan & Hardy, 2017; Rice, in press). Other examples may include examining how the legal prohibition of interracial relationships created a social landscape of fear that continues to influence how couples present themselves and interact with one another; how the women's rights movement shifted the expectations people have of romantic relationships; and contemporary legislation around abortion and trans rights may shift the social, and eventually interpersonal, landscape around what individuals value in romantic partners and seek from their relationships. Given that social issues have become so closely intertwined with political issues, assessing a partner's stance and response to highly debated topics (e.g., abortion rights) may be of critical importance for younger cohorts that are increasingly socially conscious. Notably, our discussion of historical context and romantic relationships primarily focused on relationship initiation and maintenance. We encourage future theorizing around how historical context may influence relationship dissolution across the lifespan.

REFERENCES

Afifi, T. D., Davis, S., Merrill, A. F., Coveleski, S., Denes, A., & Shahnazi, A. F. (2018). Couples' communication about financial uncertainty following the great recession and its association with stress, mental health and divorce proneness. *Journal of Family and Economic Issues*, 39(2), 205–219. https://doi.org/10.1007/s10834-017-9560-5

American Psychiatric Association. (1980). *Diagnostic and statistical manual of mental disorders* (3rd ed.). APA.

Anderson, M., Vogels, E., & Turner, E. (2020). *The virtues and downsides of online dating*. Pew Research Center: Internet, Science & Tech. https://policycommons.net/artifacts/616387/the-virtues-and-downsides-of-online-dating/1597009/

Awosan, C. I., & Hardy, K. V. (2017). Coupling processes and experiences of never married heterosexual Black men and women: A phenomenological study. *Journal of Marital and Family Therapy*, 43(3), 463–481. https://doi.org/10.1111/jmft.12215

Bayne, H. B., Impellizzeri, J., Michel, R. E., Dietlin, O., & van Doorn, K. A. (2020). Impact of the 2016 US presidential election on politically divided relationships. *Counseling and Values*, 65(2), 137–154. https://doi.org/10.1002/cvj.12134

Bengston, V. L., & Allen, K. R. (1993). The life course perspective applied to families over time. In P. Boss, W. Doherty, R. LaRossa, W. Schumm, & S. Steinmetz (Ed.), *Sourcebook of family theories and methods: A contextual approach* (pp. 469–504). Springer. https://doi.org/10.1007/978-0-387-85764-0_19

Berry, J. W., & Kalin, R. (1995). Multicultural and ethnic attitudes in Canada: An overview of the 1991 National Survey. *Canadian Journal of Behavioural Science, 27*(3), 301–320. https://doi.org/10.1037/0008-400X.27.3.30

Berscheid, E. (1999). The greening of relationship science. *American Psychologist, 54*(4), 260. https://doi/10.1037/0003-066X.54.4.260

Billedo, C. J., Kerkhof, P., & Finkenauer, C. (2015). The use of social networking sites for relationship maintenance in long-distance and geographically close romantic relationships. *Cyberpsychology, Behavior, and Social Networking, 18*(3), 152–157. https://doi.org/10.1089/cyber.2014.0469

Blair, K. L., Mckenna, O., & Holmberg, D. (2022). On guard: Public versus private affection-sharing experiences in same-sex, gender-diverse, and mixed-sex relationships. *Journal of Social and Personal Relationships, 39*(9), 2914–2938. https://doi.org/10.1177/02654075221090678

Bronfenbrenner, U. (1986). Ecology of the family as a context for human development: Research perspectives. *Developmental Psychology, 22*(6), 723–742. https://doi.org/10.1037/0012-1649.22.6.723

Brooks, J. E., & Lynch, J. (2019). Partnering across race. In R. N. Roy & A. Rollins (Eds.), *Biracial families: Crossing boundaries, blending cultures, and challenging racial ideologies* (pp. 61–79). Springer.

Brooks, J. E., Bass, J. E., & Boakye, S. (2021a). Maybe, maybe not: Racial discourse and worldview in interracial relationships. *Couple and Family Psychology: Research and Practice.* Advance online publication. http://doi.org/10.1037/cfp0000200

Brooks, J. E., Ly, L. M., & Brady, S. E. (2021b). Race talk: How racial worldview impacts discussions in interracial relationships. *Journal of Social and Personal Relationships, 38*(7), 2249–2267. https://doi.org/10.1177/02654075211011530

Bühler, J. L., & Nikitin, J. (2020). Sociohistorical context and adult social development: New directions for 21st century research. *American Psychologist, 75*(4), 457–469. https://psycnet.apa.org/doi/10.1037/amp0000611

Byrd, M. M., & Garwick, A. W. (2006). Family identity: Black-white interracial family health experience. *Journal of Family Nursing, 12*(1), 22–37. https://doi.org/10.1177/1074840705285213

Chan, L. S. (2021). Looking for politically like-minded partners: Self-presentation and partner-vetting strategies on dating apps. *Personal Relationships, 28*(3), 703–720. https://doi.org/10.1111/pere.12375

Cherlin, A. J. (2004). The deinstitutionalization of American marriage. *Journal of Marriage and Family, 66*(4), 848–861. https://doi.org/10.1111/j.0022-2445.2004.00058.x

Coontz, S. (2004). The world historical transformation of marriage. *Journal of Marriage and Family, 66*(4), 974–979. https://doi.org/10.1111/j.0022-2445.2004.00067.x

Coontz, S. (2015). Revolution in intimate life and relationships. *Journal of Family Theory & Review, 7*(1), 5–12. https://doi.org/10.1111/jftr.12061

Coontz, S. (2016). *The way we never were: American families and the nostalgia trap.* Basic Books.

Cowdery, R. S., Scarborough, N., Knudson-Martin, C., Seshadri, G., Lewis, M. E., & Mahoney, A. R. (2009). Gendered power in cultural contexts: Part II. Middle class African American heterosexual couples with young children. *Family Process, 48*(1), 25–39. https://doi.org/10.1111/j.1545-5300.2009.01265.x

Crenshaw, K. (1991). Race, gender, and sexual harassment. *Southern California Law Review, 65*, 1467–1476.

Defense of Marriage Act. (1996, September 21). *H.R.3396 - 104th Congress.* www.congress.gov/bill/104th-congress/house-bill/3396

de Guzman, N. S., & Nishina, A. (2017). 50 years of loving: Interracial romantic relationships and recommendations for future research. *Journal of Family Theory & Review, 9*(4), 557–571. https://doi.org/10.1111/jftr.12215

eHarmony.com. (n.d.). *The eHarmony compatibility score: Make your matches count.* Retrieved from www.eharmony.com/tour/what-is-compatibility-system/

Elder Jr, G. H. (1994). Time, human agency, and social change: Perspectives on the life course. *Social Psychology Quarterly, 57*(1), 4–15. https://doi.org/10.2307/2786971

Elder, G. H., & George, L. K. (2016). Age, cohorts, and the life course. In Shanahan, M., Mortimer, J., Kirkpatrick Johnson, M. (Eds.), *Handbook of the life course. Handbooks of sociology and social research* (pp. 59–86). Springer. https://doi.org/10.1007/978-3-319-20880-0_3

Evans-Campbell, T. (2008). Historical trauma in American Indian/Native Alaska communities: A multilevel framework for exploring impacts on individuals, families, and communities. *Journal of Interpersonal Violence, 23*(3), 316–338. https://doi.org/10.1177/0886260507312290

Few-Demo, A. L. (2014). Intersectionality as the "new" critical approach in feminist family studies: Evolving racial/ethnic feminisms and critical race theories. *Journal of Family Theory & Review, 6*(2), 169–183. https://doi.org/10.1111/jftr.12039

Finkel, E. J., Eastwick, P. W., Karney, B. R., Reis, H. T., & Sprecher, S. (2012). Online dating: A critical analysis from the perspective of psychological science. *Psychological Science in the Public Interest, 13*(1), 3–66. https://doi.org/10.1177/1529100612436522

Finkel, E. J., Hui, C. M., Carswell, K. L., & Larson, G. M. (2014). The suffocation of marriage: Climbing Mount Maslow without enough oxygen. *Psychological Inquiry, 25*(1), 1–41. https://doi.org/10.1080/1047840X.2014.863723

Gallup (2021, February 24). *LGBT identification rises to 5.6% in latest US estimate.* https://news.gallup.com/poll/329708/lgbt-identification-rises-latest-estimate.aspx

Gee, G. C., Walsemann, K. M., & Brondolo, E. (2012). A life course perspective on how racism may be related to health inequities. *American Journal of Public Health, 102*(5), 967–974. https://doi.org/10.2105/AJPH.2012.300666

Gone, J. P. (2013). Redressing First Nations historical trauma: Theorizing mechanisms for indigenous culture as mental health treatment. *Transcultural Psychiatry, 50*(5), 683–706. https://doi.org/10.1177/1363461513487669

Harris, T. M., & Kalbfleisch, P. J. (2000). Interracial dating: The implications of race for initiating a romantic relationship. *Howard Journal of Communication, 11*(1), 49–64. https://doi.org/10.1080/106461700246715

Hibbler, D. K., & Shinew, K. J. (2002). Interracial couples' experience of leisure: A social network approach. *Journal of Leisure Research, 34*(2), 135–156. https://doi.org/10.1080/00222216.2002.11949966

Hocker, L., Kline, K., Totenhagen, C. J., & Randall, A. K. (2021). Hold my hand: Associations between minority stress, commitment, and PDA for same-gender couples. *Journal of Social and Personal Relationships, 38*(9), 2742–2750. https://doi.org/10.1177/02654075211020501

Jenkins, A. I. C., Fredman, S. J., Le, Y., Sun, X., Brick, T. R., Skinner, O. D., & McHale, S. M. (2020). Prospective associations between depressive symptoms and marital satisfaction in Black couples. *Journal of Family Psychology, 34*(1), 12–23. https://doi.org/10.1037/fam0000573

Kelley, R. D. G. (1992). Notes on deconstructing "the folk." *The American Historical Review, 97*(5), 1400–1408. https://doi.org/10.2307/2165942

Killian, K. D. (2002). Dominant and marginalized discourses in interracial couples' narratives: Implications for family therapists. *Family Process, 41*(4), 603–618. https://doi.org/10.1111/j.1545-5300.2002.00603.x

LaRossa, R., & Reitzes, D. C. (2009). Symbolic interactionism and family studies. In P. Boss, W. J. Doherty, R. LaRossa, W. R. Schumm, & S. K. Steinmetz (Eds.), *Sourcebook of family theories and methods* (pp. 135–166). Springer. http://dx.doi.org/10.1007/978-0-387-85764-0_6

Lauer, S., & Yodanis, C. (2010). The deinstitutionalization of marriage revisited: A new institutional approach to marriage. *Journal of Family Theory & Review, 2*(1), 58–72. https://doi.org/10.1111/j.1756-2589.2010.00039.x

LeFebvre, L. E. (2018). Swiping me off my feet: Explicating relationship initiation on Tinder. *Journal of Social and Personal Relationships, 35*(9), 1205–1229. https://doi.org/10.1177/0265407517706419

Martin, P. A. (1979). Marriage and marital therapy: Psychoanalytic, behavioral and systems theory perspectives. *American Journal of Psychiatry, 136*(5), 745–745. https://doi.org/10.1176/ajp.136.5.745

McNeil Smith, S., Williamson, L. D., Branch, H., & Fincham, F. D. (2020). Racial discrimination, racism-specific support, and self-reported health among African American couples. *Journal of Social and Personal Relationships, 37*(3), 779–799. https://doi.org/10.1177/0265407519878519

McNulty J. K. (2016). Highlighting the contextual nature of interpersonal relationships. In Olson J. M. & Zanna M. P. (Eds.), *Advances in experimental social psychology* (Vol. 54, pp. 247–315). Academic Press.

Monk, J. K., & Ogolsky, B. G. (2019). Contextual relational uncertainty model: Understanding ambiguity in a changing sociopolitical context of marriage. *Journal of Family Theory & Review, 11*(2), 243–261. https://doi.org/10.1111/jftr.12325

Monto, M. A., & Carey, A. G. (2014). A new standard of sexual behavior? Are claims associated with the "hookup culture" supported by General Social Survey data? *The Journal of Sex Research, 51*(6), 605–615. https://doi.org/10.1080/00224499.2014.906031

Murty, K. S., & Roebuck, J. B. (2015). African American HBCU students' attitudes and actions toward interracial dating & marriage: A survey analysis. *Race, Gender & Class, 22*(3–4), 136–153. www.jstor.org/stable/26505353

Ogolsky, B. G., Monk, J. K., Rice, T. M., & Oswald, R. F. (2019). Personal well-being across the transition to marriage equality: A longitudinal analysis. *Journal of Family Psychology, 33*(4), 422. https://doi.org/10.1037/fam0000504

Oswald, R. F., & Kuvalanka, K. A. (2008). Same-sex couples: Legal complexities. *Journal of Family Issues, 29*(8), 1051–1066. https://doi.org/10.1177/0192513X08316274

Pew Research Center. (2016, December 15). *Americans name the 10 most significant historic events of their lifetimes.* www.pewresearch.org/politics/2016/12/15/americans-name-the-10-most-significant-historic-events-of-their-lifetimes/

Pietromonaco, P. R., & Perry-Jenkins, M. (2014). Marriage in whose America? What the suffocation model misses. *Psychological Inquiry, 25*(1), 108–113. https://doi.org/10.1080/1047840X.2014.876909

Regan, P. C. (2015). Attraction in close relationships. *Oxford Bibliographies Online: Psychology.* https://doi.org/10.1093/obo/9780199828340-0158

Redina, H. J., Jimenez, R. H., Grov, C., Ventuneac, A., & Parsons, J. T. (2014). Patterns of lifetime and recent HIV testing among men who have sex with men in New York City who use Grindr. *AIDS and Behavior, 18*(1), 41–49. https://doi.org/10.1007/s10461-013-0573-2

Rice, T. M. (in press). Echoes of slavery: Reflections on contemporary racial discrimination in Black Americans' romantic relationships. *Journal of Social and Personal Relationships.*

Riggle, E. D. B., Drabble, L. A., Bochicchio, L. A., Wootton, A. R., Veldhuis, C. B., Munroe, C., & Hughes, T. L. (2021). Experiences of the COVID-19 pandemic among African American, Latinx, and White sexual minority women: A descriptive phenomenological study. *Psychology of Sexual Orientation and Gender Diversity, 8*(2), 145–158. https://doi.org/10.1037/sgd0000510

Riggle, E. D. B., Rostosky, S. S., & Horne, S. G. (2010). Psychological distress, well-being, and legal recognition in same-sex couple relationships. *Journal of Family Psychology, 24*(1), 82–86. https://doi.org/10.1037/a0017942

Rosenfeld, M. J., Thomas, R. J., & Hausen, S. (2019). Disintermediating your friends: How online dating in the United States displaces other ways of meeting. *Proceedings of the National Academy of Sciences, 116*(36), 17753–17758. https://doi.org/10.1073/pnas.1908630116

Rostosky, S. S., Riggle, E. D., Rothblum, E. D., & Balsam, K. F. (2016). Same-sex couples' decisions and experiences of marriage in the context of minority stress: Interviews from a population-based longitudinal study. *Journal of Homosexuality, 63*(8), 1019–1040. https://doi.org/10.1080/00918369.2016.1191232

Simmons, M., & Lee, J.S. (2020). Catfishing: A look into online dating and impersonation. In Meiselwitz, G. (Ed.), *Social computing and social media. Design, ethics, user behavior, and social network analysis* (pp. 335–348). Springer. https://doi.org/10.1007/978-3-030-49570-1_24

Smith, A., & Duggan, M. (2013). *Online dating and relationships.* Pew Research Center: Internet, Science & Tech. www.pewresearch.org/internet/2013/10/21/online-dating-relationships/

Stamps, D. L., Mandell, L., & Lucas, R. (2021). Relational maintenance, collectivism, and coping strategies among Black populations during COVID-19. *Journal of Social and Personal Relationships, 38*(8), 2376–2396. https://doi.org/10.1177/02654075211025093

Stryker, S. (2008). From Mead to a structural symbolic interactionism and beyond. *Annual Review of Sociology, 34*(1), 15–31. https://doi.org/10.1146/annurev.soc.34.040507.134649

Todosijevic, J., Rothblum, E. D., & Solomon, S. E. (2005). Relationship satisfaction, affectivity, and gay-specific stressors in same-sex couples joined in civil unions. *Psychology of Women Quarterly*, 29(2), 158–166. https://doi.org/10.1111/j.1471-6402.2005.00178.x

United States Census Bureau. (2021, August 12). *2020 Census illuminates racial and ethnic composition of the country*. www.census.gov/library/stories/2021/08/improved-race-ethnicity-measures-reveal-united-states-population-much-more-multiracial.html

Zink, T., Regan, S., Jacobson Jr, C. J., & Pabst, S. (2003). Cohort, period, and aging effects: A qualitative study of older women's reasons for remaining in abusive relationships. *Violence Against Women*, 9(12), 1429–1441. https://doi.org/10.1177/1077801203259231

9

The Legal Meaning of Sex (and Romantic Relationships)

ROBIN FRETWELL WILSON, SO YOUNG PARK,
AND REBECCA VALEK

Legal changes in the regulation of sexuality and domestic relationships have contributed to public perceptions that partnerships accompanying the act of sex are a wholly private matter. In the era of no-fault divorce and increased privatizing of sexual relationships, scholars have recognized a shift from traditional marriage and morality in family law and "changes in the way law and society view humans and human relationships" (Schneider, 1985, p. 1803). The United States Supreme Court echoed this sentiment when striking down Texas' homosexual sodomy laws in *Lawrence v. Texas* (2003), when it held that the "right to liberty under the Due Process Clause gives...the full right to engage in [private, consensual sexual] conduct without intervention of government" (p. 560). "Liberty," the Court said, "protects the person from unwarranted government intrusions into a dwelling or other private places. In our tradition the State is not omnipresent in the home" (*Lawrence v. Texas*, 2003, p. 562).

And yet, lasting regulations and court opinions regarding marriage and marital dissolution suggest otherwise. In reality, the act of sex is the defining consideration separating relationships that carry duties and receive legal recognition and those that do not. Sex matters inside marriages to the dissolution of relations and annulment of marriages (Goldfarb, 2016). It matters to the creation of parent-child relationships even where the adult seeking rights is neither the biological nor the legal adoptive parent (Wilson, 2019). It matters to whether the state will protect the expectations partners have for each other and the investments made during the relationship (Hunter, 2012).

This chapter looks deeper into various laws and regulations that demonstrate the lasting significance of having sex across marriage, cohabitation, and parent-child relations.

LEGAL IMPLICATIONS OF SEXUAL BEHAVIOR AND INFIDELITY IN DISSOLUTION

Now an option in every state, no-fault divorce allows the dissolution of a marriage without any showing of wrongdoing (Nicolas, 2011). The Uniform Marriage and Divorce Act (UMDA) of 1970 provided the template by "provid[ing] unambiguously that both allocation of marital property and determinations of spousal maintenance [are to] be made 'without regard to marital misconduct'" (American Law Institute, 2002). Public opinion has moved with this trend. A survey conducted among Americans waiting for jury duty in Arizona found that the majority (65.3 percent) reported allocation of assets should be equal after a divorce, even in cases of adultery (Braver & Ellman, 2013). Despite this shift, sexual relations remain a condition of marriage, impacting marriage and marriage dissolution in a number of ways.

Having Sex Remains a Condition of Marriage

At the core of heterosexual marriage is the notion that it serves the primary purpose of procreation (Tuskey, 2006). Although this sounds dated to the modern ear, Chief Justice Roberts in *Obergefell v. Hodges* (2015), the Supreme Court's landmark decision recognizing same-sex marriage, stated that marriage, in the eyes of the state, "encourages men and women to conduct sexual relations within marriage rather than without" (pp. 689–690).

State laws engrave the centrality of sex in marriage into their code. For example, section 944.15 of the Wisconsin Statute (1973) explicitly states: "Although the state does not regulate the private sexual activity of consenting adults, the state does not condone or encourage any form of sexual conduct outside the institution of marriage."

The inability to have sex permits one to file a divorce in many states. Under the Illinois Marriage and Dissolution of Marriage Act (2015), a marriage can be declared invalid if "a party lacks the physical capacity to consummate the marriage by sexual intercourse and at the time the marriage was solemnized the other party did not know of the incapacity[.]"

In a similar vein, the failure to make oneself available for the act of sex is grounds for a fault-based divorce. It constitutes constructive abandonment, meaning that the married couple continues to live together while seeking a divorce. To constructively abandon the other, the at fault party must rupture the entire relationship – no talking to each other, no eating together, no vacationing together, and, crucially, no sex (*Lyons v. Lyons*, 1992). In *Lyons v. Lyons* (1992), the New York Supreme Court held that constructive abandonment may be granted when a spouse "repeatedly and unsuccessfully request[s] a resumption of sexual relations" for at least a year (p. 416).

A scaffold of laws reflects the view that marriage channels sexuality. From the Comstock Act and state Comstock laws banning contraceptive use among married couples, the last of which was struck in 1965 in *Griswold v. Connecticut* (1965), to sodomy and fornication laws, sex and the regulation of sex have long mattered to family law (Bailey et al., 2012; Feinberg, 2012). The court's decision in *Lawrence v. Texas* (2003) was widely seen as a shift from this traditional significance of sex, ruling that states cannot regulate private sexual relationships "absent injury to a person or abuse of an institution the law protects" (p. 6). And yet many of these adultery and fornication laws still operate today. Fornication laws banning sex outside of marriage have shrunk in number from twenty-nine states at the high-water mark to three states in 2022 (Connor, 2009; Sweeny, 2019). Adultery laws prohibiting married couples from having sexual relations outside of marriage remain good law in seventeen states (Sweeny, 2019).

To be sure, enforcement of such laws is rare but not nonexistent. In New York, one of the states with remaining adultery laws, thirteen people have been charged with this crime, only five of whom were convicted (McNiff, 2010). The thirteenth case occurred in 2010 when Suzanne Corona and Justin Amend were reported to the police for having sex in a public park in New York. Both were charged with public lewdness for this public act of fornication, and Suzanne, a married woman, received an additional charge of adultery (McNiff, 2010). This charge was only possible due to a third-party witness to the act because adultery charges cannot be made based on the testimony of either married individual. The charge was likely influenced by the public nature of the sexual infidelity (McNiff, 2010).

Although enforcement of adultery as a crime is rare, laws around adultery are more commonly enforced in divorce proceedings and alimony decisions. A weaker earning spouse's adultery is a complete bar to alimony, without regard to any other facts of the case, in a number of states like Georgia, North Carolina, and South Carolina (American Law Institute, 2002).

Six states allow alienation of affections lawsuits, which act as a back door to fault. These suits, brought upon a third party by a spouse, require the spouse to prove that their marriage had been loving and "the malicious acts of the defendant produced the loss of that love and affection" (*Pharr v. Beck*, 2001, p. 271). Proof of a loving marriage is often "documented by photographs, cards, notes, and the testimony of friends and family," while defendants in these cases attempt to show damage to the marriage prior to their affair, such as lack of a sexual relationship between the married couple (Poyner Spruill LLP, n.d.).

In *Ammarell v. France* (2018), Megan France filed a motion to dismiss the alienation of affections suit brought against her for having an affair with a married man. Ms. France's motion to dismiss was based on claims that North Carolina's "heartbalm" statutes are unconstitutional, citing *Lawrence v. Texas* (2003) as protecting her "right to private intimate conduct … with Mr.

Ammarell" (*Ammarell v. France*, 2018, p. 3). North Carolina's District Court rejected this motion, holding that "the tort claims for alienation of affection and criminal conversation pass constitutional muster" (p. 1). In this case, the liberty interests extended in *Lawrence* do not apply because the sexual relationship in question both caused "injury to a person ... [and] abuse[d] an institution which the law protects: marriage" (*Ammarell v. France*, 2018, p. 4). Because the affair violated the "fundamental right to exclusive sexual intercourse between spouses," the court held that "[t]he fundamental place held by the institution of marriage justifies the protection afforded here" (*Ammarell v. France*, 2018, p. 5).

Having sex is such a significant act that resuming sexual relations will have the effect of wiping clear the other spouse's past fault. It counts as proof of condonation. Thus, when a spouse who has been cheated on, physically abused, or otherwise "faulted" against agrees to sex, it forgives the misconduct of the offending spouse. In *Littlefield v. Littlefield* (1972), the Superior Court of Waldo County held that "the parties' engaging in acts of sexual intercourse while the divorce action was pending was not condonation per se but raised a rebuttable presumption that such actions represented forgiveness and mutual intention for restoration of all marital rights" (p. 204).

No-Fault Divorce in Sexual Violence Cases

States have walked back to no-fault divorce, recognizing that emptying fault out entirely allows deeply immoral results. Consider the case of Crystal Harris, who was raped by her husband, Shawn Harris, and was ordered to pay her husband alimony upon divorce because she earned considerably more money than he did (Chang & Litoff, 2012; *People v. Harris*, 2012). The court essentially forced her to become a debtor to her rapist, prolonging contact with him. Ms. Harris's experience prompted her to take action to reform the law in her state so that other female victims who are the breadwinners of their households do not have to pay their aggressors alimony into the future. After Ms. Harris shared her story with Assemblywoman Toni Atkins, the California Assembly amended §4324.5 of California's Family Code so that, in addition to considerations of whether a spouse "attempt[ed] to murder the other spouse or of soliciting the murder of the other spouse," a judge may take a conviction "of a specified violent sexual felony against the other spouse ... in ordering spousal support" (A.B. 1522, 2012 Cal. Legis. Serv. Ch. 718 (Cal. 2012); see also Hackbarth, 2013). When it comes to spousal support, in order to achieve the most equitable result courts need to reintroduce fault back into the equation when it comes to sexual felonies.

California is not alone; other states have passed similar laws by requiring judges to consider 'marital misconduct' when awarding spousal support (Wilson, 2009). New York's common law also considers a broad range of misconduct, notwithstanding its no-fault scheme, when the fault is of an extraordinary nature (*McCann v. McCann*, 1993). This is judicially determined, and courts have found it in cases of rape, kidnapping, and extensive physical abuse (*Howard S. v Lillian S.*, 2009; *McCann v. McCann*, 1993).

For example, in the famous case where Aftab Islam beat his wife Theresa brutally with a barbell, requiring her to have hundreds of thousands of dollars of reconstructive surgery, the defendant contended that "a spouse's egregious conduct should not be considered as a factor in equitable distribution" under no-fault divorce laws (*Havell v. Islam*, 2002, p. 343). At the time of the attack, Ms. Havell was the family's sole earner. As this case shows, at times, it is the wealthier spouse who is wronged but still has a lot to lose upon dissolution (Wilson, 2009). Here, the courts sided with Ms. Havell, awarding her over 95 percent of the marital estate. The court applied precedent from *Blickstein v. Blickstein* (1984), which allowed for consideration of fault when "the marital misconduct is so egregious or uncivilized as to bespeak of a blatant disregard of the marital relationship…compelling [the court] to invoke its equitable power to do justice between the parties" (p. 292).

Whereas domestic violence has provided just cause to wipe an abuser out financially, adultery poses a much thornier set of questions. If the law sanctioned adultery as harshly as it did Mr. Islam's domestic violence – wiping out adulterers financially – this could create incentives for the offending spouse to continue in the marriage to avoid the potential penalty of fault divorce. At some point, the penalty could become so high that people feel compelled to remain in a failing marriage lest they become insolvent. Fault in this instance could still be considered not as a mechanism for financially wiping out the adulterer but as grounds for departure from the presumptive division of marital property that would have occurred in the absence of adultery – for example, in a typical long-term marriage, grounds for departing from a 50/50 split. This disincentive to adultery would not trample on anyone's sexual liberty. The spouse who defies monogamy can always obtain a divorce on a no-fault basis before taking on new sexual partners, thereby avoiding the financial penalty entirely.

HAVING SEX CREATES DUTIES BETWEEN ADULTS

Whether social perceptions around the act of sex led to legal change or followed it has been a perennial debate in family law. Legislation has shifted with changing norms to be more inclusive of couples who live together and conduct their relationship outside of marriage, which we refer to in this chapter as cohabitation. Such legislative shifts create new rights and obligations between two people (i.e., inter se) and against third parties. In determining who has standing and who gets tagged with duties in cases involving intimate relationships, the act of sex still plays a significant role. Quite simply, those having sex can go after another for possible remedies and recourse against each other. Those without sex cannot.

Beyond Conjugality Cases

There is extensive literature and a growing number of cases that recognize the ability of non-marital couples at dissolution to recover from one another. Courts have recognized breach of contract claims as long as the contract did not "explicitly rest upon the immoral and illicit consideration of meretricious sexual services" (see seminal case, *Marvin v. Marvin*, 1976, p. 669). Courts have recognized claims in equity based on the doctrine of unjust enrichment (see *Marvin v. Marvin II*). States like Washington have created a status remedy for those even in a meretricious relationship. In *Connell v. Francisco* (1995), the Supreme Court of Washington defined a meretricious relationship as "a stable, marital-like relationship where both parties cohabit with knowledge that a lawful marriage between them does not exist" (p. 346) and awarded the cohabited petitioner the right to share in property acquired during the relationship. In 2021, the Uniform Law Commission adopted the Uniform Cohabitants Economic Remedies Act to standardize the economic rights of cohabitants and ensure consistency across states (Uniform Law Commission, 2021).

Cohabitation between two people is defined by the courts as "a relationship between two persons ... who reside together in the manner of husband and wife, mutually assuming those rights and duties usually attendant upon the marriage relationship" (American Jurisprudence Proof of Facts, 1989). Many states include sexual relations in these "rights and duties" as they do in a marital relationship. For example, the Supreme Court of Delaware held that cohabitation "has a common and accepted meaning as an arrangement existing when two persons live together in a sexual relationship when not legally married" (*Gertrude L.Q. v Stephen P.Q.*, 1983, p. 1217). Some courts have expanded this definition to include both sexual and financial aspects, defining cohabitation as "an arrangement that is ostensible, in which the man and woman engage in sexual relations with each other, and where they enjoy a measure of financial benefit from the relationship" (*Quisenberry v. Quisenberry*, 1982, p. 276). The Iowa Supreme Court went so far as to outline six factors to determine cohabitation, the first of which is "sexual relations...while sharing the same living quarters" (*State v. Kellogg*, 1996, p. 517).

It is important to note that, although the act of sex "may be a persuasive indicium of cohabitation, it is not everything" (*Taylor v. Taylor*, 1983, p. 478). In most jurisdictions, the entire content of the cohabiting relationship has to be more than just having sex. Couples must "function as would a husband and wife, either sexually or otherwise" to constitute cohabitation (*Fuller v. Fuller*, 1988, p. 1169). Many courts have emphasized the importance of shared finances over sexual relations. One court suggested that the factors that mark cohabitation – namely, "the normally accepted attributes of a marriage – a common residence which each party regards as his or her home, a common household to which each contributes, and a personal relationship that is more than casual and has significant meaning to each" – can be "measured...by living arrangements, by shared assets and expenses, and by how the parties and the community view their relationship" (*Fisher v. Fisher*, 1988, p. 1169).

Still, it is highly unlikely that couples will establish this sort of intimate and financial relationship akin to marriage in the absence of a sexual relationship. Ultimately, the act of sex serves as a sorting function to differentiate between cohabitating couples and mere roommates for whom there is nearly no legal responsibility to the other and no recognition from the state. Familial relationships are no exception. In the case of *Burden v. The United Kingdom* (2008), two sisters who lived together for thirty-one years took issue with the fact that, in the case of one of their deaths, the surviving sister "would be required to pay inheritance tax on the dead sister's share of the family home, whereas the survivor of a married couple or a homosexual relationship registered under the Civil Partnership Act 2004 would be exempt from paying inheritance tax" (pp. 2–3). In essence, they were upset because they were being treated differently simply because they did not have a sexual relationship. The Grand Chamber ruled against the sisters, finding that it does not violate Article 14 for States (protection against discrimination) to treat marriage and civil partnerships differently than relationships based on consanguinity or other cohabiting relationships (*Burden v. The United Kingdom*, 2008).

Upon learning of this case, Baroness Deech, sought to extend civil partnerships to include caretakers and cohabitees, such as these sisters. Baroness Deech argued that those who have "chosen to live together [such as these sisters] would expect a hand of equality to be offered to them" (House of Lords Debate, 2013, c.6108, para. 3). Baroness Barker took an opposing stance, saying that Baroness Deech's proposal "equates two fundamentally different sorts of relationship: those entered into freely and voluntarily as adults, and consanguine, family relationships. Those two types of relationship[s] have always been treated differently in law, for very good reason ... You have relationships with people in that family which are wholly different, and your obligations to those people are wholly different, from those in the families which you create" (House of Lords Debate, 2013, c.1611, para. 2).

Unlike inter se cases where rights and obligations between two people are at issue, third-party cases, especially against the state, are more complicated. States basically use sexual behavior to distinguish fraudulent claims from real ones in cases implicating health insurance and social benefits. This is to prevent the issue of "moral hazard" in which protected parties undermine the effectiveness of an intervention already in place, or governmental costs outweigh the benefits it intended to provide. Individuals with insurance are prone to put themselves more at risk or frequently visiting hospitals than is needed. Similarly, one's marital and fertility behavior may be affected by welfare and the level of benefits one could receive as a single parent or a married dependent (Moffitt, 1998).

The distinction of using sexual behavior to screen for cohabitation was also raised in Canada's Beyond Conjugality report (The Law Commission of Canada, 2001). In particular, the report opens debate regarding the government registration scheme in the province of Nova Scotia, which limits registration to "two individuals who are cohabiting in a conjugal relationship" (p. 119) and restricts familial or blood relationships such as adult siblings. In a post on the comments board, "thirty-six-year-old twin sisters who have never been married or had children and who live together" lamented being denied access to government tax benefits awarded to married and cohabiting couples (p. 119). These sisters raised the question about the importance of sexual behavior to governmental schemes and family law: "Should the possibility of sexual relations between two co-habitating[sic] adults…really be the yardstick by which the government, the law, and the corporation measure a citizen's entitlement to social and economic rights?" (The Law Commission of Canada, 2001, p. 119).

But many scholars would answer yes: sexual relations, or at least romantic relations, are fundamentally different from any other type of relationship. People are especially vulnerable in cohabitating relationships compared to platonic roommate relationships because "the role of intimacy involved in romantic relationships is typically deeper and more pervasive" (Kansky, 2018, p. 2). Attachment theory, traditionally applied to the child-parent relationship, can explain the increased vulnerability present in a romantic relationship. Scholars theorize that "adults may develop analogous attachment patterns to romantic partners" (*Marvin v. Marvin*, 1976, p. 684). The legal distinction between cohabitants and roommates is responding to the vulnerability and interdependency that sex and romance create in relationships.

Parent-Child Relations

The cost of having sex is greater when the person you are having sex with is a parent. Family structures in the United States have morphed since a decade ago, raising numerous questions about the nature of parentage: What features make the adult-child relationship worthy of respect and obligations under the law? Should the live-in partner of a child's adoptive or biological parent (together, "legal parent") be able to force visitation or shared custody over the legal parent's objection after the adults break up? How long should the adult have been in a child's life for the state to respect that tie when the legal parent objects? (Wilson, 2019).

Sexual Relationship and Relational Parentage

Notions of a child having two heterosexual parents to whom they are biologically related are no longer the exclusive basis of modern-day court decisions concerning parent-child relationships (Shanley, 2001). Approximately

3 million cohabiting-partner households include children in the household who are the offspring of only one partner (U.S. Census Bureau, 2021a). Other households are "mixed," containing children who are the biological or adoptive children of both parents, as well as children who are the legal child of only one of the adults (U.S. Census Bureau, 2021b). A great number of children live with only one legal parent, usually the child's mother. As a result of these many different household types, children often come into contact with adults who are transient in the legal parent's life. Twenty-nine percent of children in the United States "experience two or more mother partnerships (either marriage or cohabitation)" by the time they turn fifteen (Deal, 2021).

With seismic shifts in how families comprise themselves, courts have been presented with questions of first impression. "Who counted as one's family" was predicted by biology for mothers, biology in the case of men married to birth mothers via a nearly irrebuttable marital presumption, and adoption. Now, legal parentage has lost its value as a sole determining factor in court's determinations concerning parent-child relationships. States have used a cluster of doctrines to decide when to award rights of association, care, decision-making, and even full custody for a child to relational parents, doctrines undergirded by very different intuitions. Some rest on the nature of the bond, recognizing relationships the preservation of which will be in the child's best interests (American Law Institute, 2002); some rely on the concept of psychological parent (*McAllister v. McAllister*, 2010); and others stress the harm that will follow from disrupting the bond that has developed between the claimant and the child, often captured in the idea of "irreparable harm" to the children (*Kulstad v. Maniaci*, 2009). These claims to be legally determined the child's parent – or to receive rights in the child like those given to parents – can be grouped under the heading of "relational parentage."

There can be a number of different fact patterns giving rise to an individual claiming to continue contact with the child. However, to have standing in these types of cases, one has to have had a sexual relationship, or at least a romantic relationship, with the parent.

The United States Supreme Court has not established clear or comprehensive guidelines for states' conferral of initial legal-parent status (Meyer, 2016). However, courts, legislators, and others have used four doctrinal "hooks" – psychological parenthood, In Loco Parentis, Parent by Estoppel, and de facto parenthood – to permit an adult to press a claim for legal status as a relational parent (Meyer, 2013).

Psychological parenthood test varies by jurisdiction, but it generally requires a day-in-day-out job of parenting, which is unlikely to be fulfilled unless the parent lives with the child. In *In re Clifford K.* (2005), the West Virginia Appellate Court defines a psychological parent as "a person who, on a continuing day-to-day basis, through interaction, companionship, interplay, and mutuality, fulfills a child's psychological and physical needs for a parent and provides for the child's emotional and financial support" (p. 157). In addition, the relationship "must have begun with the consent and encouragement of the child's legal parent or guardian" (p. 157). The same rationale applied in a case involving a same-sex couple when the Supreme Court of New Jersey granted visitation rights to a former partner of the legal mother (*V.C. v. M.J.B.*, 2000). Other than kinship, the only time these claims will happen between two legal strangers is when the two have had sex and opened up to each other. *In Loco Parentis* gives standing to an adult who literally has stood in the place of a parent. It requires the assumption of parental status and the fulfilment of parental duties (*TB v. LRM*, 2001). *Parent by Estoppel* prevents a person from evading an obligation or asserting a right that contradicts what they previously said or agreed to by law. It also requires the interested party's reliance. For example, in *L.S.K. v. H.A.N.* (2002), when a same-sex partner filed a complaint for custody against her former partner, the children's biological mother, she was estopped from denying child support in a subsequent suit filed against her by the children's mother.

The *de facto parenthood test*, which the Uniform Parentage Act ("UPA") and thirty-one states have adopted in some version, acknowledges an individual's rights of the child as long as the parents cohabited and had a codependent relationship in the caretaking of the child. In *In Re Parentage of L.B.* (2005), when a woman brought an action against the biological mother of a minor, seeking to establish her co-parentage, who was conceived by artificial insemination during the woman's twelve-year intimate domestic relationship with the mother, she was granted the right for visitation. The case was initially dismissed due to her lack of standing as a psychological parent. However, the Court of Appeals later established her de facto parent status based on the parent-like relationship she had prior to separation. Similarly, in *Rubano v. DiCenzo* (1988), when the Supreme Court of Rhode Island was presented with the question of whether an agreement between the parents allowing the nonbiological parent to have visitation with the child after separation was enforceable, the Court answered in the affirmative recognizing the nonbiological parent as a de facto parent (i.e., holding a "parent-like relationship" with the child).

Legally inserting oneself into a parent-child relationship as a live-in partner is easier than one may assume. The three-part "de facto parent" test proposed by the ALI in the *Principles* is indicative of the low bar. The test requires residency, caretaking, and an agreement of equal share in caretaking, which can be implied (American Law Institute, 2002). With the belief that conforming to the lived experience of children is critically important to children's welfare (American Law Institute, 2002), the ALI's test substantially enlarged parental rights to live-in partners who share equal caretaking duties for a child for as little as two years (Wilson, 2010). This not only diminished the right and encroached on parenting decisions of the legal parent who are mothers, in most cases, but also constrained the ability of mothers to decide who has access to their children – with some potentially devastating repercussions for at least some of the children involved (Wilson, 2008). The costs of considering the parentage claims of relational parents – both to the legal parent and to the child – have received inadequate weight to date.

Some of these decisions are controversial in that outcome creates a parent-child relationship against a would-be-presumed parent's will (Harvard Law Review, 2006). Being wary of such negative outcomes, not every court has sided with the claimant. For example, in *Janice M. v. Margaret K.* (2008), a partner of a legal parent prayed for the visitation rights of her child after ending eighteen years of her romantic relationship. Maryland Court of Appeals refused to recognize "de facto parenthood" despite the fact that she jointly took care of the child for more than four years. The court was reluctant to regard her parenting role as an exceptional circumstance overriding the legal parent's liberty interest in deciding custody and care of the child. This decision was in line with legislative and court decisions to protect parents' desires to control children's upbringing without the oversight by any state agency. This holding is also consistent with the Maine Supreme Court's holding in *Pitts v. Moore* (2014), stating that "forcing a parent to expend time and resources defending against a third-party claim to a child is itself an infringement on the fundamental right to parent …." The only time you can really get tied for child support is if you were cohabiting with your partner when a child was born.

Even so, only the people who had sex with the child's parent will meet the criteria to assert a parentage claim. No other relationship will have the same standing as a live-in partner in these cases. A recent ruling granting "tri-custody" for one child shows a good example. In 2018, the Suffolk County Supreme Court granted tri-custody to a Long Island couple and a neighbor with whom they had a threesome for eighteen months (Marsh, 2017). Before conception, the three had an agreement that all would raise the child together: they went to the doctor's appointments together, fed the baby taking turns, and the son knew the two women as his mothers. New Jersey also had a similar case involving a gay male couple and a straight woman where the court recognized the partner of the biological father as a "psychological parent" (*D.G. & S.H. v. K.S.*, 2016). As a parent, sexual behavior incurs costs, and the legal effect is not insignificant to potentially impact romantic relationship decisions for single parents.

Rights without Obligations?

Although a person can demand physical custody of a child or stay in the relationship until the child emancipates by inserting themselves into a parent-child relationship that already existed, they can also get tagged for parental duties. Quite simply, because of the sexual relationship they had with their partner, they can be made to pay for a child that is not theirs. Relational parentage, in that sense, has both protective and exacting qualities. Just like legal parentage, whoever has rights has responsibilities. For example, in *Elisa B v. Superior Court* (2005), when two mothers dissolved their relationship during which they artificially inseminated and gave birth to a child, both were legally obligated to the child. Emily B., Elisa's ex-partner, who discontinued financial support, had to resume payment under the common law principle, de facto parentage. The fact that Emily consented to and participated in the insemination, causing the child's birth, held the child as her own, and co-parented the child for a substantial period of time all corroborated the decision-making. Courts preclude one from ejecting themselves from a potential risk of becoming a parent as they form a romantic and sexual relationship with another.

On the other hand, with similar facts, in *T.F. vs. B.L.* (2004), where a mother sought child support from her ex-partner who agreed to co-parent the child conceived by artificial insemination while they were together, the Massachusetts Supreme Court denied the request holding that enforcing an implied agreement to co-parent is against public policy and parenthood by contract is not in their law. However, had the petitioner argued the establishment of parentage based on her ex-partner's conduct and relationship with the child during their cohabitation rather than an operation of contract, the outcome may have been different (Walters Kluwer, 2007). Although courts may resolve the question of parentage based on the claimant's arguments and hold a different ruling because two people may never agree to co-parent absent the act of sex, sex still remains at the center of these claims. People who have to defend themselves from these types of parentage claims are typically those who had sex and opened themselves up to a parent-child situation.

To some, this may raise concern because it will cause an outcome where parenthood would "devolve upon an unwilling candidate" similar to the effect of a rebuttable presumption of paternity statute (*In re Nicholas*, 2002, p. 941).

Even with the same idea that those having sex can seek legal remedies and recourse and those who do not cannot, case outcomes have been different depending on the state and the doctrinal "hooks" they apply in rulings. Legislation and courts have dealt with cases concerning parental rights and parental duty differently, and the court's irregular response to the question of whether to impose duties of support on relational parents, especially using the *de facto parent* test, has long perplexed lawmakers.

With good intentions to protect children's sense of stability, the American Law Institute's proposal and the new UPA place relational parents in parity with legal parents regarding physical custody rights. However, the standard operates as a one-way street – it can be asserted by those seeking rights but not by those seeking continued support for a child. Section 3.03 of the ALI's proposal restricts responsibility to legal parents and those who have, in exceptional circumstances, willingly agreed to assume full parental responsibilities (American Law Institute, 2002) and leaves it to those deciding legal parentage to determine who should shoulder the responsibilities of parenthood. (Baker, 2006). Baker (2006) critiques the deep incoherency in *de facto parentage*, calling it "asymmetrical parenthood." She analyzes the *Principles'* child support provisions teasing out "precisely the kind of scenario in which someone is likely to have custody or visitation rights as de facto parent under [the ALI's custody proposal], but not have financial responsibility for a child under [its child support proposals] ...

> Fred, a widowed father of two, cohabited with Allen for five years before separating. During their cohabitation Fred and Allen shared their earnings and the children benefited from the increased household income. Assume also that Fred and Allen shared caretaking responsibilities with Allen doing as much as Fred. Allen would have custodial rights as a de facto parent but, absent affirmative conduct indicating ... an agreement to assume a parental support obligation and even then only in exception circumstances, Allen would not be responsible for any child support. (p. 133)

In an attempt to avoid punishing people for having sex, the ALI proposal gives rights without obligations to live-in partners (Wilson, 2010). Regardless of the incoherency in court decisions concerning parental obligation suits, sexual behavior is still the factor that distinguishes people who can be made responsible versus people who cannot. Absent the act of sex, two adults and a child who forms a close relationship with both seem just as emotionally and financially interdependent as a relationship involving a cohabitating sexual partner. And yet, only the people who had sex with the child's parent will need to make their presence in court to defend themselves from parental obligation suits filed by the legal parent. No roommates, nannies, or even sisters would be lumped together in the same category as ex-partners with whom the parent had a sexual relationship. To clear inconsistencies, Fineman (2004) suggests care rather than sex as a nexus for legally recognizing relationships. She argues that the system should ensure a caretaking arrangement for children at the end of any interdependent relationship that may or may not involve having sex, and questions the significance of sex as an indicator of commitment or intimacy in modern family law. Whether or not the current system requires reorientation, court decisions concerning parent-child relationship reflect the role that sexual behavior plays in distinguishing adult relationships and determining legal questions of rights and responsibilities.

CONCLUSION

Sexual behavior in romantic relationships continues to have legal impact in family law. Sex is what separates relationships that carry duties and those that do not. Having sex with another adult can create the circumstances for paying support after the break up, whether married or not. Being sexually involved with another individual can create duties to share acquired wealth, whether married or not. An intimate relationship with a child's parent opens the possibility of parent-like rights and even responsibilities toward that child – claims that would almost certainly never arise in the absence of sexual behavior with the parent. Whatever stance one takes on whether the act of sex *should matter* in the dissolution of relationships, it still does across much of America.

REFERENCES

A.B. 1522, 2012 Cal. Legis. Serv. Ch. 718 (Cal. 2012).

American Jurispurdence Proof of Facts 3d 765 (1989).

American Law Institute. (2002). *Principles of the law of family dissolution: Analysis and recommendations.*

Ammarell v. France, No. 316CV00708RJCDSC, 2018 WL 2843441, at *1 (W.D.N.C. June 11, 2018).

Bailey, M. J., Guldi, M., Davido, A., & Buzuvis, E. (2012). *Early legal access: Laws and policies governing contraceptive access, 1960–1980* [Working paper]. University of Michigan. www-personal.umich.edu/~baileymj/ELA_laws.pdf

Baker, K. K. (2006). Asymmetric Parenthood. In R. F. Wilson (Ed.), *Reconceiving the family: Critique on the American Law Institute's Principles of the law of family dissolution* (pp. 121–141). Cambridge University Press. https://doi.org/10.1017/CBO9780511617706.008

Blickstein v. Blickstein, 99 A.D.2d 287 (1984).

Braver, S. L., & Ellman, R. M. (2013). Citizen's views about fault in property division. *Family Law Quarterly, 47*(3), 419–435. https://doi.org/10.2139/ssrn.2328982.

Burden v. The United Kingdom, App. No. 13378/05, Eur. Ct. H.R. (Grand Chamber, 29 Apr. 2008). www.legislationline.org/download/id/7073/file/ECHR_Case_Burden_v_UK_2008_en.pdf

Chang, J. & Litoff, A. (2012, April 4). Sexual Assault Victim Ordered to Pay Alimony to Attacker Fights to Change California Law. *ABC News*. https://abcnews.go.com/US/sexual-assault-victim-ordered-pay-alimony-attacker-fights/story?id=16075409

Connell v. Francisco, 898 P.2d 831 (1995).

Connor, A. (2009). Is your bedroom a private place? Fornication and fundamental rights. *New Mexico Law Review, 39*(3), 507–526. https://digitalrepository.unm.edu/nmlr/vol39/iss3/4

Deal, R. L. (2021). *Marriage, family, & stepfamily statistics*. Smart Stepfamilies. www.smartstepfamilies.com/view/statistics.

D.G. & S. H. v. K.S., 2016 WL 482622 (N.J. Super. Ct., Ocean County, Aug. 24, 2015, approved for publication, Feb. 5, 2016).

Elisa B. v. Superior Court, 117 P.3d 660 (Cal. 2005).

Feinberg, J. (2012). Exposing the traditional marriage agenda. *Northwestern Journal of Law & Social Policy, 7*(2), 301–351. http://scholarlycommons.law.northwestern.edu/njlsp/vol7/iss2/3

Fineman, M. A. (2004). *The autonomy myth: A theory of dependency*. The New Press.

Fisher v. Fisher, 540 A.2d 1165 (1988).

Fuller v. Fuller, 461 N.E.2d 1348 (1983).

Gertrude L.Q. v. Stephen P.Q., 466 A.2d 1213 (Del. 1983).

Goldfarb, S. F. (2016). Divorcing marriage from sex: Radically rethinking the role of sex in marriage law in the United States. *Oñati Socio-Legal Series, 6*(6), 1276–1302. https://ssrn.com/abstract=2890997

Griswold v. Connecticut, 381 U.S. 479 (1965).

Hackbarth, K. (2013). Chapter 718: Financial protection for victims of sexually violent felonies by a spouse. *McGeorge Law Review, 44*(3), 655–660.

Harvard Law Review. (2006). Family law same-sex couple's parental rights and obligations California supreme court holds child support provisions of its uniform parentage act applicable to same-sex couples Elisa b. v. Superior court. *Harvard Law Review, 119*(5), 1614–1621.

Havell v. Islam, 301 A.D.2d 339 (2002).

House of Lords Debate. (2013, July 29). c1608. www.theyworkforyou.com/lords/?id=2013-07-29a.1546.6&s=deech+speaker%3A13524#g1608.1

House of Lords Debate. (2013, July 29). c1611. www.theyworkforyou.com/lords/?id=2013-07-29a.1546.6&s=deech+AND+Burden#g1611.0

Howard S. v Lillian S., 876 N.Y.S.2d 351 (2009).

Hunter, L. P. (2012). *Know your rights: The legal guarantees you are- and aren't - entitled to as part of a cohabitating couple*. Essence. https://facultywork.wlulaw.wlu.edu/wp-content/uploads/sites/16/2012/10/robin-wilson-in-essence-magazine1.pdf

In re Clifford K., 619 SE 2d 138 (W.Va. App. 2005).

In re Nicholas., 46 P.3d 932 (Cal. 2002).

In Re Parentage of LB, 122 P.3d 161 (Wash. 2005).

Janice M v. Margaret K., 948 A.2d 73 (2008).

Kansky, J. (2018). What's love got to do with it?: Romantic relationships and well-being. In E. Diener, S. Oishi, & L. Tay (Eds.), *Handbook of well-being* (pp. 1–24). DEF Publishers. www.nobascholar.com/chapters/10/download.pdf

Kulstad v. Maniaci, 220 P.3d 595 (Mo nt. 2009).

Lawrence v. Texas. 539 US 558 (2003).

Littlefield v. Littlefield, 292 A.2d 204 (Me. 1972).

L.S.K. v. H.A.N., 813 A.2d 872 (Pa.Super. 2002).

Lyons v. Lyons, 187 A.D.2d 415 (1992).

Marsh, J. (2017, March 10). Historic ruling grants 'tri-custody' to trio who had threesome. *New York Post*. https://nypost.com/2017/03/10/historic-ruling-grants-custody-to-dad-and-mom-and-mom/

Marvin v. Marvin, 18 Cal. 3d 660 (1976).

Marvin v. Marvin II, 122 Cal.App.3d 871 (1981).

McAllister v. McAllister, 779 N.W.2d 652 (N.D. 2010).

McCann v. McCann, 593 N.Y.S.2d 917 (1993).

McNiff, E. (2010). Woman charged with adultery to challenge New York law. *ABC News*. https://abcnews.go.com/TheLaw/woman-charged-adultery-challenge-york-law/story?id=10857437

Meyer, D. D. (2013). Family diversity and the rights of parenthood. In Linda C. McClain & Daniel Cere (Eds.), *What is parenthood: Contemporary debates about the family* (pp. 124–146). New York University Press.

Meyer, D. D. (2016). The constitutionality of 'best interests' parentage. *William & Mary Bill of Rights Journal, 14*(3), 857–881.

Moffitt, R. A. (1998). The effect of welfare on marriage and fertility. In Robert A. Moffitt (Ed.), *Welfare, the family, and reproductive behavior: Research perspectives*. National Academics Press.

Nicolas, P. (2011). The lavender letter: Applying the law or adultery to same-sex couples and same-sex conduct. *Florida Law Review*, 63(1), 97–127. https://digitalcommons.law.uw.edu/faculty-articles/291

Obergefell v. Hodges, 576 U.S. 644 (2015).

People v. Harris, No. D059126, 2012 WL 1651015 (Cal. Ct. App. May 11, 2012).

Pitts v. Moore, 90 A.3d 1169 (Me. 2014).

Pharr v. Beck, 147 N.C. App. 268 (2001).

Poyner Spruill LLP. (n.d.). *Alienation of affection & criminal conversation*. www.poynerspruill.com/for-family/family-law/alienation-of-affections-criminal-conversation/

Quisenberry v. Quisenberry, 449 A.2d 274 (Del. Fam. Ct. 1982).

Rubano v. DiCenzo, 759 A.2d 959 (1998).

Schneider, C. E. (1985). Moral discourse and the transformation of American family law. *Michigan Law Review*, 83(8), 1803–1879. www.jstor.org/stable/1288953

Shanley, M. L. (2001). *Making babies, making families: What matters most in an age of reproductive technologies, surrogacy, adoption, and same-sex and unwed parents*. Beacon Press.

State v. Kellogg, 542 N.W.2d 514 (Iowa 1996).

Sweeny, J. (2019, May 6). Adultery and fornication: Why are states rushing to get these outdated laws off the books? *Salon*. www.salon.com/2019/05/06/adulteryand-fornication-why-are-states-rushing-to-get-these-outdated-laws-off-the-books/

Taylor v. Taylor, 465 N.E.2d 476 (1983).

TB v. LRM, 786 A. 2d 913 (Pa. 2001).

T.F. v. B.L., 442 Mass. 522 (2004).

The Illinois Marriage and Dissolution of Marriage Act, 750 ILCS. 5/301(2) (2015).

The Law Commission of Canada. (December 21, 2001). *Beyond conjugality: Recognizing and supporting close personal adult relationships*. Available at SSRN: https://ssrn.com/abstract=1720747; www.againstequality.org/wp-content/uploads/2012/08/lcoc_beyond_conjugality.pdf

Tuskey, J. (2006). The elephant in the room – Contraception and the renaissance of the traditional marriage. *Regent University Law Review*, 18(2), 315–325. www.regent.edu/acad/schlaw/student_life/studentorgs/lawreview/docs/issues/v18n2/5%20Tuskey.pdf

Uniform Law Commission. The Uniform Parentage Act § 609 (2017).

U.S. Census Bureau. (2021a). Table FG6. One-Parent Unmarried Family Groups with Own Children Under 18, *America's Families and Living Arrangements: 2021*. Retrieved from www.census.gov/data/tables/2021/demo/families/cps-2021.html

U.S. Census Bureau. (2021b). Table UC3: Opposite Sex Unmarried Couples by Presence of Biological Children1 Under 18, and Age, Earnings, Education, and Race and Hispanic Origin of Both Partners, *America's Families and Living Arrangements: 2021*. Retrieved from www.census.gov/data/tables/2021/demo/families/cps-2021.html

V.C. v. M.J.B., 748 A.2d 539 (2000).

Wilson, R. F. (2008). The harmonisation of family law in the United States. In Boele-Woelki, K. & Sverdrup, T. (Eds.), *European challenges in contemporary family law* (pp. 27–52). Intersentia: Antwerp. Available at SSRN: https://ssrn.com/abstract=1031149

Wilson, R. F. (2009). Beyond the bounds of decency: Why fault continues to matter to (some) wronged spouses. *Washington and Lee Law Review*, 66(1), 503–514. https://scholarlycommons.law.wlu.edu/wlulr/vol66/iss1/12

Wilson, R. F. (2010). Trusting mothers: A critique of the American Law Institute's treatment of de facto parents. *Hofstra Law Review, 34*, 1103–1190.

Wilson, R. F. (2019). Relational parents: When adults receive rights in children because of their relationship with a parent. In J. G. Dwyer (Ed.), *The Oxford handbook of children and the law* (pp. 476–502). Oxford University Press.

Wisconsin Statute § 944.15 (1973).

Walters Kluwer. (2007). *Casenote Legal Briefs: Contracts*. Aspen Publishers.

10

Romantic Relationships and Traditional Media

JESSE FOX AND JESSICA R. FRAMPTON

Many have contemplated the role media play in romantic relationships, from poets and lovesick teens to therapists and divorce lawyers. In this chapter, we will explore scholarship on traditional media, whereas the next chapter explores digital media (McEwan & Lefebvre, this volume). Although separating "old media" and "new media" helps break this massive topic into manageable chapters, we advise reading these chapters together regardless of your research interests. As we will soon explain, this division can be counterproductive.

In this chapter, we will first establish our scope of traditional media and provide a framework for studying all media. Our literature review will begin by delving into the use of traditional media to seek partners and initiate romantic relationships. Then, we will consider how people use media to communicate within and about their romantic relationships. Next, we will consider how media consumption and media content can affect our relational beliefs, attitudes, and behaviors. Finally, we will consider how people can experience romantic relationships *with* media. In each section, we will synthesize topical research, introduce relevant theories, highlight key elements of media, and consider how media have shaped our scholarly understanding of romantic relationships.

MEDIA: A (RE)INTRODUCTION

In the twentieth century, media such as newspapers, radio, telephone, and television became embedded in the fabric of our daily lives. Yet, a skim of contemporary journal articles and academic books on romantic relationships reveals a dearth of research focused on the role of media. Most romantic relationships under study, however, have qualified as *mixed media relationships*, transpiring through and affected by multiple channels (Parks, 2017). Given the growing pervasiveness of media in modern life, it is essential for relationship researchers to consider why media are important and how they can best be studied.

For the purposes of this chapter, we use the term *traditional media* to refer to channels that require material means for communication and precede the Internet age. This conceptualization excludes face-to-face and computer-mediated communication, yet includes media that have more recently shifted to digital transmission (e.g., television, telephone calls). Specifically, we consider written or text-based messages (e.g., letters, cards, notes); literature and recorded folklore (e.g., poetry, novels, mythological/religious texts, comic books, graphic novels, manga); newspapers, magazines, and other print media; radio (broadcast as well as shortwave, citizens' band [CB], and amateur radio); audio-based exchanges (e.g., telephone calls, party lines, answering machines, voicemail, recordings); transmitted messages (e.g., telegraph, telegrams, teletype, facsimile); music recordings and artwork; television, film, and videos; and other methods (e.g., billboards, graffiti, bumper stickers). These channels entail interpersonal, group, mass (one-to-many), and masspersonal (interpersonal or group that is visible to many) communication.

Categorizing "old" and "new" media is relative, however; not too long ago, these designations separated letters from the telegraph, or newspapers from television. Although an emergent medium may seem novel, chances are it is far more similar than dissimilar to existing media. Instead of focusing on a particular medium, device, platform, or app, it is critical to determine what properties of media are significant.

An affordance-based approach is a useful lens for understanding why media are important and how they are distinct. *Affordances* are the inherent attributes of an object that emerge when a user interacts with it (Gibson, 1979). The affordances that enable or shape human interactions are known as *social affordances* (Fox & McEwan, 2017) and are critical for understanding how media function in relationship contexts.

Several affordances are presented and defined in Table 10.1 with examples of how they have been discussed or studied in relevant literature. Importantly, individual perceptions of affordances vary, and context is a critical factor in shaping perceptions (Fox & McEwan, 2017). Let's consider Sheila and Johnny, a dating couple. Sheila may perceive a phone call private when she's at home, but not at work. Johnny may also consider a phone call at home private, except when his eavesdropping roommate is around. Each partner's perception of privacy is likely to shape what they feel comfortable saying and how intimate the conversation will become, which in turn could influence relationship development and satisfaction in one or both partners. As this example illustrates, affordances allow people to understand why a particular channel may be selected and how it may affect romantic interactions and relationships.

TABLE 10.1 Key media affordances and applications to romantic relationship contexts

Affordance	Definition	Application
Accessibility	Ability to use a channel regardless of time, place, structural limitations, or other constraints	Many people could not afford to send telegrams when geographically separated (Standage, 1998)
Social presence	Feelings of togetherness and sharing the same experience with another person	Media create social presence in long-distance couples (Stafford, 2004)
Physical co-presence	Two parties are co-located in the same space	Couples talk while watching television together (Alberts et al., 2005)
Visibility/privacy	The extent to which communication can be observed by others	Communication between prisoners and their spouses is monitored and may be censored (Black, 2010)
Anonymity/identifiability	How easily a communicator can be recognized or tied to their real name or identity	CB radio operators use handles that convey relationship status or interest (Dannefer & Kasen, 1981)
Bandwidth	Number of cues that can be transmitted through a channel, contingent on modality	Video dating provides richer information than photographs or written profiles (Woll, 1986)
Synchronicity	Timing of message exchange	A marriage made by telegraph was deemed legal as vows were exchanged in real time (Marvin, 1988)
Editability	The capacity to change or revise a message	Letters can be revised before sending (Janning, 2018)
Personalization/addressivity	Tailoring a message to an individual recipient	Sentiments on mass-produced greeting cards can feel impersonal (West, 2004)
Conversational control	Managing the mechanics of an interaction (e.g., turn taking, starting or ending a dialogue)	Military spouses can initiate letters but not phone calls to their deployed mates (Carter & Renshaw, 2016)
Persistence/ephemerality	Duration of a message	Love letters are valued because they can be kept and revisited by the recipient (Janning, 2018)
Tangibility	Having a physical materiality that can be touched and manipulated	Photographs of couples are often displayed for visitors in the home (Lohmann et al., 2003)
Recordability/replicability	How easily a message can be copied or duplicated	Meaningful songs can be copied to create a mixtape for a romantic partner – and the mix duplicated for a new partner (Drew, 2016)
Scalability	How easily a message can be shared with a wider audience	Matchmaking radio shows help singles broadcast their availability to a large pool (Griffen-Foley, 2020)

MEDIATED RELATIONSHIP INITIATION: MATE SEEKING AND FINDING

Research on the communicative power and effects of media grew rapidly in the mid-twentieth century (e.g., Lazarsfeld, 1940). The predominant theoretical paradigm suggested that media were monolithic and unidirectional, and people were passive consumers. The uses and gratifications approach reframed people as active consumers who select media for specific reasons, such as information seeking, entertainment, and social purposes (Katz et al., 1973). It emphasized that researchers should examine not only what needs drive media use, but also whether media succeed in gratifying those needs.

Although romantic relationship research rarely employs the uses and gratifications framework, it often works from the same assumption that people make deliberate choices about media use and develop strategies to gratify their needs (e.g., Woll & Cozby, 1987). As Adelman and Ahuvia (1991) noted, relationship initiation "is shaped, in part, by the ways the channel facilitates the searching for, matching with, and interacting with a potential partner" (p. 274). Face-to-face, people may encounter or actively seek out mates when socializing in informal group settings (e.g., a bar, playing volleyball), events (e.g., dinner parties), or organizations (e.g., work, religious community). Alternatively, they may seek out designated social spaces designed for relationship goals (e.g., a speed dating event, singles meetup, or swingers club). Mediated opportunities for relationship initiation are similar, but offer distinct affordances. Here, we consider mate seeking and relationship initiation in four contexts: mediated socializing, personal advertising, media-based matchmaking services, and broadcast matchmaking programs.

Mediated Socializing

Compared to the extensive research on finding romance in online social settings such as chatrooms and social networking sites (see McEwan & Lefebvre, this volume), research on socializing via traditional media is limited. One possible explanation is that fewer traditional media afford group settings that allow people to encounter new potential mates.

One channel that meets this criterion is citizens' band (CB) radio, which offered everyday consumers an easily accessible masspersonal channel and mobile social connectivity before the internet and mobile phones. Arguably, CB radio is the closest ancestor to online chatrooms: people adopt a pseudonymous handle and join live, ephemeral, limited bandwidth conversations with faceless strangers whenever they wish. Romantic or sexual communication is not uncommon; some CB users even signal their relationship status or interest through handles such as Playmate, Two-Timer, and Super Stud (Dannefer & Kasen, 1981). A content analysis found that 43 percent of exchanges between men and women were sexual. Heterosexual flirtation was common, but women were also frequently subject to unsolicited date requests and sexual invitations (Dannefer & Kasen, 1981). Similar affordances may explain why findings on CB use portend later findings on online interactions.

Mediated socializing can also occur at work. In some jobs, coworkers who have never met face-to-face are in constant communication, and workplace romances have taken root. Intimate long-distance relationships developed among telegraph operators despite the limited bandwidth of tapped messages (Standage, 1998). Similarly, romantic relationships have been sparked through the constant exchanges between police officers and dispatchers over the radio.

Although designated social spaces in traditional media are rare, one notable example has been described as "adult chat," "fantasy lines," "telesex," or "dial-a-porn," which peaked in the 1990s before the internet (Hall, 1995). Many of these fee-driven telephone services advertised as private, anonymous ways to meet and chat with attractive, sexually interested women, although studies revealed these services were often deceptive (Borna et al., 1993). The women were not available singles, but paid operators. Some male patrons, however, perceived ongoing interactions with the same operator as a developing relationship (Hall, 1995). These telesex operators presaged the "cam girls" and online sex workers (e.g., Onlyfans) of today.

Personal Advertising

Perhaps the most common use of mass and masspersonal media is to advertise one's availability for a relationship. Newspapers and magazines have hosted classified advertisements with romantic goals (e.g., personals, "lonely hearts" ads, matrimonial ads) for centuries. Personal ads typically feature brief, text-based descriptions of the seeker and whom they are seeking; the low bandwidth also provides more anonymity than other channels. Several content analyses of personal ads have been conducted across several countries, examining expressed and desired characteristics (e.g., Andersen, 1958; de Sousa Campos et al., 2002), gender role expectations (Ramasubramanian & Jain, 2009), and cultural values (Zhou et al., 1997).

On singles voicemail services, users record a message describing themselves, listen to others' recorded ads, and demonstrate interest by leaving a voicemail reply (Woll & Cozby, 1987). Whereas these systems afford relative anonymity and privacy, television advertising offers a tradeoff: seekers willing to publicly broadcast their lack of success can access a larger, more diverse pool of possible mates. In China, the show *Television Red Bride* (1988) gave men (and later women) who had been unsuccessful in finding a mate locally the opportunity to advertise themselves to a broader audience (Wang, 2017). US cable company Comcast offered *Dating on Demand* wherein singles were invited to record video advertisements that were then broadcast to the metropolitan area market. One study selected three videos from this service and created an audio version and a transcript to test whether bandwidth affected viewers' attributions about the featured women. Men's perceptions that women wanted to have fun, reduce uncertainty, or develop a friendship did not differ across modalities; however, they were more likely to perceive that women wanted sex in the video and audio conditions than in the transcript condition (Henningsen et al., 2011).

Although there is limited research, it is worth noting that some individuals choose to advertise via less conventional channels, such as bumper stickers (Woll & Cozby, 1987). Romantic and sexual graffiti was found in the ruins of Pompeii (79 CE), and in the modern era, several intrepid scholars have studied its prevalence in bathroom stalls. *Latrinalia* advertisements may include self-descriptions with phone numbers or invitations with instructions (e.g., "tap your foot for..."; Matthews et al., 2012). Their success rate remains unknown.

Media-Based Matchmaking Services

A third method of identifying a romantic partner through media is via matchmaking services. Mail-based introductory services (e.g., pen pal clubs for singles) require seekers to generate a self-description or complete a questionnaire that the service uses to identify potential partners (Wallace, 1959). Some services facilitate *correspondence marriage* or *transnational marriage migration*, introducing people from different countries with complementary needs (Constable, 2003). Although many couples report positive experiences (Constable, 2003), some services disempower and commodify women. As the paying customers, men are given the power to choose among options and initiate relationships (e.g., "mail order bride" catalogs), control the channel and nature of communication during long-distance relationship development, and even govern the terms of migration and marriage (Wang & Chang, 2002).

In the 1970s, a matchmaking service offering higher bandwidth emerged: video dating. Modern scholars may be surprised to learn how similar the video dating process is to online dating (and, perhaps, that video dating still exists). First, participants provide photographs and complete a survey to generate a profile. Then, they record a video, usually an interview five to ten minutes in length. The higher bandwidth of video allows daters to observe a candidate's dynamic nonverbal expressiveness (e.g., smiling, eye contact), which Riggio and Woll (1984) identified as a predictor of videodaters' popularity. Videodaters report taking time to craft and revise their profiles and videos (Woll & Young, 1989). This process, enabled by the affordances of asynchronicity and editability, was later conceptualized as *selective self-presentation* in the online context and theorized as part of the hyperpersonal model (Walther, 1992).

Participants have identified several advantages of video dating. First, it increases accessibility and provides a much larger pool than daters have access to face-to-face (Woll & Young, 1989). Second, the amount and richness of information enables videodaters to prescreen candidates and evaluate them on a deeper level before wasting time on a date (Woll & Young, 1989). Finally, video makes it more difficult to conceal or misrepresent characteristics such as age, weight, or attractiveness, so it is perceived as a more authentic portrayal (Woll & Cozby, 1987). Studies indicate that video daters do not necessarily benefit from these advantages, however; in fact, they may backfire. Woll (1986) identified drawbacks to an abundance of choice, which many video daters found overwhelming. Although photographs are deliberately situated on the back of profiles to encourage getting to know someone before evaluating their looks, many videodaters adopted the strategy of starting with photographs and appearance judgments. Generally, videodaters made decisions based on quickly discernible characteristics such as physical attractiveness, age, and occupation, which Woll (1986) attributed to cognitive overload. Woll and Cozby (1987) also argued that the amount of information provided about a candidate may be problematic because "it produces only the *illusion* of knowledge or validity rather than actual increases in accuracy" (p. 96). They also found, however, that videodaters' judgments were more accurate when they watched a candidate's video compared to just the profile or the profile and photographs.

A final advantage cited by video daters is conversational control through mutual consent: both individuals must indicate romantic interest before the service distributes contact information (Woll & Cozby, 1987). This matching procedure is akin to the gatekeeping on dating apps like Tinder and Bumble, where both partners must express interest for communication to be enabled. Regardless of these perceived advantages over other initiation methods, Woll and Cozby (1987) estimated the success rate of video dating services as 10 percent–15 percent, which they deemed "unimpressive."

Broadcast Matchmaking Programs

A final, curious intersection of romantic relationship initiation and media is broadcast matchmaking programs. These shows play an active role in the relationship initiation process by identifying, screening, testing, or selecting potential mates. One format is the *participatory dating show*, exemplified by call in radio shows. These shows are largely unscripted, and matchmaking is not only visible to, but requires active participation from, a live audience. For example, on the Australian radio show *Midnight Matchmaker* (1982), the host would interview a caller, eliciting a personal advertisement, desired partner traits, and often personal narratives; interested listeners would call in and the host would try to facilitate a match (Griffen-Foley, 2020). Other listeners called in to offer support, advice, or criticism to mate seekers.

Dating game shows first appeared on the radio, and their formats were eventually replicated on television. These shows involve singles selected by producers, feature mate competition, and vary in how scripted they are. For example, on the Australian radio show *Blind Date* (1946), two candidates competed over the phone for a date with an unseen woman; on *Boy Meets Girl* (1947), a comedian wrangled a small group of men and women hoping to find a match (Griffen-Foley, 2020). *The Dating Game* debuted on US television in 1965 and different versions popped up around the globe. The 1990s–2000s reality television boom presented an onslaught of both episodic (e.g., *Singled Out*) and serial (e.g., *The Bachelor, Temptation Island*) competitive dating shows. One study of episodic dating shows in Israel and the United States examined the categories participants chose to screen a large group of suitors in the first round of competition (e.g., relationship goals, age, lifestyle, personality). The two most common categories selected by both men and women were sexual characteristics (e.g., bedroom behavior, breast or penis size) and physical appearance (Hetsroni & Bloch, 1999).

A final type of broadcast matchmaking is the *dating setup show*, exemplified by *Blind Date, Dating Naked,* and *Married at First Sight*. Seekers apply to the show and producers match two applicants. Cameras then capture the pair's introduction and relational development, usually with intervening "confessionals" where each partner speaks to the camera independently about their feelings or reflections. The show's presentation invites viewers to judge the relationship's potential for success or failure and often the participants themselves.

It is unclear why couples would want to publicly broadcast the private and often awkward initial stages of a romantic relationship, which may explain why a handful of studies have explored motivations for participating in dating shows. Stuart (1962) studied applicants to the United States television show, *A Chance for Romance*, and found they were primarily driven by a perceived lack of options through traditional methods such as singles clubs or meeting people through work. Women also noted that there was a greater sense of safety knowing that the television show would conduct background checks. A study by Syvertsen (2001), however, found that applicants to the Norwegian TV dating show *Reisesjekken* reported seeking publicity more than love. Given the different goals and foci of broadcast matchmaking programs, more research is warranted on participant motivations and matchmaking success.

Contributions to Romantic Relationship Research

In 1987, Woll and Cozby argued that interpersonal theorizing had largely overlooked potential differences in how mate seeking and relationship initiation transpires in mediated contexts compared to face-to-face. For example, research on initial interactions has often assumed that when two people meet, it is a face-to-face interaction between strangers who know nothing about each other. The implications are that people have access to a wide range of nonverbal cues (given high bandwidth), that the initial availability of personal information is relatively equal between partners (as they are physically co-present), and there is limited opportunity to carefully craft or revise messages (as synchronicity and co-presence limit editability). Social norms that govern face-to-face interaction, such as politeness and turn-taking, are assumed. As the research reviewed here demonstrates, these assumptions do not necessarily hold across mediated contexts, yet theoretical progress at this intersection remains torpid (for a notable exception, see Tong et al., 2016).

Why people select and avoid different channels to seek mates has also enlightened our understanding of relationship initiation. For example, Woll and Cozby (1987) argued that research too often assumes that all relationship seekers have equal access to mates and thus concludes a lack of success indicates an interpersonal deficit. Research on mediated mate-seeking has drawn attention to many obstacles to relationship initiation, such as having a concealed, stigmatized identity (e.g., LGBTQ+ individuals), constraints on time (e.g., single mothers with young children), and geographical or cultural isolation (e.g., immigrants). Collectively, research on mediated mate-seeking suggests that individual and contextual factors that shape potential mate pools and initiation possibilities warrant more attention. Further, more longitudinal research is needed on dating efforts, successes, and failures over time to interpret channel choice and decision-making in the early stages of romantic relationships.

USING MEDIA TO COMMUNICATE WITHIN ROMANTIC RELATIONSHIPS

Studies have revealed the multitude of roles that media play within romantic relationships. One relevant theory for understanding these roles is *the theory of the niche*, an offshoot of the uses and gratifications framework, which argues that people consider what channels are available to them and employ different channels to meet different, specific needs (Dimmick et al., 2000). For example, a couple may choose the phone for some relationship maintenance behaviors (e.g., tasks) but rely on face-to-face for others (e.g., relationship talk). Here, we consider how and why people employ different media during relationship escalation, maintenance, disruption, and dissolution.

Developing Relationships

From papyrus to notebook paper, written messages have fostered relationship development throughout history. In some cases, such as personal advertisements and pen pals, relationships are developed through written exchanges before face-to-face-meetings. In other cases, a couple that has met face-to-face may escalate the relationship through textual communication. Cultural customs may necessitate such formalities (Su, 2016); for example, calling cards were instrumental in arranging Victorian era courtship (Bailey, 1988). Geographical separation may also force couples to rely on written exchanges (Wyss, 2008).

Relationship development through a low bandwidth, asynchronous channel presents advantages and disadvantages. Although the slow rate of exchanged letters may frustrate some, others find the pacing and conversational control appealing (Janning, 2018). Low bandwidth and physical separation may encourage more intimate disclosures, particularly if couples' face-to-face time is chaperoned or otherwise regulated (Bailey, 1988). The tangible, persistent nature of letters also enables the recipient to keep and revisit these messages as desired (Janning, 2018).

If other channels are available, however, letters are seen as less appropriate than phone or face-to-face for attempting to escalate a relationship (Westmyer et al., 1998). The dearth of cues and communicative control also makes deception easier. Newspapers in the 1800s regularly reported incidents wherein hopeful lovers were deceived and defrauded through personal ads, letters, and telegraphs (Marvin, 1988), what is now known as *catfishing* in the digital age. One notorious catfishing case is the serial killer Belle Gunness, who placed personal ads seeking a husband in the early 1900s, luring men to her farm through love letters before robbing, murdering, and dismembering them.

The telephone has also played a significant role in romantic relationship development over the past few decades. Romantic interest is often conveyed by requesting or offering a phone number, as the telephone increases accessibility. The telephone has emerged as an important medium in the development of adolescent romantic relationships as it enables regular access and more private dyadic interaction than interactions at school or with peers. Feiring (1996) reported that adolescents talked with their partners on the phone nearly every day, and that their conversations averaged an hour. Although interactions have shifted from calling to texting, the phone still affords accessibility and privacy for adolescent couples today.

Given the diminished bandwidth, synchronous conversations on the phone present some interesting challenges for partners just getting to know each other. Women in heterosexual dating relationships reported the phone was less warm and personal than face-to-face conversation, and the reduction in nonverbal cues such as facial expressions often heightened their uncertainty about their partner's feelings (Sarch, 1993). Some felt there were benefits to lower bandwidth, however, such as not having to regulate their own nonverbals and feeling emboldened to make disclosures (Sarch, 1993). In our current, media-rich interactions, studying the role of different affordances and their gratifications would clarify how couples use and experience different channels in modern developing relationships.

Maintaining Long-Distance Relationships

Many circumstances can force couples into geographical separation: relocating for college or work, military deployment, imprisonment, hospitalization, or, as many have now experienced, quarantine. Media become a vital means of sustaining long-distance and otherwise separated relationships (Dainton & Aylor, 2002). Mediated maintenance is first determined by what channels are accessible to both partners. For example, prisoners are typically restricted in what channels they can access, and phone calls can be cost-prohibitive (Black, 2010). During Desert Storm, US soldiers could call, fax, email, record videotapes, or even videoconference; yet over a decade later in Somalia, a lack of infrastructure limited communication to email (Schumm et al., 2004). Disabilities and literacies can also limit what modalities are practicable for a couple (Wyss, 2008). When channel choice is constrained, partners may have to forge new ways of communicating. For example, couples can employ idiosyncratic linguistic codes in their letters to conceal their exchanges from their guardians or censors (e.g., in prison; Black, 2010)

Consistent with Parks's (2017) conceptualization of mixed media relationships, several studies have examined the use of multiple channels by couples. Stafford and Reske (1990) found that letters were associated with more relationship satisfaction, stronger feelings of love, and increased idealization of the relationship than communicating face-to-face or by phone. The authors hypothesized that the asynchronicity and low bandwidth of letters promoted idealization. A second possibility may be related to the symbolic nature of letters, as couples may perceive them as more meaningful than other forms of communication (Janning, 2018). A third possibility may be that letters help avoid stress or negativity. Carter and Renshaw (2016) found that for service members with lower levels of family stress, more use of synchronous channels (e.g., phone) was associated with increased relationship satisfaction, but for those with higher stress, synchronous channel use was associated with decreased satisfaction. The opposite pattern was observed for asynchronous channels such as letters, which may provide stressed couples more opportunity for regulation and stress mitigation than synchronous interpersonal channels.

Managing Relationship Disruption

Romantic relationships often face disruptions such as transitions, conflict, or turbulence. When facing a difficult conversation, partners may employ mass media content as a proxy for communicating their feelings. For instance, women use music to convey sexual desire to a disinterested partner (O'Sullivan & Byers, 1993). Likewise, greeting cards help express sentiments when the sender feels awkward or stymied (West, 2004), and dissatisfied partners use relevant television content to prompt relationship talk with their partner (Fallis et al., 1985).

One noteworthy example of mass media being repurposed for interpersonal communication is the music mixtape (Drew, 2016). A mixtape is an effortful undertaking; the creator must devote hours to find the perfect songs before recording and sequencing them just so. The personalization of mixtapes is meaningful to the recipient, but also the sender as a form of self-expression (Jansen, 2009); even naming the mix or designing the playlist insert can be a symbolic gesture of devotion (Drew, 2016). Creators report giving mixtapes to initiate, escalate, maintain, repair, and terminate romantic relationships (Drew, 2016). Mixes are also used by creators and recipients to make sense of their feelings, cope with a breakup, or ruminate over lost love. A final use is that, due to their tangibility and persistence, mixtapes are treasured as relationship artifacts that evoke memories and nostalgia (Jansen, 2009).

Terminating Relationships

Paul Simon once observed, "There must be fifty ways to leave your lover." Media have provided many storied forms for relationship dissolution, from the "Dear John" letter to breaking up with the answering machine to battling an ex-spouse on the television show *Divorce Court*. Although research on media as a breakup tool is limited, one study of college undergraduates found that although face-to-face was the most frequent channel (45.5 percent), one-fifth reported breaking up by phone call (Carter et al., 2018). In dating couples, no longer returning phone calls is understood as a passive, if impolite, method of ending the relationship (Sarch, 1993). Most adults perceive the use of media to terminate a relationship as gauche, but Gershon (2010) argued this perception is contingent on the couple's *media ecology* (media use within the relationship) and individual *media ideologies*, beliefs, and attitudes about how a medium should be used.

Practicality may also govern the use of media for relationship dissolution. Long-distance couples may lack the opportunity to break up face-to-face. Couples in the early stages of dating may not want to arrange a face-to-face date solely to end the relationship; a phone call may be perceived as merciful rather than discourteous in its efficiency (Sarch, 1993). It is also worth noting that channels lacking synchronicity and physical co-presence afford greater safety. Although more direct inquiry is needed, it appears breakup initiators are likely to consider affordances when deciding how to terminate a relationship.

Contributions to Romantic Relationship Research

This body of research demonstrates three critical points. First, media are regular, and sometimes necessary, means for enacting romantic relationships.

Second, media affordances shape our dyadic interactions through these channels and, in turn, our romantic relationships. They determine what communication is possible and influence how it is perceived. Yet, many studies of romantic relationship interactions or processes adopt a media-agnostic approach, which may overlook critical factors. Consider a romantic conflict: would you expect the conflict to transpire the same face-to-face compared to texting? Would it last the same amount of time? Would partners say the same things? Would the emotional experience be the same? Would it end the same? If the answer to any of these questions is no, would you then expect the effect on the relationship to be the same?

Another question is whether the couple only argues through a particular channel, if the couple argues across all channels, or if an argument starts in one channel and carries over to another. The *communication interdependence perspective* suggests that it is important to consider how communication across both face-to-face and mediated channels transpires within a close relationship (Caughlin & Sharabi, 2013). Our final point is that in mixed media relationships, relationship functions, and processes may be occurring across multiple channels, or they may be confined to a particular channel (e.g., due to accessibility or media ideologies). Focusing on a single channel when studying a relationship phenomenon, particularly without consideration of media perceptions and attributes (e.g., affordances), greatly limits what we can generalize to our understanding of the phenomenon, the channel, or media more broadly.

USING PUBLIC CHANNELS TO COMMUNICATE ABOUT ROMANTIC RELATIONSHIPS

In addition to using media to communicate within romantic relationships, we also use media to communicate about them. Using private channels is common, whether asking friends for relationship advice on a phone call, providing status updates in holiday cards, or sending wedding invitations. We also communicate about our relationships to public audiences, such as through tie signs like matching hoodies or wedding rings (Goffman, 1971). Here, we cover a less studied area: the use of mass and masspersonal traditional media to communicate with others about our romantic relationships.

Help Seeking

Songwriter John Prine once satirized the letter writers seeking help from advice columnists: "Dear Abby, Dear Abby, my fountain pen leaks. My wife hollers at me and my kids are all freaks .... Signed, Unhappy." Advice columns offer readers the opportunity to share their problems and seek help pseudonymously (Golia, 2021). Common romantic relationship topics mentioned by advice seekers include commitment (e.g., relationship ambivalence, infidelity), communication problems (e.g., conflict, intimacy issues), beliefs (regarding culture, gender, religion, etc.), socioeconomic stressors, and aggression (e.g., domestic violence, abuse; Barnett et al., 2020).

The content of advice columns is an artifact of the era and contemporaneous cultural norms, but studies have also demonstrated differences based on venue and columnist. Thus, some findings suggest advice columns endorse traditional cultural beliefs, gender roles, and relationship myths, whereas others find evidence that they defy oppressive norms and refute marital myths (e.g., Golia, 2021). In one illustrative study, Johnson and Holmes (2019) analyzed Abigail Van Buren's (*Dear Abby*) and Ann Landers's discussion of homosexuality from 1967 to 1982, demonstrating how historical events (e.g., Stonewall, the AIDS crisis) and shifting scientific opinions were reflected in columnists' coverage, language, and advice to readers over time. Further, Van Buren consistently demonstrated greater compassion and acceptance of homosexuality than Landers (and even criticized Landers, her twin sister, in a 1973 column).

In contrast to static print media, call in radio shows provided an opportunity for an interactive conversation with a licensed therapist. One study found that the most common reason people called into *Loveline* was seeking expert advice (Borzutzky et al., 2008). Many radio advice shows, however, involve synchronous interaction not just between the caller and the therapist, but also a host, audience members, or additional guest experts, which can impede the help-seeking process.

Daytime television talk shows were a natural progression for this genre, but they also represent a critical shift in affordances. In televised *audience participation talk shows*, help seekers are no longer nameless or faceless, and they disclose their relationship problems in front of a physically present audience that offers real-time verbal and nonverbal feedback (Timberg, 2002). *The Phil Donahue Show* and *The Oprah Winfrey Show* were early pioneers in this genre, but soon tabloid talk shows emerged. *Jerry Springer Show*, *Geraldo*, *The Montel Williams Show*, *Ricki Lake*, and *Maury* were labeled "trash TV" as they ratcheted up the sensationalism, revealing marital affairs to unwitting partners and conducting paternity tests to determine "Who's the daddy?" among a woman's sexual partners (Timberg, 2002).

Marriage, dating, sexual activity, and infidelity are common themes on talk shows, but they do not always provide experts to help (Johnson et al., 1999). A content analysis revealed that when relationship experts do appear, they provide specific advice and concrete solutions to problems more than 90 percent of the time; however, these "experts" vary considerably in their qualifications, including Ph.D.s, formally trained therapists, book authors, media personalities, and matchmakers (Johnson et al., 1999). Although anecdotal evidence exists (such as lawsuits against *The Jenny Jones Show* and *Dr. Phil*), systematic research is needed to assess how helpful (or harmful) proffered advice is for mediated help-seekers and whether the media experience itself affects participants or their relationships.

Public Declarations

Public declarations about romantic relationships are best described as masspersonal communication wherein a personalized message to one's partner is deliberately conveyed in a highly visible channel to reach a large audience. For example, radio shows like *Love Songs with Delilah* allow callers to dedicate songs to express love, gratitude, or contrition to their partner or ex-partner (Griffen-Foley, 2020). A now-common trope is the *broadcast marriage proposal*, wherein one partner uses media to propose in front of a large audience, whether over a JumboTron at a sporting event or on live television. Public declarations of love may be perceived as having greater relational significance given the additional effort and risk of public humiliation.

Status Announcements

When romantic relationships undergo certain changes, mass mediated announcements may be made for celebratory, commemorative, informative, or legal reasons. For centuries, newspapers have been a source of information about others' romantic relationships through society pages, gossip columns, and community member updates, and even now it is common practice for people to announce engagements, weddings, and anniversaries in their local newspaper. These announcements also serve a normative function. *The New York Times*'s weddings section, for example, has been perceived as a cultural hallmark (e.g., Hatch & Hatch, 1947). When the *NYT* began publishing announcements of same-sex civil unions alongside heterosexual marriages in 2002, it was viewed as a milestone in the battle for marriage equality (Donovan, 2002).

Status announcements about romantic relationships may also address disengagement, however. Couples may choose to make a public announcement about a breakup or divorce through a newspaper notice, press release, or mass mailing (e.g., Lewis, 1983). When a partner dies, newspaper obituaries may represent a status announcement for the newly widowed. In some cases, however, stigmatized romantic relationships may be omitted or concealed. During the AIDS crisis, gay men's obituaries rarely explicitly identified a partner, although some mentioned a "roommate" or "friend" alongside surviving family (Williams, 1997). In this way, public announcements can be used to confirm or deny one's relationship status or romantic partner.

Contributions to Romantic Relationship Research

These examples demonstrate how people have publicized their romantic relationships and romantic struggles, but the effects of visibility on relationships remain understudied in traditional media contexts. Arguably, our romantic relationships are more visible than ever before. Studies in social media contexts have begun exploring how greater visibility affects romantic relationships, such as making the dissolution process more stressful (Fox et al., 2021), but the effects of publicity and mass audiences remains undertheorized. Notably, the affordances of masspersonal and mass media challenge theorizing about public disclosures and audiences in some relationship models. For example, Knapp's (1978) staircase model suggests that the final stage of relationship escalation is bonding through a broadly visible, public announcement about the relationship, because it assumed it was only when a couple was engaged or married that they would make an effort at mass notification. The research reviewed here suggests that publicization of the relationship can happen much earlier, perhaps before the couple is on solid ground, or can weather the attention.

A second consideration is what it means to see everyday people like ourselves in the media. People still hold reverence for mass media, and we attribute importance to those who appear in it. Seeing common people likely affects us differently than seeing celebrities, public figures, or fictional characters. We may feel more similar to these models, and thus their problems may seem more real, their experiences more relevant, and their accomplishments more attainable (Bandura, 1986). As we will discuss in the next section, there is considerable research about romantic portrayals in movies and television shows, but it is less clear if regular people's publicized romantic experiences influence beliefs, norms, attitudes, or behaviors differently.

MASS MEDIA CONSUMPTION BY ROMANTIC PARTNERS

Throughout relationship processes, mass media consumption can serve several functions. When mate seeking, media tastes can signal attractiveness or compatibility (Zillmann & Bhatia, 1989). Media co-use allows couples to spend time together and share experiences (Ledbetter, 2013). Alternatively, differences in media consumption can become a source of relational conflict and even dissolution (Bergner & Bridges, 2002).

Mass Media and Attraction

Music is an important marker of personality and romantic compatibility, especially in adolescence (North & Hargreaves, 2008). Music is strategically used to communicate information about one's identity to others (North & Hargreaves, 2008) and to judge others' personalities during initial interactions (Rentfrow & Gosling, 2006). Genre preferences and similarity in musical tastes can influence the attractiveness of a potential partner (Zillmann & Bhatia, 1989). Music is also used as a marker of relational identity (Harris et al., 2020). Having a "couple-defining song" has been associated with higher intimacy levels, likely because listening to the song elicits positive emotions and evokes memories of happy moments in the relationship (Harris et al., 2020).

Shared and Divergent Mass Media Consumption

Media co-use can serve as a shared activity or ritual within romantic relationships. Many couples listen to music, watch television, or go to the movies together. Such media-based relational maintenance is positively associated with relationship quality (Ledbetter, 2013), particularly among couples who do not share friends (Gomillon et al., 2017). Partners may use media as a basis for conversation, and shared media experiences can help partners develop shared perspectives on life (Ledbetter et al., 2010).

On the other hand, media consumption may be a direct contributor to conflict and discord (e.g., Bergner & Bridges, 2002). Excessive media consumption has been linked to increased conflict and lower relationship satisfaction in several studies (e.g., Spencer et al., 2017), as have discrepancies in media use between partners (Dew & Tulane, 2015). For example, spouses report feeling frustrated or upset when their partner pays less attention to them or outright ignores them in favor of watching television (Morgan et al., 2017).

Several studies have examined pornography use by romantic partners. People report greater dissatisfaction when a partner's use is excessive, secretive, or detracts from a couple's interaction time (Pyle & Bridges, 2012). Heterosexual women report feeling upset by their partner's pornography use because it challenged the women's beliefs about their relationship with their partner, their view of their own self-worth and desirability, and their understanding of their partners' character and morality (Bergner & Bridges, 2002). One study of married or cohabiting heterosexual couples found that men's pornography use was associated with diminished sexual quality for both men and women, but women's pornography use was associated with women's sexual quality (Poulsen et al., 2013). Joint pornography use has also been associated with increased sexual satisfaction (Willoughby & Leonhardt, 2020).

Coping and Remembering with Mass Media

Individuals may seek out certain media to manage their mood, whether they want to wallow in sadness, engage in escapism, or cheer up. As such, media can play an important role in helping people cope with relationship dissolution (Garrido & Davidson, 2019). Media also have strong associations in our relational memory. Hearing certain songs can make us feel nostalgic about poignant romantic experiences and past loves (Garrido & Davidson, 2019).

Contributions to Romantic Relationship Research

These studies demonstrate that there are several mass media uses relevant to romantic relationships. Media co-use presents an interesting case study for the debate regarding what does and does not constitute relationship maintenance. Does merely staring at the screen together benefit relationships? Disentangling affordances may offer some insight. Is physical co-presence necessary, or does sharing a mediated experience virtually suffice? A second angle may be whether the media experience is enjoyable for both partners. A pleasant shared experience may create happy memories for both parties. Otherwise, one partner may enjoy watching spaghetti westerns whereas the other may endure the tedium as a maintenance labor of love.

A second question that arises from media consumption is its role in presumed – and actual – compatibility. Media tastes are often visible on dating profiles or part of small talk between couples getting to know each other. The research here suggests people believe these tastes to be relatively reliable cues to a target's personality and the couple's compatibility, although how strong a role these attributions play in relationship initiation and development remains understudied.

MEDIA REPRESENTATIONS OF ROMANTIC RELATIONSHIPS

Mass media have depicted themes of love and romance since ancient times, such as Greek romance novels from the first through third centuries (Ricquier, 2019), marriage guides from the eighth to fourteenth centuries in China (De Pee, 2007), and religious texts such as the Bible and Quran that are still cited to authorize, proscribe, and criminalize relationships today. In modern times, researchers analyzed romantic and sexual content across books and other media including radio (Lazarsfeld, 1940), comics (Saenger, 1955), magazines (Carpenter, 1998), music (Smiler et al., 2017), television (Anderegg et al., 2014), manga (Ito, 2002), and movies (Frampton & Linvill, 2017).

Studies emerging from the uses and gratifications tradition (Katz et al., 1973) have found that people consume romantic media for purposes such as to learn about sex (Zurbriggen & Morgan, 2006) or to relieve a sense of loneliness (Greenwood & Long, 2011). Some selective exposure theories focus on affective motivations (e.g., mood management theory, Zillmann & Bryant, 1985). Generally, these theories suggest people choose media content that helps them either maintain or change to a desired mood. Scholars have explored how people might select or avoid romantic content based on their mood (e.g., Knobloch & Zillmann, 2003). For example, one study found that people who regretted cheating on their romantic partner expressed desire to watch infidelity-related storylines (Nabi et al., 2006).

Several scholars have suggested that relational schema or knowledge structures are formed in part by observing relationships, sexual encounters, and cultural romantic norms depicted in mass media (e.g., Andersen, 1993). *Prototypes* are cognitive structures that represent "the clearest cases or best examples of category" (Fehr, 1993, p. 89). *Relational* or *sexual prototypes* comprise the features a typical marriage, partner, or sexual experience should have. People may develop *relational scripts* for routine sequences of behavior such as going on a first date, escalating a relationship, or ending a relationship (Honeycutt & Sheldon, 2018). People also develop *sexual scripts* for physical intimacy (Simon & Gagnon, 1986).

Cultivation theory (Gerbner et al., 1986) and social cognitive theory (Bandura, 1986) both explain how people might learn about relationships from media. Cultivation theory suggests frequent television viewing leads people to develop beliefs and attitudes more consistent with the televised world than the real world. For example, Segrin and Nabi (2002) found that consumption of romantic TV shows was associated with idealistic beliefs about marriage, which in turn predicted marital intentions. Similarly, Vu and Lee (2013) found that Vietnamese women's consumption of South Korean soap operas was associated with their willingness to marry a South Korean man and intentions to contact a transnational matchmaking service.

Social cognitive theory (Bandura, 1986) suggests that people learn by observing others. To learn from mass media, people must first identify and pay attention to a socially attractive model performing the behavior (Bandura, 1986). Next, they retain the behavior in memory, incorporated in a knowledge structure. People must also believe they can execute the behavior (i.e., self-efficacy). Lastly, people must be motivated to perform the behavior. Motivation is determined in part by vicarious reinforcement: when models are punished for certain behaviors, there is an inhibitory effect, but if they are rewarded, there is a disinhibitory effect. These effects occur because people come to expect the same outcomes the models received if they also perform the behavior (Bandura, 1986). However, Nabi and Clark (2008) found that people may imitate the sexual behaviors they see in mass media regardless of whether models are rewarded or punished. The researchers speculated that people develop "happily-ever-after" scripts for media content that prevent them from interpreting punishments as severe or long-lasting. Thus, media effects may be further complicated by existing media schema.

Regardless of theoretical approach, studies on the representation of romantic relationships in media and their effects have been concentrated in three areas. First, a heavy focus by scholars on violent media and aggression has yielded several studies on romantic conflict and relational aggression. A second major focus has been sexual behavior, including consent, safe sex, and consequences. A final area is idealized romantic portrayals and their effects on romantic beliefs and expectations.

Conflict and Relational Aggression

Media frequently depict interpersonal conflict and *relational aggression*, defined as "using or manipulating the relationship to harm one's romantic partner" (Coyne et al., 2011, p. 57). Exposure to interpersonal conflict on television is positively related to viewers' attempts to control their romantic partner, especially if the television content is perceived as real (Aubrey et al., 2013).

One cause of conflict often depicted in media is infidelity. Some research shows that when suspicious partners are exposed to media depictions of infidelity, they exhibit a stronger intention to end the relationship if a partner is unfaithful (Alexopoulos & Taylor, 2020). However, other research demonstrated that effects of exposure to media content depicting infidelity depend in part on whether positive or negative consequences of infidelity were also portrayed (Alexopoulos & Taylor, 2021). It is possible media that depict negative consequences of infidelity activate a script for punishing unfaithful partners. Punishment of an unfaithful partner in the form of physical abuse, verbal aggression, or counter-jealousy induction is a common theme in romantic media (Frampton & Linvill, 2017). These same media depictions often show a "happily-ever-after" ending for the on-screen couple despite the destructive response to infidelity (Johnson & Holmes, 2009), making such behaviors more likely to be imitated according to social cognitive theory (Bandura, 1986).

Media also depict domestic violence beyond the context of infidelity (e.g., Joyce & Martinez, 2017). Exposure to media depictions of domestic abuse are not only positively related to acceptance and minimization of the abuse, but also perpetration of it (Rodenhizer & Edwards, 2019). The relationship between exposure to physical violence in media and physical aggression toward romantic partners may be particularly strong for men (Coyne et al., 2011). Indeed, Moss et al. (2022) found that exposure to popular television shows and music videos is associated with the acceptance of men's use of violence toward women and that this relationship is mediated by several variables such as the endorsement of sexual objectification of women.

Zillmann and Bryant (1982) similarly found that exposure to large amounts of pornography resulted in less compassion toward rape victims and toward women in general. Pornographic content frequently depicts aggressive acts such as slapping and choking, and these actions are disproportionately targeted toward women and particularly Black women (Fritz et al., 2020). Importantly, pornography rarely shows negative consequences stemming from the aggression, as targets typically respond neutrally or positively (Fritz et al., 2020).

Sex

Since the turn of the century, sexual content has proliferated and become increasingly explicit in some countries such as the United States (e.g., Kunkel et al., 2007; Smiler et al., 2017). In more restrictive countries like China, sexual media content remains less explicit (Brown et al., 2013). In some countries, sexual media content is outlawed. In Iran, this ban extends to any media featuring relationships not approved by sharia law (e.g., cohabitation or homosexuality). Numerous studies have examined sexual media content (see Coyne et al., 2019), particularly in the United States where there is notable variation in both media regulation and sexual attitudes.

Most content analyses have focused on television programming given its accessibility to a broad audience. Sex is frequently portrayed; one study reported sexual talk or behavior in 20 percent of coded episodes (Dillman Carpentier et al., 2017) and another reported two acts of sexual intercourse per episode (Eyal & Finnerty, 2009). Content analyses of television shows have identified problematic depictions such as sexual activity without explicit consent (Jozkowski et al., 2019) or sexual assault not characterized as such (Eyal & Finnerty, 2009). Although it is increasingly common to include messages of sexual responsibility (e.g., condom use), topics related to sexual risks or responsibilities remain infrequent (Dillman Carpentier et al., 2017). Problematic depictions include sexual activity without clear consent (Jozkowski et al., 2019). Several studies have examined outcomes of sex. Positive consequences are more likely to be portrayed than negative consequences (Eyal & Finnerty, 2009). When negative consequences are depicted, they are usually emotional and social consequences rather than physical consequences such as a sexually transmitted infection (Dillman Carpentier et al., 2017). Negative consequences are usually suffered by women rather than men (Aubrey, 2004) and are more common among heterosexual characters than lesbian, gay, or bisexual characters (Bond et al., 2019).

Many people learn about sex from media, especially adolescents and emerging adults (Ward et al., 2019). Exposure to sexual media content has been linked to more permissive attitudes toward sex (Dillman Carpentier & Stevens, 2018), perceptions that peers engage in frequent sex (Ward et al., 2019), and endorsement of traditional gender roles (Zurbriggen & Morgan, 2006). Exposure to sexual content has also been linked to sexual behavior (Coyne et al., 2019). There are concerns about young adults mimicking problematic or risky sexual behaviors they see in media such as unprotected sex and sex without consent (Ward et al., 2019). For example, exposure to more sexual content on television is associated with the experience of teen pregnancy (Chandra et al., 2008), indicating adolescents may be imitating the risky sexual behaviors they see on screen.

Media also help viewers learn sexual scripts and prototypes for a "good" sexual experience, which can impact their expectations for sexual activity (Ward et al., 2019). However, sexual experiences depicted in mass media are often idealized, and real-life experiences may not live up to their on-screen counterparts, sometimes leading to regret regarding the sexual encounter (Martino et al., 2009). A meta-analysis found that pornography consumption is associated with less satisfaction with sexual partners and relationships (Wright et al., 2017). One possible explanation is contrast effects: people in pornography videos often appear more attractive, sexually adventurous, and sexually competent than one's current sexual partner. Thus, relationship alternatives become more attractive to people who view a lot of pornography (Rasmussen, 2016).

Romantic Themes and Idealized Representations

Media not only portray idealized versions of sex, they also portray idealized versions of relationships and romance (Hefner & Wilson, 2013). Television and movies frequently feature mythic ideas such as everyone has a soulmate, love can happen "at first sight," love will conquer all, and true love will last forever (Hefner & Wilson, 2013; Johnson & Holmes, 2009).

Exposure to romantic ideals in media is associated with increased endorsement of those ideals (Hefner & Wilson, 2013). Young people are especially likely to endorse romantic beliefs and ideals depicted in media if they watch for learning purposes (Hefner & Wilson, 2013). Even when adolescents acknowledge that portrayals are idealized, they still consider these portrayals to be relationship goals (Len-Ríos et al., 2016). Unfortunately, it is unlikely that a romantic partner or relationship can live up to the high standards set in romantic media. Although some media representations of relationships recognize relationships face challenges, those representations often trivialize negative consequences of problems or relational transgressions (Johnson & Holmes, 2009). Yet, in reality, unmet expectations of ideal relationships can lead to lower levels of commitment and higher perceived costs of the relationship (Osborn, 2012). In some cases, however, exposure to idealistic content may lead to greater life satisfaction than more realistic content (Kretz, 2019), presumably because the content encourages viewers to idealize their own relationship.

Contributions to Romantic Relationship Research

Media effects research has demonstrated that it is not just cultural values or interpersonal sources such as family and peers that influence our romantic beliefs and relationships. Although we readily acknowledge that much of our formal education comes through media such as textbooks, we often lose sight of the educational potential of other media, particularly entertainment media. The same things that attract consumers to certain media, such as attractive stars or a desire to learn, may increase the likelihood that content will affect relationship beliefs, attitudes, and behaviors. Future research should adopt a holistic perspective and examine media among other sources of information and influence.

In the real world, relationship models are limited by what is possible: what is normative and often most influential is what we see every day. Media can provide us with more attractive or desirable versions of what we have experienced, or offer portrayals of what we have not. Moreover, media often depict a hyperreality with impossibly impeccable partners and unattainable relationship goals. These idealized representations can shape our schema and formulate expectations that can only be disappointed – unless, perhaps, we seek a relationship with a media figure.

ROMANTIC RELATIONSHIPS WITH MEDIA FIGURES

A final intersection occurs when consumers develop romantic relationships with media. According to Horton and Wohl (1956), media like television simulate interpersonal interactions. As a result, people may develop feelings for celebrities, characters, and media figures over time that can be characterized as *parasocial relationships*. Crucially, Horton and Wohl (1956) distinguished these illusory experiences from social experiences, noting they are "one-sided, nondialetical, controlled by the performer, and not susceptible of mutual development" (p. 252).

Parasocial romantic relationships (PSRRs) occur when a person perceives intimacy with a media figure or feels like they have a strong "crush" on them (Tukachinsky Forster, 2021). Romantic attraction towards a media figure that entails idealization and intense fantasies has also been described as *obsessive fandom* or *celebrity worship*. PSRRs are characterized by an affective attachment to the figure and often include behaviors such as information seeking and repeatedly consuming media in which they are featured.

People react to PSRRs similarly to how they would react in social relationships. For example, PSRRs develop over time just like more interdependent relationships, and people engage in parasocial relational maintenance (Tukachinsky Forster, 2021). Likewise, people experience jealousy in PSRRs when the media figure becomes romantically involved with someone else (Tukachinsky Forster, 2021). People experience distress from parasocial breakups, particularly if they are lonely (Eyal & Cohen, 2006).

PSRRs are especially impactful for adolescents and may influence their development of romantic beliefs and relational scripts (Erickson & Dal Cin, 2018). Tukachinsky Forster (2021) describes two models for understanding PSRRs in adolescence: as practice for a real relationship or as compensation for a lack of one. Although many teen infatuations fade over time, one concern is how experiences in PSRRs may affect real relationships. For example, Tukachinsky and Dorros (2018) found that emotional involvement in a PSRR during adolescence was related to lower relationship satisfaction and less favorable attitudes toward subsequent romantic partners. It is possible that fantasy relationships may set unreasonably high expectations for a future partner, and their one-sided nature may belie the effort required to develop and maintain a satisfying relationship.

Contributions to Romantic Relationship Research

Although research on PSRRs is rarely cited in research on real romantic relationships, it has the potential to offer insights into several phenomena. PSRRs may be an important contributor to relationship schema and idealized romantic beliefs among media consumers, particularly among those with less romantic experience. Strong or enduring parasocial relationships may foster the development of romantic prototypes and expectations that real partners may never fulfill. Given that children develop PSRs at a very young age, PSRRs may also represent a possible step in understanding how attachment models from infancy transfer to romantic relationships.

PSRRs are inherently one-sided and require imagination and fantasy to be sustained. Understanding how people develop and maintain PSRRs may lend additional insights into unwanted relational pursuit and stalking behavior. Due to their one-sidedness, PSRRs also present an interesting context for examining perceptions of equity, power, and control within romantic relationships.

CONCLUSION

In the modern world, media are woven into the fabric of our romantic relationships as means, models, megaphones, memories, and even mates. Unquestionably, they have played a critical role in shaping, initiating, escalating, maintaining, disrupting, and dissolving romantic relationships since the emergence of mediated communication. Thus, media warrant more consideration by relationship researchers.

A second takeaway that affordances are crucial for understanding how media differ, why people choose media, and how media affect our relationships. Although many technologies undergo radical changes or become obsolete, affordances and the ways humans experience media evolve more slowly, if at all (cf., Reeves & Nass, 1996). Centering affordances and features of media instead of adopting a narrow, channel-focused approach will help researchers identify relevant findings and make theoretical contributions that will be more enduring than teletext personals.

A final, crucial lesson is that mediated relational experiences are not a novelty born of the digital age. Many phenomena scholars have erroneously described as "new" or "unique to" modern relationships were identified and studied in "old" media decades ago. To understand the future of media and romantic relationships, we must first know the past.

REFERENCES

Adelman, M. B., & Ahuvia, A. C. (1991). Mediated channels for mate seeking: A solution to involuntary singlehood? *Critical Studies in Media Communication, 8*(3), 273–289. https://doi.org/10.1080/15295039109366798

Alberts, J. K., Yoshimura, C. G., Rabby, M., & Loschiavo, R. (2005). Mapping the topography of couples' daily conversation. *Journal of Social and Personal Relationships, 22*(3), 299–322. https://doi.org/10.1177/0265407505050941

Alexopoulos, C., & Taylor, L. D. (2020). Your cheating cognitions: Young women's responses to television messages about infidelity. *Mass Communication and Society, 23*(2), 249–271. https://doi.org/10.1080/15205436.2019.1705350

Alexopoulos, C., & Taylor, L. D. (2021). If your girl only knew: The effects of infidelity-themed song lyrics on cognitions related to infidelity. *Psychology of Popular Media, 10*(4), 445–456. https://doi.org/10.1037/ppm0000326

Anderegg, C., Dale, K., & Fox, J. (2014). Media portrayals of romantic relationship maintenance: A content analysis of relational maintenance behaviors on prime time television. *Mass Communication & Society, 17*(5), 733–753. https://doi.org/10.1080/15205436.2013.846383

Andersen, H. (1958). An analysis of 777 matrimonial want ads in two Copenhagen newspapers. *Acta Sociologica, 3*(1), 173–182. www.jstor.org/stable/4193491

Andersen, P. A. (1993). Cognitive schemata in personal relationships. In S. Duck (Ed.), *Individuals in relationships* (pp. 1–29). Sage.

Aubrey, J. S. (2004). Sex and punishment: An examination of sexual consequences and the sexual double standard in teen programming. *Sex Roles, 50*(7–8), 505–514. https://doi.org/10.1023/B:SERS.0000023070.87195.07

Aubrey, J. S., Rhea, D. M., Olson, L. N., & Fine, M. (2013). Conflict and control: Examining the association between exposure to television portraying interpersonal conflict and the use of controlling behaviors in romantic relationships. *Communication Studies, 64*(1), 106–124. https://doi.org/10.1080/10510974.2012.731465

Bailey, B. L. (1988). *From front porch to back seat: Courtship in twentieth-century America*. Johns Hopkins University Press.

Bandura, A. (1986). *Social foundations of thought and action: A social cognitive theory*. Prentice Hall.

Barnett, C., Briggs, A., Osei-Tutu, A., & Dzokoto, V. (2020). How will I know if (s)he really loves me? An analysis of romantic relationship concerns in Ghanaian print media advice columns, 2000–2016. *Journal of Black Sexuality and Relationships, 6*(3), 93–125. https://doi.org/10.1353/bsr.2020.0002

Bergner, R. M., & Bridges, A. J. (2002). The significance of heavy pornography involvement for romantic partners: Research and clinical implications. *Journal of Sex and Marital Therapy, 28*(3), 193–206. https://doi.org/10.1080/009262302760328235

Black, C. F. (2010). Doing gender from prison: Male inmates and their supportive wives and girlfriends. *Race, Gender & Class, 17*(3–4), 255–271. www.jstor.org/stable/41674764

Bond, B. J., Miller, B., & Aubrey, J. S. (2019). Sexual references and consequences for heterosexual, lesbian, gay, and bisexual characters on television: A comparison content analysis. *Mass Communication and Society, 22*(1), 72–95. https://doi.org/10.1080/15205436.2018.1489058

Borna, S., Chapman, J., & Menezes, D. (1993). Deceptive nature of Dial-a-Porn commercials and public policy alternatives. *Journal of Business Ethics, 12*(7), 503–509. https://doi.org/10.1007/BF00872370

Borzutzky, C., Clark, L., & Belzer, M. (2008). Callers to a nationally syndicated commercial entertainment radio show about sex and relationships: Their questions, reasons for calling, and outcomes. *Journal of Adolescent Health, 42*(2), 32. https://doi.org/10.1016/j.jadohealth.2007.11.086

Brown, J. D., Zhao, X., Wang, M. N., Liu, Q., Lu, A. S., Li, L. J., Ortiz, R. R., Liao, S., & Zhang, G. (2013). Love is all you need: A content analysis of romantic scenes in Chinese entertainment television. *Asian Journal of Communication, 23*(3), 229–247. https://doi.org/10.1080/01292986.2012.729148

Carpenter, L. M. (1998). From girls into women: Scripts for sexuality and romance in *Seventeen* magazine, 1974–1994. *Journal of Sex Research, 35*(2), 158–168. https://doi.org/10.1080/00224499809551929

Carter, K. R., Knox, D., & Hall, S. S. (2018). Romantic breakup: Difficult loss for some but not for others. *Journal of Loss and Trauma, 23*(8), 698–714. https://doi.org/10.1080/15325024.2018.1502523

Carter, S. P., & Renshaw, K. D. (2016). Communication via different media during military deployments and post-deployment relationship satisfaction. *Military Behavioral Health, 4*(3), 260–268. https://doi.org/10.1080/21635781.2016.1153535

Caughlin, J. P., & Sharabi, L. L. (2013). A communicative interdependence perspective of close relationships: The connections between mediated and unmediated interactions matter. *Journal of Communication, 63*(5), 873–893. https://doi.org/10.1111/jcom.12046

Chandra, A., Martino, S. C., Collins, R. L., Elliott, M. N., Berry, S. H., Kanouse, D. E., & Miu, A. (2008). Does watching sex on television predict teen pregnancy? Findings from a national longitudinal survey of youth. *Pediatrics, 122*(5), 1047–1054. https://doi.org/10.1542/peds.2007-3066

Constable, N. (2003). *Romance on a global stage: Pen pals, virtual ethnography, and "mail order" marriages.* University of California Press.

Coyne, S. M., Nelson, D. A., Graham-Kevan, N., Tew, E., Meng, K. N., & Olsen, J. A. (2011). Media depictions of physical and relational aggression: Connections with aggression in young adults' romantic relationships. *Aggressive Behavior, 37*(1), 56–62. https://doi.org/10.1002/ab.20372

Coyne, S. M., Ward, L. M., Kroff, S. L., Davis, E. J., Holmgren, H. G., Jensen, A. C., Erickson, S. E., & Essig, L. W. (2019). Contributions of mainstream sexual media exposure to sexual attitudes, perceived peer norms, and sexual behavior: A meta-analysis. *Journal of Adolescent Health, 64*(4), 430–436. https://doi.org/10.1016/j.jadohealth.2018.11.016

Dainton, M., & Aylor, B. (2002). Patterns of communication channel use in the maintenance of long-distance relationships. *Communication Research Reports, 19*(2), 118–129. https://doi.org/10.1080/08824090209384839

Dannefer, D., & Kasen, J. H. (1981). Anonymous exchanges: CB and the emergence of sex typing. *Urban Life, 10*(3), 265–287. https://doi.org/10.1177/089124168101000303

De Pee, C. (2007). *The writing of weddings in middle-period China: Text and ritual practice in the eighth through fourteenth centuries.* SUNY Press.

de Sousa Campos, L., Otta, E., & de Oliveira Siqueira, J. (2002). Sex differences in mate selection strategies: Content analyses and responses to personal advertisements in Brazil. *Evolution and Human Behavior*, 23(5), 395–406. https://doi.org/10.1016/S1090-5138(02)00099-5

Dew, J., & Tulane, S. (2015). The association between time spent using entertainment media and marital quality in a contemporary dyadic national sample. *Journal of Family and Economic Issues*, 36(12), 621–632. https://doi.org/10.1007/s10834-014-9427-y

Dillman Carpentier, F. R., & Stevens, E. M. (2018). Sex in the media, sex on the mind: Linking television use, sexual permissiveness, and sexual concept accessibility in memory. *Sexuality & Culture*, 22(1), 22–38. https://doi.org/10.1007/s12119-017-9450-x

Dillman Carpentier, F. R., Stevens, E. M., Wu, L., & Seely, N. (2017). Sex, love, and risk-n-responsibility: A content analysis of entertainment television. *Mass Communication and Society*, 20(5), 686–709. https://doi.org/10.1080/15205436.2017.1298807

Dimmick, J., Kline, S., & Stafford, L. (2000). The gratification niches of personal e-mail and the telephone: Competition, displacement, and complementarity. *Communication Research*, 27(2), 227–248. https://doi.org/10.1177/009365000027002005

Donovan, J. M. (2002). Same-sex union announcements: Whether newspapers must publish them, and why we should care. *Brooklyn Law Review*, 68(3), 721–807.

Drew, R. (2016). The space between: Mix taping as a ritual of distance. *Popular Communication*, 14(3), 146–155. https://doi.org/10.1080/15405702.2015.1084627

Erickson, S. E., & Dal Cin, S. (2018). Romantic parasocial attachments and the development of romantic scripts, schemas, and beliefs among adolescents. *Media Psychology*, 21(1), 111–136. https://doi.org/10.1080/15213269.2017.1305281

Eyal, K., & Cohen, J. (2006). When good friends say goodbye: A parasocial breakup study. *Journal of Broadcasting & Electronic Media*, 50(3), 502–523. https://doi.org/10.1207/s15506878jobem5003_9

Eyal, K., & Finnerty, K. (2009). The portrayal of sexual intercourse on television: How, who, and with what consequence? *Mass Communication & Society*, 12(2), 143–169. https://doi.org/10.1080/15205430802136713

Fallis, S. F., Fitzpatrick, M. A., & Friestad, M. S. (1985). Spouses' discussion of television portrayals of close relationships. *Communication Research*, 12(1), 59–81. https://doi.org/10.1177/009365085012001003

Fehr, B. (1993). How do I love thee? Let me consult my prototype. In S. Duck (Ed.), *Individuals in relationships* (pp. 87–120). Sage.

Feiring, C. (1996). Concept of romance in 15-year-old adolescents. *Journal of Research on Adolescence*, 6(2), 181–200.

Fox, J., & McEwan, B. (2017). Distinguishing technologies for social interaction: The perceived social affordances of communication channels scale. *Communication Monographs*, 84(3), 298–318. https://doi.org/10.1080/03637751.2017.1332418

Fox, J., Frampton, J. R., Jones, E., & Lookadoo, K. (2021). Romantic relationship dissolution on social networking sites: Self-presentation and public accounts of breakups on Facebook. *Journal of Social and Personal Relationships*, 38(12), 3732–3751. https://doi.org/10.1177/2056305118800317

Frampton, J. R., & Linvill, D. L. (2017). Green on the screen: Types of jealousy and communicative responses to jealousy in romantic comedies. *Southern Communication Journal*, 82(5), 298–311. https://doi.org/10.1080/1041794X.2017.1347701

Fritz, N., Malic, V., Paul, B., & Zhou, Y. (2020). A descriptive analysis of the types, targets, and relative frequency of aggression in mainstream pornography. *Archives of Sexual Behavior*, 49(8), 3041–3053. https://doi.org/10.1007/s10508-020-01773-0

Garrido, S., & Davidson, J. W. (2019). *Music, nostalgia, and memory: Historical and psychological perspectives*. Palgrave Macmillan.

Gerbner, G., Gross, L., Morgan, M., & Signorielli, N. (1986). Living with television: The dynamics of the cultivation process. In J. Bryant & D. Zillmann (Eds.), *Perspectives on media effects* (pp. 17–40). Lawrence Erlbaum.

Gershon, I. (2010). *The breakup 2.0: Disconnecting over new media*. Cornell University Press.

Gibson, J. J. (1979). *The ecological approach to visual perception*. Houghton Mifflin.

Goffman, E. (1971). *Relations in public: Microstudies of the public order*. Harper & Row.

Golia, J. (2021). *Newspaper confessions: A history of advice columns in a pre-internet age*. Oxford University Press.

Gomillion, S., Gabriel, S., Kawakami, K., & Young, A. F. (2017). Let's stay home and watch TV: The benefits of shared media use for close relationships. *Journal of Social and Personal Relationships*, 34(6), 855–874. https://doi.org/10.1177/0265407516660388

Greenwood, D. N., & Long, C. R. (2011). Attachment, belongingness needs, and relationship status predict imagined intimacy with media figures. *Communication Research*, 38(2), 278–297. https://doi.org/10.1177/0093650210362687

Griffen-Foley, B. (2020). *Australian radio listeners and television viewers: Historical perspectives*. Palgrave.

Hall, K. (1995). Lip service on the fantasy lines. In K. Hall & M. Bucholtz (Eds.), *Gender articulated: Language and the socially constructed self* (pp. 183–216). Routledge.

Harris, C. B., Baird, A., Harris, S. A., & Thompson, W. F. (2020). "They're playing our song": Couple-defining songs in intimate relationships. *Journal of Social and Personal Relationships*, 37(1), 163–179. https://doi.org/10.1177/0265407519859440

Hatch, D. L., & Hatch, M. A. (1947). Criteria of social status as derived from marriage announcements in *The New York Times*. *American Sociological Review*, 12(4), 396–403. www.jstor.org/stable/2087283

Hefner, V., & Wilson, B. J. (2013). From love at first sight to soul mate: The influence of romantic ideals in popular films on young people's beliefs about relationships. *Communication Monographs*, 80(2), 150–175. https://doi.org/10.1080/03637751.2013.776697

Henningsen, D. D., Henningsen, M. L. M., McWorthy, E., McWorthy, C., & McWorthy, L. (2011). Exploring the effects of sex and mode of presentation in perceptions of dating goals in video-dating. *Journal of Communication*, 61(4), 641–658. https://doi.org/10.1111/j.1460-2466.2011.01564.x

Hetsroni, A., & Bloch, L. R. (1999). Choosing the right mate when everyone is watching: Cultural and sex differences in television dating games. *Communication Quarterly*, 47(3), 315–332. https://doi.org/10.1080/01463379909385562

Honeycutt, J. M., & Sheldon, P. (2018). *Scripts and communication for relationships* (2nd ed.). Peter Lang.

Horton, D., & Wohl, R. R. (1956). Mass communication and para-social interaction: Observations on intimacy at a distance. *Psychiatry*, 19(3), 215–229. https://doi.org/10.1080/00332747.1956.11023049

Ito, K. (2002). The world of Japanese ladies' comics: From romantic fantasy to lustful perversion. *Journal of Popular Culture, 36*(1), 68–85.

Janning, M. (2018). *Love letters: Saving romance in the digital age*. Routledge.

Jansen, B. (2009). Tape cassettes and former selves: How mix tapes mediate memories. In K. Bijsterveld & J. van Dijck (Eds.), *Sound souvenirs: Audio technologies, memory, and cultural practices* (pp. 43–54). Amsterdam University Press.

Johnson, A. J., Smith, S. W., Mitchell, M. M., Orrego, V. O., & Ah Yun, K. (1999). Expert advice on daytime talk television: A beneficial source of information for the general public? *Communication Research Reports, 16*(1), 91–101. https://doi.org/10.1080/08824099909388705

Johnson, K. R., & Holmes, B. M. (2009). Contradictory messages: A content analysis of Hollywood-produced romantic comedy feature films. *Communication Quarterly, 57*(3), 352–373. https://doi.org/10.1080/01463370903113632

Johnson, P. M., & Holmes, K. A. (2019). Gaydar, marriage, and rip-roaring homosexuals: Discourses about homosexuality in Dear Abby and Ann Landers advice columns, 1967–1982. *Journal of Homosexuality, 66*(3), 389–406. https://doi.org/10.1080/00918369.2017.1413274

Joyce, S. N., & Martinez, M. (2017). From social merchandising to social spectacle: Portrayals of domestic violence in TV Globo's prime-time telenovelas. *International Journal of Communication, 11*, 220–236. https://ijoc.org/index.php/ijoc/article/view/5905

Jozkowski, K. N., Marcantonio, T. L., Rhoads, K. E., Canan, S., Hunt, M. E., & Willis, M. (2019). A content analysis of sexual consent and refusal communication in mainstream films. *The Journal of Sex Research, 56*(6), 754–765. https://doi.org/10.1080/00224499.2019.1595503

Katz, E., Blumler, J. G., & Gurevitch, M. (1973). Uses and gratifications research. *The Public Opinion Quarterly, 37*(4), 509–523. www.jstor.org/stable/2747854

Knapp, M. L. (1978). *Social intercourse: From greeting to goodbye*. Allyn and Bacon.

Knobloch, S., & Zillmann, D. (2003). Appeal of love themes in popular music. *Psychological Reports, 93*(3), 653–658. https://doi.org/10.2466/pr0.2003.93.3.653

Kretz, V. E. (2019). Television and movie viewing predict adults' romantic ideals and relationship satisfaction. *Communication Studies, 70*(2), 208–234. https://doi.org/10.1080/10510974.2019.1595692

Kunkel, D., Farrar, K. M., Eyal, K., Biely, E., Donnerstein, E., & Rideout, V. (2007). Sexual socialization messages on entertainment television: Comparing content trends 1997–2002. *Media Psychology, 9*(3), 595–622. https://doi.org/10.1080/15213260701283210

Lazarsfeld, P. F. (1940). *Radio and the printed page: An introduction to the study of radio and its role in the communication of ideas*. Duell, Sloan and Pearce.

Ledbetter, A. M. (2013). Relational maintenance and inclusion of the other in the self: Measure development and dyadic test of a self-expansion theory approach. *Southern Communication Journal, 78*(4), 289–310. https://doi.org/10.1080/1041794X.2013.815265

Ledbetter, A. M., Stassen, H., Muhammad, A., & Kotey, E. N. (2010). Relational maintenance as including the other in the self. *Qualitative Research Reports in Communication, 11*(1), 21–28. https://doi.org/10.1080/17459430903413457

Len-Ríos, M. E., Streit, C., Killoren, S., Deutsch, A., Cooper, M. L., & Carlo, G. (2016). U.S. Latino adolescents' use of mass media and mediated communication in romantic relationships. *Journal of Children and Media, 10*(4), 395–410. https://doi.org/10.1 080/17482798.2016.1144214

Lewis, P. H. (1983). Innovative divorce rituals: Their psycho-social functions. *Journal of Divorce, 6*(3), 71–81. https://doi.org/10.1300/J279v06n03_06

Lohmann, A., Arriaga, X. B., & Goodfriend, W. (2003). Close relationships and placemaking: Do objects in a couple's home reflect couplehood? *Personal Relationships, 10*(3), 437–450. https://doi.org/10.1111/1475-6811.00058

Martino, S. C., Collins, R. L., Elliott M. N., Kanouse, D. E., & Berry, S. H. (2009). It's better on TV: Does television set teenagers up for regret following sexual initiation? *Perspectives on Sexual and Reproductive Health, 41*(2), 92–100.

Marvin, C. (1988). *When old technologies were new: Thinking about electric communication in the late nineteenth century.* Oxford University Press.

Matthews, N., Speers, L., & Ball, J. (2012). Bathroom banter: Sex, love, and the bathroom wall. *Electronic Journal of Human Sexuality, 15*(17), 1–11. http://mail.ejhs.org/volume15/Banter.html

Morgan, P., Hubler, D. S., Payne, P. B., Pomeroy, C., Gregg, D., & Homer, M. (2017). My partner's media use: A qualitative study exploring perceptions of problems with a partner's media use. *Marriage & Family Review, 53*(7), 683–695. https://doi.org/10 .1080/01494929.2016.1263589

Moss, L., Ward, L. M., & Overstreet, N. M. (2022). Do objectification, gender beliefs, or racial stereotypes mediate associations between Black adults' media use and acceptance of intimate partner violence? *Psychology of Violence, 12*(2), 63–73. https://doi .org/10.1037/vi0000412

Nabi, R. L., & Clark, S. (2008). Exploring the limits of social cognitive theory: Why negatively reinforced behaviors on TV may be modeled anyway. *Journal of Communication, 58*(3), 407–427. https://doi.org/10.111/j.1460-2466.2008.00392.x

Nabi, R. L., Finnerty, K., Domschke, T., & Hull, S. (2006). Does misery love company? Exploring the therapeutic effects of TV viewing on regretted experiences. *Journal of Communication, 56*(4), 689–706. https://doi.org/10.1111/j.1460-2466.2006.00315.x

North, A., & Hargreaves, D. (2008). *The social and applied psychology of music.* Oxford University Press.

O'Sullivan, L. F., & Byers, E. S. (1993). Eroding stereotypes: College women's attempts to influence reluctant male sexual partners. *Journal of Sex Research, 30*(3), 270–282. https://doi.org/10.1080/00224499309551711

Osborn, J. L. (2012). When TV and marriage meet: A social exchange analysis of the impact of television viewing on marital satisfaction and commitment. *Mass Communication & Society, 15*(5), 739–757. https://doi.org/10.1080/15205436.2011 .618900

Parks, M. R. (2017). Embracing the challenges and opportunities of mixed-media relationships. *Human Communication Research, 43*(4), 505–517. https://doi.org/10.1111/hcre.12125

Poulsen, F. O., Busby, D. M., & Galovan, A. M. (2013). Pornography use: Who uses it and how it is associated with couple outcomes. *Journal of Sex Research, 50*(1), 72–83. https://doi.org/10.1080/00224499.2011.648027

Pyle, T. M., & Bridges, A. J. (2012). Perceptions of relationship satisfaction and addictive behavior: Comparing pornography and marijuana use. *Journal of Behavioral Addictions, 1*(4), 171–179. https://doi.org/10.1556/jba.1.2012.007

Ramasubramanian, S., & Jain, P. (2009). Gender stereotypes and normative heterosexuality in matrimonial ads from globalizing India. *Asian Journal of Communication, 19*(3), 253–269. https://doi.org/10.1080/01292980903072831

Rasmussen, K. (2016). A historical and empirical review of pornography and romantic relationships: Implications for family researchers. *Journal of Family Theory & Review, 8*(2), 173–191. https://doi.org/10.1111/jftr.12141

Reeves, B., & Nass, C. (1996). *The media equation: How people treat computers, television, and new media like real people and places.* Cambridge.

Rentfrow, P. J., & Gosling, S. D. (2006). Message in a ballad: The role of music preferences in interpersonal perception. *Psychological Science, 17*(3), 236–242. https://doi.org/10.1111/j.1467-9280.2006.01691.x

Ricquier, K. (2019). The early modern transmission of the ancient Greek romances: A bibliographic survey. *Ancient Narrative, 15*, 1–34. https://doi.org/10.21827/5c643a2ff2600

Riggio, R. E., & Woll, S. B. (1984). The role of nonverbal cues and physical attractiveness in the selection of dating partners. *Journal of Social and Personal Relationships, 1*(3), 347–357. https://doi.org/10.1177/0265407584013007

Rodenhizer, K. A. E., & Edwards, K. M. (2019). The impacts of sexual media exposure on adolescent and emerging adults' dating and sexual violence attitudes and behaviors: A critical review of the literature. *Trauma, Violence, & Abuse, 20*(4), 439–452. https://doi.org/10.1177/1524838017717745

Saenger, G. (1955). Male and female relations in the American comic strip. *Public Opinion Quarterly, 19*(2), 195–205. https://doi.org/10.1086/266561

Sarch, A. (1993). Making the connection: Single women's use of the telephone in dating relationships with men. *Journal of Communication, 43*(2), 128–144. https://doi.org/10.1111/j.1460-2466.1993.tb01266.x

Schumm, W. R., Bell, D. B., Ender, M. G., & Rice, R. E. (2004). Expectations, use, and evaluation of communication media among deployed peacekeepers. *Armed Forces & Society, 30*(4), 649–662. https://doi.org/10.1080/15267431.2016.1146723

Segrin, C., & Nabi, R. L. (2002). Does television viewing cultivate unrealistic expectations about marriage? *Journal of Communication, 52*(2), 247–263. https://doi.org/10.1111/j.1460-2466.2002.tb02543.x

Simon, W., & Gagnon, J. H. (1986). Sexual scripts: Permanence and change. *Archives of Sexual Behavior, 15*(2), 97–120. https://doi.org/10.1007/BF01542219

Smiler, A. P., Shewmaker, J. W., & Hearon, B. (2017). From "I want to hold your hand" to "promiscuous": Sexual stereotypes in popular music lyrics, 1960–2008. *Sexuality & Culture, 21*(4), 1083–1105. https://doi.org/10.1007/s12119-017-9437-7

Spencer, T. A., Lambertsen, A., Hubler, D. S., & Burr, B. K. (2017). Assessing the mediating effect of relationship dynamics between perceptions of problematic media use and relationship satisfaction. *Contemporary Family Therapy, 39*(2), 80–86. https://doi.org/10.1007/s10591-017-9407-0

Stafford, L. (2004). *Maintaining long-distance and cross-residential relationships.* Erlbaum.

Stafford, L., & Reske, J. R. (1990). Idealization and communication in long-distance premarital relationships. *Family Relations*, 39(3), 274–279. https://doi.org/10.2307/584871

Standage, T. (1998). *The Victorian internet: The remarkable story of the telegraph and the nineteenth century's online pioneers*. Weidenfeld & Nicolson.

Stuart, I. R. (1962). Complementary vs. homogeneous needs in mate selection: A television program situation. *The Journal of Social Psychology*, 56(2), 291–300. https://doi.org/10.1080/00224545.1962.9919398

Su, H. (2016). Infrastructures of romantic love: Chinese love letters in the early 1900s. *Interactions: Studies in Communication & Culture*, 7(3), 265–280. https://doi.org/10.1386/iscc.7.3.265_1

Syvertsen, T. (2001). Ordinary people in extraordinary circumstances: A study of participants in television dating games. *Media, Culture & Society*, 23(3), 319–337. https://doi.org/10.1177/016344301023003003

Timberg, B. M. (2002). *Television talk: A history of the TV talk show*. University of Texas Press.

Tong, S. T., Hancock, J. T., & Slatcher, R. B. (2016). Online dating system design and relational decision making: Choice, algorithms, and control. *Personal Relationships*, 23(4), 645–662. https://doi.org/10.1111/pere.12158

Tukachinsky Forster, R. (2021). *Parasocial romantic relationships: Falling in love with media figures*. Lexington Books.

Tukachinsky Forster, R., & Dorros, S. M. (2018). Parasocial romantic relationships, romantic beliefs, and relationship outcomes in USA adolescents: Rehearsing love or setting oneself up to fail? *Journal of Children and Media*, 12(3), 329–345. https://doi.org/10.1080/17482798.2018.1463917

Vu, H. T., & Lee, T. T. (2013). Soap operas as a matchmaker: A cultivation analysis of the effects of South Korean TV dramas on Vietnamese women's marital intentions. *Journalism & Mass Communication Quarterly*, 90(2), 308–330. https://doi.org/10.1177/1077699013482912

Wallace, K. M. (1959). An experiment in scientific matchmaking. *Marriage and Family Living*, 21(4), 342–348. https://doi.org/10.2307/347108

Walther, J. B. (1992). Interpersonal effects in computer-mediated interaction: A relational perspective. *Communication Research*, 19(1), 52–90. https://doi.org/10.1177/009365092019001003

Wang, H. Z., & Chang, S. M. (2002). The commodification of international marriages: Cross-border marriage business in Taiwan and Viet Nam. *International Migration*, 40(6), 93–116. https://doi.org/10.1111/1468-2435.00224

Wang, P. (2017). Inventing traditions: Television dating shows in the People's Republic of China. *Media, Culture & Society*, 39(4), 504–519. https://doi.org/10.1177/0163443716648493

Ward, L. M., Moorman, J. D., & Grower, P. (2019). Entertainment media's role in the sexual socialization of Western youth: A review of research from 2000–2017. In S. Lamb & J. Gilbert (Eds.), *The Cambridge handbook of sexual development: Childhood and adolescence* (pp. 395–418). Cambridge University Press.

West, E. (2004). *Greeting cards: Individuality and authenticity in mass culture* [Unpublished doctoral dissertation, University of Pennsylvania]. ProQuest. www.proquest.com/docview/305146127

Westmyer, S. A., DiCioccio, R. L., & Rubin, R. B. (1998). Appropriateness and effectiveness of communication channels in competent interpersonal communication. *Journal of Communication*, 48(3), 27–48. https://doi.org/10.1111/j.1460-2466.1998.tb02758.x

Williams, J. E. (1997). Discourses on death: Obituaries and the management of spoiled identity. *OMEGA-Journal of Death and Dying*, 34(4), 301–319. https://doi.org/10.2190/ARM6-MQER-CYPV-T3W5

Willoughby, B. J., & Leonhardt, N. D. (2020). Behind closed doors: Individual and joint pornography use among romantic couples. *The Journal of Sex Research*, 57(1), 77–91. https://doi.org/10.1080/00224499.2018.1541440

Woll, S. B. (1986). So many to choose from: Decision strategies in videodating. *Journal of Social and Personal Relationships*, 3(1), 43–52. https://doi.org/10.1177/0265407586031004

Woll, S. B., & Cozby, P. C. (1987). Videodating and other alternatives to traditional methods of relationship initiation. In W. H. Jones & D. Perlman (Eds.), *Advances in personal relationships* (Vol. 1, pp. 69–108). JAI Press.

Woll, S. B., & Young, P. (1989). Looking for Mr. or Ms. Right: Self-presentation in videodating. *Journal of Marriage and the Family*, 51(2), 483–488. https://doi.org/10.2307/352509

Wright, P. J., Tokunaga, R. S., Kraus, A., & Klann, E. (2017). Pornography consumption and satisfaction: A meta-analysis. *Human Communication Research*, 43(3), 315–343. https://doi.org/10.1111/hcre.12108

Wyss, E. L. (2008). From the bridal letter to online flirting: Changes in text type from the nineteenth century to the Internet era. *Journal of Historical Pragmatics*, 9(2), 225–254. https://doi.org/10.1075/jhp.9.2.04wys

Zhou, N., Yau, O. H., & Lin, L. (1997). For love or money: A longitudinal content analysis of Chinese personal advertisements, 1984–1995. *Journal of Current Issues & Research in Advertising*, 19(2), 65–77. https://doi.org/10.1080/10641734.1997.10524438

Zillmann, D., & Bhatia, A. (1989). Effects of associating with musical genres on heterosexual attraction. *Communication Research*, 16(2), 263–288. https://doi.org/10.1177/009365089016002005

Zillmann, D., & Bryant, J. (1982). Pornography, sexual callousness, and the trivialization of rape. *Journal of Communication*, 32(4), 10–21. https://doi.org/10.1111/j.1460-2466.1982.tb02514.x

Zillmann, D., & Bryant, J. (1985). Affect, mood, and emotion as determinants of selective exposure. In D. Zillmann & J. Bryant (Eds.), *Selective exposure to communication* (pp. 157–190). Erlbaum.

Zurbriggen, E. L., & Morgan, E. M. (2006). Who wants to marry a millionaire? Reality dating television programs, attitudes toward sex, and sexual behaviors. *Sex Roles*, 54(1–2), 1–17. https://doi.org/10.1007/s11199-005-8865-2

11

Romantic Relationships and Social Media

BREE McEWAN AND LEAH E. LEFEBVRE

Social media channels serve multiple roles throughout the lifespan of relationships. Although social media has been shown to be particularly useful for maintaining relationships with weak tie relationships such as acquaintances and casual friends (Ellison et al., 2007), social media channels also have implications for romantic partners, who may vacillate in tie strength over the course of the relationship. This chapter will focus on advancements in research on romantic and sexual relationships and consider social media's influence on the message strategies and outcomes of romantic couples. Social media may offer communication opportunities for direct relational communication related to the initiation, development, and maintenance of romantic relationships as well as provide a stage for couples to communicate the state their relationship to the broader social network. In addition, social media has altered strategies related to the dissolution of romantic relationships and post-dissolution interactions.

We offer the caveat that the popularity of specific social media platforms rises and falls over time. Within the literature, much of the research thus far focuses specifically on Facebook. Yet, Facebook may not represent the way that future romantic partners engage in relational communication via social media channels. Within the chapter, we attempt to weave in research from multiple platforms. Yet, we also note that if we consider the affordances of the platform, research conducted on Facebook may still provide information about the influence of message visibility or network connectivity even if the platform falls out of favor (see also McEwan & Fox, 2022).

INITIATING RELATIONSHIPS

When exploring potential options of romantic partners, people often use social media to aid in information seeking and uncertainty reduction. These processes, facilitated through social media, have led to changes and adaptations to the relationship initiation process. Complex and diverse channels and pathways allow social media users to locate potential romantic partners and develop burgeoning romantic relationships.

Relationship Initiation

Communication technologies are able to accommodate the initiation and escalation processes used to seek, find, and communicate with potential romantic interests in-person and/or online (Sharabi & Caughlin, 2017; Van Ouystel et al., 2016). In particular, the blurring of interpersonal and mass communication offers the ability for individuals to have access to a wider network of numerous potential partners (Finkel et al., 2012; O'Sullivan & Carr, 2018). People may use online dating apps to evaluate a wide network of potential partners, social network sites (SNS) to facilitate information-seeking and disclosure processes, and messaging apps to begin relational communication.

The enhancement of communication technology affords users the ability to connect with easier accessibility and personalization, allowing for increased convenience of sending and receiving messages to a potentially wider array of possible partners. Social media can consist of public to private channels conveying impersonal to interpersonal messages. Social media are often masspersonal, in that they allow for messages that do the work of interpersonal communication while simultaneously being visible to a larger social audience (O'Sullivan & Carr, 2018). Individual motivation and communication practices may aid in locating potential romantic and/or sexual partner(s) with greater or lesser success (LeFebvre & Goodcase, 2021).

Relationship initiation is contingent on identifying available and potential partners. Prior to technological advancements in smartphones, online dating sites, and mobile dating applications, people commonly met romantic partners through the intermediation of friends and family (Coontz, 2005). These peripheral tie relationships offered the ability to bridge new connections (Granovetter, 1973). The internet increasingly altered the social arena for locating potential romantic partners. Although online dating sites or mobile dating applications[1] are typically what is thought of when we consider people seeking new romantic partners, the creation of connections (and reconnections) to potential partners can come through a variety of social media applications. Social networking sites (SNS; see boyd & Ellison, 2007) allow for unconventional platforms and channels for finding and locating partners, for instance, messaging or reconnecting on Facebook (Langlais et al., 2020; Ramirez et al., 2017), or sliding into DMs (direct messages) on Instagram, Twitter, or WhatsApp (Dibble et al., 2021; Sharabi & Hopkins, 2021). Other social media related relational behavior might involve interacting through TikTok (Vaterlaus & Winter, 2021), or watching video streams together on such platforms as Douyu, Twitch, or YouTube (Sheng & Kairam, 2020).

These and other communication technologies have modified and displaced traditional ways of meeting potential partners, especially for heterosexual individuals, who were previously relying on family members and friends (Rosenfeld & Thomas, 2012). Unlike mixed-sex couples, same-sex couples have been using mediated platforms for relational communication for several decades (Rosenfeld & Thomas, 2012), although the expansion of social and sexual platforms has afforded new opportunities for finding partner(s). Mediated platforms, whether dating apps or social media, allow LGBTQ+ adults more access to potential romantic and/or sexual partners, particularly in rural areas (Sumter & Vandenbosch, 2019).

Young adults often have the greatest access and availability to social media, and also the greatest availability of potential partners. Yet, although young adults are perceived (and often are) more technologically savvy, they are the least likely to meet potential partners using mediated platforms (Rosenfeld & Thomas, 2012). This outcome may be because young adults have access to a wide and available pool of potential dating partners through their regular social networks.

The availability of social media, including online dating apps, may alter the process of selecting romantic partners in two ways. First, when selecting potential partners offline, people tend to seek partners from within (endogamy) rather than outside (exogamy) their social groups. Social media has led to greater exogamy than was available in solely offline relational initiation (Thomas et al., 2020). In addition, social media and dating apps may allow people to find a wider pool of dating partners. This type of access to selected groups may be particularly useful for members of the LGBTQ community (Miller, 2015), especially those who live in smaller or more isolated communities (Blackwell et al., 2015). Second, in selecting romantic partners people tend towards homophily, or attraction to others they find to have similar personal qualities. Yet, research has found that couples who met online have greater interracial and interreligious connections as well as wider variation in their level of obtained education between the relationship partners (Thomas, 2020).

When using online dating platforms, individuals must understand how they want to brand themselves as well as explicitly delineate their preferences with predetermined personalized biographical descriptions, visual depictions, and parameters narrowing their potential connections (LeFebvre, 2018). These pre-interaction relational processes are generated prior to interaction and allow other users to passively consider future interaction and reduce some uncertainty (Sharabi, 2021). They break down into three stages: profile, matching, and discovery (Markowitz et al., 2018).

The profile stage involves intrapersonal decision-making processes about identity presentation and emphasizes users' curation of their motivations, authenticity, and self-promotion (Dredge & Anderson, 2021). Categorizing information about oneself for potential partners allows people to evaluate their potential, and women are more likely than men to identify their own relationship motivations, religious beliefs, and employment (Vogels & Anderson, 2020). Self-presentational practices in dating profiles may involve careful selection of photos and messages, masking identity characteristics, or even providing erroneous information (Toma et al., 2018). On the other hand, most deception on online dating apps is slight (Gibbs et al., 2006) and likely not any more egregious than deceptive practices identified in face-to-face dating (Cunningham & Barbee, 2008; Tooke & Camire, 1991). The matching stage involves the potential to initiate interpersonal communication as users determine their attractiveness and interest in other users. This stage allows users to practice swiping behaviors, which take place in seconds (Levy et al., 2019). The discovery phase occurs after a match has been made and involves mediated communication to determine if the matched parties will choose to pursue a face-to-face meeting and possible relationship.

Information Seeking, Creeping, and "Facebook Stalking"

Whether individuals meet in-person or online, relationship initiation typically involves uncertainty and information gathering to reduce that uncertainty (Knobloch & Miller, 2008). Verifying, vetting, and seeking personalized information, particularly for online matches, necessitates combing through, scouting for, and scrutinizing potential partners and is not limited to online contacts. Social media provides a mechanism for relational partners in the early relationship stages to gather information about their potential or nascent romantic partner (Fox et al., 2014; Sheldon & Bryant, 2016). These uncertainty reduction and information-seeking strategies can be applied sequentially or simultaneously to reduce uncertainty (Ramirez & Walther, 2009), and may be especially informative in relationship formation that coalesces with social media. The affordances of social media increase the persistence and searchability of the information available about potential and nascent romantic partners. The persistence of social media means that posted information endures online and then can be searched by other users, including potential new romantic partners.

This social media searching can represent a specific form of passive uncertainty reduction (see Berger & Bradac, 1982) called extractive information seeking (Ramirez et al., 2002). When locating potential partners, people are worried about others misrepresenting themselves (Gibbs et al., 2011) or deception (Sharabi & Caughlin, 2017; Toma et al., 2018). Verification processes are commonplace when many couples who meet online are perfect strangers with limited or no peripheral ties connecting them. Often individuals use information-seeking strategies (see Ramirez et al., 2002) that include passive (unobstructive available information), active (third-party sources), and extractive (non-human information sources, such as Googling prospective daters) strategies to locate information, form assumptions, and find answers (see Gibbs et al., 2011). Even if partners are aware of their potential partners through in-person interactions, they often employ other SNS sites to locate identity-verifying information including their contact information, general description, romantic history, current relational status, and even personal values (Duguay, 2017; LeFebvre et al., 2019; Weser et al., 2021). This strategy of partner vetting can help users determine interest and compatibility, as well as reduce disillusionment or potential rejection (Chan, 2021).

Seeking information about social network members including romantic relationship partners is a form of interpersonal electronic surveillance (IES, Tokunaga, 2011). In the early days of Facebook, young adults experiencing this form of surveillance often referred to as "creeping" (Fox et al., 2014) or "Facebook stalking" (Hermida & Hernández-Santaolalla, 2020). These terms are colloquialisms referring to fairly expected forms of social information collection (Hermida & Hernández-Santaolalla, 2020). Searching through social media posts may be seen as a more socially acceptable method of seeking information about new and potential partners because the information is posted publicly, which might not be perceived as violation of trust (Utz & Beukeboom, 2011). People may look for information about the compatibility of a potential romantic partner (Andrejevic, 2005), or see if the person already has a romantic partner (Fox et al., 2014). Overall, information gleaned from scanning Facebook profiles can provide information about a potential partners' friends, level of education, and hobbies that can help reduce uncertainty about the potential partner (Goldberg et al., 2022).

Although most IES through social media is likely quite benign, people with darker intentions can use social media to engage in cyberstalking (Tokunaga & Aune, 2017). Cyberstalking refers to unwanted pursuit and surveillance via social media, search engines, and even applications such as keyboard loggers or smartphone apps (Reyns et al., 2011; Spitzberg & Hoobler, 2002). Around 11 percent of US adults have personally experienced cyberstalking (Vogels, 2021). Research with German participants suggests 6.5 percent of German adults have experienced cyberstalking (Dreßing et al., 2014) Perpetrators of cyberstalking may have problems with anger and desire immediate gratification (Kuar et al., 2021). Cyberstalkers may be more likely to be narcissistic (Ménard & Pincus, 2012). Cyberstalking in male perpetrators was also correlated with machiavellianism and physical aggression, whereas cyberstalking in female perpetrators is correlated with interpersonal jealousy and discomfort with intimacy (Kuar et al., 2021). There are other gender differences in cyberstalking as well; men may be less likely to experience victimization, but also less likely to report being stalked (Berry & Bainbridge, 2017; Fansher & Randa, 2019).

Like stalking, cyberstalking is accompanied by a threat to harm. Cyberstalking is particularly worrisome as it can cause serious psychological distress for victims (Parsons-Pollard & Moriarty, 2009) and be a precursor for further harms (e.g., physical violence, reputation destruction) by the aggressor. Cyberstalking itself can be quite detrimental to victims. People being stalked through online channels may experience decreases in the quality of their eating, sleeping, and academic habits as well as increases in emotional distress, and other aspects of mental health such as anxiety, irritability and depression (see Kuar et al., 2021, for an extensive review).

RELATIONAL DEVELOPMENT

As individuals move from initiation to development, social media use related to the relationship more often associates relationship development processes (Bryant et al., 2011; Ling et al., 2012) with network display and constraints (Hall, 2020; Weser et al., 2021). In addition, the masspersonal nature of social media, often reconfigures public-private boundaries (Hjorth & Lim, 2012; Hobbs et al., 2017; O'Sullivan & Carr, 2018), creating more channels for interpersonal connection, but also opening the communication between and about the romantic partnership to a larger networked audience.

When considering the influence and impact of media on romantic relationships, it is important to highlight the distinction that many behaviors or characteristics are enabled by media (particularly SNS), whereas other behaviors and characteristics have been created because of media (Rus & Tiemensma, 2017). Some scholars have used the relational development model (see Knapp et al., 2020) to articulate how social media might affect different stages of romantic relational development (Brody et al., 2016; Fox & Anderegg, 2014; Fox & Warber, 2013; Fox et al., 2014; Goldberg et al., 2022; LeFebvre et al., 2015). The relationship developmental model (see Knapp et al., 2020) illustrated relationship movement through five coming-together stages: *initiating, experimentation, intensifying, integrating,* and *bonding* and five coming-apart stages: *differentiating, circumscribing, stagnating, avoiding, and terminating.* These stages (along with other relationship dissolution models) examined and mapped SNS behaviors onto these models. When extending these prior models, scholars considered specific relational behaviors afforded by social networking sites such as surveillance, relationship broadcasting or status determination, communicating (in)stability, photo impression management, network management, considerations for privacy and sharing, and relational communication (see Brody et al., 2016; Fox et al., 2014). These patterns delineate strategies and behaviors that are multiphasic (e.g., Brody et al., 2016), and exist beyond face-to-face communication channels. In particular, the initiating and experimenting processes include finding and locating, but also highlighted the ambiguity and uncertainty that can unfold through perpetual contact (Katz & Aakhus, 2002) and continuous connectivity (Karsay & Vandenbosch, 2021). In these stages, people may use uncertainty reduction strategies, information-seeking, and stalking practices to initiate (described above) but also describe how individuals work to manage relationships as they develop.

Early work in relationships and computer-mediated dating highlighted the process of modality switching, or when relational partners shift their communication from online-only to face-to-face (Ramirez & Zhang, 2007; Sharabi & Dykstra-DeVette). Modality switching is still an important process for online daters who to continue the relationship generally must move from purely mediated channels to face-to-face interaction. For example, Ramirez et al. (2015) found that online daters fared the best when they switched modalities around 14–21 days after first meeting online. This finding is likely explained by the fact that online daters needed enough time to learn a bit about each other, but not spend so much time purely online so that they began to form overly idealized or hyperpersonal impressions (see Walther, 1996).

With current forms of mediated communication, it is unlikely that daters move from purely online communication to purely offline communication. Rather, the communication driving the formation of interpersonal relationships likely occurs through a tapestry of modalities. Even relationships that start online weave various forms of social media throughout their relational communication (McEwan, 2021). Social media users may use messaging and image sharing features to display their relationship to the broader network. They may share gifs or TikToks with each other to highlight their perceived similarity. They can use social media postings to seek information and reduce uncertainty about each other.

Overall, social media may lead people to consider how to share and integrate their relationship in current public and private spheres. During these stages, relational partners may begin to make choices about how they will portray their relationship on social media. Public social media messages often bring different network segments together into a single audience, creating context collapse (see Marwick & boyd, 2011). For romantic relationships, context collapse may require couples to navigate posting messages that are appropriate for friends, but also family members, and perhaps work colleagues. Partners may need to discuss their preferences and requirements for managing messages for their social media audience.

Earlier research on social media focused on Facebook, which offered the ability to sign a relationship connection by going *Facebook official* (see Fox et al., 2014; Papp et al., 2012). By adding a relational status, this action prompted an important display of commitment, especially in young adult romantic relationships (Fox & Warber, 2013; Lane et al., 2016). Today, social media users have moved away from the idea of "Facebook official" for dating relationships (although many still update statuses for marriages and engagements), yet users still create posts to broadcast the status of their relationship to their broader network. For example, people might upload a new profile picture that includes their romantic partner or relationship pictures (Toma & Choi, 2015).

As couples begin to integrate, they also begin the process of managing impressions not only of themselves but also of the relationship (Sharabi & Hopkins, 2021). Representations of the relationship on social media can serve as a sign of partners' commitment to the relationship. Relational posts signal the existence and importance of the relationship to the broader social network (Ito et al., 2021). This visual public intimacy may demonstrate a critical relational turning point by signifying the disclosure of a developing relationship (Brody et al., 2016). However, for some partners, the intimacy loses its status when advertised broadly on social media (Miguel, 2016). The privilege of posting visual intimacy often highlights heteronormative relationships, and even if individuals and partners may want to display their developing relationship, the public-private norms may not allow their relationship openness. It should be noted that research findings in this area are primarily from studies with young adult samples. Although older demographics are becoming steady adopters (Auxier & Anderson, 2021) further relationship development scholarship should explore how adults of all ages navigate romantic relationships and social media.

The display of romantic relationship status on social media may have particularly positive outcomes for members of the LGBTQ community. Positive feedback via comments and likes on relational status posts can lead to greater feelings of resilience and well-being for same-sex partners (Bond, 2015). Viewing posts of others in sexual minority relationships can also serve as identity-affirming experiences for people whose LGBTQ-related aspects of identity are emerging. Social media content can provide representation of everyday regular life that goes beyond stereotyped and fetishized LGBTQ representations found within mass media (Fox & Ralston, 2016).

Social Media Relational Maintenance Behaviors

The observation of the relationship development model draws in and highlights relationship maintenance as relational partners demonstrate behaviors and routines through social media. All relationships require some type of maintenance to remain in existence and ideally in a mutually satisfactory state. Relational maintenance behaviors are the strategic and routine behaviors that couples engage in to keep their relationship in a desired state (Dindia, 2003). These behaviors or tactics have been sorted into various strategies such as positivity (cheerful and upbeat messages), assurances (messages related to relational commitment), openness (discussions about the relationship), and more (see Canary et al., 1993; Stafford, 2011).

Although the formation and dissolution processes in relationships often garner the most attention, couples spend the most time in their relationships maintaining that relationship. Social media, particularly SNS, can facilitate maintenance behaviors across a variety of relational types, including romantic couples. As people began to adopt social media platforms more widely, relational maintenance was a frequently cited motivation (Sheldon, 2008). Indeed, Ramirez and Walther (2009) noted that Facebook's "greatest utility" was likely relational maintenance.

In regard to specific studies of relational maintenance via social media, McEwan et al. (2014) developed a measure of Facebook relational maintenance. However, that measure has primarily been used to study platonic Facebook connections, and other scholars have adapted versions of general relational maintenance measures for social media contexts. For example, Stewart et al. (2014) examined sharing messages related to positivity, openness, and assurances and found that relational satisfaction was correlated with engaging in higher amounts of Facebook positivity and assurances. People may also use private channels provided through social media (e.g., Facebook messenger, Instagram DMs, Snapchat) to share maintenance messages (Langlais et al., 2020). More recent qualitative studies have found that young adults still use Facebook to maintain their romantic relationships. Goldberg et al. (2022) found social media such as Facebook and Instagram allowed users to create a sense of togetherness, but that Facebook was perceived as a better choice to display relational events as the Facebook audience is often a more closed network of friends, family, and social acquaintances whereas Instagram posts are often for the purpose of creating a particular aesthetic for a more public, less known audience.

Partners can tag each other as a type of electronic tie-sign (Goldberg et al., 2022; Ito et al., 2021; Tong & Walther, 2011). Engaging with each other's content through likes and comments can show that a partner endorses and confirms particular activities and identity displays (Goldberg et al., 2022). Other research has found that people may display their relationship on social media by posting pictures of gifts they have exchanged. Interestingly, motivations for posting gift pictures may vary by platform. Chinchanachokchai and Pusaksrikit (2021) found that people were more likely to post gifts they thought represented themselves on Facebook and use Instagram to post gifts that were high status. Overall, the utility of social media sites appears to be connected to the maintenance strategy of network connectivity. Social media allows a couple to display their relationship and commitment to their broader network. As one of Fox et al.'s (2014) participants noted, Facebook posts can be "the ultimate PDA [public display of affection], 'cause everyone can see it."

Ongoing Partner Surveillance

SNS can also serve as a site of ongoing surveillance of romantic partners (Fox et al., 2014; Tokunaga, 2016). SNS have several affordances including the visibility and persistence of posted information as well as increasing the perception of network associations that can lead to increased partner surveillance.

Through social media, romantic partners can monitor each other's posts and activity (Rueda et al., 2015).

Relational partners may use social media monitoring more when they are experiencing uncertainty about the relationship (Stewart et al., 2014). Relational uncertainty can be particularly high in the early stages of a relationship as partners get to know each other. In this stage, gathering information from a partner's or potential partner's social media feed may be a relatively benign way to get to know the person better. However, high levels of uncertainty later in the relationship may lead to jealousy-related reasons for monitoring a partner's social media behavior (Dainton & Berkoski, 2013; Dainton & Stokes, 2015; Stewart et al., 2014). SNS in particular may be breeding grounds for relational jealousy because the platforms provide easy access to survey network connections and interactions, facilitate relational maintenance with potential rivals, and produce more ambiguous social situations that could result in misunderstandings (Bevan, 2013).

Multiple studies have found that social media use can lead to conflict and jealousy when partners respond to potential rivals' posts, view profiles of potential rivals, and reconnect or post pictures with exes (Clayton et al., 2013; Muise et al., 2014). Seidmen et al. (2019) found that for couples with low levels of jealousy social media monitoring was perceived to be helpful for the relationship, but for those who were very jealous, monitoring did not improve the relationship. The persistence of social media information also allows partners to dig through previous posts and photos to find virtual artifacts and possessions or digital remnants such as social media evidence left over from previous romantic relationships (Frampton & Fox, 2018; LeFebvre et al., 2015; Robards & Lincoln, 2016). For some romantic partners, these virtual possessions or remnants may induce retroactive jealousy, which occurs when someone feels jealous about their partner's romantic history even though previous partners are not actively interfering in the current relationship (Elphinston & Noller, 2011; Frampton & Fox, 2018; LeFebvre et al., 2015).

Another way social media may contribute to increased jealousy in relationships is through hyperperception effects (Carpenter & Spottswood, 2021, see Walther 1996 for a review of the foundational hyperpersonal model). Hyperperception occurs when romantic partners view their partners' interactions with potential rivals on social media and perceive those interactions to be more intimate than they actually are. These effects can occur because (a) there is a limited amount of information available via social information and (b) social media tends to have a positivity bias where people post primarily positive content. Thus, if the observing partner perceives that their romantic partner and the potential rival are frequently engaging in positive interactions on SNS the observer may interpret this to mean that one or both members of the dyad are attempting to escalate their relationship. Actively seeking out interactions between partners and rivals, as well as engaging in a feedback loop (feeling that observing some of the partner/rival interaction led the observer to actively look for more of their interactions) was associated with greater feelings of jealousy (Carpenter & Spottswood, 2021).

Conflict

As can be seen from the findings on surveillance and jealousy, social media does not always have a positive effect on romantic couples. Although jealousy and finding out information about one's partner or potential rivals may be a main driver of social media related conflict (Arikewuyo et al., 2020), social media interactions can contribute to other conflicts as well. For example, in interviews with Latino adolescents, Len-Rios et al. (2016) found that respondents felt that sites such as Facebook or Instagram could have negative effects on their relationships as the increased ability to monitor their partners' posts could lead to finding potential causes of conflict. Partners may also use social media to check up on their partners' claims and activities if there is a lack of trust in the relationship (Frampton & Fox, 2018). Another potential source of conflict is disagreement over what partners consider appropriate to post on social media (Fox et al., 2014). Posts, pictures, and public communication with others can all lead to relational conflict episodes between romantic partners and Facebook related conflict has been shown to be negatively correlated with relational satisfaction, commitment, and love (Rahaman, 2015).

RELATIONSHIPS END, SOCIAL MEDIA LIVES ON

The process of de-coupling from a romantic entanglement typically has involved the lessening of communication frequency and intensity (Baxter, 1984; Knapp et al., 2020). Social media influences multiple aspects of relational dissolution (Gershon, 2020). When breaking up, romantic partners must determine how to disconnect or disengage their identities and shared memories. Former romantic couples need to disentangle the many ways they have woven their digital lives together, including managing virtual relational possession (Brody et al., 2020; LeFebvre et al., 2020). They also need to manage the increased uncertainty that comes with the end of the relationship and consider how much they want to engage with their former partner's social media content (Fox & Tokunaga, 2015). Mediated communication channels can influence the choices regarding how partners communicate relational termination to each other as well as how to reduce or cut off communication post-break up. Former partners can make active social media choices such as unfriending, blocking, deleting, and hiding or passive tactics such as ghosting, or cutting off communication with no explanation.

Social media can also influence how people manage the broader social network's impression of the breakup (Frampton & Fox, 2018). They may turn to social media to broadcast their side of the story or to post imagery of successfully moving on to the larger network. Social media also provides a persistent record of the relationship, by creating a visible chronology of previous communication, social interactions, and relational memory (Fox et al., 2021). This aspect of people's past must be managed as part of their own identity presentation and for what the record communicates to potential and future partners. The dissolution of a romantic relationship can be an incredibly distressing event in a person's life (Kendler et al., 2003). With the advent of social media, people now must manage public performances of the breakup, multiple communication channels connecting them to their break-up partner, and the potential for continue interaction and/or observance of the partner via social platforms.

Uncertainty Management

Often increased uncertainty bubbles up during the dissolution phase of a relationship (Planalp & Honeycutt, 1985). For those who did not initiate the break-up, experiencing dissolution can increase uncertainty about their understanding of the relationship and their former partner. In this high-uncertainty situation, people may be drawn to monitor their former partner's social media as an uncertainty management strategy (Fox & Tokunaga, 2015; Tong, 2013). Unfortunately, social media monitoring of exes is associated with greater distress for the surveyor. Taking a break from an ex-partner's social media content may be a better choice to facilitate moving on from the former relationship (Fox & Tokunaga, 2015; Fox & Warber, 2013). However, due to the integration of their social media presences, partners will have to negotiate how much social media contact they wish to have with their ex (Gershon, 2020). Different couples negotiate this in different ways, with some remaining friendly on the group messaging app, and others choosing to cut off all contact.

Relational Curation

Earlier in the chapter, we outlined how people use posts on social media to maintain the relationship and present an impression of the relationship to the network. During relational dissolution, couples must decide what happens to these digital artifacts. Some people choose to delete every virtual possession connected to the relationship, others choose to selectively remove relationship-related artifacts, and still others choose to keep the social media record fully intact (Herron et al., 2017). The variance in keeping and deleting behaviors may represent different approaches to the relational curation process (LeFebvre et al., 2020).

When people based curation decisions on their connection with their ex-partner, they were more likely to choose to keep those artifacts (LeFebvre et al., 2020). This choice may reflect a partner still connecting their identity with that relationship. However, keeping these artifacts may make adjusting to post-dissolution life more difficult (Sas & Whittaker, 2013) and lead to increased rumination regarding the failed relationship. On the other hand, people often delete virtual possessions in order to prepare for future relationships (LeFebvre et al., 2015; Frampton & Fox, 2018). Social media users who based their curation decision on potential future partners, were more likely to delete virtual possessions connected to their former partner. People who delete social media artifacts may be able to move on from the past relationship more quickly (Brody et al., 2020). Yet, the ability to encapsulate the past or hold onto memories that deal with past relationship social media (Garde-Hansen, 2009; LeFebvre et al., 2015) can call into question whether they can end or simply continue to exist through our social media.

Network Impression Management and Grave Dressing

The curation process articulates that relational identities can remain on social media long after the relationships have ended (McDaniel et al., 2021). Couples often have shared memories through social media and mutual connections making it more difficult to disentangle themselves (McDaniel et al., 2021; Zhang et al., 2020). Relational information on SNS may be particularly difficult to manage post-dissolution as the persistence of past communication about the relationship conflicts with the current relational status. Former romantic partners may use social media to communicate their experience to the broader network. Whereas relationship curation typically occurs behind the scenes, the grave-dressing process prioritizes the need to present their version of the story of the breakup to a social audience.

This narrative, grave-dressing process is not new (see Duck, 1998), but social media may complicate its deployment. The masspersonal nature of SNS can lead to an audience expecting fairly fixed, consistent, and coherent identity expressions (see McEwan, 2015). Yet, relational dissolution narratives indicate a change in relationships, reconstruction of part of the identity of the former relational partners, and introduces the possibility of the former partners presenting conflicting narratives to the social media audience.

Social media allows people to follow relationships as they develop and dissolve in real time (Fox et al., 2021; Seraj et al., 2021). The public audience represented on SNS can alter the way memories are created in the grave dressing process (Brody et al., 2020). Networks on SNS tend to be comprised of large audiences of weak ties and it may be difficult to craft messages that are appropriate for all segments of the network (Marwick & boyd, 2011). The presence of these ties representing a wide variety of contexts may make it difficult to perform the narrative tasks related to the end of a relationship. In addition, the persistence of digital items that represent cues to relationship memories and associated emotions can make it difficult to move on from past relationships (Herron et al., 2017; Sas & Whittaker, 2013).

Perhaps for these reasons, mediated sharing about a breakup may not have the same benefits as a face-to-face conversation. In a study of college students, Choi and colleagues (2017) found that discussing a breakup with friends in a face-to-face setting was related to feelings of personal growth but sharing via mediated channels did not have the same relationship to personal growth. When people are moving through their breakup, they must make decisions about what their digital items represent, how and which social networks to maintain, and how to organize their own relationship and individual identity moving forward.

Social Media-Related Break-Up Strategies

At times people may also use mediated channels to facilitate their break-up communication. Breaking up via mediated technology can generate physical and psychological separation (Sprecher et al., 2010). People may choose a particular medium in an effort to alter their message (Ledbetter, 2014) or maximize difference in perceived channel affordances (Fox & McEwan, 2017). In a study of college students, Choi et al. (2017) found that although most couples in a geographically-close relationship had a face-to-face conversation to break up, some chose texting instead. For long-distance romantic relationships, texting was a more popular choice for breaking up than a face-to-face conversation. Interestingly, a voice phone call was the least popular choice regardless of the partners' proximity to each other.

In other cases, people may avoid all communication with a former or potential partner and end the relationship with a strategy known as "ghosting." The term ghosting first appeared in 2006 in the Urban Dictionary as "the act of disappearing on your friends without notice or canceling plans with little or no choice." However, over time the term morphed into the concept of halting communication with a romantic partner or potential partner with no explanation. Based on qualitative interview data, LeFebvre et al. (2019) define the process as "unilaterally ceasing communication (temporarily or permanently) in an effort to withdraw access to individual(s) prompting relationship dissolution (suddenly or gradually) commonly enacted via one or multiple technological mediums." The individual withholding the communication is the ghoster, and the partner being avoided is the ghostee.

Ghosting is not an entirely new phenomenon; Planalp and Honeycutt (1985) include unexplained loss of contact such as the partner moving away in their typology of uncertainty-increasing events. However, the accessibility of social media and other forms of mediated communication makes it obvious to the ghostee that the ghoster could resume communication if they so choose. Thus, ghosting is typically thought of in connection with mediated contexts and channels (LeFebvre & Fan, 2020). In addition, mediated channels make ghosting an ambiguous loss. There is a physical and psychological absence, yet there remains a form of ambient access, the knowledge via digital technology that the person continues to exist (LeFebvre, 2018).

Ghosting may occur on a continuum; sudden ghosting occurs when communication suddenly ceases and gradual ghosting involves slowly spacing out communication episodes until they eventually cease altogether. In any case, most people feel that ghosting is an inappropriate break-up strategy, but it should be noted that people ghost anyway (LeFebvre et al., 2019). There are cases where ghosting may be seen as more appropriate such as in very early stages. As one of LeFebvre et al.'s (2019) participants noted, "I definitely think it's appropriate if you find someone on like Tinder. You start talking for a little bit but if you're not into it, you can just start ghosting them" (p. 134). In these cases, ghosters may feel that not enough has been invested into the relationship to go to the trouble of investing the time and energy required for a more explicit break-up discussion. Ghosting may also be seen as more appropriate if the ghostee begins behaving oddly or in a way that seems dangerous (Manning et al., 2019). In such a case, cutting off communication quickly and completely may be a safer dissolution strategy than attempting to explain the need for a dissolution in a face-to-face setting.

However, sometimes people ghost merely out of convenience or finding their attraction to the person has dissipated or not materialized. People who have strong implicit theories about destiny may be more likely to ghost than people who believe that relationship can grow and change over time (Freedman et al., 2019). In these cases, ghosting may create difficulties for the ghostee in that they likely experience ambiguity, uncertainty, and a lack of closure (Koessler et al., 2019; LeFebvre et al., 2019). Ghostees aim to make sense of the relationship itself often before transitioning to a new relationship; however, ghostees may engage in increased privacy settings (e.g., blocking of previous partners or social networks, deleting messages) in order to control the process of grave-dressing and begin resurrection (Pancani et al., 2021).

CONCLUSION

Throughout the lifespan of a relationship, romantic partners weave together communication through a variety of channels, including social media (McEwan, 2021).

Social media does not greatly alter the processes involved in romantic relationships; people still need to locate potential partners, form and maintain relationships, and dissolve those relationships. However, the affordances of social media, in particular persistence and network connectivity, often change the audience and rigidity of these messages. Mediated channels can allow for opportunities such as an increased pool of potential partners available via dating apps but also challenges such as experiencing conflict or jealousy related to a partners' social media posts. Much of the research on romantic relationships and social media thus far has occurred within the context of Facebook (although there is starting to be more work on other platforms e.g., Instagram, Snapchat). Whether Facebook remains an important social channel or not, young adults in particular are likely to weave their relational communication through many different mediated channels. Within this chapter, we have attempted to consider how relational processes and channel affordance intersect to make meaning in romantic relationships. Future research focusing on specific affordances can help us continue to increase our understanding of how the context of social media accommodates, amplifies, or alters relational communication processes (McEwan & Fox, 2022).

NOTE

1 It is an open question whether online dating applications are "social media." Using Carr and Hayes (2015) definition we would argue that many dating applications are Internet-based, they are disentrained (communication can send messages in real time or asynchronously from differing locations), and derive value primarily by connecting different users to each others' content. Thus, dating apps could reasonably be counted as social media.

REFERENCES

Andrejevic, M. (2005). The work of watching one another: Lateral surveillance, risk, and governance. *Surveillance & Society*, 2(4), 479–497. https://doi.org/10.24908/ss.v2i4.3359

Arikewuyo, A. O., Lasisi, T. T., Abdulbaqi, S. S., Omoloso, A. I., & Arikewuyo, H. O. (2020). Evaluating the use of social media in escalating conflicts in romantic relationships. *Journal of Public Affairs*, 22(1), e2331. https://doi.org/10.1002/pa.2331

Auxier, B., & Anderson, M. (2021). Social media use in 2021. *Pew Research Center*. www.pewresearch.org/internet/2021/04/07/social-media-use-in-2021/

Baxter, L. A. (1984). Trajectories of relationship disengagement. *Journal of Social and Personal Relationships*, 1(1), 29–48. https://doi.org/10.1177/0265407584011003

Berger, C. R., & Bradac, R. (1982). *Language and social knowledge: Uncertainty in interpersonal relations*. Arnold.

Berry, M. J., & Bainbridge, S. L. (2017). Manchester's Cyberstalked 18–30s: Factors affecting cyberstalking. *Advances in Social Sciences Research Journal*, 4(18).

Bevan, J. L. (2013). *The communication of jealousy*. Peter Lang.

Blackwell, C., Birnholtz, J., & Abbott, C. (2015). Seeing and being seen: Co-situation and impression formation using Grindr, a location-aware gay dating app. *New Media & Society*, 17(7), 1117–1136. https://doi.org/10.1177/1461444814521595

Bond, B. J. (2015). The mediating role of self-discrepancies in the relationship between media exposure and well-being among lesbian, gay, and bisexual adolescents. *Media Psychology*, *18*, 51–73. https://doi.org/10.1080/15213269.2014.917591

Boyd, d. m., & Ellison, N. B. (2007). Social network sites: Definition, history, and scholarship. *Journal of Computer-Mediated Communication*, *13*(1), 210–230. https://doi.org/10.1111/j.1083-6101.2007.00393.x

Brody, N., LeFebvre, L., & Blackburn, K. (2016). Social networking site behaviors across the relational lifespan: Measurement and association with relationship escalation and de-escalation. *Social Media + Society*, *2*(4).

Brody, N., LeFebvre, L. E., & Blackburn, K. (2020). Holding on and letting go: Virtual memory, nostalgia, and the effects of virtual possession management practices in post-breakup adjustment. *Journal of Social and Personal Relationships*, *37*(7), 2229–2249.

Bryant, E. M., Marmo, J., & Ramirez, A., Jr. (2011). A functional approach to social networking sites. In K. B. Wright & L. M. Webb (Eds.), *Computer-mediated communication in personal relationships* (pp. 3–20). Peter Lang.

Canary, D. J., Stafford, L., Hause, K. S., & Wallace, L. A. (1993). An inductive analysis of relational maintenance strategies: Comparisons among lovers, relatives, friends, and others. *Communication Research Reports*, *10*(1), 3–14. https://doi.org/10/1080/08824099309359913

Carpenter, C. J., & Spottswood, E. L. (2021). Extending the hyperpersonal model to observing others: The hyperperception model. *Journal of Communication Technology*, *4*(2), 58–81. https://doi.org/10.51548/joctec-2021-010

Chan, L. S. (2021). Looking for politically like-minded partners: Self-presentation and partner-vetting strategies on dating apps. *Personal Relationships*. Advanced online version. https://doi.org/10.1111/pere.12375

Chinchanachokchai, S., & Pusaksrikit, T. (2021). The role of self-construal in romantic gift posting across social networking sites. *Computers in Human Behavior*, *117*, 106665, https://doi.org/10.1016/j.chb.2020.106665.

Choi, M., Toma, C. L., Reinecke, L., & Eden, A. (2017). Social sharing with friends and family after romantic breakups: Patterns of media use and effects on psychological well-being. *Journal of Media Psychology: Theories, Methods, and Applications*, *29*(3), 166–172. https://doi.org/10.1027/1864-1105/a000226

Clayton, R. B., Nagurney, A., & Smith, J. R. (2013). Cheating, breakup, and divorce: Is Facebook use to blame?. *Cyberpsychology, Behavior, and Social Networking*, *16*(10), 717–720. https://doi.org/10.1089/cyber.2012.0424

Coontz, S. (2005). *Marriage, a history: How love conquered marriage*. Penguin Books.

Cunningham, M., & Barbee, A. (2008). Prelude to a kiss: Nonverbal flirting, opening gambits, and other communication dynamics in the initiation of romantic relationships. In S. Sprecher, A. Wenzel, & J. Harvey, (Eds.), *Handbook of Relationship Initiation* (pp. 109–132). Psychology Press.

Dainton, M., & Berkoski, L. (2013). Positive and negative maintenance behaviors, jealousy, and Facebook: Impacts on college students' romantic relationships. *Pennsylvania Communication Annual*, *69*(1), 35–50.

Dainton, M., & Stokes, A. (2015). College students' romantic relationships on Facebook: Linking the gratification for maintenance to Facebook maintenance activity and the experience of jealousy. *Communication Quarterly*, *63*(4), 365–383. https://doi.org/10.1080/01463373.2015.1058283

Dibble, J. L., Banas, J. A., & Drouin, M. (2021). Fanning the flames of back burner relationships electronically: Implications for romances and well-being among adults. *Atlantic Journal of Communication.* https://doi.org/10.1080/15456870.2021.1991349

Dindia, K. (2003). Definitions and perspectives on relational maintenance communication. In D. J. Canary & M. Dainton (Eds.), *Maintaining relationships through communication: Relational, contextual, and cultural variations* (pp. 1–30). Lawrence Erlbaum.

Dredge, R., & Anderson, J. (2021). The qualitative exploration of social competencies and incompetencies on mobile dating applications. *Personal Relationships, 28*(3), 627–651. https://doi.org/10.1111/pere.12378

Dreßing, H., Bailer, J., Anders, A., Wagner, H., & Gallas, C. (2014). Cyberstalking in a large sample of social network users: Prevalence, characteristics, and impact upon victims. *Cyberpsychology, Behavior, and Social Networking, 17*(2), https://doi.org/10.1089/cyber.2012.0231

Duck, S. W. (1998). *Human relationships* (3rd ed.). Sage.

Duguay, S. (2017). Dressing up Tinderella: Interrogating authenticity claims on the mobile dating app Tinder. *Information, Communication & Society, 20*(3), 351–367. https://doi.org/10.1080/1369118X.2016.1168471

Ellison, N. B., Steinfeld, C., & Lampe, C. (2007). The benefits of Facebook "friends": Social capital and college students' use of online social network sites. *Journal of Computer-Mediated Communication, 12*(4), 1143–1168. https://doi.org/10.1111/j.1083-6101.2007.00367.x

Elphinston, R. A., & Noller, P. (2011). Time to face it! Facebook intrusion and the implications for romantic jealousy and relationship satisfaction. *Cyberpsychology, Behavior, and Social Networking, 14*(11), 631–635. https://doi.org/10.1089/cyber.2010.0318

Fansher, A. K., & Randa, R. (2019). Risky social media behaviors and the potential for victimization: A descriptive look at college students victimized by someone met online. *Violence and Gender, 6*(2), 115–123. https://doi.org/10.1089/vio.2017.0073

Finkel, E. J., Eastwick, P. W., Karney, B. R., Reis, H. T., & Sprecher, S. (2012). Online dating: A critical analysis from the perspective of psychological science. *Psychological Science in the Public Interest, 13*(1), 3–66. https://doi.org/10.1177/1529100612436522

Fox, J., & Anderegg, C. (2014). Romantic relationship stages and social networking sites: Uncertainty reduction strategies and perceived relational norms on Facebook. *Cyberpsychology, Behavior, and Social Networking, 17*(11), 685–691. https://doi.org/10.1089/cyber.2014.0232

Fox, J., & McEwan, B. (2017). Distinguishing technologies for social interaction: The perceived social affordances of communication channels scale. *Communication Monographs, 84*(3), 298–318. https://doi.org/10.1080/03637751.2017.1332418

Fox, J., & Ralston, R. (2016). Queer identity online: Informal learning and teaching experiences of LGBTQ individuals on social media. *Computers in Human Behavior, 65,* 635–642. https://doi.org/10.1016/j.chb.2016.06.009

Fox, J., & Tokunaga, R. S. (2015). Romantic partner monitoring after breakups: Attachment, dependence, distress, and post-dissolution online surveillance via social networking sites. *Cyberpsychology, Behavior, and Social Networking, 18*(9), 491–498. https://doi.org/10.1089/cyber.2015.0123

Fox, J., & Warber, K. M. (2013). Romantic relationship development in the age of Facebook: An exploratory study of emerging adults' perceptions, motives, and behaviors. *Cyberpsychology, Behavior, and Social Networking, 16*(1), 3–7. https://doi.org/10.1089/cyber.2012.0288

Fox, J., Frampton, J. R., Jones, E., & Lookadoo, K., (2021). Romantic relationship dissolution on social networking sites: Self-presentation and public accounts of breakups on Facebook. *Journal of Social and Personal Relationships, 38*(12), 3732–3751. https://doi.org/10.1177/02654075211052247

Fox, J., Osborn, J. L., & Warber, K. M. (2014). Relational dialectics and social networking sites: The role of Facebook in romantic relationship escalation, maintenance, conflict, and dissolution. *Computers in Human Behavior, 35*(12), 527–534. https://doi.org/10.1016/j.chb.2014.02.031

Frampton, J. R., & Fox, J. (2018). Social media's role in romantic partners' retroactive jealousy: Social comparison, uncertainty, and information seeking. *Social Media + Society, 4*(3). https://doi.org/10.1177/2056305118800317

Freedman, G., Powell, D. N., Le, B., & Williams, K. D. (2019). Ghosting and destiny: Implicit theories of relationships predict beliefs about ghosting. *Journal of Social and Personal Relationships, 36*(3), 905–924. https://doi.org/10.1177/0265407517748791

Garde-Hansen, J. (2009). MyMemories?: Personal digital archive fever and Facebook. In J. Garde-Hansen, A. Hoskins, & Reading, A. (Eds.), *Save as .... Digital memories* (pp. 135–150). Palgrave Macmillan. https://doi.org/10.1057/9780230239418_8

Gershon, I. (2020). The breakup 2.1: The ten-year update. *Information Society, 36*(5), 279–289.

Gibbs, J. L., Ellison, N. B., & Heino, R. D. (2006). Self-presentation in online personals: The role of anticipated future interaction, self-disclosure, and perceived success in internet dating. *Communication Research, 33*(2). https://doi.org/10.1177/0093650205285368

Gibbs, J. L., Ellison, N. B., & Lai, C.-H. (2011). First comes love, then comes google: An investigation of uncertainty reduction strategies and self-disclosure in online dating. *Communication Research, 38*(1), 70–100. https://doi.org/10.1177/0093650210377091

Goldberg, S., Yeshua-Katz, D., & Marciano, A. (2022). Online construction of romantic relationships on social media. *Journal of Social and Personal Relationships.* Advanced online version.

Granovetter, M. S. (1973). The strength of weak ties. *American Journal of Sociology, 78*(6), 1360–1380. www.jstor.org/stable/2776392

Hall, J. A. (2020). *Relating through technology: Advances in Personal Relationships.* Cambridge University Press.

Hermida, A., & Hernández-Santaolalla, V. (2020). Horizontal surveillance, mobile communication and social networking sites: Lack of privacy in young people's daily lives. *Communication & Society, 33*(1), 139–152. https://hdl.handle.net/10171/62402

Herron, D., Moncur, W., & van den Hoven, E. (2017). *Digital decoupling and disentangling: Towards design for romantic breakup.* Proceedings of the 2017 Conference on Designing Interactive Systems, 1175–1185.

Hjorth, L., & Lim, S. S. (2012). Mobile intimacy in an age of affective mobile media. *Feminist Media Studies, 12*(4), 477–484. https://doi.org/10.1080/14680777.2012.741860

Hobbs, M., Owen, S., & Gerber, L. (2017). Liquid love?: Dating apps, sex, relationships and digital transformation of intimacy. *Journal of Sociology, 53*(2), 271–284. https://doi.org/10.1177/1440783316662718

Ito, K., Yang, S., & Li, L. M. W. (2021). Changing Facebook profile pictures to dyadic photos: Positive association with romantic partners' relationship satisfaction via perceived partner commitment. *Computers in Human Behavior, 120,* 106748. https://doi.org/10.1016/j.chb.2021.106748

Karsay, K., & Vandenbosch, L. (2021). Endlessly connected: Moving forward with agentic perspectives of mobile media. *Mass Communication and Society, 24*(6), 779–794. https://doi.org/10.1080/15205436.2021.1974785

Katz, J. E., & Aakhus, M. (2002). *Perpetual contact: Mobile communication, private talk, public performance.* Cambridge University Press.

Kendler, K. S., Hettema, J. M., Butera, F., Gardner, C. O., & Prescott, C. A. (2003). Life event dimensions of loss, humiliation, entrapment, and danger in the prediction of onsets of major depression and generalized anxiety. *Archives of General Psychiatry, 60*(8), 789–796. https://doi.org/10.1001/archpsyc.60.8.789

Knapp, M. L., Vangelisti, A. L., & Caughlin, J. P. (2020). *Interpersonal communication and human relationships* (8th ed.). Allyn & Bacon.

Knobloch, L. K., & Miller, L. E. (2008). Uncertainty and relationship initiation. In S. Sprecher, A. Wenzel, & J. Harvey (Eds.), *Handbook of relationship initiation* (pp. 121–134). Psychology Press.

Koessler, R. B., Kohut, T., & Campbell, L. (2019). When your boo becomes a ghost: The association between breakup strategy and breakup role in experiences of relationship dissolution. *Collabra: Psychology, 5*(1), 29. https://doi.org/10.1525/collabra.230

Kuar, P., Dhir, A., Tandon, A., Alzeiby, E. A., & Abohassan, A. (2021). A systematic literature review on cyberstalking. An analysis of past achievements and future promises. *Technological Forecasting and Social Change, 163,* https://doi.org/10.1016/j.techfore.2020.120426

Langlais, M. R., Seidman, G., & Bruxvoort, K. M. (2020). Adolescent romantic relationship-oriented Facebook behaviors: Implications for self-esteem. *Youth & Society, 52*(4), 661–683. https://doi.org/10.1177/0044118X18760647

Lane, B. L., Piercy, C. W., & Carr, C. T. (2016). Making it Facebook official: The warranting value of online relationship status disclosures on relational characteristics. *Computers in Human Behavior, 56,* 1–8. https://doi.org/10.1016/j.chb.2015.11.016

Ledbetter, A. (2014). The past and future of technology in interpersonal communication theory and research. *Communication Studies, 65*(4), 456–459.

LeFebvre, L. E. (2018). Swipe me off my feet: Explicating relationship initiation on Tinder. *Journal of Social and Personal Relationships, 35*(9), 1205–1229. https://doi.org/10.1177/0265407517706419

LeFebvre, L. E., & Fan, X. (2020). Ghosted?: Navigating strategies for reducing uncertainty and implications from ambiguous loss. *Personal Relationships, 27*(2), 433–459. https://doi.org/10.111/pere.12322

LeFebvre, L. E., & Goodcase, E. T. (2021). *The impact of rejection on mobile dating: Moderated mediation path analysis.* Paper presented at the 10th Society for the Study of Emerging Adults virtual conference.

LeFebvre, L. E., Allen, M., Rasner, R., Garstad, S., Wilms, A., & Parrish, C. (2019). Ghosting in emerging adults' romantic relationships: The digital disappearance dissolution strategy. *Imagination, Cognition, and Personality, 39*(2), 125–150.

LeFebvre, L. E., Blackburn, K., & Brody, N. (2015). Navigating romantic relationships on Facebook: Extending the relational dissolution model to account for social networking environments. *Journal of Social and Personal Relationship, 32*(1), 78–98. https://doi.org/10.1177/0265407514524848

LeFebvre, L. E., Brody, N., & Blackburn, K. G. (2020). How concerns about former or future partners influence virtual possession management: Examining relational curation in the relational dissolution model. *Communication Research Reports, 37*(4), 161–171. https://doi.org/10.1080/08824096.2020.1796617

LeFebvre, L. E., Ramirez, A., Hayes, J., & Gabrielson, G. (2019). *Finding, seeking, and communicating in relationship initiation: Exploring the pathway of modality switching and information-seeking*. Paper presented to the Human Communication and Technology Division at the National Communication Association Conference in Baltimore, Maryland.

Len-Ríos, M. E., Streit, C., Killoren, S., Deutsch, A., Cooper, M. L., & Carlo, G. (2016). US Latino adolescents' use of mass media and mediated communication in romantic relationships. *Journal of Children and Media, 10*(4), 395–410.

Levy, J., Markell, D., Cerf, M. (2019). Polar similars: Using massive mobile dating data to predict synchronization and similarity in dating preferences. *Frontiers in Psychology, 10*. www.frontiersin.org/articles/10.3389/fpsyg.2019.02010/full

Ling, R., Bertel, T., & Sundsøy, P. (2012). The socio-demographics of texting: An analysis of traffic data. *New Media & Society, 14*(2), 280–297. https://doi.org/10.1177/1461444811412711

Manning, J., Buchanan, C., & Denker, K. J. (2019). *Ghosting: Defining a relational communication phenomena*. In Meeting of the International Communication Association, Washington, DC.

Markowitz, D., Hancock, J., & Tong, S. (2018). Interpersonal dynamics in online dating: Profile, matching, and discovery. In Z. Papacharissi (Ed.), *A networked self and love* (pp. 50–61). Routledge.

Marwick, A. E., boyd, d. (2011). I tweet honestly, I tweet passionately: Twitter users, context collapse, and the imagined audience. *New Media & Society, 13*, 114–133. https://doi.org/10.1177/1461444810365313

McDaniel, B. T., Drouin, M., Dibble, J., Galovan, A. M., & Merritt, M. (2021). Are you going to delete me? Latent profiles of post-relationship breakup social media use and emotional distress. *Cyberpsychology, Behavior, and Social Networking, 24*(7), 464–472. https://doi.org/10.1089/cyber.2020.0714

McEwan, B. (2015). *Navigating new media networks: Understanding and managing communication challenges in a networked society*. Lexington Books.

McEwan, B. (2021). Modality switching to modality weaving: Updating theoretical perspectives for expanding media affordances. *Annals of the International Communication Association, 45*(1), 1–19. https://doi.org/10.1080/23808985.2021.1880958

McEwan, B., & Fox, J. (2022). Before the how: The whats and whys of studying social media. In A. Quan-Hasse and L. Sloan (Eds.), *Social media research methods* (2nd ed., pp. 27–39). Sage.

McEwan, B., Fletcher, J., Eden, J., & Sumner, E. (2014). Development and validation of a Facebook relational maintenance measure. *Communication Methods and Measures, 8*(4), 244–263. https://doi/org/10.1080/19312458.2014.967844

Ménard, K. S., & Pincus, A. L. (2012). Predicting overt and cyber stalking perpetration by male and female college students. *Journal of Interpersonal Violence, 27*(11), 2183–2207. https://doi.org/10.1177/0886260511432144

Miguel, C. (2016). Visual intimacy on social media: From selfies to the co-construction of intimacies through shared pictures. *Social Media + Society, 2*(2). https://doi.org/10.1177/2056305116641705

Miller, B. (2015). "They're the modern-day gay bar": Exploring the uses and gratifications of social networks for men who have sex with men. *Computers in Human Behavior, 51,* 476–482. https://doi.org/10.1016/j.chb.2015.05.023

Muise, A., Christofides, E., & Desmarais, S. (2014). "Creeping" or just information seeking: Gender differences in partner monitoring in response to jealousy on Facebook. *Personal Relationships, 21*(1), 33–50.

O'Sullivan, P. B., & Carr, C. T. (2018). Masspersonal communication: A model bridging the mass-interpersonal divide. *New Media & Society, 20*(3), 1161–1180. https://doi.org/10.1177/1461444816686104

Pancani, L., Mazzoni, D., Aureli, N., & Riva, P. (2021). Ghosting and orbiting: An analysis of victims' experiences. *Journal of Social and Personal Relationships, 38*(7), 1987–2007. https://doi.org/10.1177/02654075211000417

Papp, L. M., Danielewicz, J., & Cayemberg, C. (2012). "Are we Facebook official?" Implications of dating partners' Facebook use and profiles for intimate relationship satisfaction. *Cyberpsychology, Behavior, and Social Networking, 15*(2), 85–90. https://doi.org/10.1089/cyber.2011.0291

Parsons-Pollard, N., & Moriarty, L. J. (2009). Cyberstalking: Utilizing what we do know. *Victims and Offenders, 4*(4), 435–441. https://doi.org/10.1080/15564880903227644

Planalp, S., & Honeycutt, J. M. (1985). Events that increase uncertainty in personal relationships. *Human Communication Research, 11*(4), 593–604. https://doi.org/10.1111/j.1468-2958.1985.tb00062.x

Rahaman, H. S. (2015). Romantic relationship length and its perceived quality: Mediating role of Facebook-related conflict. *Europe's Journal of Psychology, 11*(3), 395. https://doi.org/10.5964/ejop.v11i3.932

Ramirez, A., Jr., & Walther, J. B. (2009). New technologies and new directions in online relating. In S. W. Smith & S. W. Wilson (Eds.), *New directions in interpersonal communication research* (pp. 264–284). Sage.

Ramirez, A., Jr., & Zhang, S. (2007). When online meets offline: The effect of modality switching on relational communication. *Communication Monographs, 74*(3), 287–310. https://doi.org/10.1080/03637750701543493

Ramirez, A. Jr., Sumner E. M., Fleuriet, C., & Cole, M. (2015). When online dating partners meet offline: The effect of modality switching on relational communication between online daters. *Journal of Computer-Mediated Communication, 20*(1), 99–114. https://doi.org/10.1111/jcc4.12101

Ramirez, A., Jr., Sumner, E. M., & Spinda, J. (2017). The relational reconnection function of social network sites. *New Media & Society, 19*(6), 807–825. https://doi.org/10.1177/1461444815614199

Ramirez, A., Jr., Walther, J. B., Burgoon, J. K., & Sunnafrank, M. (2002). Information-seeking strategies, uncertainty, and computer-mediated communication. *Human Communication Research, 28*(2), 213–228. https://doi.org/10.1111/j.1468-2958.2002.tb00804.x

Reyns, B. W., Henson, B., & Fisher, B. S. (2011). Being pursued online: Applying cyber-lifestyle–routine activities theory to cyberstalking victimization. *Criminal Justice and Behavior, 38*(11), 1149–1169. https://doi.org/10.1177/0093854811421448

Robards, B., & Lincoln, S. (2016). Making it "Facebook official": Reflecting on romantic relationships through sustained Facebook use. *Social Media + Society, 2*(4). https://doi.org/10.1177/2056305116672890

Rosenfeld, M. J., & Thomas, R. J. (2012). Searching for a mate: The rise of the internet as a social intermediary. *American Sociological Review, 77*(4), 523–547. https://doi.org/10.1177/0003122412448050

Rueda, H. A., Lindsay, M., & Williams, L. R. (2015). "She posted it on Facebook": Mexican American adolescents' experiences with technology and romantic relationship conflict. *Journal of Adolescent Research, 30*(4), 419–445. https://doi.org/10.1177/0743558414565236

Rus, H. M., & Tiemensma, J. (2017). "It's complicated." A systematic review of associations between social network site use and romantic relationships. *Computers in Human Behavior, 75*, 684–703. https://doi.org/10.1016/j.chb.2017.06.004

Sas, C., & Whittaker, S. (2013). Design for forgetting: Disposing of digital possessions after a breakup. In *Proceedings of the SIGCHI conference on human factors in computing systems* (pp. 1823–1832). ACM. https://doi.org/10.1145/2470654.2466241

Seidman, G., Langlais, M., & Havens, A. (2019). Romantic relationship-oriented Facebook activities and the satisfaction of belonging needs. *Psychology of Popular Media Culture, 8*(1), 52–62.

Seraj, S., Blackburn, K. G., & Pennebaker, J. W. (2021). Language left behind on social media exposes the emotional and cognitive costs of a romantic breakup. *Proceedings of the National Academy of Science, 118*(7), 1–7. https://doi.org/10.1073/pnas.2017154118

Sharabi, L. L. (2021). Online dating profiles, first-date interactions, and the enhancement of communication satisfaction and desires in future interaction. *Communication Monographs, 88*(2), 131–153. https://doi.org/10.1080/03637751.2020.1766094

Sharabi, L. L., & Caughlin, J. P. (2017). What predicts first date success? A longitudinal study of modality switching in online dating. *Personal Relationships, 24*(2), 370–391. https://doi.org/10.1111/pere.12188

Sharabi, L. L., & Hopkins, A. (2021). Picture perfect? Examining associations between relationship quality, attention to alternatives, and couples' activities on Instagram. *Journal of Social and Personal Relationships.* https://doi.org/10.1177/0265407521991662

Sheldon, P. (2008). Student favorite: Facebook and motives for its use. *Southwestern Mass Communication Journal, 23*(2).

Sheldon, P., & Bryant, K. (2016). Instagram: Motives for its use and relationship to narcissism and contextual age. *Computers in Human Behavior, 58*, 89–97. https://doi.org/10.1016/j.chb.2015.12.059

Sheng, J. T., & Kairam, S. R. (2020). From virtual strangers to irl friends: Relationship development in livestreaming communities on twitch. *Proceedings of the ACM on Human-Computer Interaction, 4*(CSCW2), 1–34. http://doi.org/10.1145/3415165

Sprecher, S., Zimmerman, C., & Abrahams, E. M. (2010). Choosing compassionate strategies to end a relationship: Effects of compassionate love for partner and the reason for the breakup. *Social Psychology, 41*(2), 66–75. https://doi.org/10.1027/1864-9335/a000010

Spitzberg, B. H., & Hoobler, G. (2002). Cyberstalking and the technologies of interpersonal terrorism. *New Media & Society, 4*(1), 71–92. https://doi.org/10.1177/14614440222226271

Stafford, L. (2011). Measuring relationship maintenance behaviors: Critique and development of the revised relationship maintenance behavior scale. *Journal of Social and Personal Relationships, 28*(2), 278–303. https://doi.org/10.1177/0265407510378125

Stewart, M. C., Dainton, M., & Goodboy, A. K. (2014). Maintaining relationships on Facebook: Associations with uncertainty, jealousy, and satisfaction. *Communication Reports, 27*(1), 13–26. https://doi.org/10.1080/08934215.2013.84675

Sumter, S. R., & Vandenbosch, L. (2019). Dating gone mobile: Demographic and personality-based correlates of using smartphone-based dating applications among emerging adults. *New Media & Society, 21*(3), 655–673. https://doi.org/10.1177/1461444818804773

Thomas, R. (2020). Online exogamy reconsidered: Estimating the internet's effects on racial, educational, religious, political and age assortative mating. *Social Forces, 98*(3), 1257–1286, https://doi.org/10.1093/sf/soz060

Tokunaga, R. S. (2011). Social networking site or social surveillance site? Understanding the use of interpersonal electronic surveillance in romantic relationships. *Computers in Human Behavior, 27*(2), 705–713

Tokunaga, R. S. (2016). Interpersonal surveillance over social network sites: Applying a theory of negative relational maintenance and the investment model. *Journal of Social and Personal Relationships, 33*(2), 171–190. https://doi.org/10.1177/0265407514568749

Tokunaga, R. S., & Aune, K. S. (2017). Cyber-defense: A taxonomy of tactics for managing cyberstalking. *Journal of Interpersonal Violence, 32*(10), 1451–1475. https://doi.org/10.1177/0886260515589564

Toma, C. L., & Choi, M. (2015). The couple who Facebooks together, stays together: Facebook self-presentation and relationship longevity among college-aged dating couples. *Cyberpsychology, Behavior, and Social Networking, 18*, 367–372. https://doi.org/10.1089/cyber.2015.0060

Toma, C. L., Jiang, L. C., & Hancock, J. T. (2018). Lies in the eye of the beholder: Asymmetric beliefs about one's own and others' deceptiveness in mediated and face-to-face communication. *Communication Research, 45*(8), 1167–1192.

Tong, S. T. (2013). Facebook use during relationship termination: Uncertainty reduction and surveillance. *Cyberpsychology, Behavior, and Social Networking, 16*(11), 788–793. https://doi.org/10.1089/cyber.2012.0549

Tong, S. T., & Walther, J. B. (2011). Relational maintenance and CMC. *Computer-Mediated Communication in Personal Relationships, 53*(9), 1689–1699.

Tooke, W., & Camire, L. (1991). Patterns of deception in intersexual and intrasexual mating strategies. *Ethology and Sociobiology, 12*(5), 345–364. https://doi.org/10.1016/0162-3095(91)90030-T

Utz, S., & Beukeboom, C. J. (2011). The role of social network sites in romantic relationships: Effects on jealousy and relationship happiness. *Journal of Computer-Mediated Communication, 16*(4), 511–527. https://doi.org/10.1111/j.1083-6101.2011.01552.x

Van Ouytsel, J., Van Gool, E., Walrave, M., Ponnet, K., & Peeters, E. (2016). Exploring the role of social networking sites within adolescent romantic relationships and dating experiences. *Computers in Human Behavior, 55*(Part A), 76–86. https://doi.org/10.1016/j.chb.2015.08.042

Vaterlaus, J. M., & Winter, M. (2021). TikTok: An exploratory study of young adults' uses and gratifications. *Social Science Journal*. Advanced online version. https://doi.org/10.1080/03623319.2021.1969882

Vogels, E. A. (2021). The state of online harassment. *Pew Research Center*. Retrieved from www.pewresearch.org/internet/2021/01/13/the-state-of-online-harassment/

Vogels, E. A., & Anderson, M. (2020). Dating and relationships in the digital age. *Pew Research Center*. www.pewresearch.org/internet/2020/05/08/dating-and-relationships-in-the-digital-age/

Walther, J. B. (1996). Computer-mediated communication: Impersonal, interpersonal, and hyperpersonal interaction. *Communication Research, 23*(1), 3–43. https://doi.org/10.1177/009365096023001001

Weser, V. U., Opara, I., Sands, B E., Fernandes, C. F., & Hieftje, K. D. (2021). How Black teen girls navigate social media to form romantic relationships. *Social Media + Society, 7*(3), 1–9.

Zhang, E., Freeman, G., & McNeese, N. J. (2020). Breakups and social media: Social behaviors and dilemmas. *CSCW '20 Companion*.

12

Situating Latinx Immigrant Romantic Relationships in the Context of Illegality

Using a Socioculturally Attuned Lens

BETHANY L. LETIECQ AND J. MARIA BERMUDEZ

Over the past two decades, there have been significant advances in research with Latinx immigrant families residing in the United States (Romero & Umaña-Taylor, 2018). This research has included to a limited degree a focus on intimate partner romantic relationships, with most studies examining relationships among Mexican-origin couples and young people (e.g., Brady et al., 2009; Helms et al., 2014; Killoren et al., 2022; Pila, 2016). Although immigrants from Mexico comprise the largest share of Latinx immigrants in the United States, in more recent years, the Latinx immigrant population has become more heterogeneous, especially with the growth of immigrants hailing from Central America (Capps et al., 2020). Scholars have begun to document the lived experiences of Central American immigrants to the United States (e.g., Abrego, 2014; Menjívar et al., 2016); however, more research is needed to understand and contextualize romantic relationship formation, pathways to commitment, and relational health and functioning among diverse Latinx immigrants and their partners vis-à-vis their country of origin and where they settle in the United States.

Additionally, given how US immigration laws and policies shape and stratify Latinx immigrant experiences (Hall et al., 2019; Menjívar, 2021), family scholars must consider the ways in which varied and liminal legal statuses (among other factors related to immigration) condition and constrain the romantic relationships of Latinx immigrants residing in the United States. Importantly, research is needed to delineate how undocumented Latinx immigrants and their partners respond and adapt to, cope with, and resist nativist, anti-immigrant, and hostile laws and policies that threaten their livelihoods while they also pursue their individual and family goals and a better life (Menjívar & Kantsroom, 2014; Walsdorf et al., 2019).

In this chapter, we review the nascent research on Latinx immigrant romantic relationships in the context of illegality, with a particular focus on Central American immigrants living in the United States. We offer a socioculturally attuned lens to reflect on the ways in which illegality shapes romantic relationships between partners, where at least one person is undocumented (Abrego, 2014; Menjívar et al., 2016; Pila, 2016). Illegality is a term used to refer to the United States immigration laws, policies, and practices that foment and expose immigrants and their families to discrimination, exploitation, victimization, violence and abuse, criminalization, detainment, deportation, and family separation based on their legal status (Abrego et al., 2017; De Genova & Peutz, 2010; Golash-Boza & Hondagneu-Sotelo, 2013; Menjívar & Kantsroom, 2014; Sampaio, 2015). We argue in this chapter that illegality is a powerful structural force that transcends cultural explanations of Latinx immigrant romantic relationships. We draw upon a recent study by Letiecq et al. (2022) to apply our socioculturally attuned lens and underscore how illegality conditions and constrains the relational experiences and opportunities of Central American immigrants residing in the Washington, DC region.

Before we delve into this review, we first detail our positionalities as authors of this chapter and researchers of Latinx immigrant family life and discuss the conceptual framing that guides our work. Then, we review the changing immigration landscape and the immigration laws and policies that have produced and sustain illegality and immigrant marginalization and exploitation in the United States. We come to this work as family scientists and critical feminist scholars with deep commitments to antiracism, decolonizing research methods, and social justice.

AUTHORS' POSITIONALITY

Bethany

As a family scholar and research methodologist, I have spent the last twenty years studying and using community-based participatory action research (CBPAR) approaches to partner with immigrant and other minoritized and marginalized families (e.g., Letiecq et al., 2022). As a White cisgender heterosexual woman and US-born citizen with settler roots (my great grandparents immigrated to the United States from Portugal and Quebec, Canada), I hold many positions of intersectional privilege and power. Using CBPAR offers the possibility of sharing power with and taking action alongside people marginalized by the racialized, gendered, and classed/caste systems that reproduce social inequalities and maintain systems of White supremacy (Letiecq, 2019; Vaughn et al., 2016; Wallerstein et al., 2018; Walsdorf et al., 2019). I also practice critical reflexivity and cultural humility, orientations to community engagement that are based on an openness to interrogate the self vis-à-vis others, hold the self and others accountable to redressing unequal power relations, and be guided by people who are the experts of their own lived experiences of social, cultural, and legal marginalization and family life (Tervalon

& Murray-Garcia, 1998). My goal is to understand how structural forces (i.e., laws, policies, regulations, and rules) reproduce and maintain family marginalization and oppression at the intersections of race, gender, class, and nation in order to take action as part of an inclusive multi-racial and gender diverse collective to advance social justice.

Maria

I am a cisgender, White, heterosexual woman who holds many privileges due to my race, ability and immigration status, and education. I am originally from Honduras and was reared in the United States. My family and I had the fortune to lawfully immigrate together in 1970, become legal residents, and later US citizens, which is something that as a family we never took for granted. My father was unable to adapt to the United States, so he returned to Honduras, leaving my mother to parent alone and shifting our family dynamics to become a transnational family. We were able to benefit from a modest middle-class lifestyle, mostly due to my mother's hard work as an accountant and my brothers as skilled carpenters. Although most of my family resides in the United States lawfully, I have family members who are undocumented, are DACA recipients, and/or experience the liminal space of being under-documented due to financial and legal barriers to US citizenship. My experiences as an immigrant Latina growing up in the United States has helped me maintain my cultural roots and embrace my bi-cultural identity, with humility and a heightened awareness and sensitivity of my position of power, social location, and sense of agency. I bring these experiences to my life as a scholar and family therapist who has devoted her career to conducting studies to better understand and empower the lives of Latinx immigrant women and their families.

SOCIOCULTURAL ATTUNEMENT AS FAMILY SCHOLARS

We are informed by the many critical lenses (i.e., intersectional feminism, Latinx and transnational feminism, borderland theory, critical geography, critical race theory, queer theory) that are the foundation of socioculturally attuned family therapy and family science. This work was first proposed by McDowell and colleague (2018) in their book, "Socioculturally Attuned Family Therapy: Guidelines for Equitable Theory and Practice." The intention of socioculturally attuned family therapy is for it to serve as a transtheoretical framework that can be applied to existing couple and family therapy models in ways that encourage equity-based practice. McDowell and colleagues define sociocultural attunement as awareness of the relationship between societal systems, culture, and power, along with the intention to persistently attend and respond to and resist what is unjust. Using this lens/approach and maintaining this stance requires scholars to seek interdisciplinary concepts to deepen our understanding of the impact of culture, power relations, and societal systems on individuals, couples, families, and communities. Sociocultural attunement goes beyond essentializing groups or analyzing between-group dynamics within a single society, to understanding the politics of difference across local, national, and global contexts and the impact of these on relationship processes (McDowell et al., 2018). Socioculturally attuned family scholars support cultural democracy while promoting just relationships. As such, it is important to carefully consider how individual and relational needs, interests, motivations, and wellbeing are reflected in the social forces that organize relationships. There is an emphasis on respecting and integrating a family's cultural values and idiosyncratic perspectives, while simultaneously challenging relational inequities and oppression at every level. This is especially important for family scholars today, whose work toward equity and social justice is at odds with strong sociopolitical forces working to maintain the status quo of White supremacy (Walsdorf et al., 2020).

McDowell and colleagues contend that sociocultural attunement paves the way for third order thinking and praxis (Knudson-Martin et al., 2019; McDowell et al., 2019). Third order thinking requires scholars and practitioners to connect the dots between a person's personal and relational problems and the broader social world and environmental context in which they are embedded. To do this, we have to maintain a keen awareness of how we organize and make sense of vast amounts of information, including how our perspectives constrain and limit our understanding and work with couples and families. Third order thinking enables one to attune to the experience of each individual within the complexities of interconnected identities and relationships within social, economic, political, and environmental contexts. This requires us to attune to the effects of uneven distribution of resources and inequitable societal structures. In essence, third order thinking helps scholars map the effects of social forces, beliefs, practices and power processes within and across cultural contexts and take collective action alongside community members to foment transformative systemic change (McDowell et al., 2018). Navigating this tension between research and action is especially important for scholars examining and witnessing the unjust effects of illegality on the lives of Latinx immigrant couples and families (Letiecq et al., 2022; Menjívar & Kantsroom, 2014).

CULTURAL VALUES VERSUS STRUCTURAL FORCES

Research on Latinx immigrant family life often points to cultural values as explanations for family dynamics and outcomes. For example, Hall et al. (2019) noted that a strong orientation toward family is a "common explanation for Latinx immigrants' early family formation transitions, relatively high rates of marriage, and higher likelihood of living in extended households"

(p. 83). Yet Hall et al. (2019), among others (e.g., Menjívar et al., 2016; Pinto & Ortiz, 2018), have questioned the relevance of arguments suggesting that the family formation behaviors and lived experiences of Latinx immigrant families are driven by cultural orientations toward the family alone. For example, Hall et al. (2019) found differences between the family and household dynamics of documented and undocumented immigrants originating from the same countries and presumably sharing similar cultural traditions regarding family life. For example, the researchers found that undocumented immigrants were less likely than documented immigrants to live with a spouse or child and more likely to live with distant kin and nonrelatives. Undocumented immigrants also experienced greater household instability, crowding, and change than their documented counterparts. Such findings suggest that structural forces, including immigration laws and policies that stratify, marginalize, oppress, and criminalize undocumented immigrants, shape the relational, familial, and household experiences of these groups (Abrego et al., 2017).

The United States immigration system, produced by a complex web of interlocking laws and policies, has varied effects on Latinx immigrant families with varied or mixed legal statuses within their family systems (Menjívar et al., 2016). Mixed statuses result when one member of the couple or family has legal authorization to be in the United States, or was born in the United States (and is therefore automatically a US citizen), whereas others are undocumented because they arrived or stayed in the United States without legal authorization or because their liminal legal status changed (Gonzales & Raphael, 2017; Terrazas et al., 2020; Walsdorf et al., 2019). It is estimated that 4.1 million US citizen children under the age of eighteen years reside with at least one undocumented immigrant parent (Capps et al., 2016). The 2011 American Communities Survey (ACS) found that one in every thirteen married couples in the United States, representing over 4 million households, are mixed status couples. López (2022) suggested that the ACS likely underestimated the numbers of mixed status couples, as it does not include, for example, cohabiting couples or families with a naturalized citizen partner and a foreign-born, non-naturalized partner. These data reflect the complexity and heterogeneity of immigrant family life in the United States – family life structurally influenced by immigration laws and policies that often focus on individuals rather than the family systems of which they are a part (López, 2022).

Although exploring the cultural values and beliefs that shape immigrants' lives is important, it is imperative for scholars to use a sociocultural lens to carefully examine and attune to the social forces (above and beyond culture) that condition and constrain lived experiences as well. This is especially critical when studying romantic relationships among Latinx immigrants in the United States, who have been consistently minoritized and marginalized by powerful structural forces undergirding the construction of illegality (Gonzales & Raphael, 2017; Menjívar et al., 2016). It is also important to document the processes of adaptation, resilience, and resistance used by those marginalized by White supremacy in order to understand, uplift, and amplify the ways in which they navigate their intimate and familial relationships, even under harsh, punishing circumstances such as those produced by illegality (Bermudez & Mancini, 2013; Heidbrink, 2020; Tuck, 2009; Vesely et al., 2017).

THE CHANGING LANDSCAPE FOR LATINX IMMIGRANTS IN THE UNITED STATES

Although the majority of Latinx people in the United States are native born (Pew Research Center, 2019), there are an estimated 11 million undocumented individuals in the United States, most of whom are from Mexico (Capps et al., 2020). Indeed, for decades, Mexico was the largest sending country. However, in more recent years, immigration from the Northern Triangle region of Central America, including El Salvador, Honduras, and Guatemala, has increased (Capps et al., 2020). It is estimated that 3.4 million Central Americans immigrants reside in the United States to date and are among the fastest growing subpopulations of immigrants (Lesser & Batalova, 2017; Meyer & Taft-Morales, 2019). Among Central American immigrants in the United States, it is estimated that 1.74 million are undocumented (Capps et al., 2020). The push factors or those that force people to leave their countries of origin (e.g., poverty, war, gang violence, political corruption, natural disasters, climate crises), the pull factors or those that encourage or entice people to immigrate (e.g., better wages, family reunification), and the means and motivations of people making the decision to journey to the United States vary from place to place (Heidbrink, 2020; Jones, 2016). Immigration and related law and policy changes in the United States and around the globe likewise can greatly influence immigration flows and settlements (Menjívar et al., 2016).

From Open Borders and Circular Migration to Settlement and Illegality

Since the nineteenth century, for people living in the US-Mexico borderlands, the border was a permeable line that allowed for the movement of people and exchange of goods and services across the border with little concern or oversight. In her book, *How Immigration Became Illegal*, Aviva Chomsky (2014) explained that:

Until 1924, the new border between the United States and Mexico was virtually unpoliced, and migration flowed openly. Mexicans were exempt from the immigration restrictions passed into law before 1965. [However], because they were not considered migrants, Mexicans were also permanently deportable and were, in fact, singled out for mass deportations in the 1930s and 1950s. (p. 10)

Later, between 1965 and 1986, an estimated 28 million undocumented immigrants, mainly from Mexico, participated in what is referred to as "circular migration" (Massey et al., 2002). Mexican migrants entered the United States to work, stayed for relatively short periods of time, returned to Mexico to live with their families, and then returned seasonally to work in the United States again. Those migrants who did not migrate based on the season and chose instead to remain in the United States were often exposed to poor living conditions, segregated work camps and barrios, underfunded schools, and poor working conditions (Chomsky, 2014; Spickard, 2007). Importantly, those harsh conditions fueled the Chicano Movement of the 1960s and 1970s, the largest civil rights movement led by people of Mexican descent in the United States. The Chicano Movement, which coincided with the Civil Rights Movement, saw some significant gains, including the unionization of and better and more dignified working conditions and pay for farmworkers (Barajas, 2012).

However, in 1986, to stem the flow of unauthorized immigration, Congress passed the Immigration Reform and Control Act (IRCA). While IRCA provided for the legalization of more than three million people, it also made it illegal for the first time in US history for employers to knowingly hire an undocumented immigrant. According to Gonzales and Raphael (2017):

The logic of IRCA was clear. The policy wiped the slate clean for those unauthorized immigrants with established lives in the United States, and made a major concession to a key class of employers (growers in particular) via a legalization for seasonal agricultural workers. At the same time, by creating a sanction system for employers and prohibiting the hiring of the unauthorized, IRCA attempted to eliminate the major pull factor that had long attracted many undocumented immigrants to the United States, namely, the prospects of higher and perhaps more stable earnings. (p. 4)

IRCA also fortified the United States-Mexico border, and according to Massey et al. (2002), resulted in unintended consequences, including the growth and stability of undocumented immigrant settlements in the United States. As noted by Gonzales and Raphael (2017), by the mid-1990s, the number of undocumented immigrants settling in the United States not only grew substantially, but immigrants crossed borders with their family members, deepening ties to Latinx immigrant communities in the United States, and growing their families by bearing US-born children who are by law US citizens.

While IRCA had the unintended effect of increasing the permanence of undocumented immigrants settling in the United States, it also fomented an inhospitable policy context, where life became increasingly hostile and challenging for those in the United States without legal authorization. Undocumented immigrants were scapegoated as harming the economic opportunities of US citizens and became the targets of a "formidable deportation machine" run by the United States Immigration and Customs Enforcement or ICE (Gonzales & Raphael, 2017, p. 6). The treatment of Mexican workers over time "underlies the apparent paradox between the United States as a so-called country of migrants and its xenophobia and restrictive immigration policies" (Chomsky, 2014, p. 10). As we discuss next, IRCA and a series of other US immigration and interlinked social welfare laws and policies successfully transformed immigration family life in the United States, producing the current context of illegality and deportability that shapes the everyday lives of immigrants in the United States, including how they form and sustain romantic relationships.

The Production of Illegality, Deportability, and Multigenerational Punishment

The United States has a long history of creating structurally-racist and value-based immigration laws and policies that conceived of immigrants as being either legal or illegal (Tourse et al., 2018). In the most recent anti-immigrant era, the United States not only passed IRCA but also implemented the 1996 Illegal Immigration Reform and Immigrant Responsibility Act (IIRIRA). Together, these acts greatly affected the everyday lives of undocumented individuals and their family members, including children (Yoshikawa, 2011). These laws denied undocumented immigrants opportunities and resources and used the threat of deportation as a cudgel to force immigrants into the shadows (Vesely et al., 2019a).

Prior to the modern era of illegality, deportations were less common, hovering around 10,000–30,000 annually, depending on the decade (US Department of Homeland Security, 2019). However, post IRCA and IIRIRA, deportations began rising steadily, reaching over 400,000 annually by 2012. Mass deportations have continued to the present (US Department of Homeland Security, 2019), criminalizing and punishing unauthorized immigrants – and especially men from Mexico and Central America – and creating high levels of stress among immigrant families with undocumented members (De Genova & Peutz, 2010; Golash-Boza & Hondagneu-Sotelo, 2013; Gonzales & Raphael, 2017). Critical scholars attuned to the sociocultural context of immigration argue that deportations enforce a prejudiced and racialized migratory system that favors certain migrant groups, while denying entry to other migrants based on a racialized paradigm against migrants of color (Enríquez, 2015; Estévez, 2012; Sampaio, 2015; Valdéz, 2016). In this context of racialized illegality, legal status serves as an axis of stratification and oppression, constraining and threatening Latinx immigrant intimate partner relationships, marriages, and familial experiences (Menjívar, 2021). Indeed, in the past, marriage to a US citizen could resolve legal status problems and protect against deportation and family separation; however, current immigration policies do not allow undocumented spouses and partners to obtain legal status, which perpetuates familial instability and relational uncertainties to the detriment of individual and family wellbeing (López, 2022; Pila, 2016).

Other policies, such as Deferred Action for Childhood Arrivals (DACA) and Temporary Protected Status (TPS), create other hierarchies of legality and mixed statuses within families (Del Real, 2019). Although DACA grants undocumented immigrants who came to the United States as children (under the age of sixteen) temporary status to remain in the United States and authorizes DACA recipients to work legally and attend public universities, the authorization must be renewed every two years and does not offer any protections for the undocumented parents of DACA recipients. Today, it is estimated that there are 646,000 immigrants with DACA residing in the United States (Capps et al., 2020). These young adults occupy a liminal space between belonging and uncertainty about their futures while also fearing parental detention, deportation, and family separation.

Like DACA, Temporary Protection Status (TPS) also grants eligible immigrants temporary and conditional authorization to live and work in the United States (Menjívar et al., 2016); however, this status is limited to a small subpopulation of immigrants and affects women and men differently. The majority of TPS holders are Salvadoran and Honduran and are also disproportionately men (Adams, 2021). Undocumented Central American immigrant women who are ineligible for TPS have few to no other pathways to regularize their status, which can create gendered hierarchies of legality and differential vulnerabilities within relationships and families (Menjívar et al., 2016). The mixed statuses created within families by US immigration laws and policies like DACA and TPS can contribute to unequal, exploitative, and abusive relationships within families, in the workplace, and in the broader society (Del Real, 2019; Letiecq et al., 2022; Parrado et al., 2005).

US immigration laws and policies, when interlinked with social welfare and health-related policies, such as the 1996 Personal Responsibility and Work Opportunity Reconciliation Act (PRWORA) and the 2010 Affordable Care Act (ACA), can further shape and constrain immigrant romantic relationships and family experiences (Letiecq et al., 2022; Menjívar et al., 2016). PRWORA, ACA, and many other US laws and policies preclude undocumented immigrants from taking up most federal benefits and social services, including Temporary Aid for Needy Families, Supplemental Social Security Income, food stamps, housing assistance, non-emergency Medicaid, Medicare, health insurance through ACA exchanges, and COVID-19 relief funds, among others (Menjívar et al., 2016; Vesely et al., 2019a). Denying these benefits also curtails benefits and health care access among immigrants' children, who are most often US citizens, because of parents' fear that pursuit of benefits and care for children could result in deportation and family separation. This sociocultural context can result in what Enriquez (2015) calls "multigenerational punishment," in which entire family systems are exposed to economic marginalization and are made vulnerable to poor health outcomes (Vesely et al., 2019a).

THE EFFECTS OF LEGAL STATUS ON LATINX IMMIGRANT ROMANTIC RELATIONSHIPS

Because of the complex US immigration system and its collusion with other social welfare and health care systems to exclude, punish, and marginalize undocumented Latinx immigrants, Latinx immigrant romantic relationships – from dating and forming partnerships to sustaining committed unions – must be understood in sociocultural context (McDowell et al., 2018). First and foremost, undocumented Latinx immigrants, and especially men from Mexico and Central America, must contend with being targeted, criminalized, detained, deported, and separated from their partners, children, and kin by US Immigration and Customs Enforcement (Berger Cardoso et al., 2014; De Genova & Peutz, 2010; Golash-Boza & Hondagneu-Sotelo, 2013). But, in the context of illegality, legal status also conditions and constrains the living and working conditions, educational pursuits, and everyday experiences of undocumented Latinx immigrants residing in the United States (e.g., Abrego, 2014; Donato & Armenta, 2011; Dreby, 2015; Glick, 2010; Hall et al., 2019; Menjívar et al., 2016; Stuesse, 2016; Vesely et al., 2019b). In the next section of this chapter, we draw upon and review research on undocumented immigrant approaches to dating, forming intimate partnerships, and sustaining their commitments and romantic relationships over time (e.g., Abrego, 2014; Enriquez, 2017; Fuller & García Coll, 2010; Letiecq et al., 2022; López, 2022; Menjívar et al., 2016; Pila, 2016). This review is not exhaustive, but illustrates how a sociocultural-attuned lens is useful to situate Latinx immigrant romantic relationships in the context of illegality.

Dating and Making Commitments

Research documenting friendship navigation and dating at the intersections of legal status and gender suggests that liminal and undocumented legal statuses can condition and constrain dating and romantic relationship formation in significant ways and challenge gendered dating norms and values (Cho, 2021; Enriquez, 2017; Gonzales et al., 2019). Dating, in general, engages gendered expectations; however, in the context of illegality, it is important to interlink such expectations with legal status complexity. For example, in her qualitative study of immigrant women and men from ten countries (majority from Mexico), Pila (2016) found that undocumented men expressed difficulty and frustration in adhering to gendered expectations regarding dating, such as paying for meals and activities or driving to and from a venue. Living in the United States without legal authorization significantly challenges immigrants' opportunities to earn wages, forcing many to work "under the table" for low-wages and in jobs that may not be stable and may be exploitive. Additionally, many immigrant children may feel pressure to contribute their earnings to their family, whether living in the United States or in the form of remittances in their country of origin (Orellana et al., 2001). In many parts of the United States, undocumented immigrants cannot obtain a driver's license, which also creates significant transportation challenges, stress, and shame (Straut-Eppeteiner, 2021). The men in Pila's (2016) study reported that, although they felt pressured to pay for dates and provide transportation, their legal status often made meeting gendered cultural expectations difficult. Some men stated that they were creative in resolving these dating challenges by, for example, searching for free venues that were accessible by foot.

Women likely experience dating expectations differently than men in the context of illegality. In Pila's (2016) study, some women worried about disclosing their status for fear that such information could be used to control them by threatening deportation and family separation. Indeed, as we discuss more fully below, research findings suggest that immigrant women are vulnerable to abuse and legal violence because their legal status can be used against them (Edelson et al., 2007). Being undocumented also likely constrains the establishment of egalitarian relationships, particularly if only one partner has legal authorization to live and work in the United States (Menjívar, 1999). For example, whereas undocumented men may assert their independence through their dating decisions, women's choices may be more constrained.

The challenges of dating "without papers" also can constrain making commitments. As Pila (2016) found, fear of detention and deportation can result in stalled relationships and breakups. Women in Pila's (2016) study also reported feeling like they were "saddling their partners unfairly with their legal status problems" (p. 150) and feared they would be a burden to their partners if US citizens even after marriage, unable to build a "normal life" (p. 152) because marriage does not guarantee one can change their legal status. Women also worried that their legal status could mean that they were not viable dating partners or that their status would create hardships for or hold back potential mates. Women worried about their limited earnings potential as undocumented immigrants in the labor market and other constraints, such as not being able to travel abroad with their partners.

In another study, Romo and Hurtado (2022) found that Mexican-origin mothers discussed these dating and romantic relationship realities with their daughters (71 percent US-born; 29 percent born in Mexico; legal status not reported), highlighting how dating is a family affair. Based on data from 132 mother-daughter dyads, the researchers found that mothers were instrumental in promoting positive decision-making and dating among their daughters, advising them to take their time, choose partners wisely, insist on respect from boys, maintain autonomy in relationships, pursue education goals, and develop a sense of self-worth. They also found that mothers were especially concerned about their daughters having unwanted sex, which led to deeper discussion about negative partner dynamics and self-protective behaviors.

However, mothers were less likely to discuss the positive aspects of sexuality or vulnerabilities to dating violence and abuse. Less is known about parent-adolescent communication among undocumented youth. More research focused not only on the dating and mating experiences of Latinx immigrants with varied legal statuses, but also on how parents can help their children navigate illegality and liminal legal statuses, dating, making commitments, and relational wellbeing is needed.

Mixed-Citizenship Coupling

Latinx immigrant romantic relationship research among mixed-citizenship couples where one partner is undocumented and the other is a US citizen is likewise sparse (Schueths, 2014). Recently, López (2022) studied relational narratives of fifty-six mixed-citizenship couples and found that participants "found each other in the same way as other, 'normal' couples. They met at bars and birthday parties, at church and work, online and on vacation" (p. 13). López asserted that mixed-citizenship American couples followed similar trends of meeting and relating as those of same-citizenship American couples, yet each mixed-citizenship relationship was shaped and challenged by legal status matters. López (2022) also pointed out that the complexity of US immigration laws and policies resulted in quite diverse trajectories for the study participants. For some, commitments were challenged by deportations and created what Berger Cardoso et al. (2014) call "involuntary transnational families" (p. 197). For others with greater privilege, access to resources and skilled legal teams led to regularizing a partners' legal status and stabilizing their relational experiences. Less is known about the dating lives and commitments made by undocumented partners who meet in the United States and how they navigate illegality together.

Dating Violence

In general, undocumented immigrants are placed at heightened risk of experiencing multiple forms of violence and trauma (e.g., violence crossing borders, deportation and family separation; Kaltman et al., 2011). Likewise, research suggests that Latinx adolescents and adults are at risk of experiencing dating violence, and that legal status is a risk factor (Edelson et al., 2007; Menjívar et al., 2016; Pila, 2016; Shaffer et al., 2018). Dating violence experiences in the context of illegality may be related to a complex web of structural and cultural factors (e.g., acculturation, gender role expectations; see Shaffer et al., 2018). For example, adolescents' definitions of problematic or abusive behaviors were found to be related to traditional gender roles, and these cultural beliefs may explain acceptance of harmful dating behaviors towards females (Ulloa et al., 2008). Yet immigration laws and policies may also create dating violence vulnerabilities at the structural level when one partner is undocumented. Researchers have noted how undocumented youth and women were wary of disclosing their status when entering relationships with others (e.g., US citizens) and may fear being exploited, manipulated, or harmed because of their legal status (Cho, 2021; Pila, 2016). Moreover, Edelson and colleagues (2007) found that Latinas who had been victims of intimate partner violence had significantly greater trauma-related symptoms, depression, and lower social and personal self-esteem than non-Latina women. It is also noted that despite greater symptoms, Latinas are less likely than women of other ethnicities to seek support and social services due to language barriers and lack of knowledge about laws and services (Vidales, 2010).

Sustaining Romantic Relationships under the Weight of Structural Oppression

In the context of illegality, structural forces affect committed romantic partners as well. Not only must they contend with threats of deportation and forced separations and other forms of violence, but also with interlocking structural forces that shape and constrain opportunities that are foundational to one's livelihood and capacity to provide for one's self and others, including opportunities to engage in the labor and housing markets. For example, in the labor market, undocumented immigrants are typically relegated to a handful of jobs that are often low-paying, physically demanding, unbenefited, unprotected, and nonstandard in terms of hours (Abrego 2014; Stuesse, 2016). This restrictive context holds implications for engaging in and sustaining romantic relationships and how couples navigate work-family conflict (Straut-Eppsteiner, 2021).

Yet, the context of illegality operates differently at the intersections of race/ethnicity and gender. Racialized and gendered illegality renders undocumented Latina immigrant women, and especially mothers, particularly limited in their employment opportunities and the wages they can generate (Abrego, 2014; Menjívar, 1999). While undocumented immigrant men typically work in construction, other building trades, or the restaurant industry and can command higher wages, undocumented Latina immigrants often are consigned to lower-paying jobs in the cleaning, food services, and childcare sectors (Adams, 2021). Without many childcare options, labor market exploitation also positions undocumented immigrant women as dependent on men (and their wages) in heterosexual unions, rendering women, and especially mothers, vulnerable to both relational and workplace abuses (Del Real, 2019; Menjívar et al., 2016; Parrado et al., 2005; Pinto & Ortiz, 2018).

A person's immigration status can also condition and constrain where and how a person lives (Hall et al., 2019). Ineligible for any public housing supports, undocumented immigrants must engage in the private housing sector to secure a place to live. As we discuss later in the chapter, without the required documentation and credit histories to secure housing, many undocumented immigrants may experience overcrowded housing circumstances, further complicating relational and familial functioning (Hall et al., 2019). Additionally, Schueths' study in 2019 showed that among her participants who were US citizen women in mixed-status marriages, the deportation of their husbands placed them at high risk for poverty. That is they often found themselves in an emotionally and physically distressing situation of being separated from their spouse and having to rely on public assistance, placing them on what she coined the "deportation to welfare pathway for US citizen mothers."

Immigration also creates a shift in marital roles and expectations. Many women and families put their lives at risk to migrate for a better way of life, often (re)negotiating the traditional male-worker migration patterns. This migrant gender shift has been called by scholars the feminization of undocumented migrants (Belliveau, 2012). However, as Menjívar et al. (2016) noted, while gendered expectations of women are significantly transformed in the process of migration, changes "do not always occur in the direction of equality" (p. 80). Indeed, in an early study of Salvadoran immigrant women residing in San Francisco, Menjívar (1999) found that even when women contributed financially to the family – and sometimes earned more than their partners – the division of labor at home did not become more egalitarian because women did not want to challenge men's patriarchal authority. As such, relationship dissolution is always a looming possibility. Findings show that when couples experience pressures in fast-growing communities, it can make it more difficult to sustain their marriages, putting immigrant couples more at risk for marital dissolution or lowered marital satisfaction (Baca Zinn & Wells, 2008; Oropesa & Landale, 2004; Padilla & Borrero, 2006). According to Wood et al. (2021) couples who experience different pressures due to economic marginalization and cultural factors in their "non-shared environments," are adversely affected in their marriages.

A CLOSER LOOK AT CENTRAL AMERICAN IMMIGRANT ROMANTIC RELATIONSHIPS

To examine more closely Central American immigrant romantic relationships in the context of illegality and further illustrate the use of a sociocultural attuned lens, we discuss the findings from a recent study conducted by Letiecq and colleagues (2022). In this study, Letiecq et al. utilized a CBPAR approach and, in partnership with Latina immigrants, examined the narratives of twenty-two undocumented Central American immigrant women (along with data from 134 interviewer-assisted surveys). The majority of women in the study were in a committed heterosexual romantic relationship and were living with their partners. Findings situated romantic partners in their community context (a low-income immigrant enclave located in the Washington, DC region) and within a labor and housing market that was economically-marginalizing, oppressive, and stratified by legal status. As we discussed earlier, undocumented Central American immigrants in this study likewise were relegated to low wage jobs that left them, and especially women, fiscally precarious. Undocumented Latina immigrants also confronted workplace abuses, such as harassment, discrimination, and threats of deportation.

In the region known for high housing costs, the majority of study participants lived with their partners and children in overcrowded apartments. Most were subletters and were vulnerable to unequal power dynamics, exploitation, harassment, and threats of eviction in addition to threats of deportation. Most couples occupied a single bedroom with their children – in some instances, rooms were filled with mattresses for sleeping and little else – and shared 1–2 bedroom apartments with other immigrants, whether single men or other family units. In these spaces, privacy was difficult to come by. When asked how couples maintained relational intimacy, one woman shared that it was difficult when sharing a room with her male partner and their two children. Another mother shared that she slept in the same bed with her husband and her son, but was hoping to find her son his own bed soon so the couple could have more space. Another woman shared that if she and her husband were in a conflict, they locked themselves in the bathroom out of earshot from their children or other apartment dwellers to resolve issues in private.

Beyond confronting the labor and housing market challenges, Letiecq et al. (2022) found that partners who were in solidarity with one another, were focused on their shared goals for a better life, especially for their children, and were working in tandem, synchronizing work schedules and childcare demands to make it in the United States. These couples often were structured as traditional nuclear family systems (i.e., male-breadwinner, female-caregiver), but some participants expressed a desire for a more egalitarian union. However, with few childcare options and women's gendered economic marginalization in the labor market, most women in the study were dependent on their male partners financially to survive US illegality. And while their family systems mirrored a traditional nuclear model, women who were dependent on undocumented immigrant men for their economic and housing stability were vulnerable, as one women stated, to "being ruined" if their partners were to be detained, incarcerated, or deported.

As has been documented in other studies (e.g., Abrego, 2014; Bermúdez et al., 2011; Menjívar et al., 2016), Letiecq et al. (2022) also heard stories of what happened when men were detained and deported, leaving behind undocumented immigrant women and their children to face economic precarity, housing insecurity, and great uncertainty in the United States as single-mother-headed families. Women in the study were keenly aware of their vulnerable positionality in their relationships, in the labor market, and in the context of illegality and several discussed feeling trapped in unfulfilling or abusive relationships, unable to leave unhealthy relationships and make it on their own. One woman in the study shared how she was aware of her partner's infidelity but could not leave him because she could not care for her two sons and her four-month-old child by herself. While infidelity and relational conflict are common experiences in romantic relationships in general, undocumented women are particularly vulnerable to getting trapped in relationships that, if they could, they would exit.

Letiecq et al. (2022) also highlighted narratives of Central American immigrant women who were single and found that some women in their study sought singlehood to secure their liberation. Such a finding raises important questions for future research regarding Latinx immigrant romantic relationships in the context of racialized and gendered illegality. Beyond cultural values and gendered expectations, for example, how do immigration laws and policies reproduce and maintain structural inequalities that condition and constrain gender equity, relational health, and functionality? And if we as a society wish to promote individual, relational, and family health and wellbeing, what kinds of structural reforms are necessary to advance such ends? Clearly, US immigration laws and policies constructing legal statuses and then targeting unauthorized immigrants for deportation, family separation, and economic marginalization are inconsistent with the government's interest in and promotion of healthy relationships and stable families. Socioculturally attuned family researchers and practitioners must work to both advance understanding of Latinx immigrant resilience, persistence and resistance in the context of racialized and gendered illegality and translate research to action for immigrant justice (McDowell et al., 2019; Vesely et al., 2017).

CONCLUSION

As can be seen, the context of Latinx immigrant romantic relationships, especially among those with liminal, mixed, or undocumented statuses, is complex and made more so by the harsh and punitive US immigration system. Currently, there is a great need for scholars to more fully understand how the confluence of immigration status and hostile policies adversely affect the lives of intimate partners and their families. Likewise, there is a great need for scholars to interrogate the ways in which immigrant partners respond to, adapt, and resist structural (or socially constructed) anti-immigrant adversity and reproduce healthful relationships, intimacy, and enduring love. As noted by Hall et al. (2019), legal status not only stratifies immigrant experiences within families and across immigrant communities, it is a *sociorelational* determinant of health (McDowell et al., 2022) that shapes and constrains immigrants' lived experiences, the trajectories of their lives, and the ways in which they form and maintain intimate partner and familial relationships (Abrego, 2014;

Hall et al., 2019; López, 2022; Menjívar et al., 2016; Pila, 2016). Currently, immigration is a contentious political issue; a social ailment, criminalized by detention and incarceration, often resulting in forced family separation, deportation, and forced transnational and mixed status families. These processes and outcomes can be changed with a strong commitment to relational and societal justice. Having a heightened critical sociocultural attunement as a family scholar can enact the third order change necessary for systems to transform systems (McDowell et al., 2022). Without it, families in vulnerable and marginalized social standing will continue to suffer the effects of immigration laws and policies that are xenophobic, racist, oppressive, financially exploitive, and ultimately deadly. We urge family and relationship scholars to utilize a socioculturally attuned lens and see their work as a form of praxis (consciousness in action) and as a commitment to social justice and third order change. This work is essential to advance Latinx immigrant relational and family health and immigrant justice.

REFERENCES

Abrego, L. (2014). *Sacrificing families: Navigating laws, labor, and love across borders.* Stanford University Press.

Abrego, L., Coleman, M., Martínez, D., Menjívar, C., & Slack, J. (2017). Making immigrants into criminals: Legal processes of criminalization in the post-IIRIRA era. *Journal on Migration and Human Security,* 5(3), 694–715.

Adams, L. (2021). *Pulling back the curtain: Analysis of new government data on temporary protected status.* Temporary Protected Status Working Group. https://nationalimmigrationproject.org/PDFs/practitioners/practice_advisories/pr/2021_31Mar_pulling-back-curtain.pdf

Baca Zinn, M., & Wells, B. (2008). Diversity within Latino families: New lessons for family social science. In S. Coontz (Ed.), *American families: A multicultural reader* (2nd ed., pp. 222–244). Routledge.

Barajas, F. (2012). *Curious unions: Mexican American workers and resistance in Oxnard, California, 1898–1961.* University of Nebraska Press.

Belliveau, M. A. (2012). Engendering inequity? How social accounts create vs. merely explain unfavorable pay outcomes for women. *Organization Science,* 23(4), 1154–1174. www.jstor.org/stable/23252454

Berger Cardoso, J., Hamilton, E. R., Rodriguez, N., Eschbach, K., & Hagan, J. (2014). Deporting fathers: Involuntary transnational families and intent to remigrate among Salvadoran deportees. *International Migration Review,* 50(1), 197–230.

Bermudez, J. M., & Mancini, J. (2013). 'Familias fuertes': Resilience among Latino families. In D. Becvar (Ed.). *Handbook of family resilience* (pp. 215–227). Springer.

Bermúdez, J. M., Stinson, M, A., & Zak-Hunter, L. M. & Abrams, B. (2011). *Mejor sola que mal acompañada*: Strengths and challenges of Mexican origin mothers parenting alone. *Journal of Divorce & Remarriage,* 52(8), 622–641.

Brady, S. S., Tschann, J. M., Ellen, J. M., & Flores, E. (2009). Infidelity, trust, and condom use among Latino youth in dating relationships. *Sexually Transmitted Diseases,* 36(4), 227–231.

Capps, R., Gelatt, J., Ruiz Soto, A., & Van Hook, J. (2020). *Unauthorized immigrants in the United States: Stable numbers, changing origins*. Migration Policy Institute.

Capps, R., Koball, H., Bachmeier, J. D., Ruiz Soto, A., Zong, J., & Gelatt, J. (2016). *Deferred action for unauthorized immigrant parents: Analysis of DAPA's potential effects on families and children*. Migration Policy Institute.

Cho, E. Y. (2021). Selective disclosure as a self-protective process: Navigating friendships as Asian and Latino undocumented young adults. *Social Forces*, 100(2), 540–563.

Chomsky, A. (2014). *Undocumented: How immigration became illegal*. Beacon Press.

De Genova, N., & Peutz, N. (Eds.). (2010). *The deportation regime: Sovereignty, space, and freedom of movement*. Duke University Press.

Del Real, D. (2019). Toxic ties: The reproduction of legal violence within mixed-status intimate partners, relatives, and friends. *International Migration Review*, 53(2), 548–570.

Donato, K. M., & Armenta, A. (2011). What we know about unauthorized migration. *Annual Review of Sociology*, 37(1), 529–543.

Dreby, J. (2015). *Everyday illegal: When policies undermine immigrant families*. University of California Press.

Edelson, M. G., Hokoda, A., & Ramos-Lira, L. (2007). Differences in effects of domestic violence between Latina and non-Latina women. *Journal of Family Violence*, 22(1), 1–10.

Enriquez, L. E. (2015). Multigenerational punishment: Shared experiences of undocumented immigration status within mixed-status families. *Journal of Marriage and Family*, 77(4), 939–953.

Enriquez, L. E. (2017). Gendering illegality: Undocumented young adults' negotiation of the family formation process. *American Behavioral Scientist*, 61(10), 1153–1171.

Estévez, A. (2012). *Human rights, migration, and social conflict: Towards a decolonized global justice*. Springer.

Fuller, B., & García Coll, C. (2010). Learning from Latinos: contexts, families, and child development in motion. *Developmental Psychology*, 46(3), 559–565. https://doi.org/10.1037/a0019412

Glick, J. E. (2010). Connecting complex processes: A decade of research on immigrant families. *Journal of Marriage and Family*, 72(3), 498–515

Golash-Boza, T., & Hondagneu-Sotelo, P. (2013). Latino immigrant men and the deportation crisis: A gendered racial removal program. *Latino Studies*, 11(3), 271–292.

Gonzales, R. G., & Raphael, S. (2017). Illegality: A contemporary portrait of immigration. *RSF: The Russell Sage Foundation Journal of the Social Sciences*, 3(4), 1–17. https://doi.org/10.7758/rsf.2017.3.4.01

Gonzales, R. G., Brant, K., & Roth, B. (2019). DACAmented in the age of deportation: Navigating spaces of belonging and vulnerability in social and personal live. *Ethnic and Racial Studies*, 43(1), 60–79.

Hall, M., Musick, K., & Yi, Y. (2019). Living arrangements and household complexity among undocumented immigrants. *Population and Development Review*, 45(1), 81–101.

Heidbrink, L. (2020). *Migranthood: Youth in a new era of deportation*. Stanford University Press

Helms, H. M., Supple, A. J., Su, J., Rodriguez, Y., Cavanaugh, A. M., & Hengstebeck, N. D. (2014). Economic pressure, cultural adaptation stress, and marital quality among Mexican-origin couples. *Journal of Family Psychology*, 28(1), 77–87.

Jones, R. C. (2016). Harbingers of migration regression: Global trends and a Mexican case study. *Social Science Quarterly, 97*(2), 293–310.

Kaltman, S., Hurtado de Mendoza, A., Gonzales, F. A., Serrano, A., & Guarnaccia, P. J. (2011). Contextualizing the trauma experience of women immigrants from Central America, South America, and Mexico. *Journal of Traumatic Stress, 24*(6), 635–642.

Killoren, S. E., Monk, J. K., Rivero, A., Quinn, D., & Kline, G. C. (2022). Romantic partners' weight criticism and Latina/o/x young adults' relationship instability. *Journal of Social and Personal Relationships, 39*(2), 264–284.

Knudson-Martin, C., McDowell, T., & Bermudez, J. M. (2019). From knowing to doing: Guidelines for socioculturally attuned family therapy. *Journal of Marital and Family Therapy, 45*(1), 47–60.

Lesser, G., & Batalova, J. (2017). *Central American immigrants in the United States.* Migration Policy Institute. Retrieved from www.migrationpolicy.org/article/central-american-immigrants-united-states

Letiecq, B. L. (2019). Family privilege and supremacy in family science: Toward justice for all. *Journal of Family Theory and Review, 11*(3), 398–411. https://doi.org/10.1111/jftr.12338

Letiecq, B. L., Davis, E., Vesely, C. K., Goodman, R. D., Zeledon, D., & Marquez, M. (2022). Central American immigrant mothers' narratives of intersecting oppressions: A resistant knowledge project. *Journal of Marriage and Family, 84*(5), 1–23.

López, J. L. (2022). *Unauthorized love: Mixed-citizenship couples negotiating intimacy, immigration, and the state.* Stanford University Press.

Massey, D. S., Durand, J., & Malone, N. J. (2002). *Beyond smoke and mirrors: Mexican immigration in an era of economic integration.* Russell Sage Foundation

McDowell, T., Knudson-Martin, C., & Bermudez, J. M. (2018). *Socioculturally attuned family therapy: Guidelines for equitable theory and practice.* Routledge/Taylor & Francis.

McDowell, T., Knudson-Martin, C., & Bermudez, J. M. (2019). Third order thinking in family therapy: Addressing social justice across family therapy practice. *Family Process, 58*(1), 9–22.

McDowell, T., Knudson-Martin, C., & Bermudez, J. M. (2022). *Socioculturally attuned family therapy: Guidelines for equitable theory and practice* (2nd ed.). Routledge/Taylor & Francis.

Menjívar, C. (1999). The intersection of work and gender: Central American immigrant women and employment in California. *The American Behavioral Scientist, 42*(4), 601–627.

Menjívar, C. (2021). The racialization of illegality. *Daedalus: Journal of the American Academy of Arts & Sciences, 150*(2), 91–105.

Menjívar C., & Kantsroom, D. (2014). *Constructing immigrant "illegality": Critiques, experiences, and responses.* Cambridge University Press.

Menjívar, C., Abrego, L. J., & Schmalzbauer, L. (2016). *Immigrant families.* Polity Press.

Meyer, P. J., & Taft-Morales, M. (2019). Central American migration: Root causes and US Policy. *Congressional Research Service in Focus, IF11151.* Retrieved from: https://crsreports.congress.gov/

Orellana, M. F., Thorne, B., Chee, A., & Lam, W. S. E. (2001). Transnational childhoods: The participation of children in processes of family migration. *Social Problems, 48*(4), 572–591.

Oropesa, R. S., & Landale, N. S. (2004). The future of marriage and Hispanics. *Journal of Marriage and Family, 66*(4), 901–920. https://doi.org/10.1111/j.0022-2445.2004.00061.x

Padilla, A. M., & Borrero, N. E. (2006). The effects of acculturative stress on the Hispanic family. In P. T. P. Wong., L. C. J. Wong, & W. J. Lonner (Eds.), *Handbook of multicultural perspectives on stress and coping* (pp. 299–317). Springer.

Parrado, E. A., Flippen, C. A., & McQuiston, C. (2005). Migration and relationship power among Mexican women. *Demography, 42*(2), 347–372.

Pew Research Center. (2019). *Facts on Latinos in the U.S.* Retrieved from www.pewresearch.org/hispanic/fact-sheet/latinos-in-the-u-s-fact-sheet/

Pila, D. (2016). "I'm not good enough for anyone": Legal status and the dating lives of undocumented young adults." *Sociological Forum, 31*(1), 138–158.

Pinto, K., & Ortiz, V. (2018). Beyond cultural explanations: Understanding the gendered division of household labor in Mexican American families. *Journal of Family Issues, 39*(16).

Romero, A. J., & Umaña-Taylor, A. J. (2018). Introduction to special issue on research methods and design considerations with Latinx populations. *Journal of Latina /o Psychology, 6*(4), 259–263. https://doi.org/10.1037/lat0000124

Romo, L. F., & Hurtado, A. (2022). "Know your worth and play it safe:" messages to daughters from Mexican-origin mothers in conversations about dating and romantic relationships. *Culture, Health & Sexuality, 24*(6), 812–826.

Sampaio, A. (2015). *Terrorizing Latino immigrants: Race, gender, and immigration politics in the age of security*. Temple University Press.

Schueths, A. M. (2014). 'It's almost like White supremacy': Interracial mixed-status couples facing racist nativism. *Ethnic and Racial Studies, 37*(13), 2438–2456. https://doi.org/10.1080/01419870.2013.835058

Schueths, A. M. (2019). Not really single: The deportation to welfare pathway for US citizen mothers in mixed-status marriage. *Critical Sociology, 45*(7–8), 1075–1092.

Shaffer, C. M., Corona, R., Sullivan, T. N. et al. (2018). Barriers and supports to dating violence communication between Latina adolescents and their mothers: A qualitative analysis. *Journal of Family Violence, 33*(2), 133–145. https://doi.org/10.1007/s10896-017-9936-1

Spickard, P. (2007). *Almost all aliens: Immigration, race, and colonialism in American history and identity*. Routledge.

Straut-Eppsteiner, H. (2021). Undocumented mothers and work–family conflict in restrictive policy contexts. *Journal of Marriage and Family, 83*(3), 865–880.

Stuesse, A. (2016). *Scratching out a living: Latinos, race, and work in the Deep South* (Vol. 38). University of California Press.

Terrazas, J., Muruthi, B. A., Thompson Cañas, R. E, Jackson, J. B., & Bermudez, J. M. (2020). Liminal legality among mixed-status Latinx families: Considerations for critically engaged clinical practice. *Contemporary Family Therapy, 42*, 360–368.

Tervalon M., & Murray-Garcia, J. (1998). Cultural humility versus cultural competence: A critical distinction in defining physician training outcomes in multicultural education. *Journal of Health Care Poor Underserved, 9*(2), 117–125. https://doi.org/10.1353/hpu.2010.0233

Tourse, R. W. C., Hamilton-Mason, J., & Wewiorski, N. J. (2018). *Systemic racism in the United States: Scaffolding as social construction*.

Tuck, E. (2009). Suspending damage: A letter to communities. *Harvard Educational Review*, 79(3), 409–427. https://doi.org/10.17763/haer.79.3.n0016675661t3n15

Ulloa, E. C., Jaycox, L. H., Skinner, S. K., & Orsburn, M. M. (2008). Attitudes about violence and dating among Latino/a boys and girls. *Journal of Ethnic & Cultural Diversity in Social Work*, 17(2), 157–176. https://doi.org/10.1080/15313200801941721

U.S. Department of Homeland Security. (2019). *Yearbook of immigration statistics 2019*. U.S. Department of Homeland Security. Office of Immigration Statistics.

Valdéz, I. (2016). Punishment, race, and the organization of U.S. immigration exclusion. *Political Research Quarterly*, 69(4), 640–654. https://doi.org/10.1177/1065912916670515

Vaughn, L. M., Jacquez, F., Linquist-Gantz, R., Parsons, A., & Milink, K. (2016). Immigrants as research partners: A review of immigrants in Community-Based Participatory Research (CBPR). *Journal of Immigrant and Minority Health*, 19, 1457–1468.

Vesely, C. K., Letiecq, B., & Goodman, R. (2017). Immigrant family resilience in context: Using a community-based approach to build a new conceptual model. *Journal of Family Theory and Review*, 9(1), 93–110.

Vesely, C. K., Bravo, D. Y., & Guzzardo, M. T. (2019a). Immigration: Policy issues across the life course. *NCFR Policy Brief*. National Council on Family Relations. www.ncfr.org/system/files/2019-07/Immigrant_Families_Policy_Brief_July_23_2019.pdf

Vesely, C. K., Letiecq, B., & Goodman, R. (2019b). "Parenting across two worlds": Low-income Latina immigrants' adaptation to motherhood in the US. *Journal of Family Issues*, 40(6), 711–738.

Vidales, G. (2010). Arrested justice: The multifaceted plight of immigrant Latinas who faced domestic violence. *Journal of Family Violence*, 25(6), 533–544.

Wallerstein, N., Duran, B., Oetzel, J., & Minkler, M. (Eds.). (2018). *Community-based participatory research for health* (3rd ed.). Jossey-Bass.

Walsdorf, A. A., Jordan, L. S., McGeorge, C. R., & Caughy, M. O. (2020). White supremacy and the web of family science: Implications of the missing spider. *Journal of Family Theory & Review*, 12(1), 64–79.

Walsdorf, A. A., Machado, Y., & Bermudez, J. M. (Nov. 2019, published online). Undocumented and mixed-status Latinx families: Sociopolitical considerations for systemic practice. *Journal of Family Psychotherapy*, 30(4), 245–271.

Wood, C. A., Helms, H. M., Supple, A. J., Rodriguez, Y., Hengstebeck, N. D., & Siskind, D. (2021). Examining patterns of Mexican immigrant spouses' Contextual pressures and links with marital satisfaction and negativity. *Marriage & Family Review*, 57(5), 442–471.

Yoshikawa, H. (2011). *Immigrants raising citizens: Undocumented parents and their children*. Russell Sage Foundation. www.jstor.org/stable/10.7758/9781610447072

13

Romantic Relationships during a Global Pandemic

PAULA R. PIETROMONACO AND NICKOLA C. OVERALL

The COVID-19 pandemic and its associated restrictions and isolation raise multiple challenges for individuals, couples, and families. People have been faced with developing and maintaining relationships separated from family and friendship networks outside of those living under the same roof while coping with disruptions in work, childcare, and daily routines. Pandemic-related restrictions also have limited the ability to initiate new relationships and maintain developing relationships. Thus, the stressors associated with the COVID-19 pandemic can threaten the ability to successfully navigate romantic relationships at all phases of relationship development, and as a consequence, potentially impair individuals' emotional and physical health (Pietromonaco & Collins, 2017).

To understand and organize the numerous processes affecting relationship maintenance and development, we apply a major relationship theory, the vulnerability-stress-adaptation model (VSA; Karney & Bradbury, 1995), which focuses on identifying the key predictors of relationship outcomes in existing couple relationships (also see Pietromonaco & Overall, 2021). The VSA model suggests that relationship quality and stability depend on the severity of life stressors together with enduring personal vulnerabilities. Our aim in this chapter is to review new and emerging research that examines shifts in romantic relationship processes associated with stress linked to the COVID-19 pandemic as well as personal vulnerabilities. We evaluate the extent to which the findings support the VSA model. We also extend the VSA model to consider how pandemic-related stress and other life stress together with enduring personal vulnerabilities may impact the initiation of romantic relationships among those not in established relationships.

In this chapter, we first provide an overview of the application of the VSA model to understanding romantic relationship processes over the course of the COVID-19 pandemic. Second, we review emerging research examining stress from the COVID-19 pandemic and relationship outcomes in established relationships, and how those outcomes are shaped by enduring personal vulnerabilities. Our review focuses primarily on research that compares relationship outcomes prior to and during the pandemic or shifts in relationship outcomes over the course of the pandemic, which provide methodological advantages over studies examining outcomes at only one point in time. Third, we discuss processes that may mitigate disruptions in established relationships and promote resilience. Fourth, we consider how stress from the COVID-19 pandemic may impact relationship initiation and newly developing relationships. Finally, we discuss several directions for future research that will be critical for understanding the longer-term implications of the pandemic for both ongoing and newly developing romantic relationships.

VULNERABILITY-STRESS-ADAPTATION MODEL

The original VSA model suggested that both external stressors and enduring personal vulnerabilities shape adaptive relationship processes, which in turn, impact both relationship quality and stability. Our framework modifies the VSA model to take into account the unique stressors associated with the COVID-19 pandemic (e.g., concern about the disease, quarantine-related social isolation, financial setbacks), and extends the model to consider how initiating and nurturing new romantic relationships might be impacted by the pandemic. Figure 13.1 illustrates the modified conceptual framework (adapted from the original model in Karney & Bradbury, 1995 and modified models in Pietromonaco & Overall, 2021, 2022b, in press), which suggests that the COVID-19 pandemic will give rise to multiple external stressors (Path A). These stressors can impact both relationship initiation attempts (a new component in the current framework) as well as adaptive dyadic relationship processes, which in turn, can amplify the effect of external stressors (Path B). Furthermore, difficulties with relationship initiation also can interfere with the development of adaptive relationship processes (Path C). When adaptive dyadic relationship processes are impaired, relationship quality and stability are threatened (Paths F and G). In addition, enduring personal vulnerabilities (e.g., attachment insecurity, emotional and physical health), as well as strengths (Pietromonaco & Overall, 2022a), can shape relationship initiation and adaptive dyadic relationship processes and amplify (or reduce) the impact of external stressors (Paths D and E).

EXTERNAL STRESS, RELATIONSHIP PROCESSES IN ESTABLISHED RELATIONSHIPS, AND RELATIONSHIP QUALITY (PATHS A, B, C, F, G)

A large body of research reveals that external stress in general (e.g., economic strain, job loss) is associated with less adaptive relationship processes, such as being hostile, critical or unsupportive, along with declines in

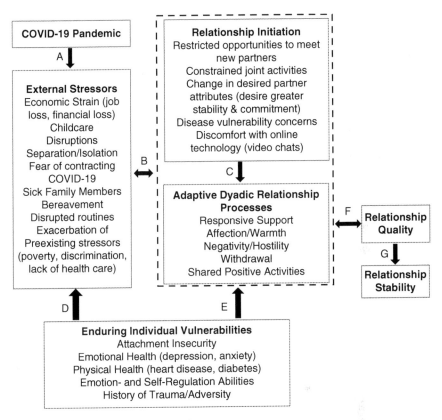

FIGURE 13.1 Potential impact of the COVID-19 pandemic on relationship processes and outcomes. The framework (Adapted from Karney & Bradbury, 1995 and Pietromonaco & Overall, 2021) suggests that the COVID-19 pandemic will create a variety of external stressors that may shape both relationship initiation and adaptive dyadic relationship processes, which can intensify the adverse impact of external stressors, lower relationship quality, and threaten relationship stability. The impact of pandemic-related stressors can be exacerbated by preexisting stressors (e.g., low income or experiencing discrimination). Couples in which one or both members have enduring vulnerabilities (e.g., attachment insecurity, depression) will be more likely to experience greater negative and fewer positive interactions, and the impact of external stressors may be heightened. The figure was adapted and modified from "Applying relationship science to evaluate how the COVID-19 pandemic may impact couples' relationships" by P. R. Pietromonaco and N. C. Overall, 2021, *American Psychologist*, 76(3), 440 (https://doi.org/10.1037/amp0000714), Copyright 2021 by the American Psychological Association.

relationship satisfaction over time (Neff & Karney, 2009, 2017; Nguyen et al., 2020; Pietromonaco & Overall, 2021; Williamson et al., 2013). Although living with a close other (e.g., romantic partner) is associated with greater well-being and less distress both before and during the first 6 months of the COVID-19 pandemic (Sisson et al., 2021), even those living with romantic partners must cope with multiple stressors arising from the COVID-19 pandemic, including disruptions in social life, finances, and work life, social distancing, the need to balance work demands in the face of no child care, and the frustration associated with loss of control and routines across many domains. This stress occurs in a context in which, compared to before the pandemic, people assign greater importance to the family but also expect greater relational conflict during the pandemic (Funder et al., 2021). The continuing stress across multiple domains will tax many individuals' cognitive and emotional resources, and this depletion is likely to impair their ability to effectively connect with new romantic partners and to respond constructively in their relationship interactions when problems arise (Buck & Neff, 2012; Neff & Karney, 2017).

Research on relationship functioning before and during the COVID-19 pandemic shows adverse effects on established romantic relationships, including declines in relationship satisfaction (Haydon & Salvatore, 2022; Pauly et al., 2022; Schmid et al., 2020), and decreased relationship functioning and family functioning among couple members who experienced greater stress (e.g., financial status, work, living conditions) during the first mandatory COVID-19 lockdown in New Zealand during March 28–April 28, 2020 (Overall, Chang, et al., 2022). One of the few studies of individuals ($N = 411$ individuals) in same-sex relationships during the pandemic revealed a similar pattern (Li & Samp, 2021): Individuals who perceived greater threat from COVID-19 or who reported a great negative impact of the pandemic on their daily life (e.g., on finances, resources, health care access, social activities) expressed greater complaint avoidance (i.e., avoiding letting their partner know when they had a problem), lower relationship satisfaction, and reported being more likely to end the relationship. Furthermore, the association between experiencing a more negative impact of the pandemic on daily life (assessed across a variety of domains including finances, resources, health care, and social activities) and lower relationship satisfaction was more pronounced for persons of color (vs. non-Hispanic White individuals) or individuals with a high (vs. low) level of internalized homophobia. Although there is also evidence that relationship satisfaction prior to the pandemic predicted greater stress during the pandemic (Pauly et al., 2022), these studies, taken together, align with the theoretical framework presented in Figure 13.1: More adverse effects of the pandemic appear to be associated with poorer relationship outcomes among individuals in mixed-gender and same-gender relationships.

Some evidence also suggests that interpersonal violence victimization increased during the pandemic. Individuals in romantic relationships (the majority were married) who experienced greater stress related to the COVID-19 pandemic also reported greater interpersonal violence victimization during the pandemic (Gresham et al., 2021). Similarly, individuals reported engaging more frequently in acts of interpersonal aggression during shelter-in-place

COVID-19 restrictions compared to their retrospective reports of interpersonal aggression during the six months prior to those restrictions (Parrott et al., 2022). Not all evidence, however, points to an increase in interpersonal aggression. A study using police reports of domestic violence incidents (vs. the self-reports of behavior used in most studies) in New Orleans, Louisiana did not find an increase in domestic violence from the year before the pandemic to the initial shelter-in-place order (March 16–May 15, 2020), or during the first reopening (May 16–June 12, 2020); however, reports did increase during the second reopening (June 13–September 29, 2020), especially in areas where domestic violence incidents were typically higher (Shariati & Guerette, 2022). Moreover, examining other types of psychological aggression, parents experiencing greater stress during the first mandatory lockdown in New Zealand reported increased verbal aggression toward their partner, taking into account their level of verbal aggression prior to the lockdown (Overall, Chang, Cross, et al., 2021).

Parents may be especially taxed by the pandemic because they often are trying to manage childcare and online schooling while fulfilling job responsibilities from home, being isolated from important others and support networks, as well as dealing with losses (e.g., economic, health, routine, space, time). This idea is supported by a study of Australian parents that found that, compared to data from parents in cohorts prior to the pandemic, parents reporting on their mental health during the pandemic (April 2020) showed an increase in depression, anxiety, and stress as well as in the use of alcohol. Parents also reported greater strain in their relationship with their partner, and experienced more irritability with their children and less expression of positive feelings in the family (Westrupp et al., 2021). Similarly, a Canadian study using longitudinal data from over 1,000 women that included three waves of data collection before the pandemic (collected from April 2012–October 2019) and one wave during the pandemic (May 20–July 15, 2020) found that mothers showed increases in both depression and anxiety during the pandemic compared to each of the three pre-pandemic timepoints (Racine et al., 2021). Parents' declines in emotional well-being during the early pandemic months may partly reflect the difficulties couples face as they attempt to negotiate parenting and balance work and family roles amid the constraints of the pandemic.

Additional research illustrates that couples experienced difficulties with both parenting and relationship quality. In a study examining parental stress prior to the COVID-19 pandemic and during the first lockdown (April 2020) in the Netherlands, increased parenting stress during the pandemic was associated with increases in coercive parenting and declines in constructive coparenting (Lucassen et al., 2021). Similarly, in a study assessing parents prior to a pandemic lockdown and during a mandatory lockdown (March 26–April 28, 2020) in New Zealand, difficulty with sharing the increased housework and parenting as a result of the pandemic was associated with greater relationship problems and dissatisfaction (Waddell et al., 2021). These results early in the pandemic contrast with a recent review of cross-sectional and longitudinal evidence suggesting that the declines observed in emotional health early in the pandemic may have returned to baseline by the middle of 2020 (Aknin et al., 2021). However, this analysis of *average* declines did not evaluate whether the effects were stronger for some individuals and families and buffered for others. Aknin et al. (2021) point out that several studies (conducted in the first half of the 2020 after the onset of the pandemic) found that individuals who spent more time taking care of children or managing their homeschooling during the pandemic experienced lower well-being and greater distress (Bu et al., 2021; Giurge et al., 2021; Lades et al., 2020), and variables such as these need to be considered as potential moderators of emotional health trajectories over the course of the pandemic.

This point reinforces the importance of examining both emotional health and relationship outcomes as parents and families endure stress as the pandemic progresses. To illustrate, in the New Zealand study described above, parents who were more distressed during a lockdown (March–April, 2020) reported greater harsh parenting (e.g., yelling or shouting at their child) controlling for both pre-pandemic distress and parenting, but only when they also perceived less support from their partner (McRae et al., 2021). Parents who were more distressed during lockdown also showed lower warm/responsive parenting, but only if they reported a lower level of cooperative parenting. Moreover, additional assessments on these families in another lockdown in the second year of the pandemic (August–September 2021) illustrated that parents showed declines in psychological (greater depressive symptoms, lower well-being) and physical health and in couple (reduced commitment and greater problem severity) and family functioning (reduced family cohesion; family chaos) across the first 1.5 years of the pandemic (Overall, Low, et al., 2022).

Yet, although these studies generally reveal adverse effects of the pandemic on relationships, growing evidence suggests that how the pandemic impacts relationships will vary widely rather than have a uniform effect on all couples' relationships. In line with this idea, data collected in May 2020 from a sample of over 3,000 individuals in Australia indicated that, among those with a living with a partner, 30.7 percent reported that their relationship had improved during the pandemic, and 15.7 percent reported that their relationship had become worse (Biddle et al., 2020; for similar findings, see Vowels et al., 2021). Variation across couples also is evident from findings in a study of couples (117 mixed-gender couples) that showed an increase in relationship instability (e.g., the extent to which individuals thought about breaking up with their partner) from early in the pandemic (Wave 1 during May 2020) to six months later but only when individuals also perceived greater general stress in their lives at Wave 1 (Ogan et al., 2021). (This association was not found when individuals perceived more economic pressure or expressed greater concerns about the pandemic at Wave 1.)

Further evidence for variability comes from data on divorce rates. Counter to predictions that divorce rates would surge as a result of the pandemic, the best evidence so far indicates that divorce rates have declined. Specifically, in twenty US states with available data, divorce rates in eighteen states were actually lower than expected in 2020 compared to pre-pandemic change from 2018 to 2019 (Westrick-Payne et al., 2022). On the one hand, this evidence may suggest that many couples were more resilient than expected during the pandemic and perhaps benefitted from strengths such as entering the pandemic with fewer vulnerabilities, or by engaging in relationship-enhancing behaviors such as spending more quality time together. On the other hand, it is also possible that economic and situational constraints prevented some couples from filing for divorce. Moreover, although the joint challenge of the pandemic enhanced stability for many couples who were functioning well, it may also have increased the vulnerability of a smaller proportion of couples who entered the pandemic with more difficulties and less social reserves. Additional data over a longer period of time are needed to fully evaluate the impact of the pandemic on the divorce rate as well as on relationship breakup in non-marital romantic relationships.

Moreover, for some couples, adaptive relationship processes may help to buffer the effects of pandemic stress on relationship quality. For example, evidence from an Australian longitudinal study of 502 parents indicates that those who experienced high levels of support from their partner, family, and friends up to fourteen years *prior to* the pandemic evidenced higher relationship quality during the pandemic (Biden et al., 2021). Other work suggests that the pandemic may also open opportunities to bolster adaptive relationship processes such as by working together as a team to combat external threats (Pietromonaco & Overall, 2021). This idea may explain why a study of 654 individuals in marital, cohabiting, or dating relationships found no differences in relationship satisfaction or partner blaming, and neither variable was associated with pandemic-related stress (Williamson, 2020). Similarly, a three-week diary study of seventy-two Israeli couples (Bar-Kalifa et al., 2021) found that COVID-related stress was not associated with either daily perceived partner responsiveness or daily relationship satisfaction, even though daily reports of COVID-related stress were associated with lower positive mood and higher negative mood.

Recent work also suggests that couples in which one partner is exposed to patients with COVID-19 as part of their job may show greater resilience when individuals believe that their partner holds similar views about the world during the pandemic. A study of frontline health care workers and their partners showed that health care workers and their partners who reported having a shared reality (e.g., that their partner shared their thoughts, feelings, and concerns about the world during the pandemic) also reported greater perceived support (health care workers) or support provision (partners), which in turn, was associated with their greater relationship satisfaction (Enestrom & Lydon, 2021). In addition, when the partners of health care workers reported having a shared reality, health care workers perceived greater support, which predicted health care workers' greater relationship satisfaction (Enestrom & Lydon, 2021).

Although all of this evidence suggests some resilience in the face of the pandemic, a host of factors is likely to shape the extent to which couples can remain resilient or collapse under the added strain of the pandemic. Some of the emerging research indicates that couples facing greater stress, such as simultaneously managing the demands of work and care for children in the absence of regular childcare and school (Overall, Chang, Cross, et al., 2021; Overall, Chang, et al., 2022; Schmid et al., 2020), dealing with preexisting stressors such as discrimination (Li & Samp, 2021) or prior experiences of domestic violence (Shariati & Guerette, 2022), are likely to experience greater difficulty during the pandemic.

ENDURING PERSONAL VULNERABILITIES (PATHS D AND E)

As shown in Figure 13.1, a variety of preexisting enduring personal vulnerabilities (e.g., attachment insecurity, depression) can shape how people perceive and respond to pandemic-related stress as well as how they engage in relationship initiation and adaptive dyadic processes. A growing set of studies illustrate the impact of personal vulnerabilities on relationship processes during the pandemic.

Attachment insecurity – either attachment anxiety or avoidance – is a vulnerability that disrupts relationship functioning, especially under stress (Mikulincer & Shaver, 2017; Simpson & Rholes, 2017), and therefore is particularly likely to interfere with relationship dynamics during the pandemic (Pietromonaco & Overall, 2021). Attachment anxiety is associated with experiencing and expressing greater distress, relying excessively on partners for reassurance and support, and worrying that partners will not be responsive enough. These tendencies give rise to a host of problematic relationship behavior, including destructive communication patterns, difficulty resolving problems, and lower relationship quality (Campbell et al., 2005; Jayamaha et al., 2017; Overall et al., 2014; Simpson et al., 1996). Attachment avoidance is associated with the expectation that partners will not be responsive, and as a result, highly avoidant individuals downplay distress, limit closeness and support, and withdraw from conflict and/or express hostility (Beck et al., 2014; Girme et al., 2015; Overall et al., 2013, 2015; Pietromonaco & Barrett, 1997; Tan et al., 2012). These strategies maintain distance at the expense of intimacy, problem-solving, effective communication, and relationship quality (Overall et al., 2013, 2015; Tan et al., 2012).

These attachment patterns are especially likely to emerge in the face of stress, such as the stress experienced as a result of the COVID-19 pandemic. Providing supportive evidence, research assessing relationship functioning during the pandemic suggests that greater attachment anxiety and avoidance are associated with lower relationship quality (Eder et al., 2021), and greater attachment avoidance is associated with poorer perceived support (Vowels & Carnelley, 2020). Individuals' attachment insecurities and their associated reactions also are likely to impact their partners, who must cope with demands such as needs for excessive reassurance in the case of anxious-attachment, or for distance in the case of avoidance. In general, when people have partners who are anxiously attached, they tend to have more difficulties communicating effectively, problem-solving, and being responsive, and are less satisfied in the relationship (Butzer & Campbell, 2008; Carnelley et al., 1996; Overall et al., 2015; Tan et al., 2012). Similarly, when people have partners who are avoidantly attached, they also are less effective in communication and problem-solving, and are less satisfied in the relationship (Beck et al., 2013; Girme et al., 2015; Overall et al., 2013, 2015). Partners are especially likely to have difficulty managing the needs of insecurely attached individuals in the context of pandemic quarantines in which couple members are confined together and isolated from others in their social network and may be experiencing additional stress themselves.

In recent work, we examined the extent to which attachment insecurity, along with stress experienced as a result of enduring a COVID-19 lockdown, predicted relationship and family functioning during the early months of the pandemic (March–April 2020), controlling for pre-pandemic assessments (Overall, Chang, Pietromonaco, et al., 2021). Individuals higher in attachment anxiety showed an increase in relationship problem severity during the COVID-19 lockdown, but in line with a diathesis-stress perspective (Simpson & Rholes, 2017), this pattern emerged only when they also experienced higher stress related to the lockdown (Overall, Chang, Pietromonaco, et al., 2021). The impact of individuals' attachment anxiety also spilled over to their partners: Partners of anxiously attached individuals showed decreases in relationship satisfaction, relationship commitment, and family cohesion, and an increase in the severity of relationship problems, but only in the context of experiencing higher pandemic-related stress. Attachment avoidance was associated with partners reporting reduced problem-solving effectiveness and less family cohesion, regardless of individuals' level of pandemic-related stress (Overall, Chang, et al., 2022).

Preexisting vulnerabilities also include broader attitudes that are connected to how couples manage power in their relationship. Hostile sexism reflects the belief that men, and not women, should hold social power and authority within the family (Glick & Fiske, 1996). Men who endorse beliefs consistent with hostile sexism are more likely to perpetrate aggression in their relationships, particularly when they feel a loss of control or power (Cross et al., 2019), as may happen when couple members lack control over the many constraints associated with the pandemic or experience problems in their family relationships. Consistent with this idea, men who endorsed beliefs consistent with hostile sexism prior to the pandemic also reported engaging in greater aggressive behavior toward their romantic partners and children during a COVID-19 lockdown (April–March 2020), especially when they experienced loss of power in their couple relationship or poorer quality parent-child relationships (Overall, Chang, Cross, et al., 2021).

A variety of other personal vulnerabilities such as poor emotion regulation (Low et al., 2021) and neuroticism (Kroencke et al., 2020) predict greater distress during the pandemic, and thus are candidates for interfering with adaptive relationship processes. Depression and anxiety rose during the early months of the pandemic (Aknin et al., 2021; Twenge & Joiner, 2020), and individuals with vulnerabilities such as insecure-anxious attachment have shown an increase in depression and anxiety from before the COVID-19 outbreak and associated lockdowns (mid-January to March 2020) to during the pandemic (April–May 2020) in the UK (Vowels et al., 2022). Furthermore, emotional distress can heighten perceptions of pandemic-related stress (Westrupp et al., 2021) and undermine adaptive relationship processes (Barry et al., 2019; Gordon et al., 2013; Knobloch-Fedders et al., 2013; Overall & Hammond, 2013; Pietromonaco et al., 2022). Similarly, having a preexisting physical health condition, such as those associated with greater susceptibility to COVID-19 (e.g., cardiovascular disease, diabetes) and more severe illness (Alyammahi et al., 2021), has been linked to greater stress and distress during the pandemic (Westrupp et al., 2021), increasing the likelihood that relationship disruptions will occur. Additional work is needed to examine how these vulnerabilities may shape couples' relationship dynamics and outcomes before and during the pandemic as well as after recovery.

VARIATION ACROSS COUPLES IN ESTABLISHED RELATIONSHIPS: MINIMIZING RELATIONSHIP DISRUPTIONS AND FACILITATING RESILIENCE

We have proposed that couples' trajectories over the course of the pandemic will vary from chronic, prolonged distress to stable resilience (Pietromonaco & Overall, 2021, 2022b), similar to the variation seen in individuals' responses to loss and trauma (Bonanno, 2004). As suggested in Figure 13.1, and consistent with the research reviewed here, couples' trajectories will depend on the severity of pandemic-related and other stressors, enduring personal vulnerabilities, and the extent to which couples are able to engage in adaptive relationship processes.

Couples who entered the pandemic with relatively low risk (economically stable, few individual vulnerabilities, and generally adaptive relationship strategies) and who experienced minimal personal and social losses as a result of the pandemic may be most likely to show resilience. They may even reap benefits from opportunities during lockdowns to spend more time together in novel and/or relaxing activities that promote relationship growth and intimacy (Gable et al., 2006; Girme et al., 2014). This idea remains to be examined in empirical studies within the context of the pandemic, but one qualitative study of open-ended survey responses ($N = 200$) and semi-structured interview responses ($N = 48$) during the early months of the pandemic (March 30–April 21, 2020) in the UK offers some indirect support. Among participants who indicated that their relationships had improved during the pandemic (28.6 percent), some individuals noted that their relationships benefitted from spending quality time together in meaningful activities (e.g., shared activities such as playing board games), as well as from appreciation of their partner and working together as a team (Vowels et al., 2021). Coping effectively with pandemic-related adversities, such as through teamwork (Vowels et al., 2021), may help couple members feel closer and more supported by each other. This idea is suggested by recent findings showing that individuals experiencing moderate-intensity exposure (e.g., experiencing power outages, disruptions to daily routine) to a disaster (Hurricane Sandy) showed increased perceptions of social support, less distress, and less attachment avoidance relative to two matched comparison cohorts (Mancini et al., 2021).

Most couples, however, will face more significant challenges, and how their relationship trajectories unfold will rest on their ability to practice adaptive relationship processes throughout the crisis (Neff & Broady, 2011; Pietromonaco & Overall, 2021). The literature on relationship processes in general, along with the research reviewed above, suggests potential intervention points for reducing destructive relationship processes and promoting resilience. These include effective communication, avoiding hostility/blame/criticism, banding together as a team to combat problems, and overcome obstacles, and both partners being committed and motivated to improve the situation. When both partners are supportive and cooperate as a team to overcome parenting obstacles during COVID-19 lockdowns, the risk of declines in relationship and family functioning is reduced (McRae et al., 2021). In addition, blaming factors outside of the relationship reduces the association between stress and lower relationship satisfaction (Diamond & Hicks, 2012). In line with this idea, diary data collected for fourteen days early in the pandemic (April and May 2020; eighty-one couples and twenty-nine individuals) and again seven months later (November and December 2020; fifty-five couples and twenty-four individuals) revealed that on days when women experienced greater stress, they were more likely to report more negative relationship behaviors and lower relationship satisfaction, but this association was reduced for women (but not men) who assigned greater blame to the pandemic for their stress (Neff et al., 2022). This effect for women was similar across the earlier and later wave of the pandemic.

Being supportive and responsive to each other's needs can foster resilience (Feeney & Collins, 2015; Pietromonaco & Collins, 2017; Reis et al., 2004) and dampen the ill effects of external stress (Pietromonaco et al., 2022). For example, greater perceived partner support predicted better psychological health and couple and parenting outcomes during the early months of the pandemic (Brown et al., 2020; Donato et al., 2021; Holmstrom et al., 2021; McRae et al., 2021; Ogan et al., 2021; Randall et al., 2022). Moreover, although parents on average experienced declines in couple and family functioning across mandatory lockdowns in 2020 and 2021, these declines were not evident for parents who perceived higher levels of support from their partners (Overall, Low, et al., 2022). Similarly, a longitudinal study examining couple members at the beginning of the pandemic (end of March 2020) and three months later found that those who experienced greater stress showed poorer relationship functioning, but this association was reduced among those who at the initial wave perceived their partners to be highly responsive (Balzarini et al., 2022). Support, however, must be calibrated to the partner's needs because too much support can make individuals feel inadequate (Zee & Bolger, 2019), and being highly responsive can be taxing for those under high stress and with some personal vulnerabilities such as avoidant attachment (Smallen et al., 2021). Other routes to resilience include sharing positive experiences (Gable & Reis, 2010; Gable et al., 2004), engaging together in novel, fun activities (Aron et al., 2000; Girme et al., 2014), and expressing gratitude (Algoe et al., 2010), all of which can promote relationship growth and intimacy.

Recommendations from a clinical perspective, informed by experiences conducting virtual couple therapy as well as informal survey observations, complement our suggestions regarding how to mitigate disruptions in established relationships and facilitate resilience (O'Reilly Treter et al., 2021). O'Reilly Treter et al. point to multiple challenges faced by couples, including assessing how to spend quality time together, balancing needs for time alone and together with less personal space, coping with pandemic-related anxiety and stress, and the potential increase in conflict and conflict escalation as well as interpersonal violence that may follow from pandemic-related stress (Bradbury-Jones & Isham, 2020; Gresham et al., 2021). Their recommendations for clinicians performing virtual couple therapy are equally relevant for couples themselves. They recommend that (a) even though couples may be spending more time together, it is vital that they incorporate *quality* time together that will enhance closeness and intimacy and set aside critical decisions and conflict for another time, (b) couples need to negotiate personal and shared time and space, (c) individuals' anxiety and concerns about the pandemic may need to be addressed, and (d) couples should be encouraged to use constructive techniques to manage disagreements, including separating problem discussions to assess the issues from problem-solving itself (O'Reilly Treter et al., 2021).

Couples who entered the pandemic with greater challenges (e.g., economic hardship, systemic inequality, and discrimination, more personal vulnerabilities) and who face multiple and more extreme stressors (e.g., loss of income, loss of housing, food insecurity) as a result of the pandemic will likely have the most difficulty maintaining adaptive relationship processes (Pietromonaco & Overall, 2021). These couples are likely to require more than guidance about effective couple communication and support strategies, which cannot solve intractable economic and social problems that are likely to be amplified by the pandemic (Pietromonaco & Overall, 2021). These couples are most likely to benefit from societal and structural support including economic and employment assistance, housing, childcare, and health care (Karney et al., 2018; Lavner et al., 2015) that will provide a foundation for couples to nurture and strengthen their relationships by practicing adaptive relationship strategies.

PANDEMIC-RELATED STRESS AND RELATIONSHIP INITIATION (PATHS B, C, E, AND F)

The original VSA model did not discuss relationship initiation, and most research on the COVID-19 pandemic and relationships has focused on married or cohabiting couples. However, an important and understudied question concerns how the pandemic may have shaped the way in which people initiate romantic relationships and their expectations and goals for those relationships. A few studies suggest how the development of new relationships may be affected by the pandemic and its associated stress. Similar to couples in established marital or cohabiting relationships, college students in dating relationships reported experiencing more adverse relationship outcomes during the pandemic compared to four months earlier, including greater relational turbulence (e.g., more chaotic, more stressful; Goodboy et al., 2021). The pandemic also was associated with less partner interference and less partner facilitation probably because of fewer opportunities for contact. However, to the extent that partners interfered more, relationship turbulence was greater during the pandemic; and to the extent that partners facilitated more, relationship turbulence was less during the pandemic (Goodboy et al., 2021).

For those seeking to begin a relationship, the pandemic may alter what they desire in a romantic partner. Individuals who evidenced greater concern about COVID-19 assigned increased importance to attributes related to partner stability (e.g., having financial resources, being faithful) and family commitment (parenting qualities, desire for children) after social distancing began compared to before it began (Alexopoulos et al., 2021). The threat associated with the pandemic may shift priorities to more stable committed relationships, but also create dynamics that limit the emergence of these connections. For example, research conducted prior to the COVID-19 pandemic found that people with greater perceived vulnerability to disease showed less affiliation (e.g., individuals rate their partner's behavior as more withdrawn and less friendly) and less attraction to potential partners (Sawada et al., 2018). This work may indicate that those who perceive greater vulnerability to COVID-19 may be more withdrawn and less friendly as well as feel less attraction when engaging with potential dating partners.

Other research also indicates that pandemic-related stress may amplify the need to connect with others, but reduce the ability to connect effectively with others, including potential romantic partners. In a ten-day experience sampling study examining anxiety and social processes during the pandemic, participants provided six reports at random times during each day as well as an end of the day report. Anxiety related to the COVID-19 pandemic was associated with daily reports of greater loneliness and wishing for more interactions with others when alone, but also with greater conflict with others and being more distracted when communicating with others (Merolla et al., 2021). Daily interactions in this study captured many different kinds of interpersonal interactions and did not focus specifically on those with potential or existing romantic partners. However, if these findings are applicable to romantic relationships, they suggest the possibility that people who are more distressed about the pandemic may be more likely to feel lonely and long for romantic connections while also being more likely to experience conflict as a relationship develops.

Computer-mediated communication such as video chats became commonplace during the height of the pandemic (Brown & Greenfield, 2021), and represents a typical way of meeting a new romantic partner during the pandemic while social distancing. Although this form of communication may work well for some people, recent work suggests that those who are apprehensive about video chatting also are more likely to worry about their relationships and feel lonelier (Curran & Seiter, 2021). For these individuals, attempting to get to know a new partner online may trigger feelings of loneliness or disconnection. Furthermore, communication with potential romantic partners via Tinder may be changing as a result of the pandemic. In a qualitative interview study of twenty-nine individuals, participants reported that they were more likely than prior to the pandemic to directly discuss concerns about health in general and sexual health as well as the possibility of transmitting COVID-19 (Noland, 2021).

The limited research on relationship initiation indicates that the pandemic and associated constraints are linked to greater turbulence in dating relationships, shifts toward desiring partners who are likely to be more stable and family-oriented, and more use of technology to meet new partners (vs. meeting them in person). Furthermore, those who are more anxious about

COVID-19 may engage in less adaptive relationship behaviors that create greater conflict, which may impact how adaptive relationship processes evolve over the course of the relationship. In addition, some vulnerabilities – such as being anxious about virtual meetings with a partner – may undermine interactions with potential partners and lead individuals to feel more disconnected and lonelier. Our review primarily reveals that we still have much to learn about how the pandemic is shaping relationship initiation and newly developing relationships.

DIRECTIONS FOR FUTURE RESEARCH

The current perspective highlights the importance of taking into account multiple features of individuals' and couples' situations in evaluating the potential impact of the pandemic on relationship functioning, including the amount and severity of pandemic-related stress, enduring personal vulnerabilities, and adaptive relationship processes both before and during the pandemic. Most of the research has taken place in the early months of the pandemic and associated lockdowns, and further work is needed to understand how the pandemic may shape relationships and relationship processes throughout the remainder of the pandemic as well as afterward. Will some patterns persist even after the pandemic ends? Will couples who experienced declines during the pandemic recover as the strains of the pandemic lessen?

We have focused primarily on studies that examined relationship outcomes both before and during the pandemic. The importance of this comparison is illustrated by recent work examining age-related differences in emotional experience. Older adults typically experience more positive emotion (Carstensen et al., 2011), and older couples (compared to younger couples) typically are more affectionate and show less negativity during conflict (Carstensen et al., 1995). This greater emotional well-being among older adults also has been found in studies examining emotion across different ages during the COVID-19 pandemic (Carstensen et al., 2020; Sun & Sauter, 2021). However, in one study examining *within-person* age-related differences in emotion from before to during the COVID-19 pandemic, the age advantage for experiencing less negative emotion was reduced from before to during the pandemic (Sun & Sauter, 2021), possibly because the context of the pandemic makes it harder for older adults to regulate negative emotion by avoiding stressful situations. This example highlights the importance of examining, when possible, how individuals and couples were functioning prior to the pandemic and how that functioning may change over the course of the pandemic and during recovery.

In addition, it will be important to examine how the pandemic shapes relationship functioning throughout the pandemic and during recovery. Some work suggests that, in the face of a natural disaster (Hurricane Harvey), married couples (231 couples at the initial wave), on average, showed an increase in marital satisfaction from before to after the disaster, but that this increase returned to pre-disaster levels as recovery ensued (Williamson et al., 2021). Indeed, although we have outlined many studies that have shown that couples members' relationship satisfaction declined during the pandemic, compared to prior to the pandemic, others studies have found no differences (Williamson, 2020). In addition to differences in stress and enduring vulnerabilities determining relative levels of risk versus resilience, most of the available evidence involves examining changes in relationships within the early stages of the pandemic. Risk of declines in relationship functioning may not be fully evident early in the pandemic as most couple are able to meet the challenge of a novel external threat, but they may more clearly emerge as couples endure pandemic-related difficulties across time. Providing supporting evidence for this idea, the first examination of changes in couple and family functioning over the first 1.5 years of the pandemic found that the pandemic had been accompanied by average declines in relationship functioning, such as greater relationship problems and poorer family cohesion (Overall, Low, et al., 2022). These findings underscore the importance of examining relationship processes over the course of the pandemic, including tracking relationship functioning as well as breakup and divorce rates after the recovery period.

Our review revealed that the majority of studies examining the impact of the pandemic on relationships have focused on established couples, and that there is a major gap in understanding the extent to which the pandemic has impacted relationship initiation, including what people value in a long-term partner. How will the experience of the pandemic impact the development of new romantic relationships? During the pandemic, the use of online dating apps (e.g., Tinder, OKCupid, Bumble) rose sharply (Gibson, 2021), and this trend may continue even after the pandemic comes to an end (Wiederhold, 2021). Furthermore, the COVID-19 pandemic has amplified individuals' perceptions of health risks such that any sexual encounter may seem risky (Bowling et al., 2021), and therefore interfere with the development of both emotional and sexual intimacy in new relationships. Important research directions will be to understand whether pandemic-related shifts such as this one will change how people get to know and select partners, how they establish and negotiate intimacy, how they balance the development of intimacy with concerns about health risks and contagion (Gibson, 2021), and whether and how such shifts may influence longer-term relationship outcomes.

The conceptual framework in Figure 13.1 points to the importance of life context during the pandemic and this context is not independent from pre-existing contextual stressors such as economic adversity and discrimination. Recent work examining same-gender couples indicates that adverse effects of the pandemic on relationship satisfaction are amplified for individuals from racial/ethnic groups likely to experience discrimination as well as among those with greater internalized homophobia (Li & Samp, 2021). There is a pressing need for research on the connection between pandemic-related stress and relationship processes that includes diverse samples that vary along a range of dimensions, including in race/ethnicity, sexual orientation, age, socioeconomic status, country, and culture. The COVID-19 pandemic has amplified inequality worldwide, including exacerbating the effects of poverty, health conditions and mortality, and violence against women (Sidik, 2022), pointing to the importance of examining relationship processes and outcomes across contexts that are not well-represented in the current literature. Doing so will advance an understanding of how the COVID-19 crisis may create different trajectories for couples who enter the pandemic with different contexts, personal vulnerabilities, and relationship strengths and weaknesses.

A key insight is that the pandemic has affected not only couples' relationships but spills over to the family (Browne et al., 2021; McRae et al., 2021; Overall, Chang, et al., 2022; Prime et al., 2020). Spillover can occur from the couples' relationship to other family members (e.g., children) but stress manifested in children or other family members also can reciprocally spill over to the couple (Overall, Pietromonaco, et al., 2022). Researchers can capitalize on datasets including assessments before, during, and after the pandemic to better understand how stress generated by the pandemic may reverberate through the family, affecting the interplay among couples' relationships, parenting, and children's behavior.

CONCLUSIONS

The COVID-19 pandemic has resulted in myriad challenges for established relationships as well as initiating and developing new relationships. Consistent with the VSA model, research examining the effects of the pandemic indicate that the quality of relationship functioning will depend on individuals' and couples' life contexts, enduring personal vulnerabilities, and the extent to which they already engaged in adaptive relationship processes prior to the pandemic. As a result, relationship trajectories across the pandemic and into pandemic recovery will vary considerably depending on the conditions that people were experiencing at the start of the pandemic. Research within the context of the pandemic offers the opportunity for strong tests of the value of relationship science theories for understanding relationship risk and resilience during real-world crises. Relationship science theories also highlight important further research directions to fully understand how social relationships have been altered by the pandemic along with the ramifications for health and well-being.

REFERENCES

Aknin, L., De Neve, J.-E., Dunn, E., Fancourt, D., Goldberg, E., Helliwell, J. F., Jones, S. P., Karam, E., Layard, R., Lyubomirsky, S., Rzepa, A., Saxena, S., Thornton, E. M., VanderWeele, T. J., Whillans, A. V., Zaki, J., Karadag Caman, O., & Ben Amor, Y. (2021). Mental health during the first year of the COVID-19 pandemic: A review and recommendations for moving forward. *Perspectives on Psychological Science.* https://ora.ox.ac.uk/objects/uuid:eb6e61dd-9e50-48d1-b64b-5d9106b6225d

Alexopoulos, C., Timmermans, E., Sharabi, L. L., Roaché, D. J., Croft, A., Hall, E. D., James-Hawkins, L., Lamarche, V., & Uhlich, M. (2021). Settling down without settling: Perceived changes in partner preferences in response to COVID-19. *Journal of Social and Personal Relationships, 38*(6), 1901–1919. https://doi.org/10.1177/02654075211011527

Algoe, S. B., Gable, S. L., & Maisel, N. C. (2010). It's the little things: Everyday gratitude as a booster shot for romantic relationships. *Personal Relationships, 17*(2), 217–233. https://doi.org/10.1111/j.1475-6811.2010.01273.x

Alyammahi, S. K., Abdin, S. M., Alhamad, D. W., Elgendy, S. M., Altell, A. T., & Omar, H. A. (2021). The dynamic association between COVID-19 and chronic disorders: An updated insight into prevalence, mechanisms and therapeutic modalities. *Infection, Genetics and Evolution, 87,* 104647. https://doi.org/10.1016/j.meegid.2020.104647

Aron, A., Norman, C. C., Aron, E. N., McKenna, C., & Heyman, R. E. (2000). Couples' shared participation in novel and arousing activities and experienced relationship quality. *Journal of Personality and Social Psychology, 78*(2), 273–284. https://doi.org/10.1037/0022-3514.78.2.273

Balzarini, R. N., Muise, A., Zoppolat, G., Di Bartolomeo, A., Rodrigues, D. L., Alonso-Ferres, M., Urganci, B., Debrot, A., Bock Pichayayothin, N., Dharma, C., Chi, P., Karremans, J. C., Schoebi, D., & Slatcher, R. B. (2022). Love in the time of COVID: Perceived partner responsiveness buffers people from lower relationship quality associated with COVID-related stressors. *Social Psychological and Personality Science,* 19485506221094436. https://doi.org/10.1177/19485506221094437

Bar-Kalifa, E., Randall, A. K., & Perelman, Y. (2021). Daily dyadic coping during COVID-19 among Israeli couples. *Emotion, 22*(8). https://doi.org/10.1037/emo0000971

Barry, R. A., Barden, E. P., & Dubac, C. (2019). Pulling away: Links among disengaged couple communication, relationship distress, and depressive symptoms. *Journal of Family Psychology, 33*(3), 280–293. https://doi.org/10.1037/fam0000507

Beck, L. A., Pietromonaco, P. R., DeBuse, C. J., Powers, S. I., & Sayer, A. G. (2013). Spouses' attachment pairings predict neuroendocrine, behavioral, and psychological responses to marital conflict. *Journal of Personality and Social Psychology, 105*(3), 388–424. https://doi.org/10.1037/a0033056

Beck, L. A., Pietromonaco, P. R., DeVito, C. C., Powers, S. I., & Boyle, A. M. (2014). Congruence between spouses' perceptions and observers' ratings of responsiveness: The role of attachment avoidance. *Personality & Social Psychology Bulletin, 40*(2), 164–174. https://doi.org/10.1177/0146167213507779

Biddle, N., Edwards, B., Gray, M., & Sollis, K. (2020). *Mental health and relationships during the COVID-19 pandemic.* The Australian National University. https://csrm.cass.anu.edu.au/research/publications/mental-health-and-relationships-during-covid-19-pandemic

Biden, E. J., Greenwood, C. J., Macdonald, J. A., Spry, E. A., Letcher, P., Hutchinson, D., Youssef, G. J., McIntosh, J. E., & Olsson, C. A. (2021). Preparing for future adversities: Lessons from the covid-19 pandemic in Australia for promoting relational resilience in families. *Frontiers in Psychiatry*, 12, 1319. https://doi.org/10.3389/fpsyt.2021.717811

Bonanno, G. A. (2004). Loss, trauma, and human resilience: Have we underestimated the human capacity to thrive after extremely aversive events? *American Psychologist*, 59(1), 20–28. https://doi.org/10.1037/0003-066X.59.1.20

Bowling, J., Montanaro, E., Gattuso, J., Gioia, D., & Guerrero Ordonez, S. (2021). "Everything feels risky now": Perceived "risky" sexual behavior during COVID-19 pandemic. *Journal of Health Psychology*, 13591053211004684. https://doi.org/10.1177/13591053211004684

Bradbury-Jones, C., & Isham, L. (2020). The pandemic paradox: The consequences of COVID-19 on domestic violence. *Journal of Clinical Nursing* (John Wiley & Sons, Inc.), 29(13/14), 2047–2049. https://doi.org/10.1111/jocn.15296

Brown, G., & Greenfield, P. M. (2021). Staying connected during stay-at-home: Communication with family and friends and its association with well-being. *Human Behavior and Emerging Technologies*. https://doi.org/10.1002/hbe2.246

Brown, S. M., Doom, J. R., Lechuga-Peña, S., Watamura, S. E., & Koppels, T. (2020). Stress and parenting during the global COVID-19 pandemic. *Child Abuse & Neglect*, 110(Pt 2), 104699. https://doi.org/10.1016/j.chiabu.2020.104699

Browne, D. T., Wade, M., May, S. S., Jenkins, J. M., & Prime, H. (2021). Covid-19 disruption gets inside the family: A two-month multilevel study of family stress during the pandemic. *Developmental Psychology*, 57(10), 1681–1692.

Bu, F., Steptoe, A., Mak, H. W., & Fancourt, D. (2021). Time use and mental health in UK adults during an 11-week COVID-19 lockdown: A panel analysis. *British Journal of Psychiatry*, 219(4), 551–556. https://doi.org/10.1192/bjp.2021.44

Buck, A. A., & Neff, L. A. (2012). Stress spillover in early marriage: The role of self-regulatory depletion. *Journal of Family Psychology*, 26(5), 698–708. https://doi.org/10.1037/a0029260

Butzer, B., & Campbell, L. (2008). Adult attachment, sexual satisfaction, and relationship satisfaction: A study of married couples. *Personal Relationships*, 15(1), 141–154. https://doi.org/10.1111/j.1475-6811.2007.00189.x

Campbell, L., Simpson, J. A., Boldry, J., & Kashy, D. A. (2005). Perceptions of conflict and support in romantic relationships: The role of attachment anxiety. *Journal of Personality and Social Psychology*, 88(3), 510–531. https://doi.org/10.1037/0022-3514.88.3.510

Carnelley, K. B., Pietromonaco, P. R., & Jaffe, K. (1996). Attachment, caregiving, and relationship functioning in couples: Effects of self and partner. *Personal Relationships*, 3(3), 257–277. https://doi.org/10.1111/j.1475-6811.1996.tb00116.x

Carstensen, L. L., Gottman, J. M., & Levenson, R. W. (1995). Emotional behavior in long-term marriage. *Psychology and Aging*, 10(1), 140–149. https://doi.org/10.1037/0882-7974.10.1.140

Carstensen, L. L., Shavit, Y. Z., & Barnes, J. T. (2020). Age advantages in emotional experience persist even under threat from the COVID-19 pandemic. *Psychological Science*, 31(11), 1374–1385. https://doi.org/10.1177/0956797620967261

Carstensen, L. L., Turan, B., Scheibe, S., Ram, N., Ersner-Hershfield, H., Samanez-Larkin, G. R., Brooks, K. P., & Nesselroade, J. R. (2011). Emotional experience improves with age: Evidence based on over 10 years of experience sampling. *Psychology and Aging*, 26(1), 21–33. https://doi.org/10.1037/a0021285

Cross, E. J., Overall, N. C., Low, R. S. T., & McNulty, J. K. (2019). An interdependence account of sexism and power: Men's hostile sexism, biased perceptions of low power, and relationship aggression. *Journal of Personality and Social Psychology*, 117(2), 338–363. https://doi.org/10.1037/pspi0000167

Curran, T., & Seiter, J. S. (2021). The role of relational worry due to COVID-19 in the links between video chat apprehension, loneliness, and adhering to CDC guidelines. *Journal of Social & Personal Relationships*, 38(6), 1869–1876. https://doi.org/10.1177/0265407520985264

Diamond, L. M., & Hicks, A. M. (2012). "It's the economy, honey!" couples' blame attributions during the 2007–2009 economic crisis. *Personal Relationships*, 19(3), 586–600. https://doi.org/10.1111/j.1475-6811.2011.01380.x

Donato, S., Parise, M., Pagani, A. F., Lanz, M., Regalia, C., Rosnati, R., & Iafrate, R. (2021). Together against covid-19 concerns: The role of the dyadic coping process for partners' psychological well-being during the pandemic. *Frontiers in Psychology*, 11. www.frontiersin.org/article/10.3389/fpsyg.2020.578395

Eder, S. J., Nicholson, A. A., Stefanczyk, M. M., Pieniak, M., Martínez-Molina, J., Pešout, O., Binter, J., Smela, P., Scharnowski, F., & Steyrl, D. (2021). Securing your relationship: Quality of intimate relationships during the COVID-19 pandemic can be predicted by attachment style. *Frontiers in Psychology*, 12. www.frontiersin.org/article/10.3389/fpsyg.2021.647956

Enestrom, M. C., & Lydon, J. E. (2021). Relationship satisfaction in the time of COVID-19: The role of shared reality in perceiving partner support for frontline health-care workers. *Journal of Social & Personal Relationships*, 38(8), 2330–2349. https://doi.org/10.1177/02654075211020127

Feeney, B. C., & Collins, N. L. (2015). A new look at social support: A theoretical perspective on thriving through relationships. *Personality and Social Psychology Review*, 19(2), 113–147. https://doi.org/10.1177/1088868314544222

Funder, D. C., Lee, D. I., Baranski, E., & Baranski, G. G. (2021). The experience of situations before and during a COVID-19 shelter-at-home period. *Social Psychological and Personality Science*. https://doi.org/10.1177/1948550620985388

Gable, S. L., Gonzaga, G. C., & Strachman, A. (2006). Will you be there for me when things go right? Supportive responses to positive event disclosures. *Journal of Personality and Social Psychology*, 91(5), 904–917. https://doi.org/10.1037/0022-3514.91.5.904

Gable, S. L., & Reis, H. T. (2010). Good news! Capitalizing on positive events in an interpersonal context. In M. P. Zanna (Ed.), *Advances in experimental social psychology* (Vol. 42, 2012-14612-004, pp. 195–257). Academic Press.

Gable, S. L., Reis, H. T., Impett, E. A., & Asher, E. R. (2004). What do you do when things go right? The intrapersonal and interpersonal benefits of sharing positive events. *Journal of Personality and Social Psychology*, 87(2), 228–245. https://doi.org/10.1037/0022-3514.87.2.228

Gibson, A. F. (2021). Exploring the impact of COVID-19 on mobile dating: Critical avenues for research. *Social and Personality Psychology Compass*, 15(11). https://doi.org/10.1111/spc3.12643

Girme, Y. U., Overall, N. C., & Faingataa, S. (2014). "Date nights" take two: The maintenance function of shared relationship activities. *Personal Relationships*, 21(1), 125–149. https://doi.org/10.1111/pere.12020

Girme, Y. U., Overall, N. C., Simpson, J. A., & Fletcher, G. J. O. (2015). "All or nothing": Attachment avoidance and the curvilinear effects of partner support. *Journal of Personality and Social Psychology*, 108(3), 450–475. https://doi.org/10.1037/a0038866

Giurge, L. M., Whillans, A. V., & Yemiscigil, A. (2021). A multicountry perspective on gender differences in time use during COVID-19. *Proceedings of the National Academy of Sciences of the United States*, 118(12), 1aa. https://doi.org/10.1073/pnas.2018494118

Glick, P., & Fiske, S. T. (1996). The Ambivalent Sexism Inventory: Differentiating hostile and benevolent sexism. *Journal of Personality and Social Psychology*, 70(3), 491–512. https://doi.org/10.1037/0022-3514.70.3.491

Goodboy, A. K., Dillow, M. R., Knoster, K. C., & Howard, H. A. (2021). Relational turbulence from the COVID-19 pandemic: Within-subjects mediation by romantic partner interdependence. *Journal of Social & Personal Relationships*, 38(6), 1800–1818. https://doi.org/10.1177/02654075211000135

Gordon, A. M., Tuskeviciute, R., & Chen, S. (2013). A multimethod investigation of depressive symptoms, perceived understanding, and relationship quality. *Personal Relationships*, 20(4), 635–654. https://doi.org/10.1111/pere.12005

Gresham, A. M., Peters, B. J., Karantzas, G., Cameron, L. D., & Simpson, J. A. (2021). Examining associations between COVID-19 stressors, intimate partner violence, health, and health behaviors. *Journal of Social & Personal Relationships*, 38(8), 2291–2307. https://doi.org/10.1177/02654075211012098

Haydon, K. C., & Salvatore, J. E. (2022). A prospective study of mental health, well-being, and substance use during the initial covid-19 pandemic surge. *Clinical Psychological Science*, 10(1), 58–73. https://doi.org/10.1177/21677026211013499

Holmstrom, A. J., Shebib, S. J., Boumis, J. K., Allard, A., Mason, A. J., & Lim, J. I. (2021). Support gaps during the COVID-19 pandemic: Sex differences and effects on well-being. *Journal of Social and Personal Relationships*, 38(10), 2985–3009. https://doi.org/10.1177/02654075211041539

Jayamaha, S. D., Girme, Y. U., & Overall, N. C. (2017). When attachment anxiety impedes support provision: The role of feeling unvalued and unappreciated. *Journal of Family Psychology*, 31(2), 181–191. https://doi.org/10.1037/fam0000222

Karney, B. R., & Bradbury, T. N. (1995). The longitudinal course of marital quality and stability: A review of theory, methods, and research. *Psychological Bulletin*, 118(1), 3–34. https://doi.org/10.1037/0033-2909.118.1.3

Karney, B. R., Bradbury, T. N., & Lavner, J. A. (2018). Supporting healthy relationships in low-income couples: Lessons learned and policy implications. *Policy Insights from the Behavioral and Brain Sciences*, 5(1), 33–39. https://doi.org/10.1177/2372732217747890

Knobloch-Fedders, L. M., Knobloch, L. K., Durbin, C. E., Rosen, A., & Critchfield, K. L. (2013). Comparing the interpersonal behavior of distressed couples with and without depression. *Journal of Clinical Psychology*, 69(12), 1250–1268. https://doi.org/10.1002/jclp.21998

Kroencke, L., Geukes, K., Utesch, T., Kuper, N., & Back, M. D. (2020). Neuroticism and emotional risk during the COVID-19 pandemic. *Journal of Research in Personality*, 89. https://doi.org/10.1016/j.jrp.2020.104038

Lades, L. K., Laffan, K., Daly, M., & Delaney, L. (2020). Daily emotional well-being during the COVID-19 pandemic. *British Journal of Health Psychology*, 25(4), 902–911. https://doi.org/10.1111/bjhp.12450

Lavner, J. A., Karney, B. R., & Bradbury, T. N. (2015). New directions for policies aimed at strengthening low-income couples. *Behavioral Science and Policy*, 1(2), 13–24. https://issuu.com/behavioralsciencepolicyassociation/docs/bsp_vol1is2__lavner/1

Li, Y., & Samp, J. A. (2021). The impact of the COVID-19 pandemic on same-sex couples' conflict avoidance, relational quality, and mental health. *Journal of Social and Personal Relationships*, 38(6), 1819–1843. https://doi.org/10.1177/02654075211006199

Low, R. S. T., Overall, N. C., Chang, V. T., Henderson, A. M. E., & Sibley, C. G. (2021). Emotion regulation and psychological and physical health during a nationwide COVID-19 lockdown. *Emotion*, 21(8), 1671–1690. https://doi.org/10.1037/emo0001046

Lucassen, N., de Haan, A. D., Helmerhorst, K. O. W., & Keizer, R. (2021). Interrelated changes in parental stress, parenting, and coparenting across the onset of the COVID-19 pandemic. *Journal of Family Psychology*, No Pagination Specified-No Pagination Specified. https://doi.org/10.1037/fam0000908

Mancini, A. D., Westphal, M., & Griffin, P. (2021). Outside the Eye of the Storm: Can Moderate Hurricane Exposure Improve Social, Psychological, and Attachment Functioning? *Personality & Social Psychology Bulletin*, 146167221990488. https://doi.org/10.1177/0146167221990488

McRae, C. S., Overall, N. C., Low, R. S. T., & Chang, V. T. (2021). Parents' distress and poor parenting during COVID-19: The buffering effects of partner support and cooperative coparenting. *Developmental Psychology*. https://doi.org/10.1037/dev0001207

Merolla, A. J., Otmar, C., & Hernandez, C. R. (2021). Day-to-day relational life during the COVID-19 pandemic: Linking mental health, daily relational experiences, and end-of-day outlook. *Journal of Social & Personal Relationships*, 38(8), 2350–2375. https://doi.org/10.1177/02654075211020137

Mikulincer, M., & Shaver, P. R. (2017). *Attachment in adulthood: Structure, dynamics and change* (2nd ed.). Guilford Publications.

Neff, L. A., & Broady, E. F. (2011). Stress resilience in early marriage: Can practice make perfect? *Journal of Personality and Social Psychology*, 101(5), 1050–1067. https://doi.org/10.1037/a0023809

Neff, L. A., Gleason, M. E. J., Crockett, E. E., & Ciftci, O. (2022). Blame the pandemic: Buffering the association between stress and relationship quality during the covid-19 pandemic. *Social Psychological and Personality Science*, 13(2), 522–532. https://doi.org/10.1177/19485506211022813

Neff, L. A., & Karney, B. R. (2009). Stress and reactivity to daily relationship experiences: How stress hinders adaptive processes in marriage. *Journal of Personality & Social Psychology*, 97(3), 435–450. https://doi.org/10.1037/a0015663

Neff, L. A., & Karney, B. R. (2017). Acknowledging the elephant in the room: How stressful environmental contexts shape relationship dynamics. *Current Opinion in Psychology*, 13, 107–110. https://doi.org/10.1016/j.copsyc.2016.05.013

Nguyen, T. P., Karney, B. R., & Bradbury, T. N. (2020). When poor communication does and does not matter: The moderating role of stress. *Journal of Family Psychology, 34*(6), 676–686. https://doi.org/10.1037/fam0000643

Noland, C. M. (2021). Negotiating desire and uncertainty on tinder during the covid-19 pandemic: Implications for the transformation of sexual health communication. *CyberPsychology, Behavior & Social Networking, 24*(7), 488–492. https://doi.org/10.1089/cyber.2020.0685

Ogan, M. A., Monk, J. K., Kanter, J. B., & Proulx, C. M. (2021). Stress, dyadic coping, and relationship instability during the COVID-19 pandemic. *Journal of Social and Personal Relationships, 38*(10), 2944–2964. https://doi.org/10.1177/02654075211046531

O'Reilly Treter, M., River, L. M., & Markman, H. J. (2021). Supporting romantic relationships during COVID-19 using virtual couple therapy. *Cognitive and Behavioral Practice*. https://doi.org/10.1016/j.cbpra.2021.02.002

Overall, N. C., Chang, V. T., Cross, E. J., Low, R. S. T., & Henderson, A. M. E. (2021). Sexist attitudes predict family-based aggression during a COVID-19 lockdown. *Journal of Family Psychology, 35*(8), 1043–1052. https://doi.org/10.1037/fam0000834

Overall, N. C., Chang, V. T., Pietromonaco, P. R., Low, R. S. T., & Henderson, A. M. E. (2021). Partners' Attachment Insecurity and Stress Predict Poorer Relationship Functioning During COVID-19 Quarantines. *Social Psychological and Personality Science*, 1948550621992973. https://doi.org/10.1177/1948550621992973

Overall, N. C., Chang, V. T., Pietromonaco, P. R., Low, R. S. T., & Henderson, A. M. E. (2022). Partners' attachment insecurity and stress predict poorer relationship functioning during COVID-19 quarantines. *Social Psychological and Personality Science, 13*(1), 285–298. https://doi.org/10.1177/1948550621992973

Overall, N. C., Fletcher, G. J. O., Simpson, J. A., & Fillo, J. (2015). Attachment insecurity, biased perceptions of romantic partners' negative emotions, and hostile relationship behavior. *Journal of Personality and Social Psychology, 108*(5), 730–749. https://doi.org/10.1037/a0038987

Overall, N. C., Girme, Y. U., Lemay, E. P. Jr., & Hammond, M. D. (2014). Attachment anxiety and reactions to relationship threat: The benefits and costs of inducing guilt in romantic partners. *Journal of Personality and Social Psychology, 106*(2), 235–256. https://doi.org/10.1037/a0034371

Overall, N. C., & Hammond, M. D. (2013). Biased and accurate: Depressive symptoms and daily perceptions within intimate relationships. *Personality and Social Psychology Bulletin, 39*(5), 636–650. https://doi.org/10.1177/0146167213480188

Overall, N. C., Low, R. S. T., Chang, V. T., Henderson, A. M. E., McRae, C. S., & Pietromonaco, P. R. (2022). Enduring COVID-19 lockdowns: Risk versus resilience in parents' health and family functioning across the pandemic. *Journal of Social and Personal Relationships, 39*(11), 3296–3319.

Overall, N. C., Pietromonaco, P. R., & Simpson, J. A. (2022). Buffering and spillover of romantic attachment insecurity in couple and family relationships. *Nature Reviews Psychology, 1*(2), 101–111.

Overall, N. C., Simpson, J. A., & Struthers, H. (2013). Buffering attachment-related avoidance: Softening emotional and behavioral defenses during conflict discussions. *Journal of Personality and Social Psychology, 104*(5), 854–871. https://doi.org/10.1037/a0031798

Parrott, D. J., Halmos, M. B., Stappenbeck, C. A., & Moino, K. (2022). Intimate partner aggression during the COVID-19 pandemic: Associations with stress and heavy drinking. *Psychology of Violence, 12*(2), 95–103. https://doi.org/10.1037/vio0000395

Pauly, T., Lüscher, J., Berli, C., & Scholz, U. (2022). *Dynamic associations between stress and relationship functioning in the wake of COVID-19: Longitudinal data from the German family panel (pairfam)*. https://journals-sagepub-com.silk.library.umass.edu/doi/full/10.1177/02654075221092360

Pietromonaco, P. R., & Barrett, L. F. (1997). Working models of attachment and daily social interactions. *Journal of Personality and Social Psychology, 73*(6), 1409–1423. https://doi.org/10.1037/0022-3514.73.6.1409

Pietromonaco, P. R., & Collins, N. L. (2017). Interpersonal mechanisms linking close relationships to health. *American Psychologist, 72*(6), 531–542. https://doi.org/10.1037/amp0000129

Pietromonaco, P. R., & Overall, N. C. (2021). Applying relationship science to evaluate how the COVID-19 pandemic may impact couples' relationships. *American Psychologist, 76*(3), 438–450. https://doi.org/10.1037/amp0000714

Pietromonaco, P. R., & Overall, N. C. (2022a). How far is the reach of personality in relationship functioning during COVID-19? Reply to Pfund and Hill (2022). *American Psychologist, 77*(1), 145–146. https://doi.org/10.1037/amp0000941

Pietromonaco, P. R., & Overall, N. C. (2022b). Implications of social isolation, separation, and loss during the COVID-19 pandemic for couples' relationships. *Current Opinion in Psychology, 43*, 189–194. https://doi.org/10.1016/j.copsyc.2021.07.014

Pietromonaco, P. R., & Overall, N. C. (in press). How will couples adapt to stress from the COVID-19 pandemic? A relationship science perspective. In M. K. Miller (Ed.), *The social science of the COVID-19 pandemic: A call to action for researchers*. Oxford University Press.

Pietromonaco, P. R., Overall, N. C., & Powers, S. I. (2022). Depressive symptoms, external stress, and marital adjustment: The buffering effect of partner's responsive behavior. *Social Psychological and Personality Science, 13*(1), 220–232. https://doi.org/10.1177/19485506211001687

Prime, H., Wade, M., & Browne, D. T. (2020). Risk and resilience in family well-being during the COVID-19 pandemic. *American Psychologist, 75*(5), 631–643. https://doi.org/10.1037/amp0000660

Racine, N., Hetherington, E., McArthur, B. A., McDonald, S., Edwards, S., Tough, S., & Madigan, S. (2021). Maternal depressive and anxiety symptoms before and during the COVID-19 pandemic in Canada: A longitudinal analysis. *The Lancet Psychiatry, 8*(5), 405–415. https://doi.org/10.1016/S2215-0366(21)00074-2

Randall, A. K., Leon, G., Basili, E., Martos, T., Boiger, M., Baldi, M., Hocker, L., Kline, K., Masturzi, A., Aryeetey, R., Bar-Kalifa, E., Boon, S. D., Botella, L., Burke, T., Carnelley, K. B., Carr, A., Dash, A., Fitriana, M., Gaines Jr., S. O., & Galdiolo, S. (2022). Coping with global uncertainty: Perceptions of COVID-19 psychological distress, relationship quality, and dyadic coping for romantic partners across 27 countries. *Journal of Social & Personal Relationships, 39*(1), 3–33. https://doi.org/10.1177/02654075211034236

Reis, H. T., Clark, M. S., & Holmes, J. G. (2004). Perceived partner responsiveness as an organizing construct in the study of intimacy and closeness. In D. J. Mashek & A.

P. Aron (Eds.), *Handbook of closeness and intimacy* (2004-00238-012; pp. 201–225). Lawrence Erlbaum Associates Publishers.

Sawada, N., Auger, E., & Lydon, J. E. (2018). Activation of the behavioral immune system: Putting the brakes on affiliation. *Personality and Social Psychology Bulletin*, 44(2), 224–237. https://doi.org/10.1177/0146167217736046

Schmid, L., Wörn, J., Hank, K., Sawatzki, B., & Walper, S. (2020). Changes in employment and relationship satisfaction in times of the COVID-19 pandemic: Evidence from the German family Panel. *European Societies*, 23(sup 1), S743–S758. https://doi.org/10.1080/14616696.2020.1836385

Shariati, A., & Guerette, R. T. (2022). Findings from a natural experiment on the impact of COVID-19 residential quarantines on domestic violence patterns in new orleans. *Journal of Family Violence*. https://doi.org/10.1007/s10896-022-00380-y

Sidik, S. M. (2022). How COVID has deepened inequality – In six stark graphics. *Nature*, 606(7915), 638–639.

Simpson, J. A., & Rholes, W. S. (2017). Adult attachment, stress, and romantic relationships. *Current Opinion in Psychology*, 13, 19–24. https://doi.org/10.1016/j.copsyc.2016.04.006

Simpson, J. A., Rholes, W. S., & Phillips, D. (1996). Conflict in close relationships: An attachment perspective. *Journal of Personality and Social Psychology*, 71(5), 899–914. https://doi.org/10.1037/0022-3514.71.5.899

Sisson, N. M., Willroth, E. C., Le, B. M., & Ford, B. Q. (2021). The benefits of living with close others: A longitudinal examination of mental health before and during a global stressor. *Clinical Psychological Science*, 21677026211053320. https://doi.org/10.1177/21677026211053320

Smallen, D., Eller, J., Rholes, W. S., & Simpson, J. A. (2021). Perceptions of partner responsiveness across the transition to parenthood. *Journal of Family Psychology*, 36(4), 618–629. https://doi.org/10.1037/fam0000907

Sun, R., & Sauter, D. (2021). Sustained stress reduces the age advantages in emotional experience of older adults: Commentary on Carstensen et al (2020). *Psychological Science*, 32(12), 2035–2041. https://doi.org/10.1177/09567976211052476

Tan, R., Overall, N. C., & Taylor, J. K. (2012). Let's talk about us: Attachment, relationship-focused disclosure, and relationship quality. *Personal Relationships*, 19(3), 521–534. https://doi.org/10.1111/j.1475-6811.2011.01383.x

Twenge, J. M., & Joiner, T. E. (2020). U.S. Census Bureau-assessed prevalence of anxiety and depressive symptoms in 2019 and during the 2020 COVID-19 pandemic. *Depression & Anxiety (1091–4269)*, 37(10), 954–956. https://doi.org/10.1002/da.23077

Vowels, L. M., & Carnelley, K. B. (2020). Attachment styles, negotiation of goal conflict, and perceived partner support during covid-19. *Personality and Individual Differences*. https://doi.org/10.1016/j.paid.2020.110505

Vowels, L. M., Carnelley, K. B., & Stanton, S. C. E. (2022). Attachment anxiety predicts worse mental health outcomes during COVID-19: Evidence from two studies. *Personality and Individual Differences*, 185. https://doi.org/10.1016/j.paid.2021.111256

Vowels, L. M., Francois-Walcott, R. R. R., Perks, R. E., & Carnelley, K. B. (2021). "Be free together rather than confined together": A qualitative exploration of how relationships changed in the early COVID-19 pandemic. *Journal of Social & Personal Relationships*, 38(10), 2921–2943. https://doi.org/10.1177/02654075211041412

Waddell, N., Overall, N. C., Chang, V. T., & Hammond, M. D. (2021). Gendered division of labor during a nationwide COVID-19 lockdown: Implications for relationship problems and satisfaction. *Journal of Social & Personal Relationships, 38*(6), 1759–1781. https://doi.org/10.1177/0265407521996476

Westrick-Payne, K. K., Manning, W. D., & Carlson, L. (2022). Pandemic Shortfall in Marriages and Divorces in the United States. *Socius, 8,* 23780231221090190. https://doi.org/10.1177/23780231221090192

Westrupp, E. M., Bennett, C., Berkowitz, T., Youssef, G. J., Toumbourou, J. W., Tucker, R., Andrews, F. J., Evans, S., Teague, S. J., Karantzas, G. C., Melvin, G. M., Olsson, C., Macdonald, J. A., Greenwood, C. J., Mikocka-Walus, A., Hutchinson, D., Fuller-Tyszkiewicz, M., Stokes, M. A., Olive, L., ... Sciberras, E. (2021). Child, parent, and family mental health and functioning in australia during COVID-19: Comparison to pre-pandemic data. *European Child & Adolescent Psychiatry.* https://doi.org/10.1007/s00787-021-01861-z

Wiederhold, B. K. (2021). How COVID has changed online dating – And what lies ahead. *CyberPsychology, Behavior & Social Networking, 24*(7), 435–436. https://doi.org/10.1089/cyber.2021.29219.editorial

Williamson, H. C. (2020). Early effects of the COVID-19 pandemic on relationship satisfaction and attributions. *Psychological Science, 31*(12), 1479–1487. https://doi.org/10.1177/0956797620972688

Williamson, H. C., Bradbury, T. N., & Karney, B. R. (2021). Experiencing a natural disaster temporarily boosts relationship satisfaction in newlywed couples. *Psychological Science, 32*(11), 1709–1719. https://doi.org/10.1177/09567976211015677

Williamson, H. C., Karney, B. R., & Bradbury, T. N. (2013). Financial strain and stressful events predict newlyweds' negative communication independent of relationship satisfaction. *Journal of Family Psychology, 27*(1), 65–75. https://doi.org/10.1037/a0031104

Zee, K. S., & Bolger, N. (2019). Visible and invisible social support: How, why, and when. *Current Directions in Psychological Science, 28*(3), 314–320. https://doi.org/10.1177/0963721419835214

INDEX

adolescence, 29, 72, 74, 81, 92–94, 177, 183, 188–190, 211, 237
adoption, 151, 158, 159
adultery, 80, 152, 153, 155
affair, 153, 154, 181
affection, 39, 42, 117, 120, 124, 142, 153, 154, 209
African American, 15–17, 21, 22, 36, 40, 57, 98, 106
aggression, 96, 104, 143, 181, 186, 187, 205, 250, 256
aging, 35, 63
anxiety, 29, 105, 206, 251, 254–256, 258, 260
Asian, 3, 7, 30, 31, 34, 36–43, 81, 92, 106
attraction, 35, 66, 72, 75, 115, 117, 190, 203, 215, 260
attractive, 63, 73, 172, 186, 189, 190
attractiveness, 15, 73, 174, 183, 204

binary, 55, 57, 59, 60
bisexual, 188
breakup, 17, 65, 71, 104, 158, 179, 182, 190, 211, 213, 214, 252, 253, 262

catfishing, 143, 177
cheating, 101, 185
China, 30, 31, 33–35, 41, 55, 172, 185, 187
cognition, 36, 43, 106, 122, 174, 185–187, 250
cohabit, 4, 14, 17, 18, 30, 32, 33, 35, 62, 63, 71, 75–78, 82, 90, 92–96, 98–101, 103, 106, 151, 155–163, 184, 188, 230, 253, 259
collectivist, 34, 37, 55, 81
colorism, 21
commitment, 5, 41, 56, 62, 64, 75, 80, 90, 95–97, 99, 101–103, 106, 136, 142, 163, 180, 189, 207–209, 211, 226, 242, 252, 255, 259
compatibility, 34, 42, 76, 93, 144, 183, 185, 205
conflict, 38–40, 62, 65, 71, 78, 96, 102, 104, 116, 122–124, 126, 141, 178, 180, 183, 184, 186, 187, 210, 211, 216, 238, 240, 241, 250, 254, 258, 260, 261

consensual non-monogamous, 63, 64
consensual non-monogamy, 60, 63, 65
coparenting, 251
courtship, 93, 177
culture, 1, 2, 30, 36–40, 42–44, 64, 81, 82, 136, 181, 228, 230, 263
custody, 64, 158–162

digital, 73, 168, 169, 177, 191, 210–215
discrimination, 7, 13, 15, 16, 20, 21, 33, 41, 42, 61, 64, 66, 120, 137, 139, 141, 157, 227, 240, 254, 259, 262
dyad, 1, 61, 77, 98, 100, 101, 210, 236
dyadic, 1, 60–62, 64, 96, 99, 102, 177, 180, 248, 254

egalitarian, 17, 94, 95, 126, 236, 239, 240
emotion, 34, 36, 38, 39, 43, 62, 256, 261
equality, 32, 33, 42, 79, 142, 143, 157, 182, 239
equity, 8, 22, 44, 78, 79, 154–156, 191, 228, 241
European, 2, 3, 29, 30, 32, 33, 35, 36, 38–40, 42, 43, 59, 78, 81, 96, 106
exchange, 61, 66, 119, 127, 169–172, 176–178, 231, 234
extradyadic, 63

Facebook, 121, 201, 202, 204, 205, 207, 209, 211, 216
fertility, 127, 157
Fincham, F. D., 95, 101, 102
friendship, 31, 64, 65, 80, 123, 141, 153, 173, 180, 184, 201–203, 205, 207, 209, 214, 235, 247, 253

gay, 59, 60, 65, 76, 79, 144, 161, 182, 188
ghosting, 5, 211, 214, 215
gratitude, 31, 40, 102, 182, 258

happiness, 43, 101
heteronormativity, 3, 4, 55–57, 60–66, 72, 208

Index

heterosexual, 21, 57, 61, 64, 65, 71, 72, 78, 79, 81, 83, 90, 92, 94, 100, 106, 152, 158, 177, 182, 184, 188, 203, 227, 228, 238, 239
homosexuality, 142, 151, 157, 181, 188
hookup, 74, 144
housework, 78, 79, 83, 251

immigrant families, 5, 226, 227, 229, 230, 233
immigration, 5, 226–228, 230–235, 237, 238, 241
inclusion, 2, 7
individualist, 34, 35, 42
inequality, 8, 18, 20, 41, 59, 60, 77, 79, 118, 119, 126, 227, 241, 259, 263
inequity, 16, 79, 81, 229
infidelity, 90, 97, 101, 102, 104–106, 153, 180, 181, 185, 187, 241
interdependence, 1, 36–40, 42, 43, 60, 61, 158, 163, 180, 190
international, 20
intersectionality, 1–3, 22, 56, 58–60, 64–66, 136, 138, 227, 228
intervention, 8, 42, 100, 106, 151, 157, 257
intimate partner violence, 1, 5, 41, 74, 80, 90, 96, 106, 155, 181, 187, 237, 238, 251, 254
Iran, 101–103, 105, 188

Japan, 30, 31, 33, 35, 41

Karney, B. R., 2, 43, 72, 76, 80, 81, 247–249, 259

Latinx, 5, 106, 117, 143, 211, 226–233, 235, 237–241
LGBTQ+, 56, 65, 75, 81, 124, 176, 203, 208
lifespan, 8, 18, 21, 136, 145, 201, 215

maintaining, 7, 15, 33, 36, 38–40, 44, 58, 63, 79, 95, 104, 121, 136, 140–142, 179, 185, 191, 201, 208, 209, 212, 214, 215, 227–229, 236, 241, 247, 254, 259
marginalization, 1, 3, 7, 9, 10, 56, 64–66, 138, 227, 230, 231, 234, 239–242
matchmaking, 171, 173–175, 181, 186
mates, 34, 35, 37, 73, 170–172, 174, 176, 191, 236
mating, 77, 79, 93, 237
migration, 35, 126, 173, 231, 232, 239
minoritized, 3, 9, 13, 227, 230
minority, 1, 13, 22, 56, 61, 82, 94, 117, 127, 142, 143, 208
money, 64, 75, 80, 83, 123, 154
multicultural, 141
multiracial, 141
Muslim, 92, 94, 106

neighborhoods, 2, 16, 20, 71, 72, 81, 82
network, 37, 39, 41, 99, 137, 141, 201–203, 205–215, 247, 251, 255
newlyweds, 96, 101

Ogolsky, B. G., 1, 2, 56, 143
oppression, 5, 7, 9, 12, 14, 17, 19, 21, 59, 61, 140, 181, 228, 229, 233, 240, 242

parasocial, 190, 191
parenting, 66, 74, 80, 159–161, 251, 252, 257–259, 263
partnering, 63, 66, 136, 137, 140, 143
phone, 169, 170, 173, 175–180, 202, 205, 214
policy, 2, 22, 33, 116, 162, 231, 232
pornography, 172, 184, 187, 188
power, 1, 7, 12, 17, 20, 58–62, 66, 80, 116–120, 125, 137, 139, 155, 171, 173, 191, 227–229, 240, 255, 257
prayer, 90, 99, 101–103
praying, 18, 96, 102, 104, 106
premarital, 17, 104
privilege, 9–11, 19, 20, 33, 57, 59–61, 119, 135, 208, 227, 228, 237

queer, 56, 60, 61, 64, 65, 142, 228

race, 1, 2, 7, 8, 11, 19, 20, 22, 56, 58–60, 63, 74, 78, 82, 117, 125, 139–141, 228, 238, 263
reciprocity, 40, 103, 105, 263
ritual, 92, 138, 184
romance, 4, 12, 13, 20, 30, 34, 41, 71, 125, 158, 171, 185, 189
romantic, 1, 3–5, 7–16, 18–22, 29, 30, 32, 35, 37–40, 42–44, 56–58, 60–66, 71, 72, 74, 75, 81, 82, 90–93, 95, 97, 99–106, 115–117, 118, 120–127, 135–140, 145, 158, 159, 161–163, 168–177, 179, 180, 182–187, 189–191, 201–215, 226, 230, 233–239, 241, 247–250, 253, 256, 259, 260, 262
rural, 33, 35, 73, 81, 203

school, 55, 72, 75, 177, 232, 251, 252, 254
scientists, 1, 43, 44, 91, 107, 227
security, 16, 63, 64, 76, 81, 103, 106, 136, 239, 241
sexuality, 3, 55–58, 60, 63–66, 92, 101, 106, 118, 151, 153, 237
sibling, 158
singlehood, 14, 16, 32, 35, 59, 63, 126, 144, 170–173, 175, 241
Snapchat, 209, 216
social exchange theory, 124
sociocultural, 3, 5, 7, 10, 12–14, 16, 17, 22, 63, 92, 228–230, 233–235, 239, 242
socioculturally, 226, 228, 242
socioeconomic status, 1, 2, 72, 74–77, 79–81, 83, 263
spouse, 22, 31, 32, 37, 77, 91, 96, 99, 101–105, 152–155, 170, 179, 184, 230, 233, 239
stereotypes, 10, 12, 106, 208
stigma, 17, 41, 42, 124, 144
stigmatized, 35, 64, 176, 182

Index

straight, 59, 60, 161
stressor, 4, 12, 13, 103, 104, 142, 143, 181, 247, 248, 250, 254, 256, 259, 262

technology, 1, 124, 143, 144, 202, 214, 215, 260
televison, 175, 181, 186
texting, 177, 180, 214
TikTok, 202
Tinder, 72, 174, 215, 260, 262
trauma, 138–140, 237, 256

trust, 64, 117, 205, 211
Twitter, 202

uncertainty, 15, 56, 58, 136, 143, 173, 177, 201, 203–207, 210–212, 214, 215, 234, 240

victimization, 74, 205, 227, 250

wife, 17, 31, 78, 79, 90, 95, 96, 99, 102, 140, 155, 156, 180

Printed in the United States
by Baker & Taylor Publisher Services